ROBYN HOOD OUTLAW

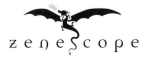

zenescope

ROBYN HOOD OUTLAW

Story **DAVE FRANCHINI** & **HOWARD MACKIE** Writer **HOWARD MACKIE**

Artwork **BABISU KOURTIS** Colors **JUAN MANUEL RODRIGUEZ**

Letters **TAYLOR ESPOSITO** (OF GHOST GLYPH STUDIOS)

Editor **KELLIE SUPPLEE** Art Direction & Design **CHRISTOPHER COTE**

Cover Artwork **MARCO MASTRAZZO**

Grimm Universe created by **JOE BRUSHA** & **RALPH TEDESCO**

This volume reprints Robyn Hood: Outlaw issues 1-6 and the short story *Robyn Hood: Side Job* from Grimm Universe presents 2019 published by Zenescope Entertainment. First Edition, February 2020 • ISBN: 978-1951087012

zenescope
WWW.ZENESCOPE.COM

Joe Brusha • President & Chief Creative Officer
Ralph Tedesco • VP Film & Television
Christopher Cote • Art Director
Dave Franchini • Editor
Kellie Supplee • Assistant Editor
Rachel Bishop • Assistant Editor
Ashley Vanacore • Graphic Designer

Lauren Klasik • Director of Sales & Marketing
Jennifer Bermel • Business Development & Licensing Manager
Jason Condeelis • Direct Sales Representative
Stu Kropnick • Operations Manager
Bria Holmes • E-Commerce Coordinator
Chris Samson • Tradeshow Manager

Robyn Hood: Outlaw Trade Paperback, February, 2020. First Printing. Published by Zenescope Entertainment Inc., 433 Caredean Drive, Ste. C, Horsham, Pennsylvania 19044.

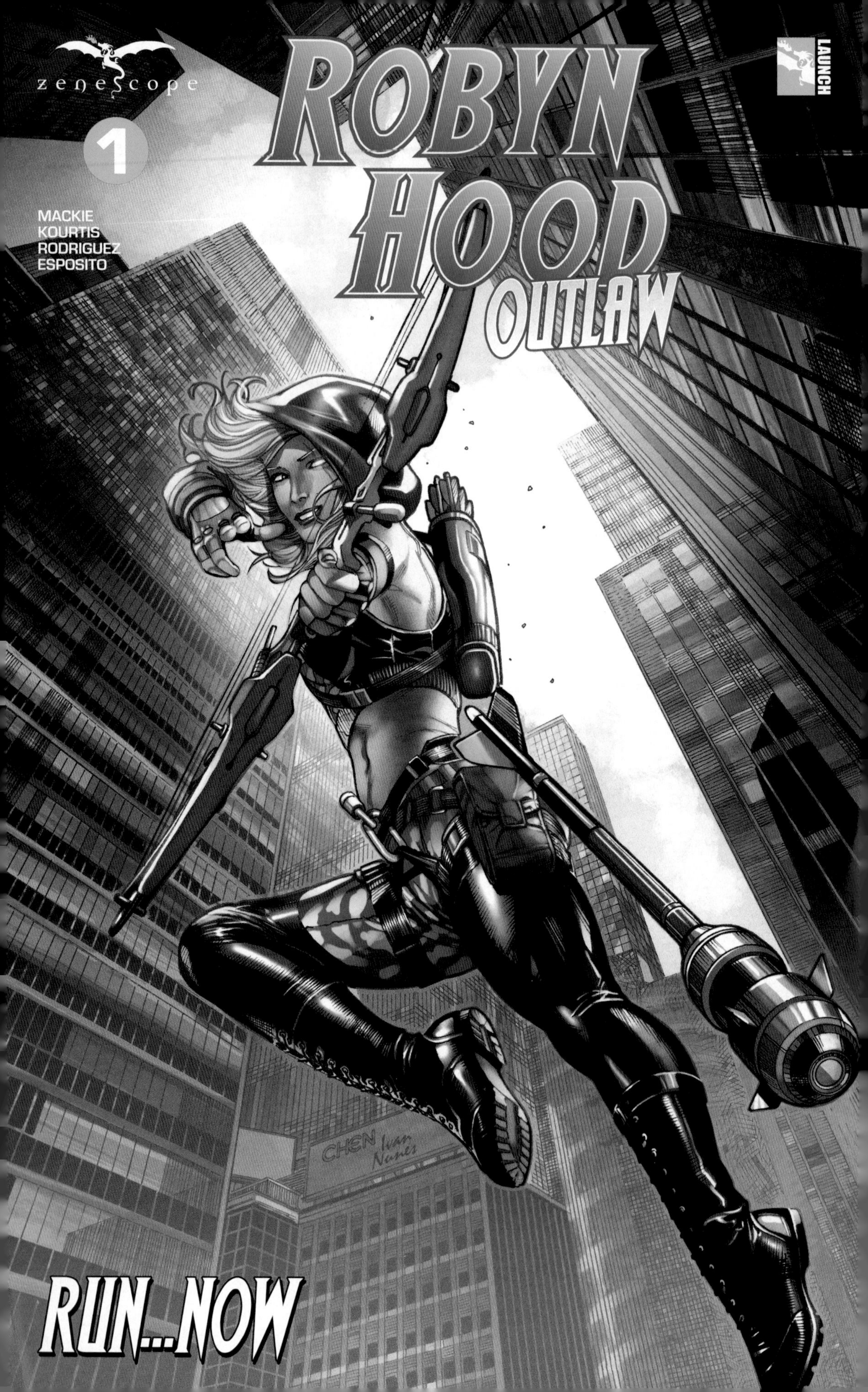
zenescope
1
ROBYN HOOD
OUTLAW
MACKIE
KOURTIS
RODRIGUEZ
ESPOSITO
LAUNCH
CHEN
Ivan Nunes
RUN...NOW

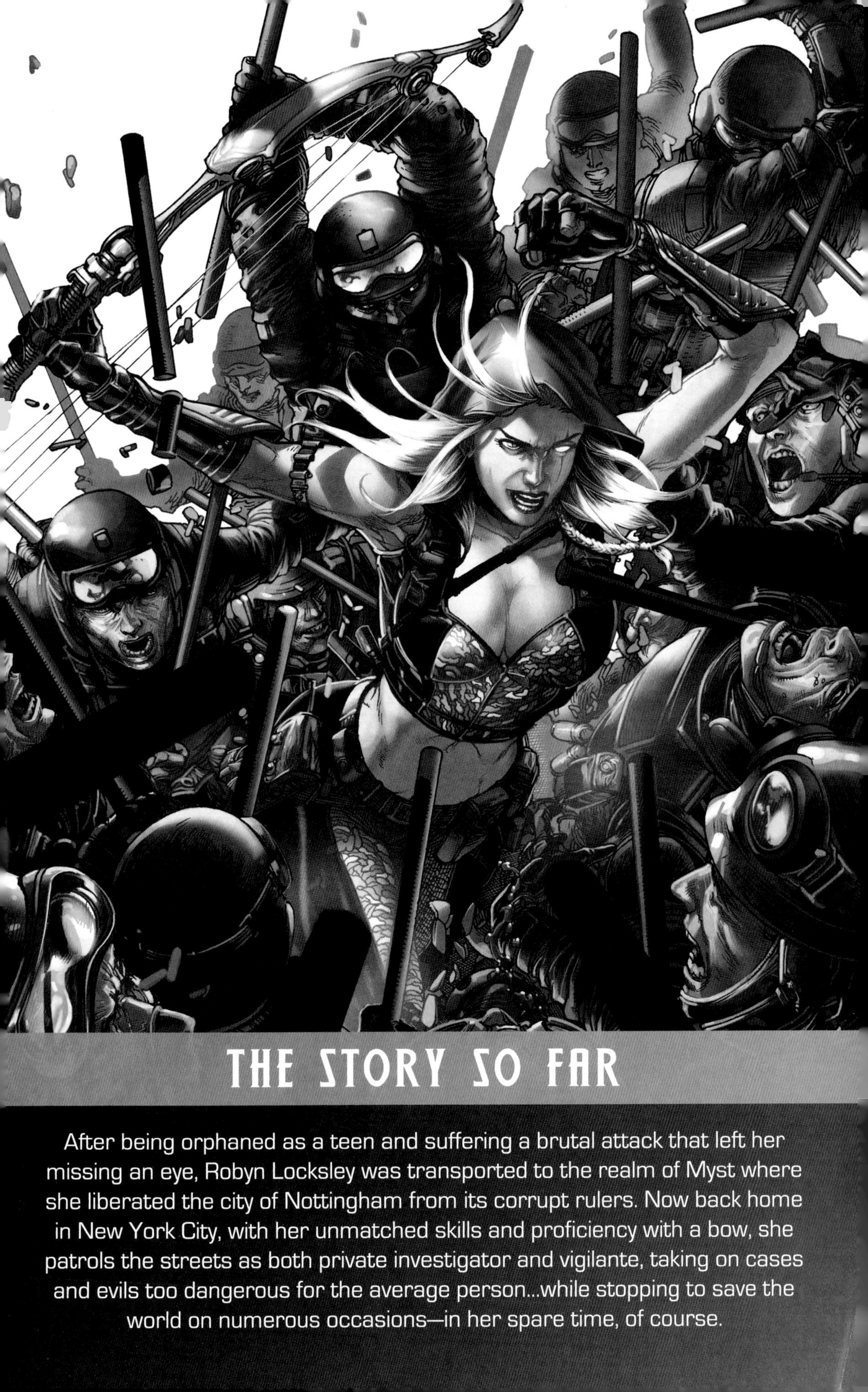

THE STORY SO FAR

After being orphaned as a teen and suffering a brutal attack that left her missing an eye, Robyn Locksley was transported to the realm of Myst where she liberated the city of Nottingham from its corrupt rulers. Now back home in New York City, with her unmatched skills and proficiency with a bow, she patrols the streets as both private investigator and vigilante, taking on cases and evils too dangerous for the average person...while stopping to save the world on numerous occasions—in her spare time, of course.

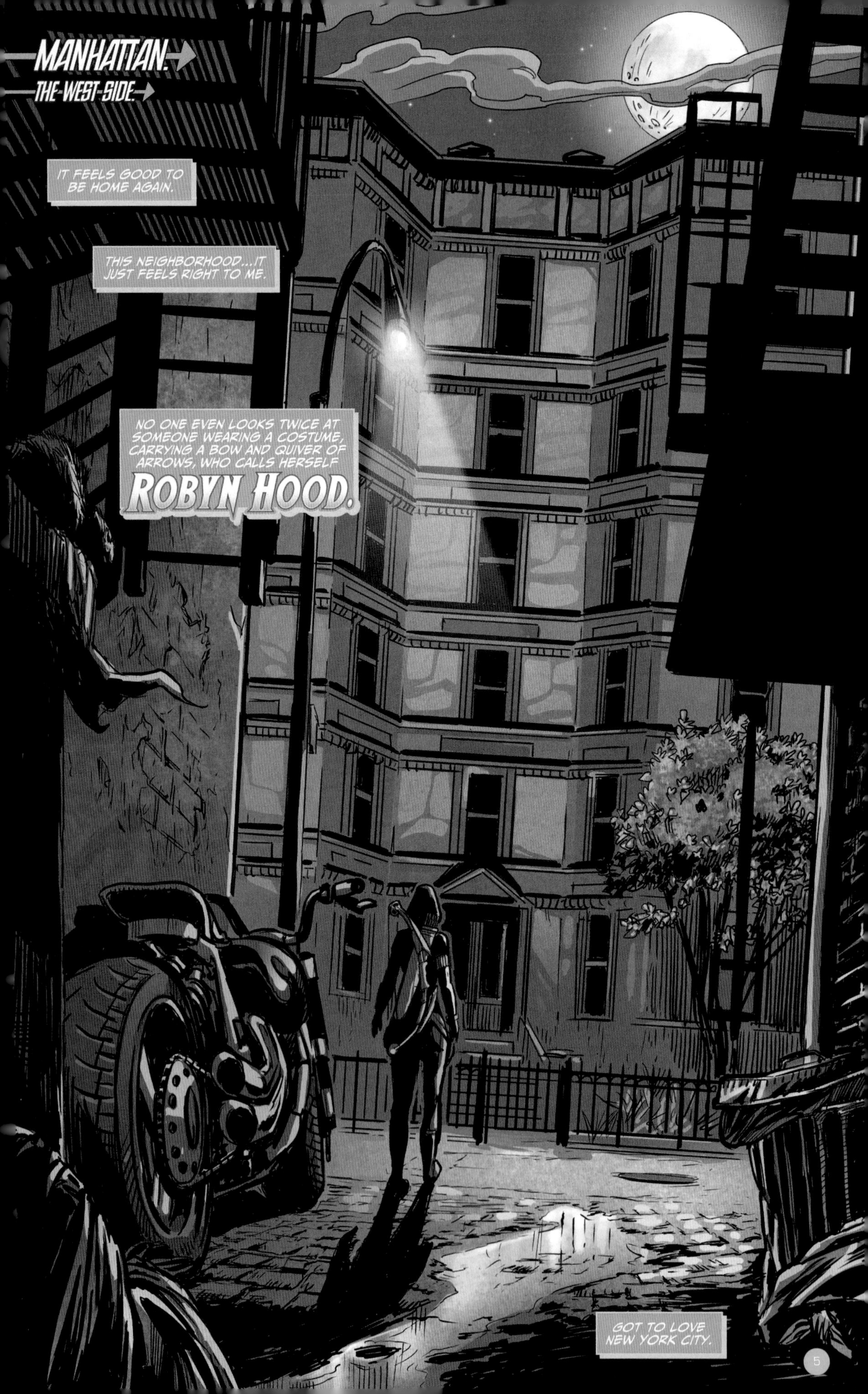
MANHATTAN.
THE WEST SIDE.
IT FEELS GOOD TO BE HOME AGAIN.
THIS NEIGHBORHOOD...IT JUST FEELS RIGHT TO ME.
NO ONE EVEN LOOKS TWICE AT SOMEONE WEARING A COSTUME, CARRYING A BOW AND QUIVER OF ARROWS, WHO CALLS HERSELF
ROBYN HOOD.
GOT TO LOVE NEW YORK CITY.

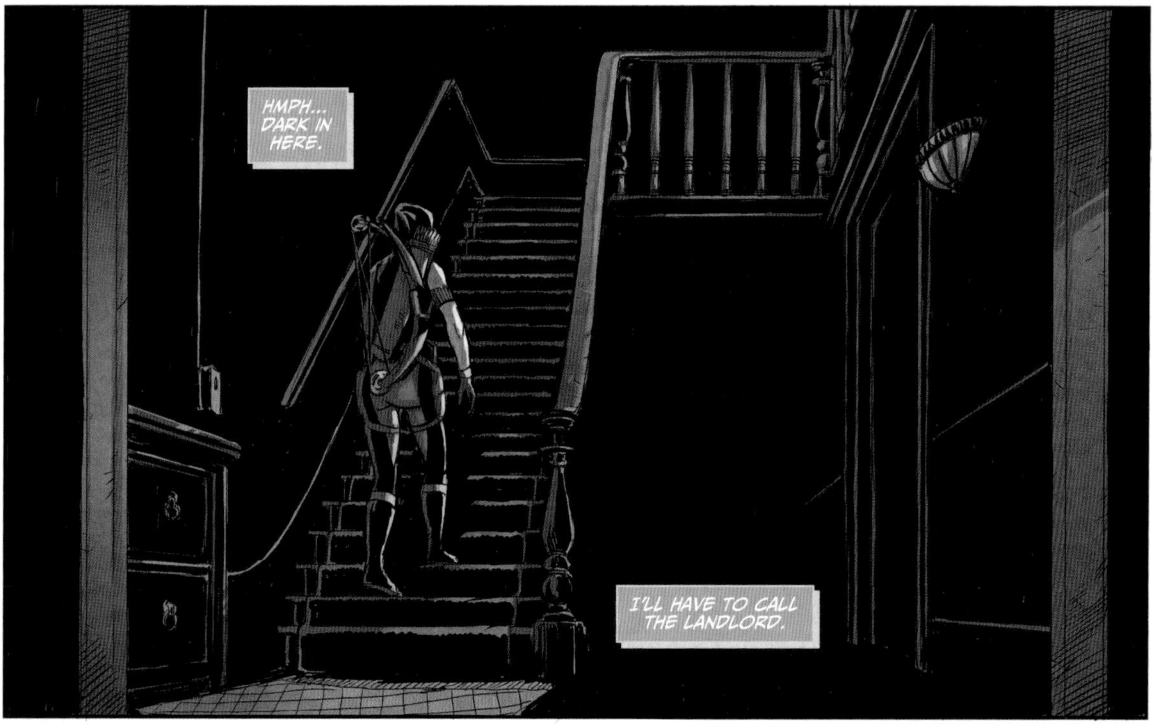
HMPH... DARK IN HERE.
I'LL HAVE TO CALL THE LANDLORD.

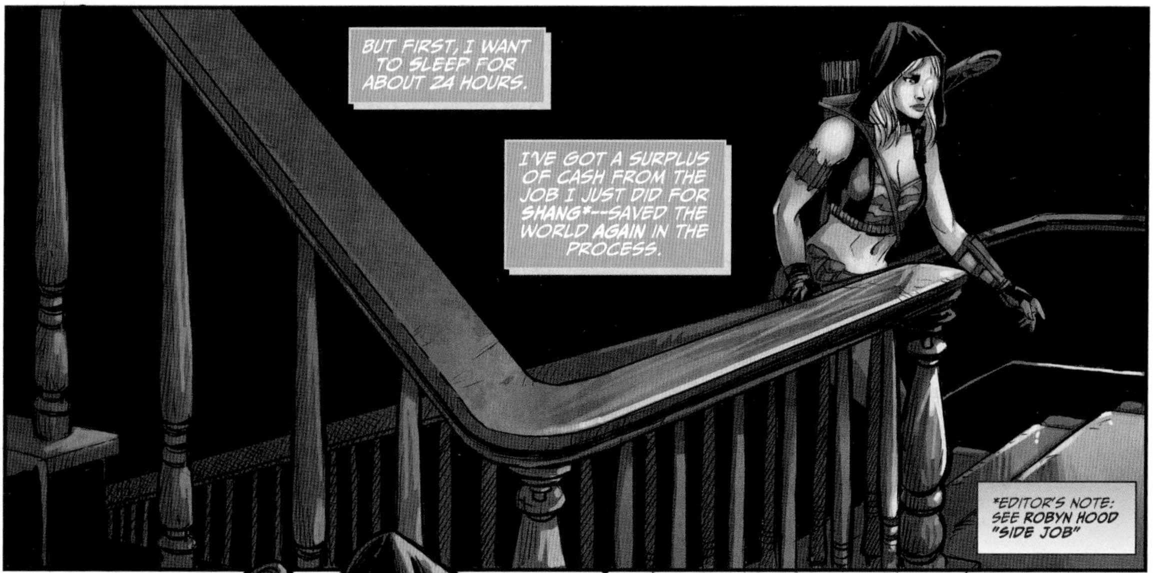
BUT FIRST, I WANT TO SLEEP FOR ABOUT 24 HOURS.
I'VE GOT A SURPLUS OF CASH FROM THE JOB I JUST DID FOR SHANG*--SAVED THE WORLD AGAIN IN THE PROCESS.
*EDITOR'S NOTE: SEE ROBYN HOOD "SIDE JOB"

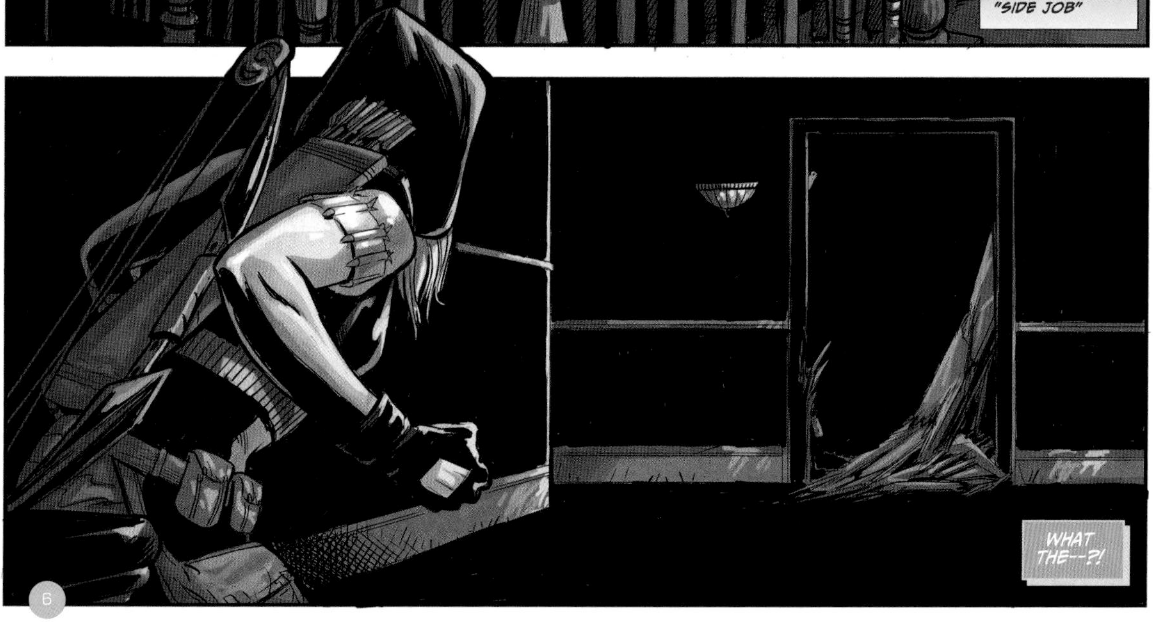
WHAT THE--?!

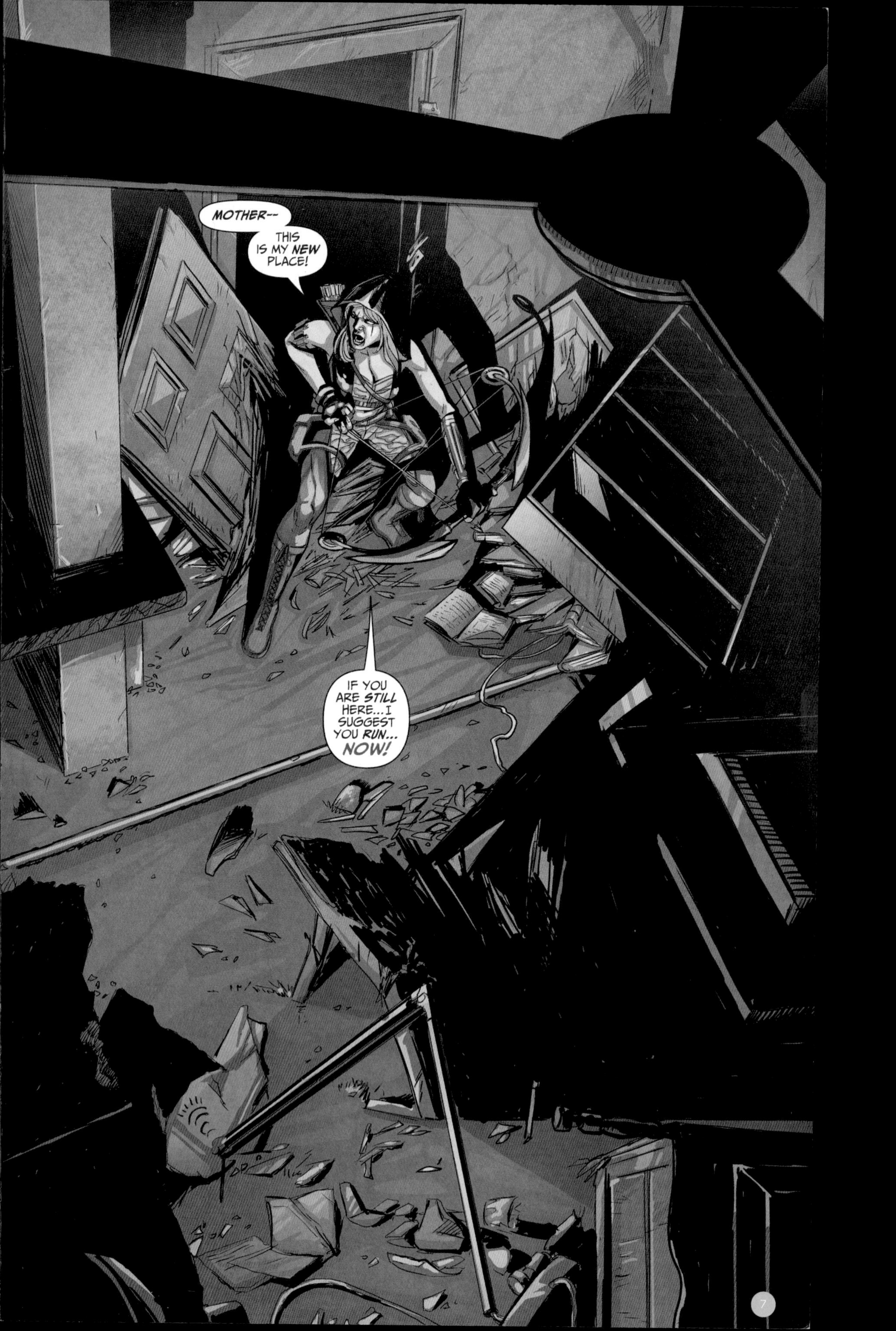
MOTHER--
THIS IS MY NEW PLACE!
IF YOU ARE STILL HERE...I SUGGEST YOU RUN... NOW!

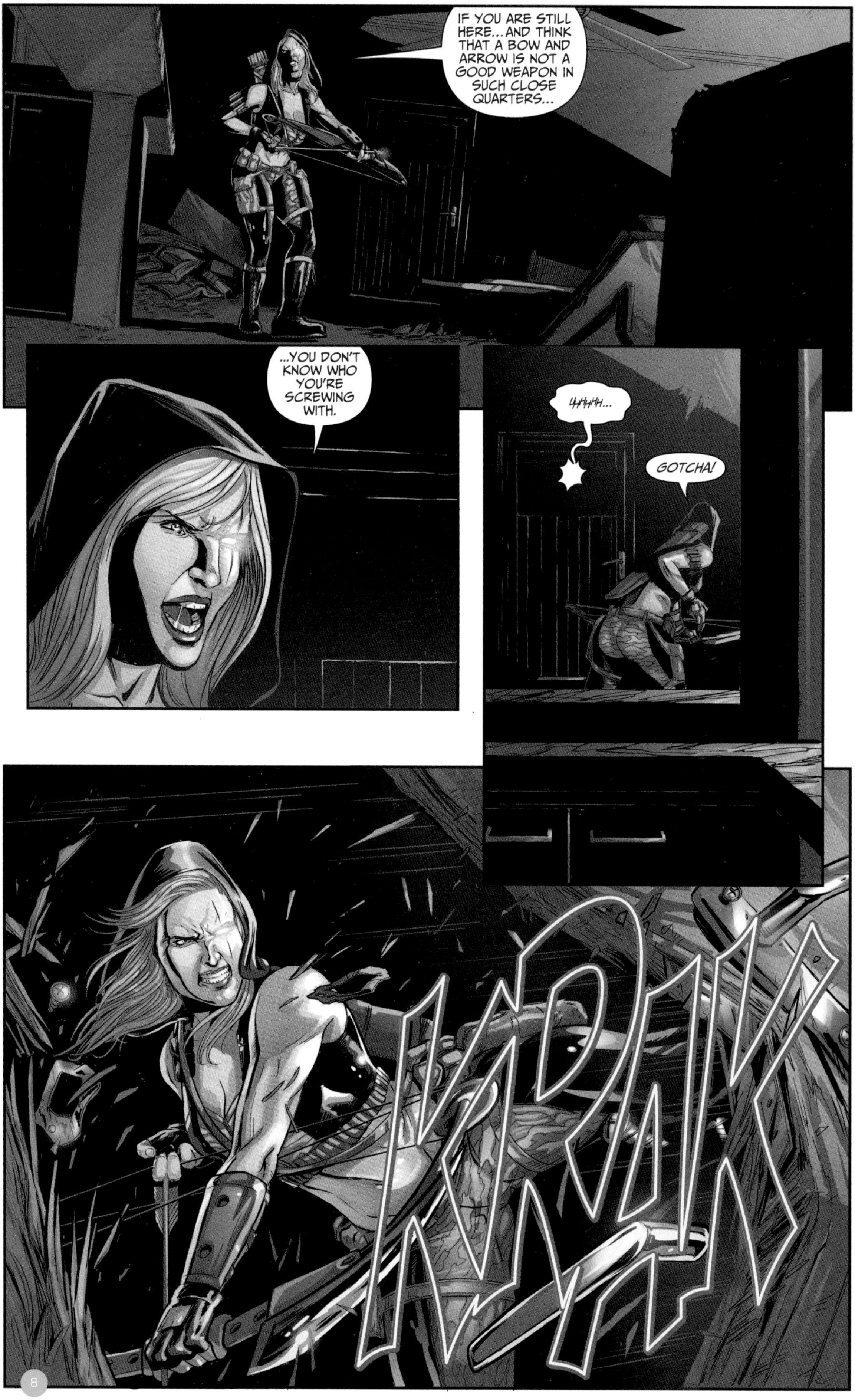
IF YOU ARE STILL HERE...AND THINK THAT A BOW AND ARROW IS NOT A GOOD WEAPON IN SUCH CLOSE QUARTERS...
...YOU DON'T KNOW WHO YOU'RE SCREWING WITH.
UHHHH...
GOTCHA!
KADAK
KAK

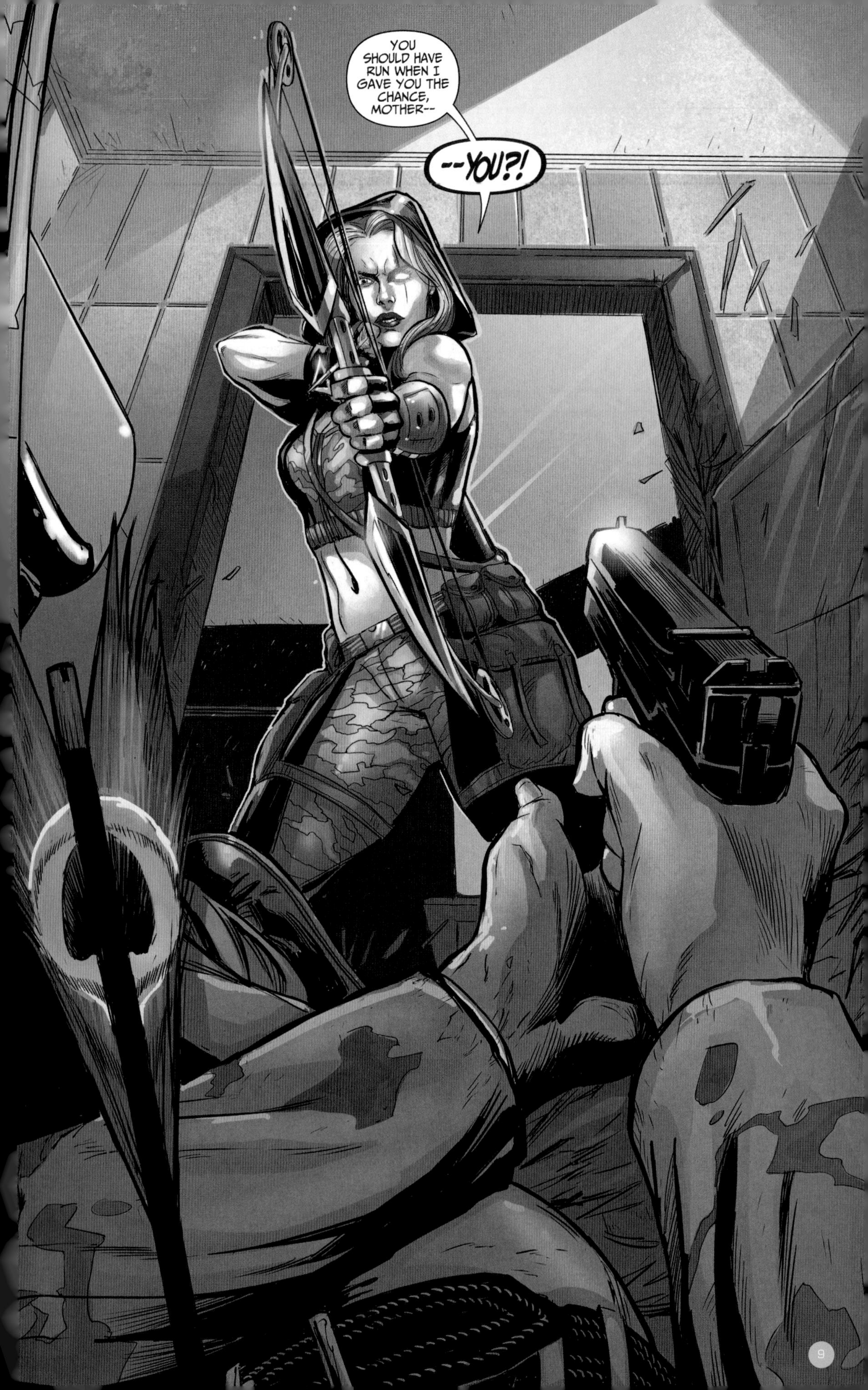

YOU SHOULD HAVE RUN WHEN I GAVE YOU THE CHANCE, MOTHER--
--YOU?!

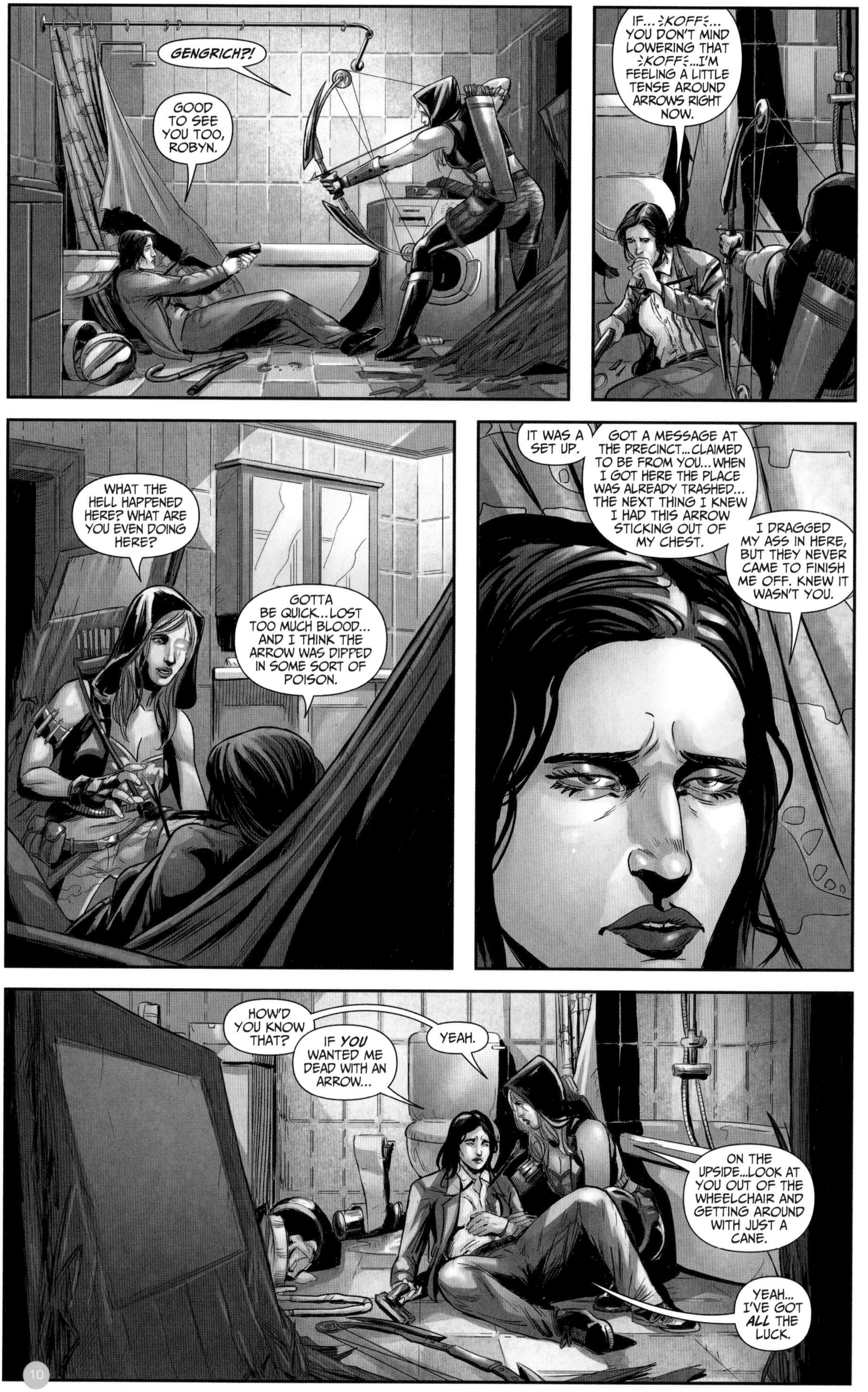
GENGRICH?!
GOOD TO SEE YOU TOO, ROBYN.
IF... ⸾KOFF⸾... YOU DON'T MIND LOWERING THAT ⸾KOFF⸾...I'M FEELING A LITTLE TENSE AROUND ARROWS RIGHT NOW.
WHAT THE HELL HAPPENED HERE? WHAT ARE YOU EVEN DOING HERE?
GOTTA BE QUICK...LOST TOO MUCH BLOOD... AND I THINK THE ARROW WAS DIPPED IN SOME SORT OF POISON.
IT WAS A SET UP.
GOT A MESSAGE AT THE PRECINCT...CLAIMED TO BE FROM YOU...WHEN I GOT HERE THE PLACE WAS ALREADY TRASHED... THE NEXT THING I KNEW I HAD THIS ARROW STICKING OUT OF MY CHEST.
I DRAGGED MY ASS IN HERE, BUT THEY NEVER CAME TO FINISH ME OFF. KNEW IT WASN'T YOU.
HOW'D YOU KNOW THAT?
IF YOU WANTED ME DEAD WITH AN ARROW...
YEAH.
ON THE UPSIDE...LOOK AT YOU OUT OF THE WHEELCHAIR AND GETTING AROUND WITH JUST A CANE.
YEAH... I'VE GOT ALL THE LUCK.

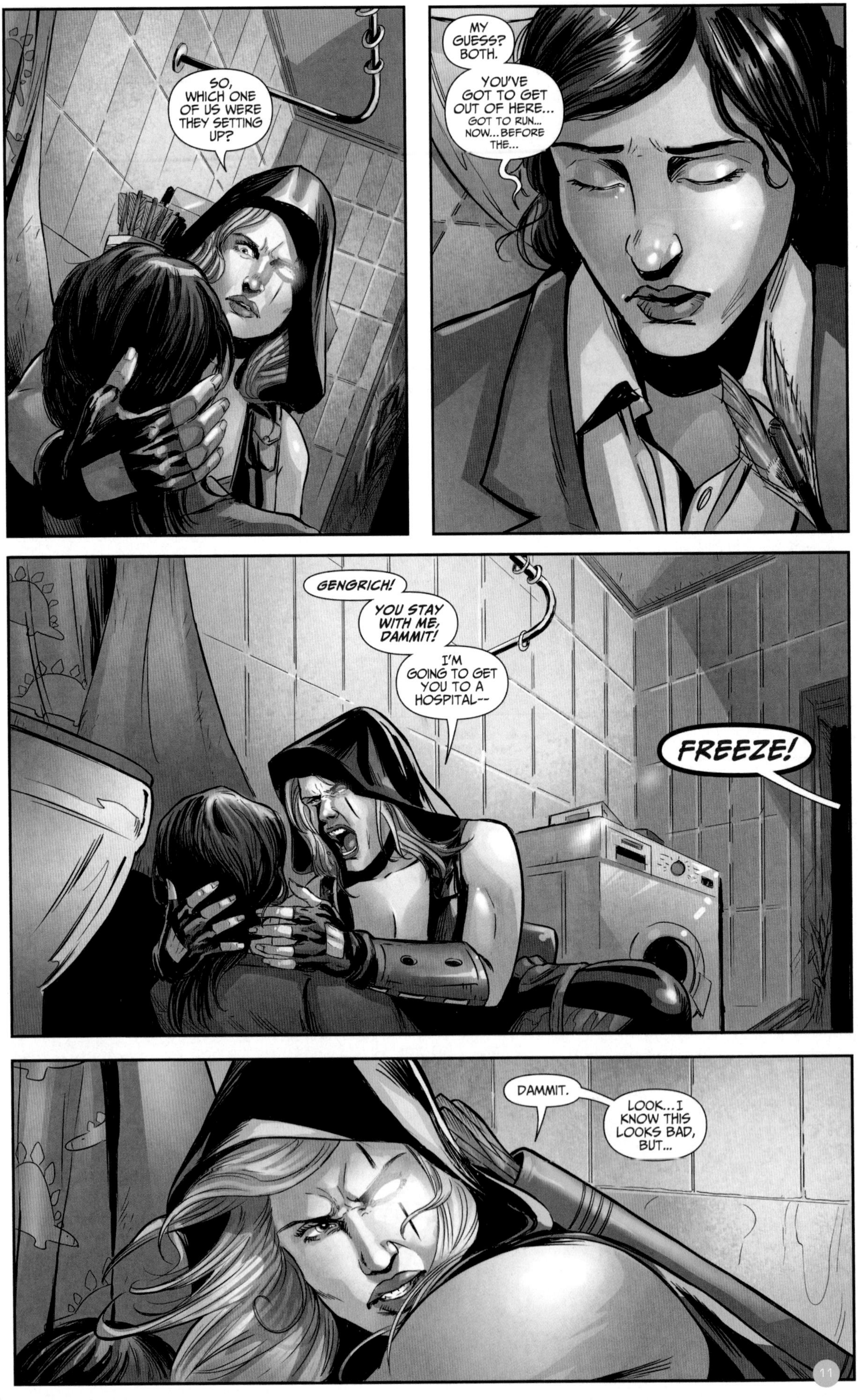
SO, WHICH ONE OF US WERE THEY SETTING UP?
MY GUESS? BOTH.
YOU'VE GOT TO GET OUT OF HERE... GOT TO RUN... NOW...BEFORE THE...
GENGRICH!
YOU STAY WITH ME, DAMMIT!
I'M GOING TO GET YOU TO A HOSPITAL--
FREEZE!
DAMMIT.
LOOK...I KNOW THIS LOOKS BAD, BUT...

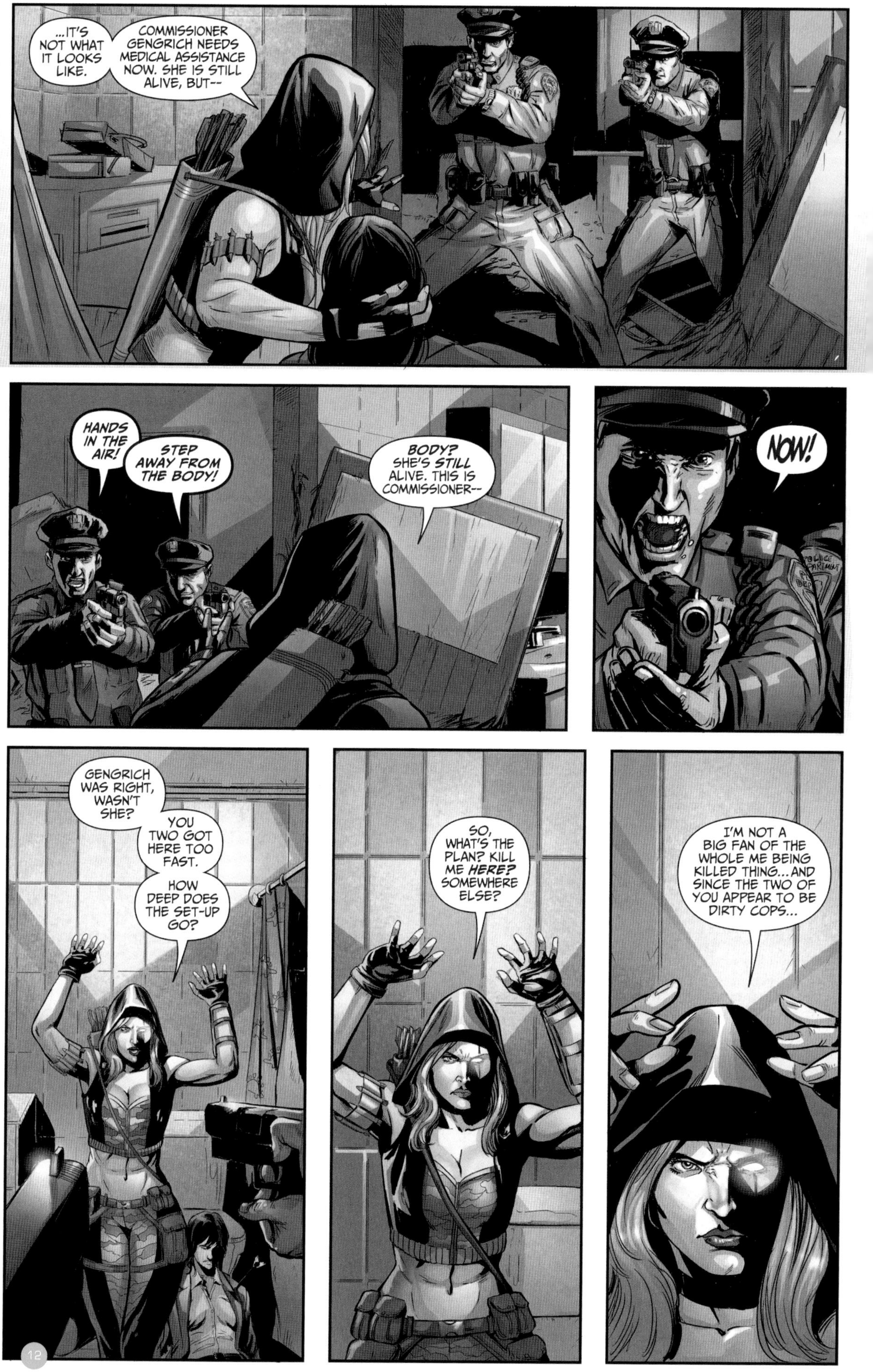
...IT'S NOT WHAT IT LOOKS LIKE.
COMMISSIONER GENGRICH NEEDS MEDICAL ASSISTANCE NOW. SHE IS STILL ALIVE, BUT--
HANDS IN THE AIR!
STEP AWAY FROM THE BODY!
BODY? SHE'S STILL ALIVE. THIS IS COMMISSIONER--
NOW!
GENGRICH WAS RIGHT, WASN'T SHE?
YOU TWO GOT HERE TOO FAST.
HOW DEEP DOES THE SET-UP GO?
SO, WHAT'S THE PLAN? KILL ME HERE? SOMEWHERE ELSE?
I'M NOT A BIG FAN OF THE WHOLE ME BEING KILLED THING...AND SINCE THE TWO OF YOU APPEAR TO BE DIRTY COPS...

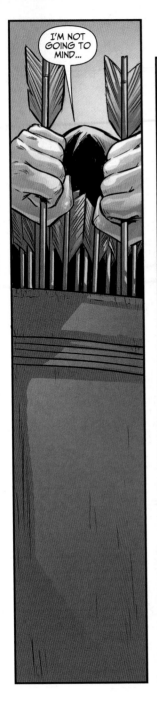

I'M NOT GOING TO MIND...

...IF THE TWO OF YOU...

...GET A LITTLE BUSTED UP.

BY THE WAY... I ASSUME YOU KNOW BETTER THAN TO PULL THOSE TRIGGERS.

THAT'D GET PRETTY NASTY.

NOW... LET'S SAY WE HAVE A LITTLE FUN?

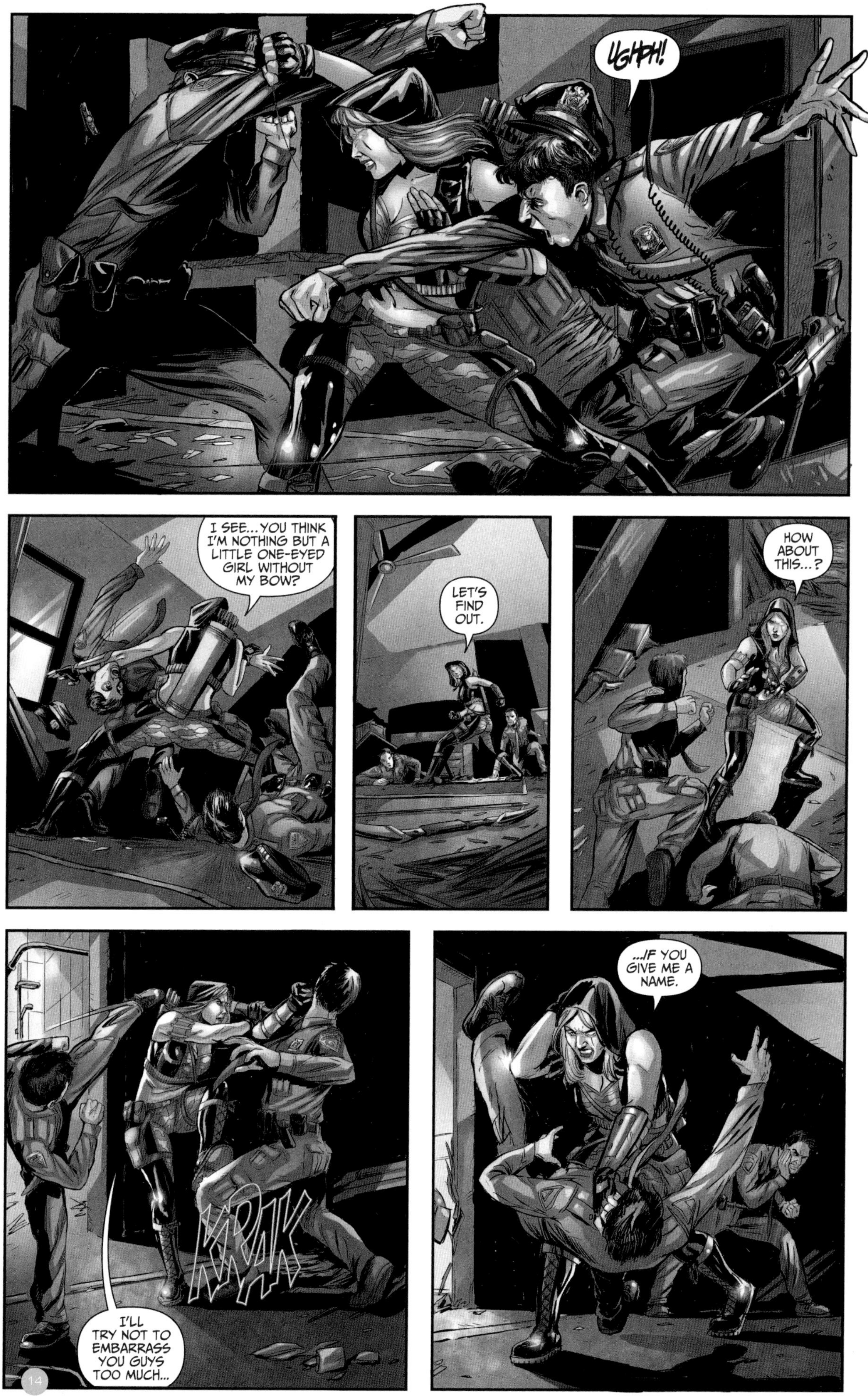
UGHPH!
I SEE...YOU THINK I'M NOTHING BUT A LITTLE ONE-EYED GIRL WITHOUT MY BOW?
LET'S FIND OUT.
HOW ABOUT THIS...?
I'LL TRY NOT TO EMBARRASS YOU GUYS TOO MUCH...
KRAK
...IF YOU GIVE ME A NAME.

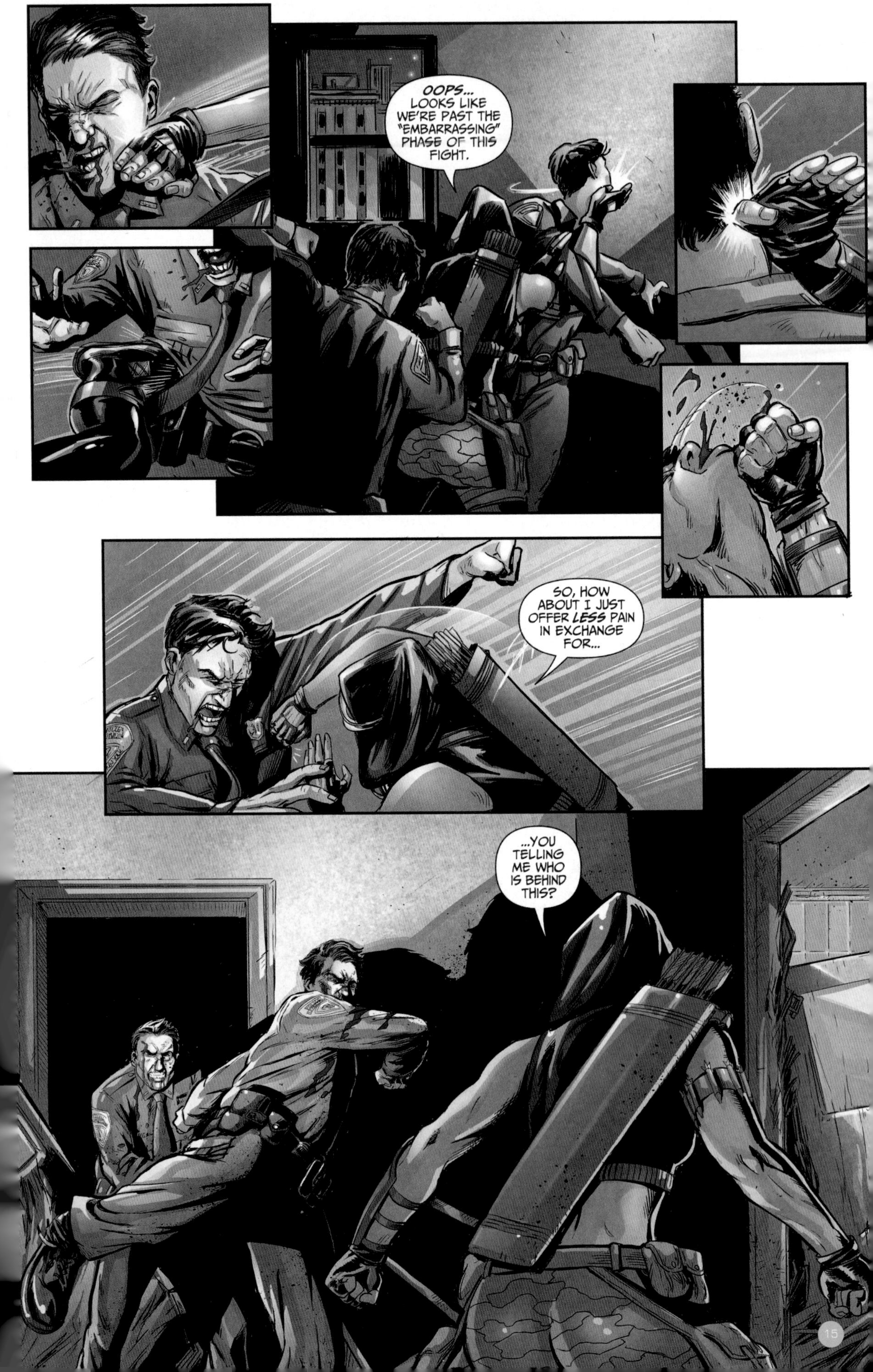
OOPS... LOOKS LIKE WE'RE PAST THE "EMBARRASSING" PHASE OF THIS FIGHT.
SO, HOW ABOUT I JUST OFFER LESS PAIN IN EXCHANGE FOR...
...YOU TELLING ME WHO IS BEHIND THIS?

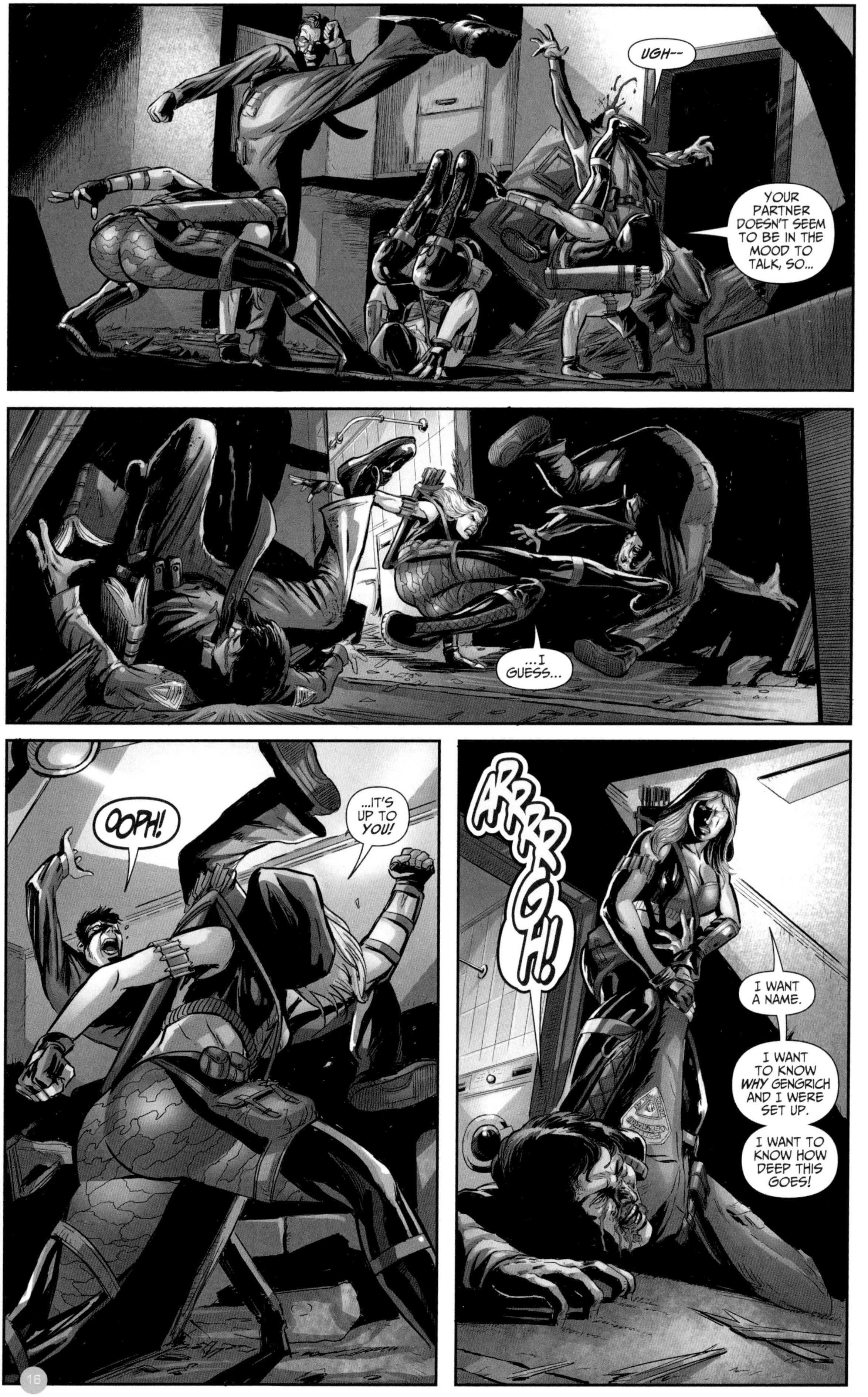

UGH--
YOUR PARTNER DOESN'T SEEM TO BE IN THE MOOD TO TALK, SO...
...I GUESS...
OOPH!
...IT'S UP TO *YOU!*
ARRRRGH!
I WANT A NAME.
I WANT TO KNOW *WHY* GENGRICH AND I WERE SET UP.
I WANT TO KNOW HOW DEEP THIS GOES!

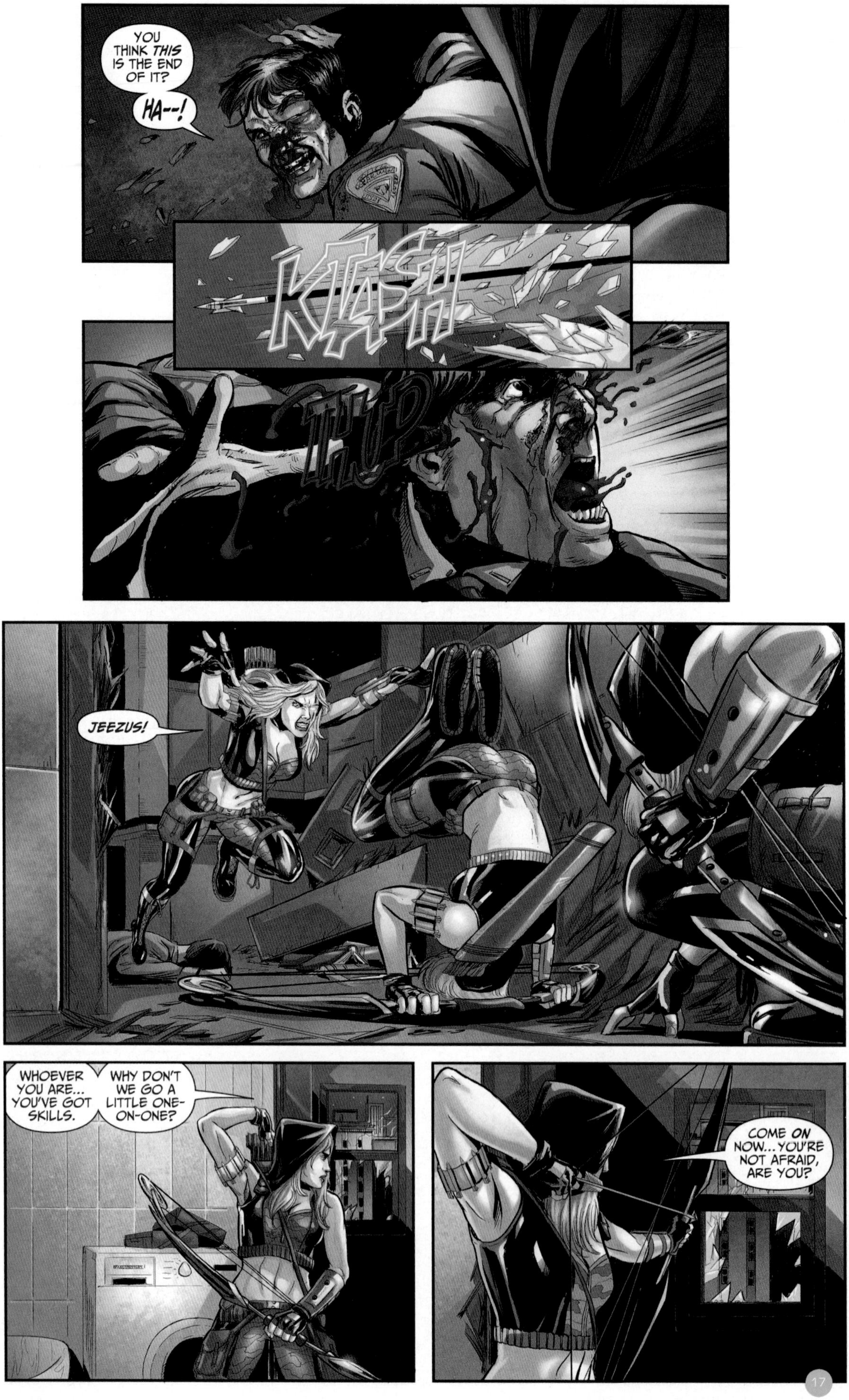
YOU THINK THIS IS THE END OF IT?
HA--!
KTASH
THUP
JEEZUS!
WHOEVER YOU ARE... YOU'VE GOT SKILLS.
WHY DON'T WE GO A LITTLE ONE-ON-ONE?
COME ON NOW... YOU'RE NOT AFRAID, ARE YOU?

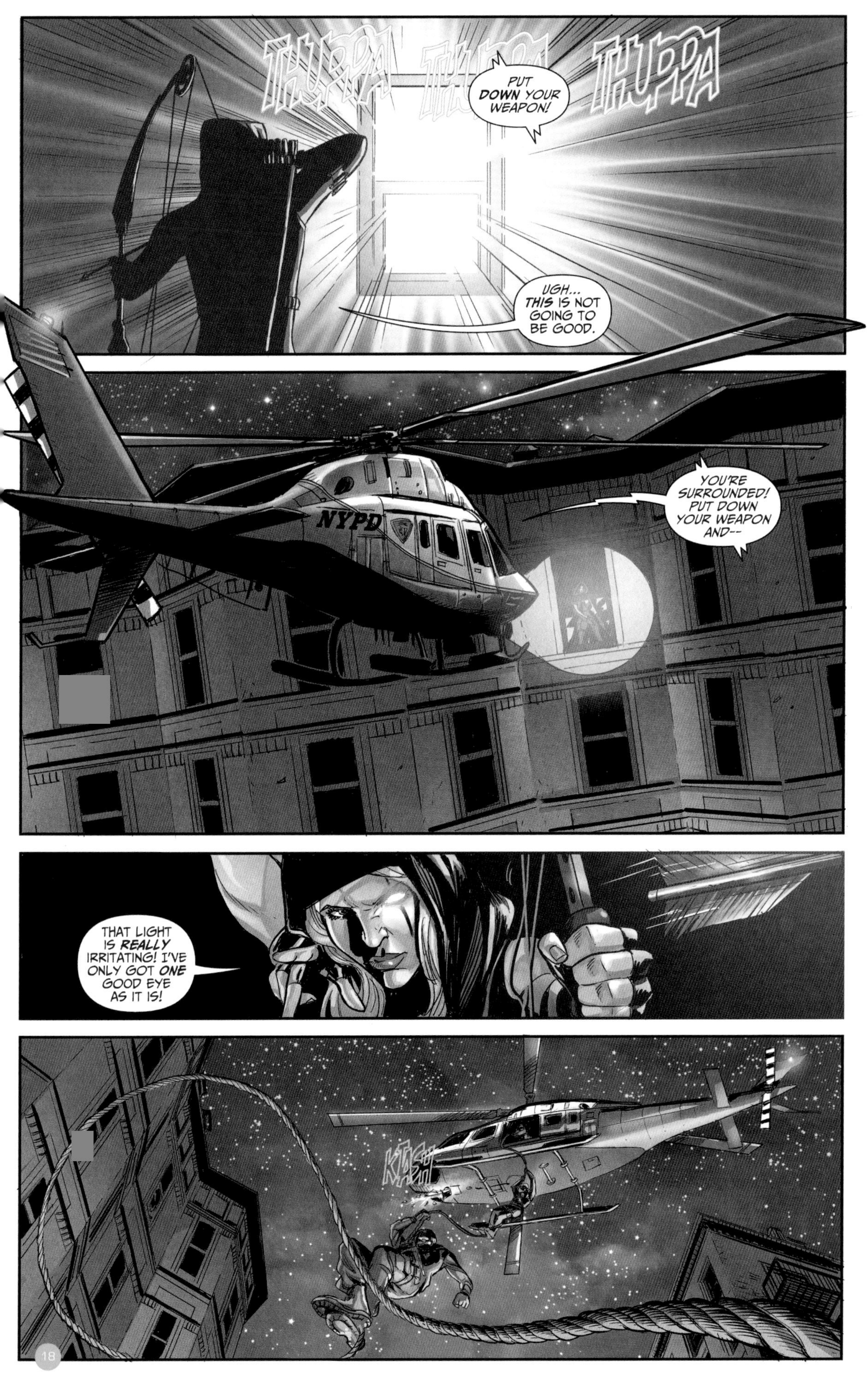
THUPPA THUPPA THUPPA
PUT DOWN YOUR WEAPON!
UGH... THIS IS NOT GOING TO BE GOOD.
NYPD
YOU'RE SURROUNDED! PUT DOWN YOUR WEAPON AND--
THAT LIGHT IS REALLY IRRITATING! I'VE ONLY GOT ONE GOOD EYE AS IT IS!
KASH

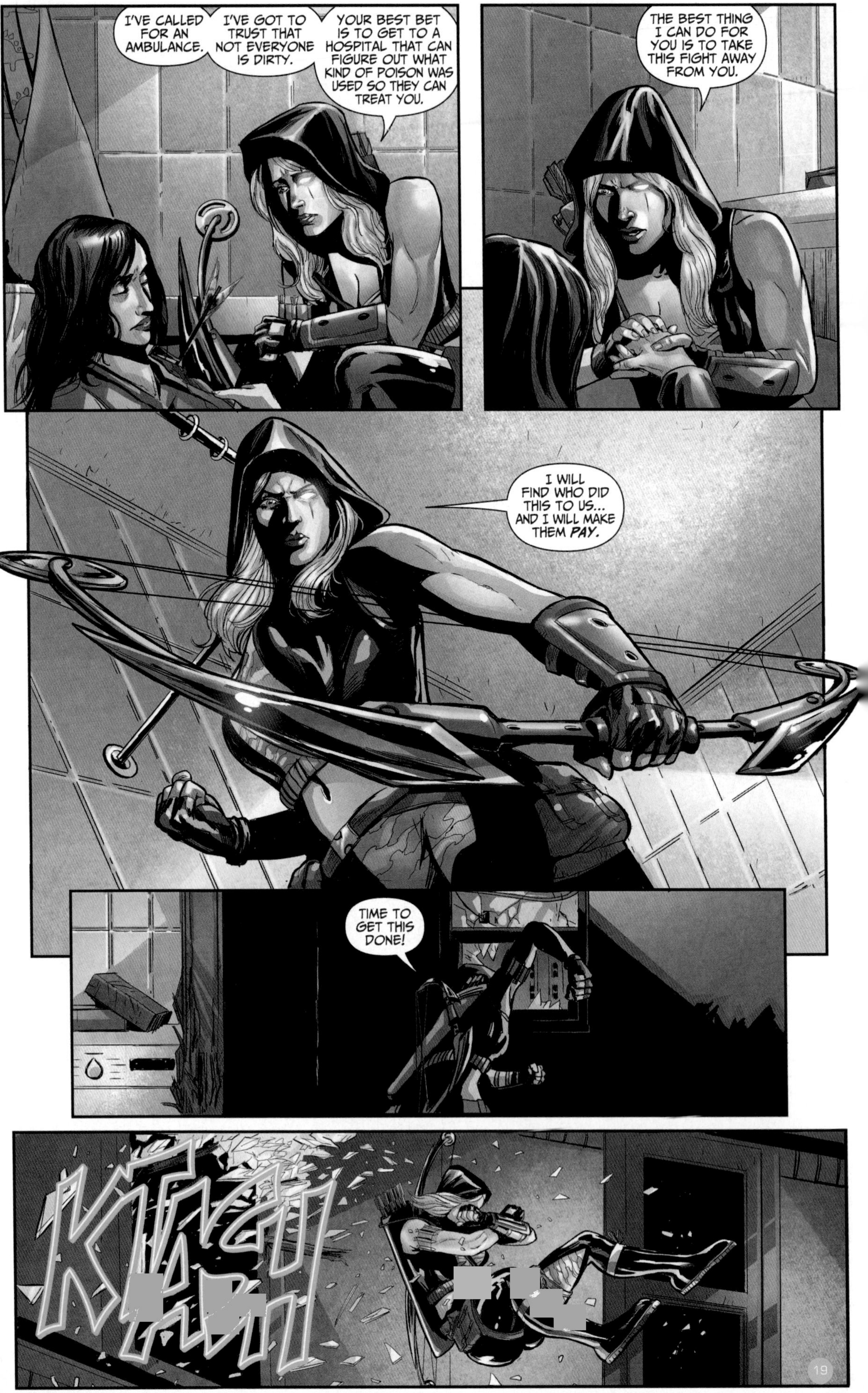
I'VE CALLED FOR AN AMBULANCE.
I'VE GOT TO TRUST THAT NOT EVERYONE IS DIRTY.
YOUR BEST BET IS TO GET TO A HOSPITAL THAT CAN FIGURE OUT WHAT KIND OF POISON WAS USED SO THEY CAN TREAT YOU.
THE BEST THING I CAN DO FOR YOU IS TO TAKE THIS FIGHT AWAY FROM YOU.
I WILL FIND WHO DID THIS TO US... AND I WILL MAKE THEM *PAY.*
TIME TO GET THIS DONE!

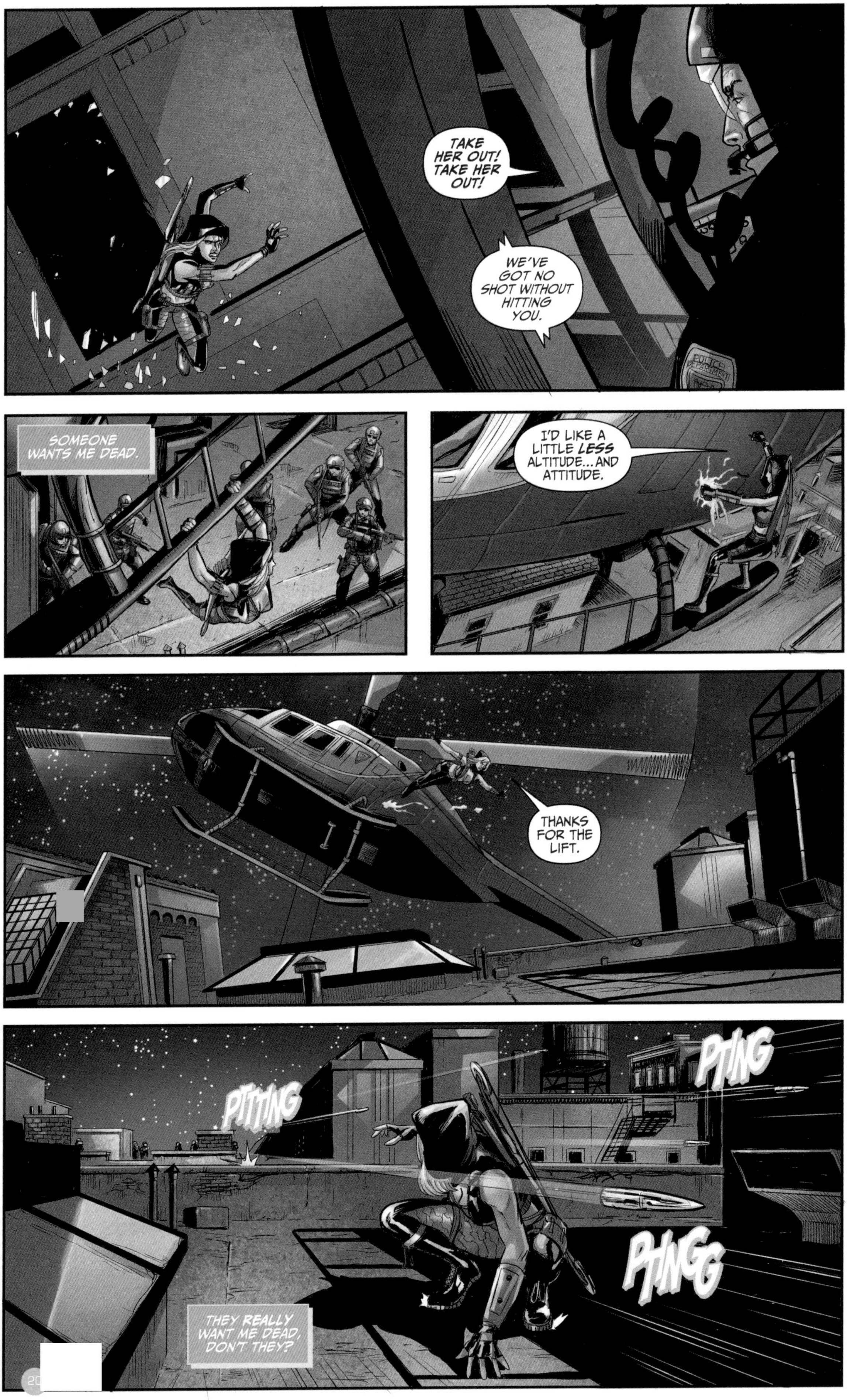
TAKE HER OUT! TAKE HER OUT!
WE'VE GOT NO SHOT WITHOUT HITTING YOU.
SOMEONE WANTS ME DEAD.
I'D LIKE A LITTLE LESS ALTITUDE... AND ATTITUDE.
THANKS FOR THE LIFT.
PTITING
PTING
PHINGG
THEY REALLY WANT ME DEAD, DON'T THEY?

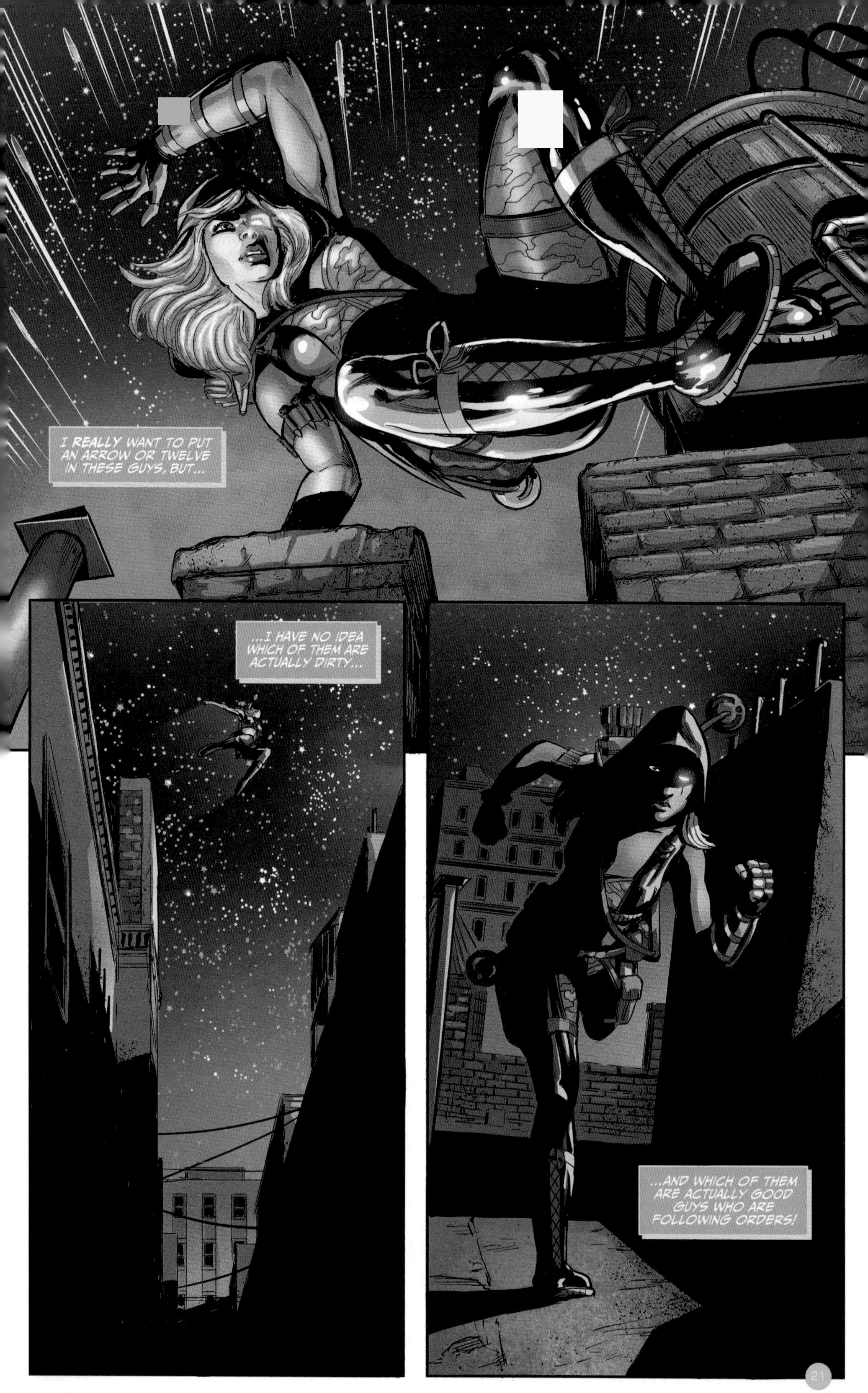
I REALLY WANT TO PUT AN ARROW OR TWELVE IN THESE GUYS, BUT...
...I HAVE NO IDEA WHICH OF THEM ARE ACTUALLY DIRTY...
...AND WHICH OF THEM ARE ACTUALLY GOOD GUYS WHO ARE FOLLOWING ORDERS!

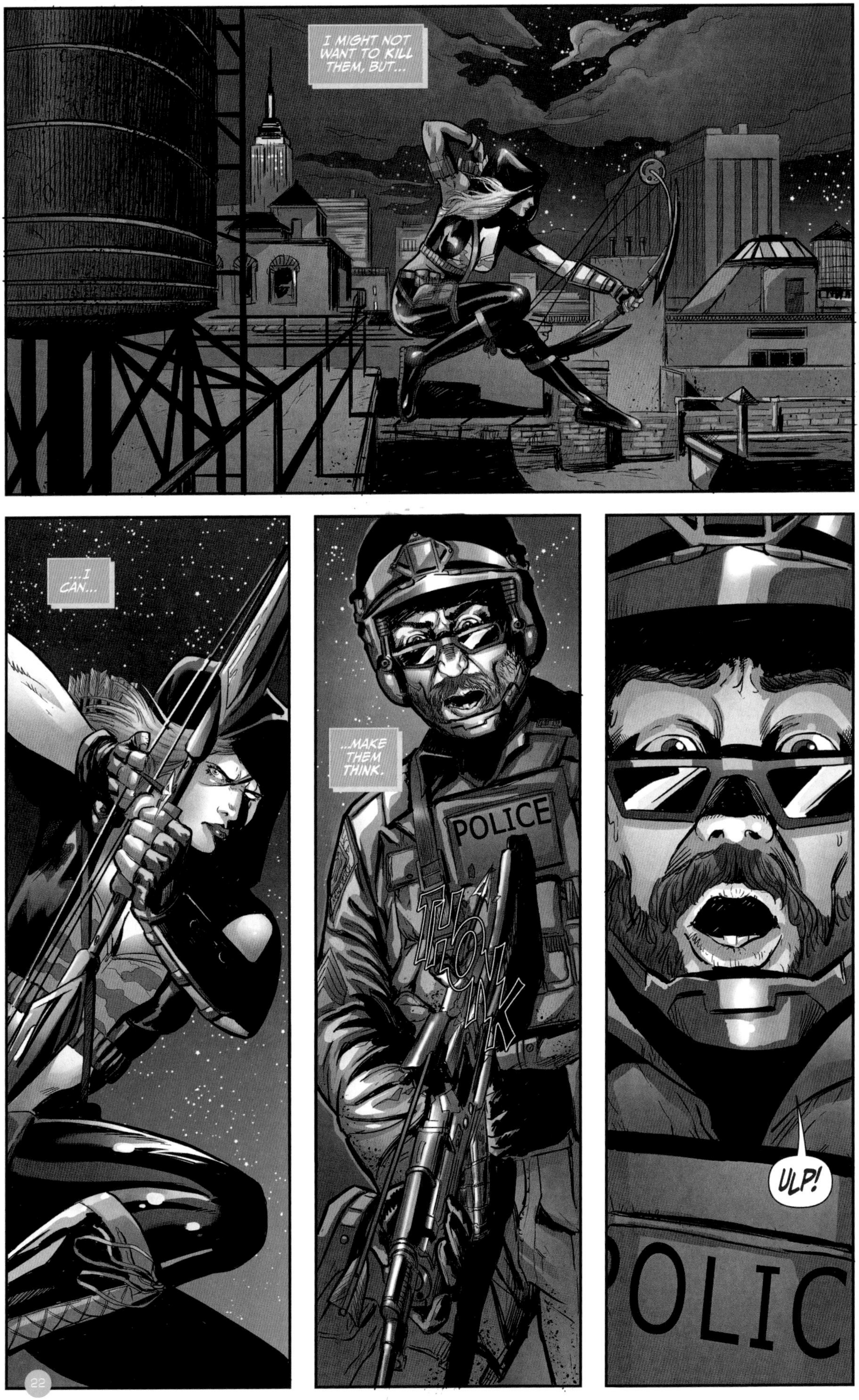
I MIGHT NOT WANT TO KILL THEM, BUT...
...I CAN...
...MAKE THEM THINK.
POLICE
THONK
ULP!
POLIC

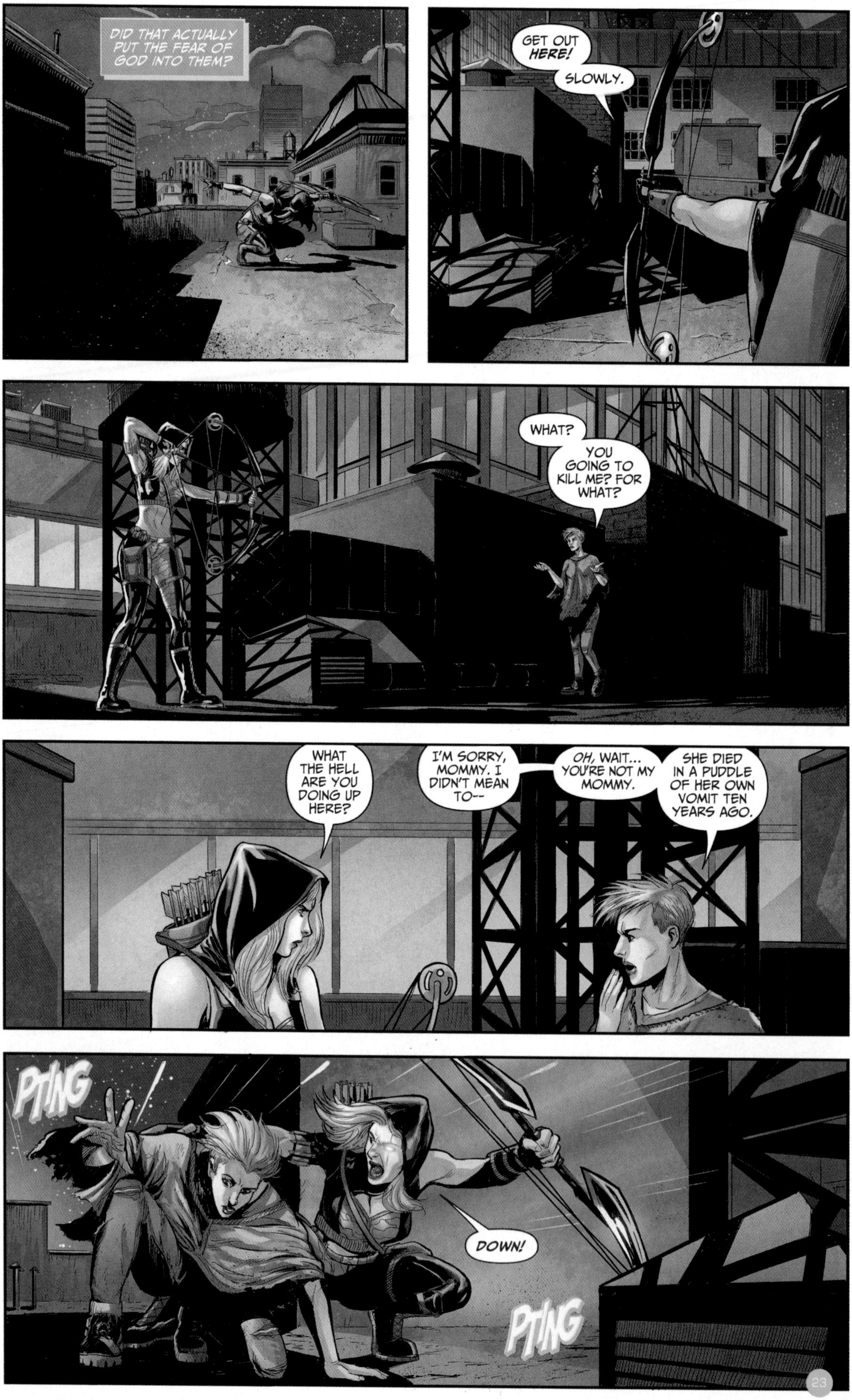
DID THAT ACTUALLY PUT THE FEAR OF GOD INTO THEM?
GET OUT HERE!
SLOWLY.
WHAT?
YOU GOING TO KILL ME? FOR WHAT?
WHAT THE HELL ARE YOU DOING UP HERE?
I'M SORRY, MOMMY. I DIDN'T MEAN TO--
OH, WAIT... YOU'RE NOT MY MOMMY.
SHE DIED IN A PUDDLE OF HER OWN VOMIT TEN YEARS AGO.
PTING
DOWN!
PTING

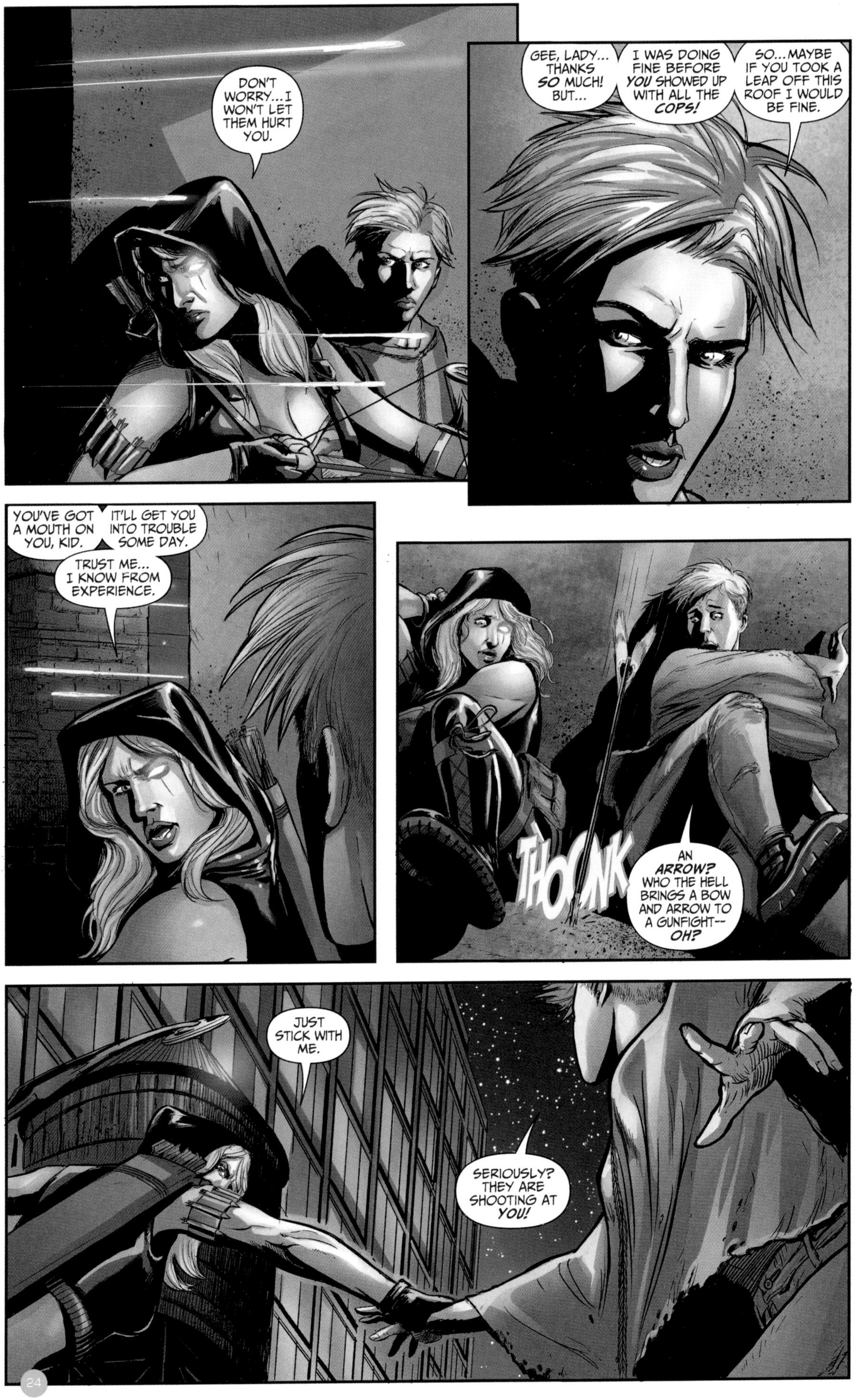
DON'T WORRY...I WON'T LET THEM HURT YOU.
GEE, LADY... THANKS SO MUCH! BUT...
I WAS DOING FINE BEFORE YOU SHOWED UP WITH ALL THE COPS!
SO...MAYBE IF YOU TOOK A LEAP OFF THIS ROOF I WOULD BE FINE.
YOU'VE GOT A MOUTH ON YOU, KID.
IT'LL GET YOU INTO TROUBLE SOME DAY.
TRUST ME... I KNOW FROM EXPERIENCE.
THOONK
AN ARROW? WHO THE HELL BRINGS A BOW AND ARROW TO A GUNFIGHT-- OH?
JUST STICK WITH ME.
SERIOUSLY? THEY ARE SHOOTING AT YOU!

JUST LEAVE ME THE *HELL* ALONE!

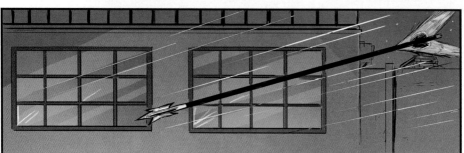

THANKS. I WANTED ONE OF THESE.

DAMMIT! YOU SAVED MY FREAKING LIFE.

YOU'RE WELCOME?

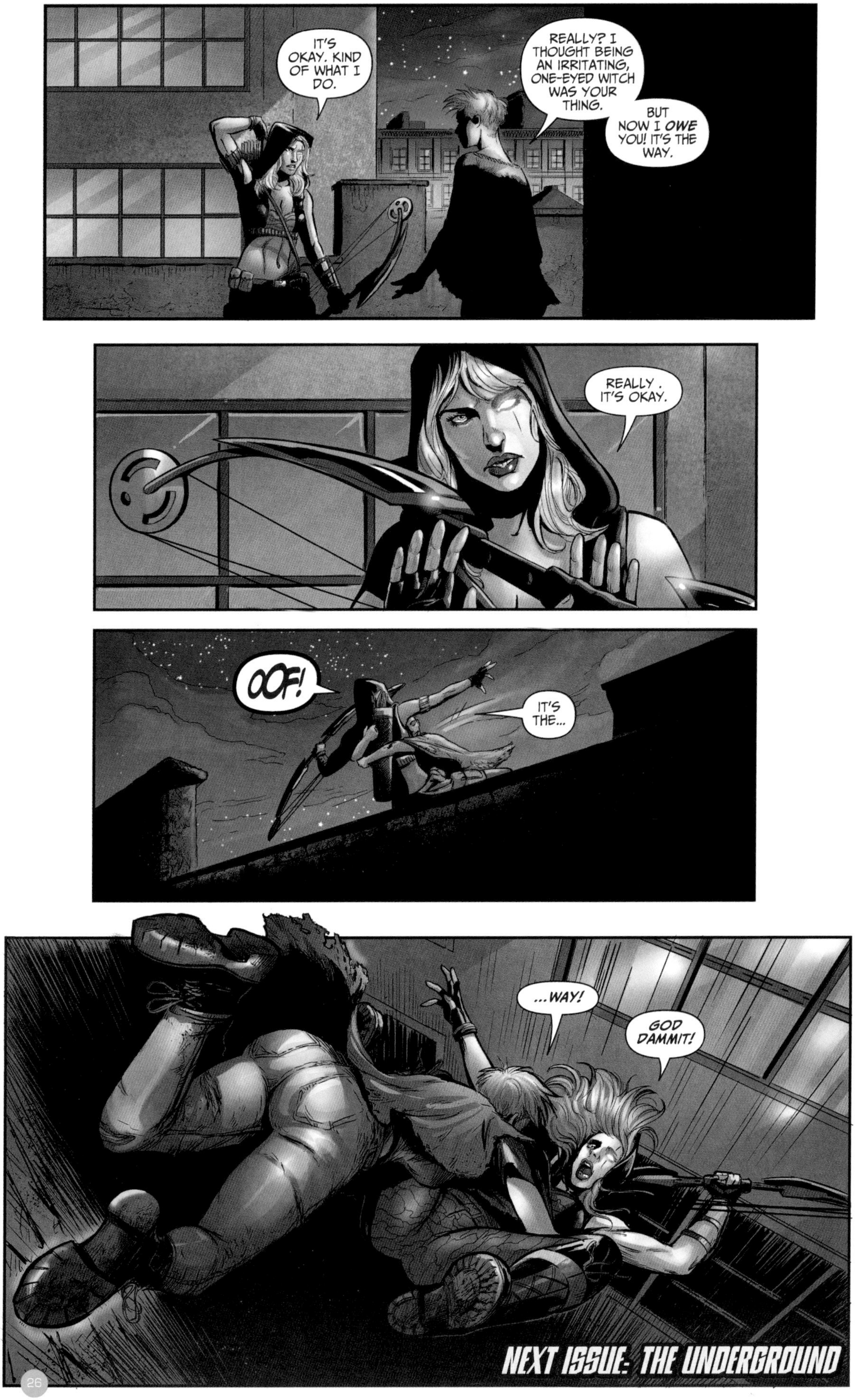
IT'S OKAY. KIND OF WHAT I DO.
REALLY? I THOUGHT BEING AN IRRITATING, ONE-EYED WITCH WAS YOUR THING.
BUT NOW I *OWE* YOU! IT'S THE WAY.
REALLY . IT'S OKAY.
OOF!
IT'S THE...
...WAY!
GOD DAMMIT!
NEXT ISSUE: THE UNDERGROUND

ROBYN HOOD
OUTLAW

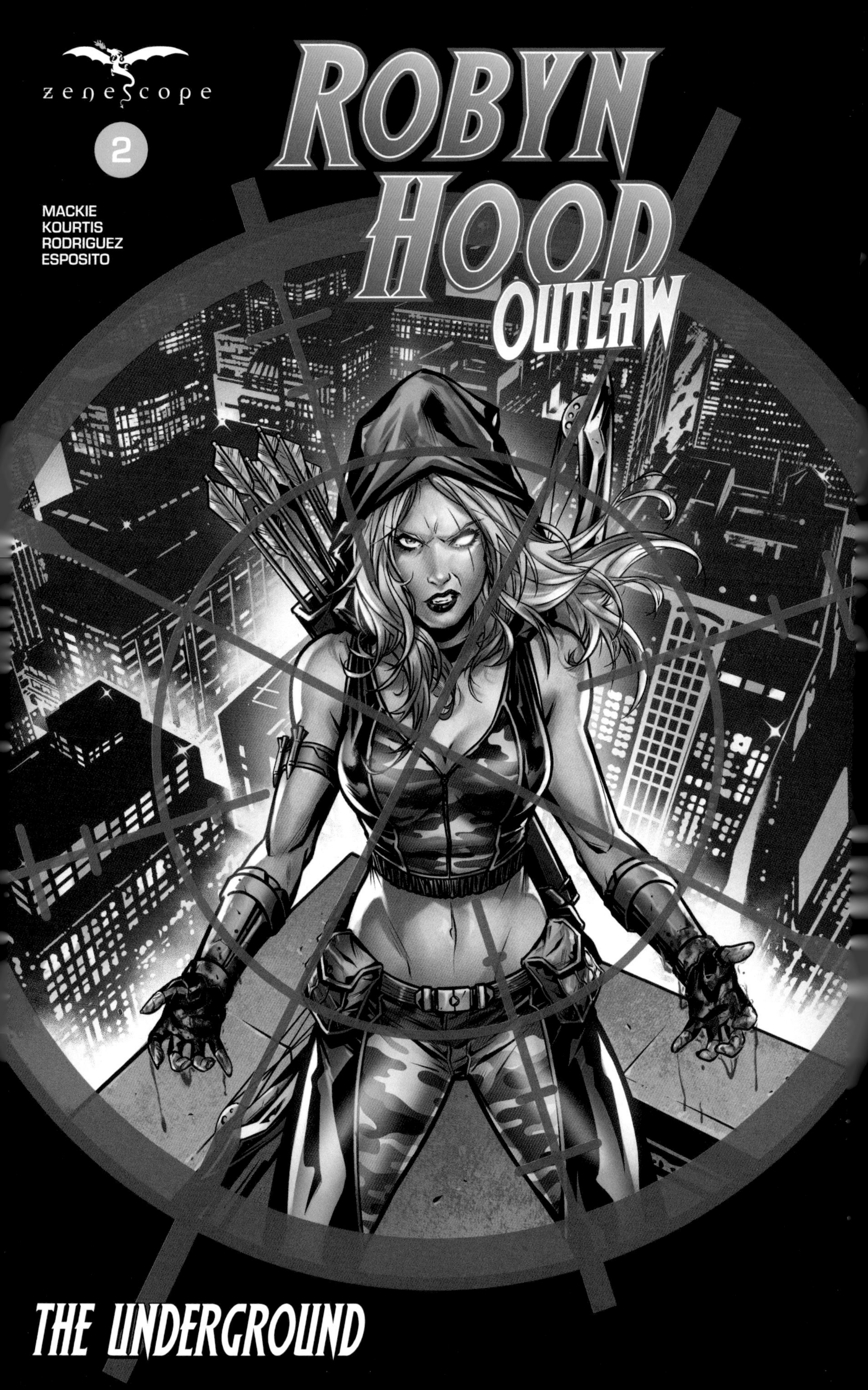
zenescope
2
MACKIE
KOURTIS
RODRIGUEZ
ESPOSITO
ROBYN HOOD
OUTLAW
THE UNDERGROUND

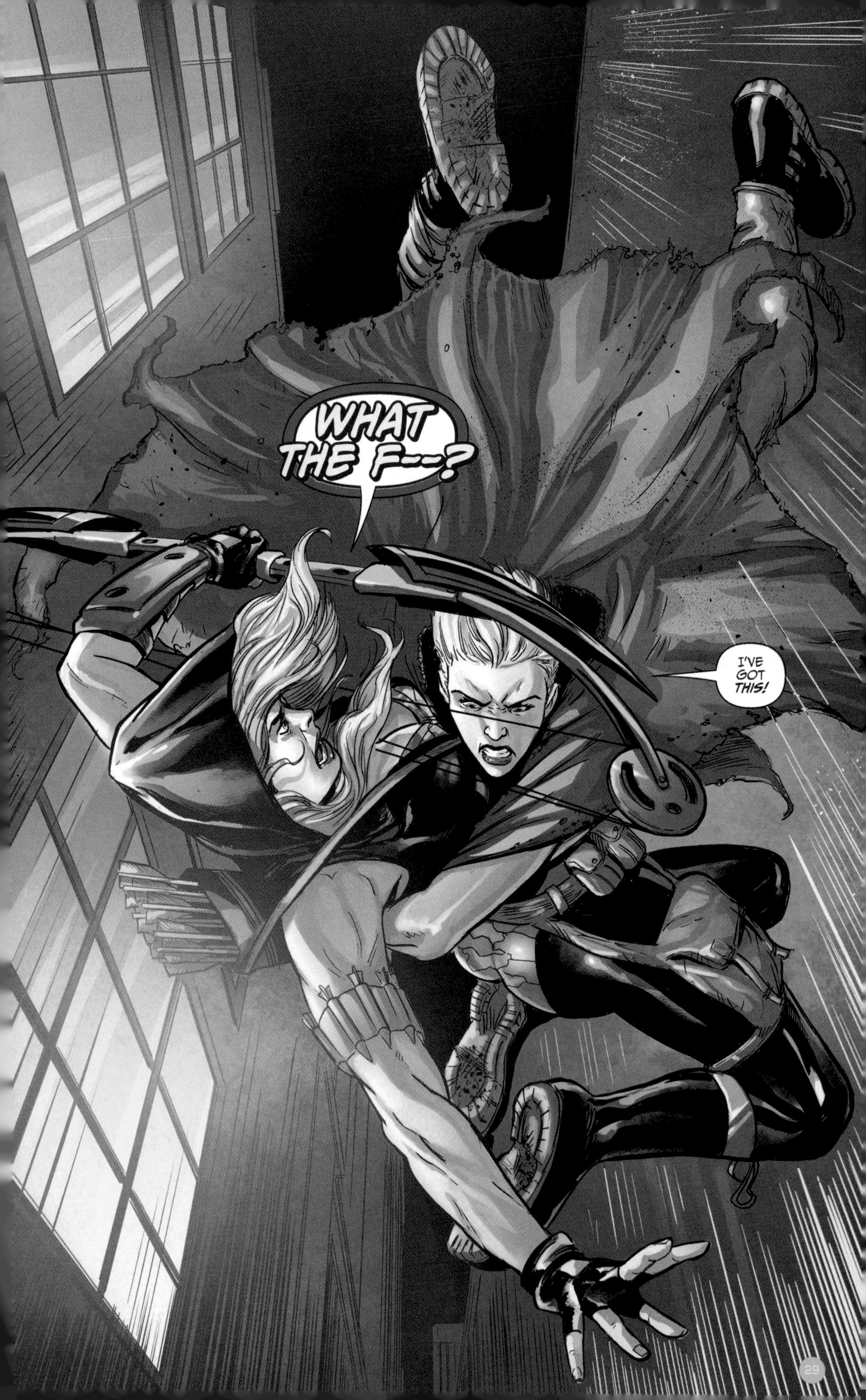
WHAT THE F--?
I'VE GOT THIS!

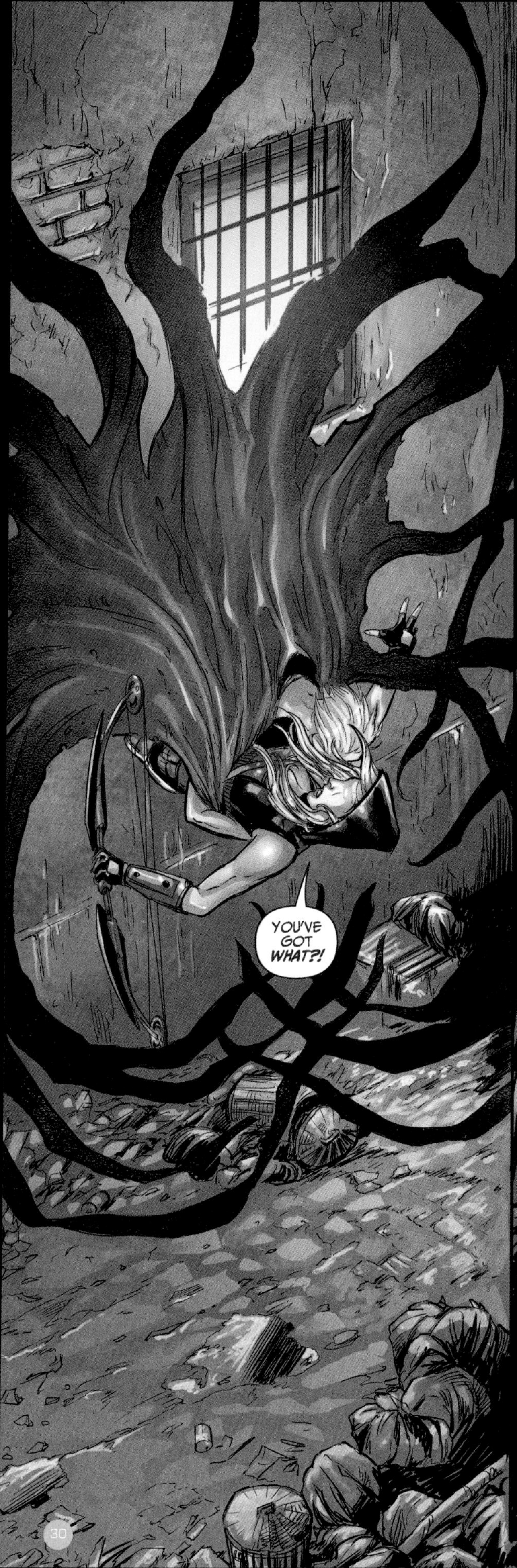
YOU'VE GOT WHAT?!
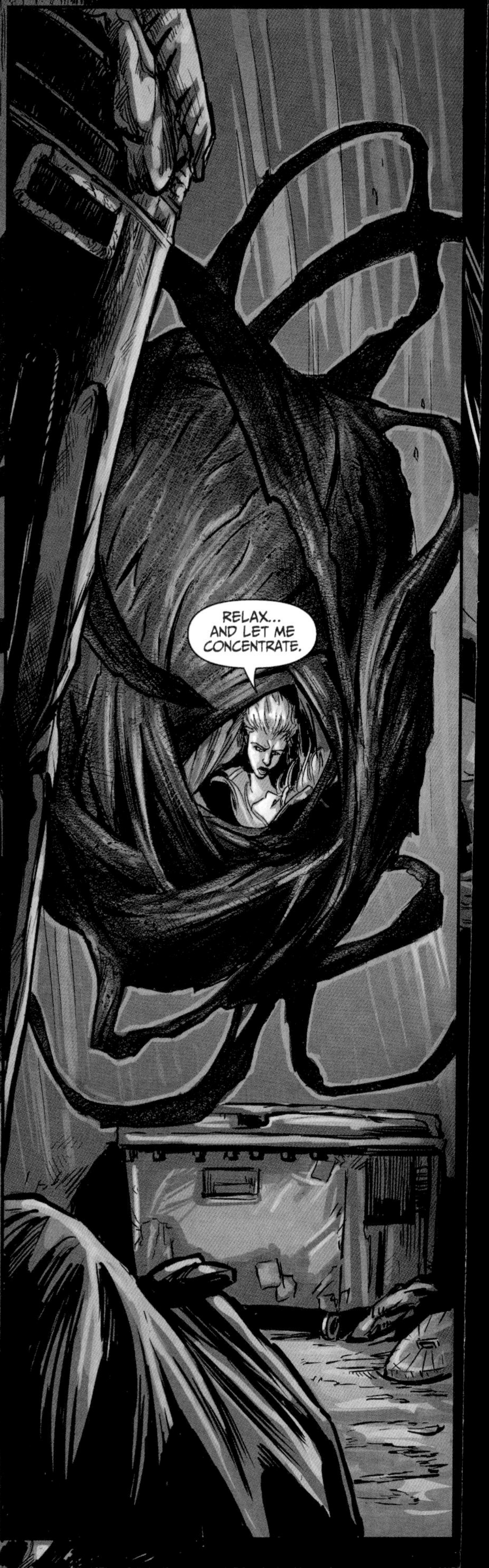
RELAX... AND LET ME CONCENTRATE.

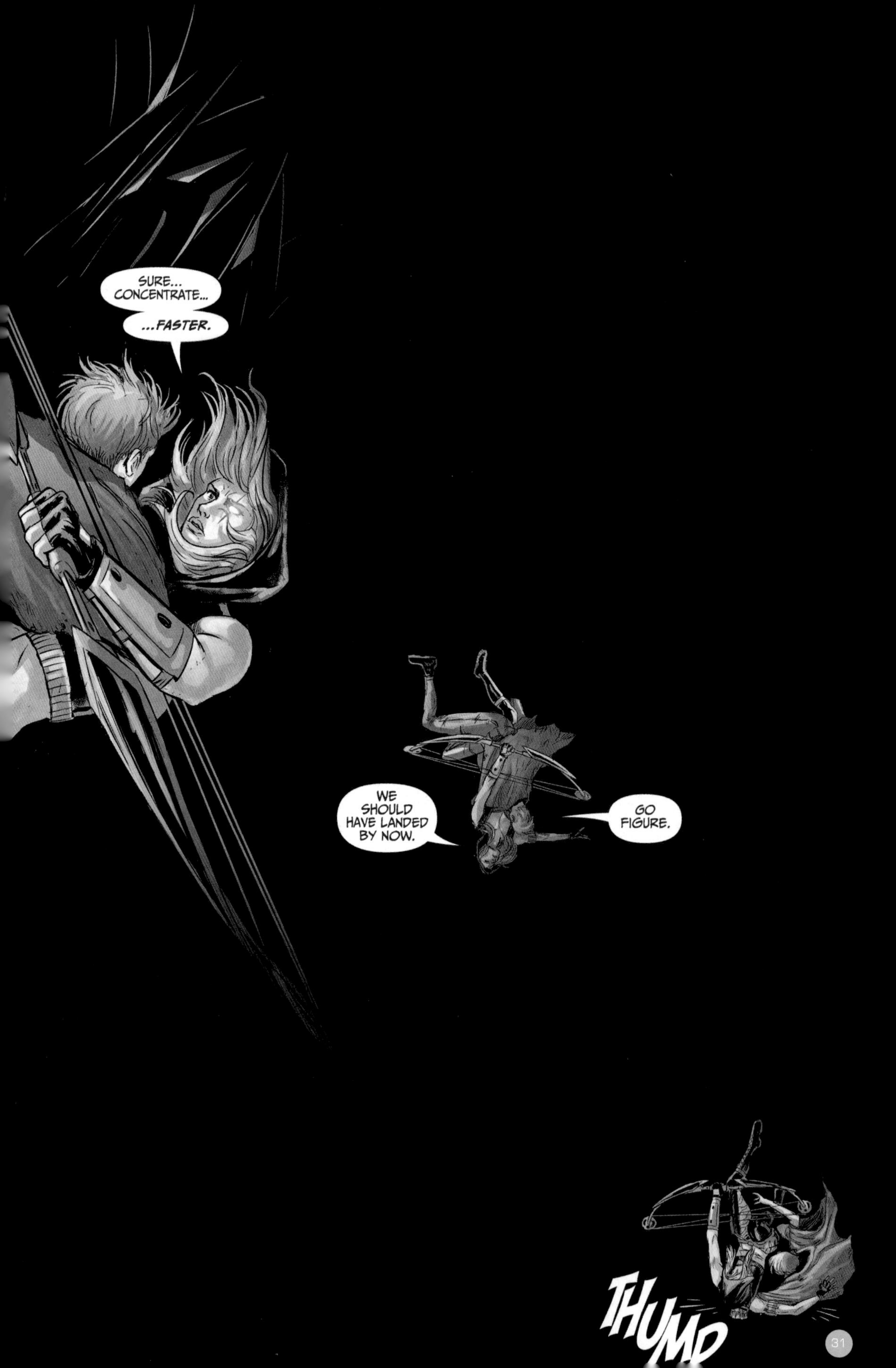
SURE... CONCENTRATE...
...FASTER.
WE SHOULD HAVE LANDED BY NOW.
GO FIGURE.
THUMP

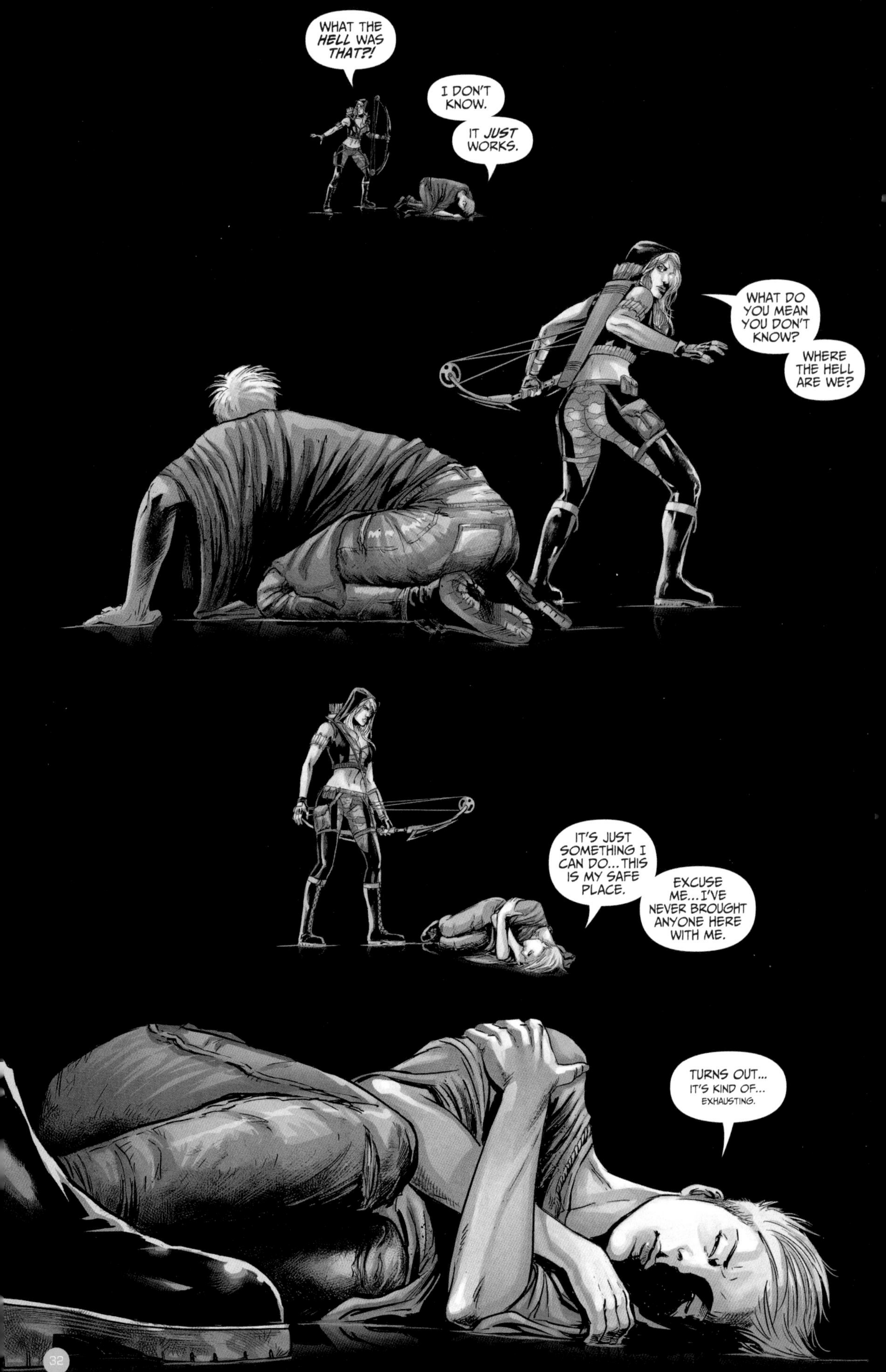
WHAT THE HELL WAS THAT?!
I DON'T KNOW.
IT JUST WORKS.
WHAT DO YOU MEAN YOU DON'T KNOW?
WHERE THE HELL ARE WE?
IT'S JUST SOMETHING I CAN DO... THIS IS MY SAFE PLACE.
EXCUSE ME... I'VE NEVER BROUGHT ANYONE HERE WITH ME.
TURNS OUT... IT'S KIND OF... EXHAUSTING.

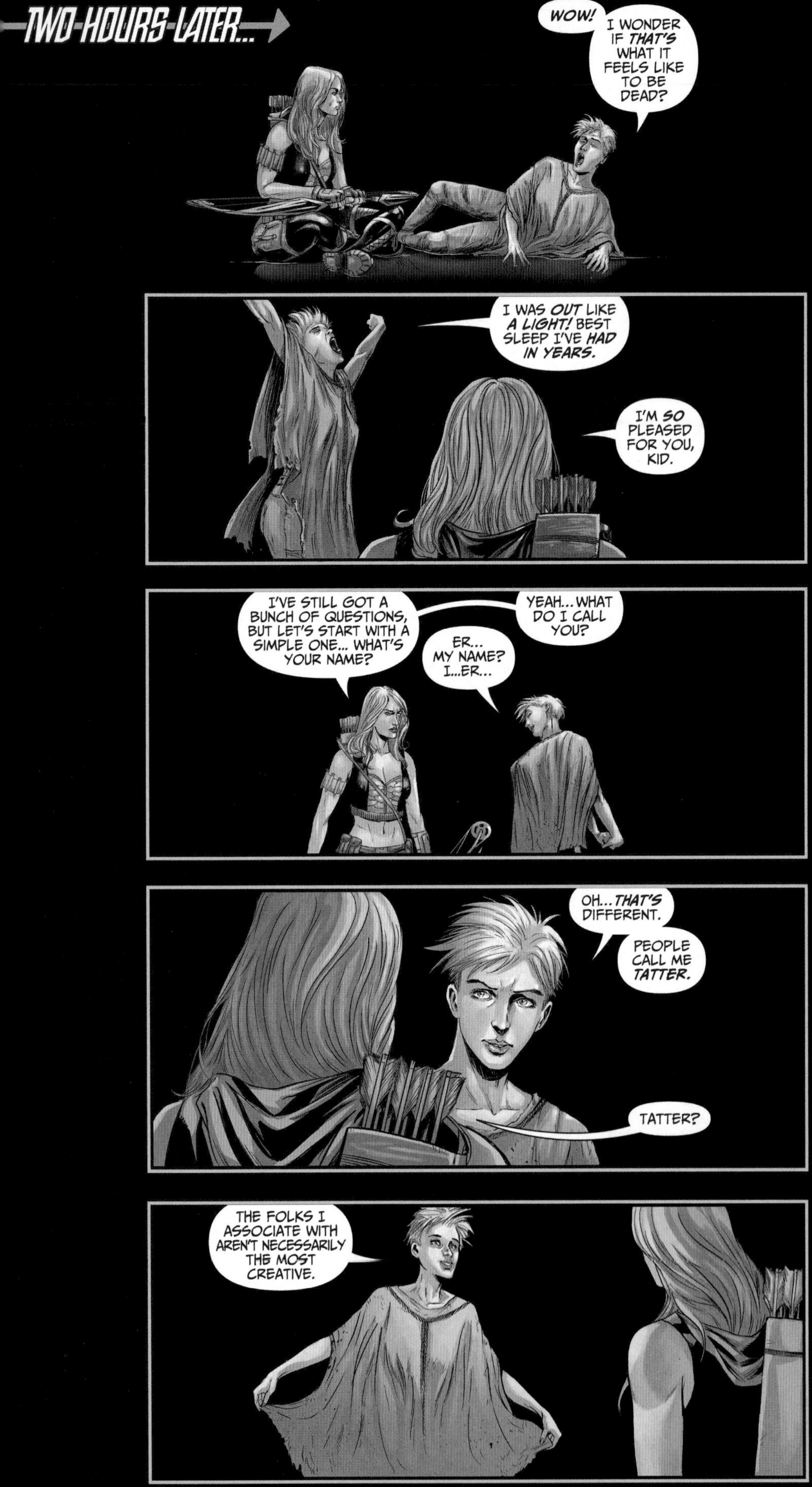
TWO HOURS LATER...
WOW!
I WONDER IF *THAT'S* WHAT IT FEELS LIKE TO BE DEAD?
I WAS *OUT* LIKE *A LIGHT!* BEST SLEEP I'VE *HAD IN YEARS.*
I'M *SO* PLEASED FOR YOU, KID.
I'VE STILL GOT A BUNCH OF QUESTIONS, BUT LET'S START WITH A SIMPLE ONE... WHAT'S YOUR NAME?
YEAH... WHAT DO I CALL YOU?
ER... MY NAME? I...ER...
OH... *THAT'S* DIFFERENT.
PEOPLE CALL ME *TATTER.*
TATTER?
THE FOLKS I ASSOCIATE WITH AREN'T NECESSARILY THE MOST CREATIVE.

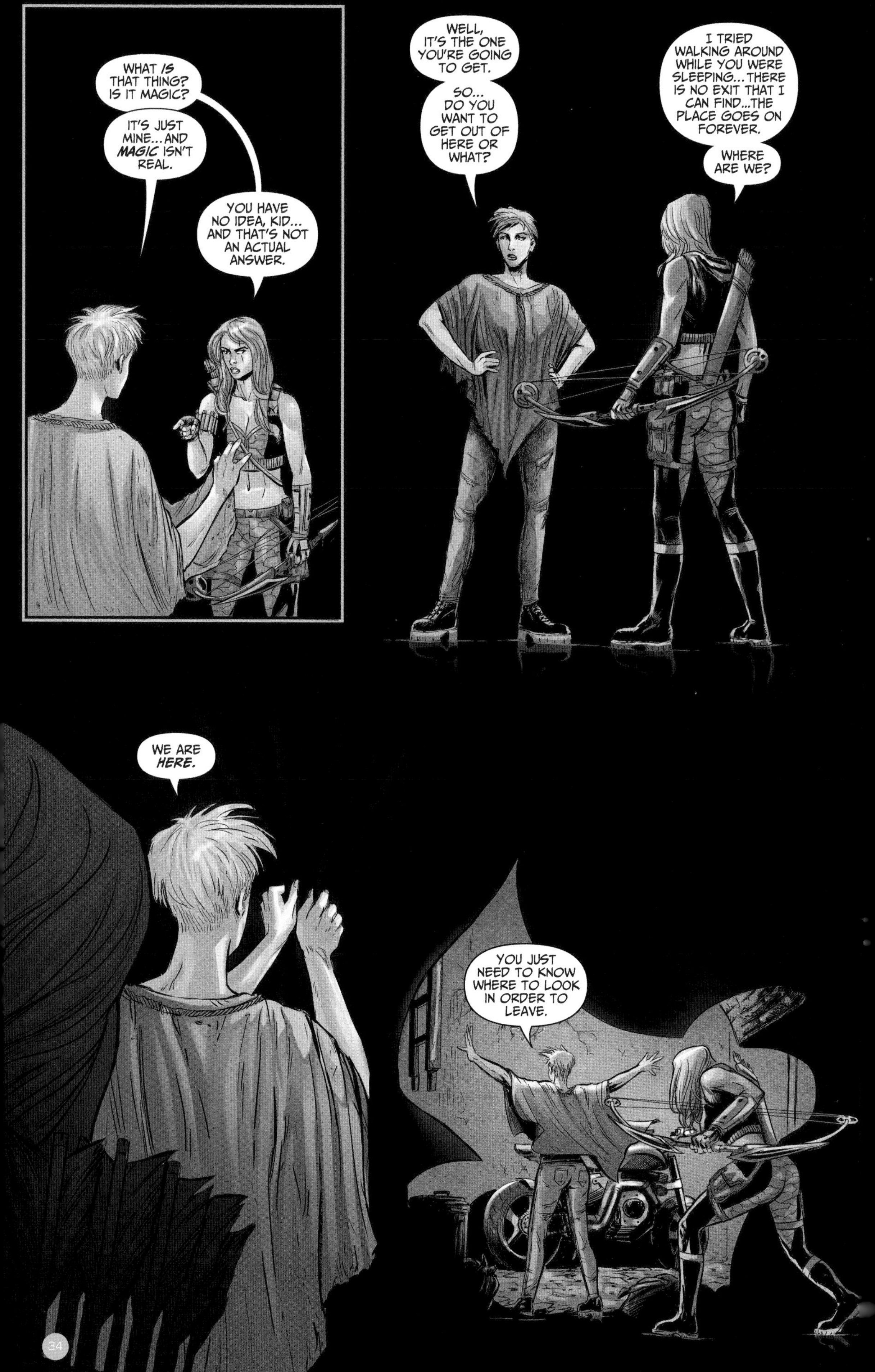
WHAT *IS* THAT THING? IS IT MAGIC?
IT'S JUST MINE... AND *MAGIC* ISN'T REAL.
YOU HAVE NO IDEA, KID... AND THAT'S NOT AN ACTUAL ANSWER.
WELL, IT'S THE ONE YOU'RE GOING TO GET.
SO... DO YOU WANT TO GET OUT OF HERE OR WHAT?
I TRIED WALKING AROUND WHILE YOU WERE SLEEPING... THERE IS NO EXIT THAT I CAN FIND...THE PLACE GOES ON FOREVER.
WHERE ARE WE?
WE ARE *HERE.*
YOU JUST NEED TO KNOW WHERE TO LOOK IN ORDER TO LEAVE.

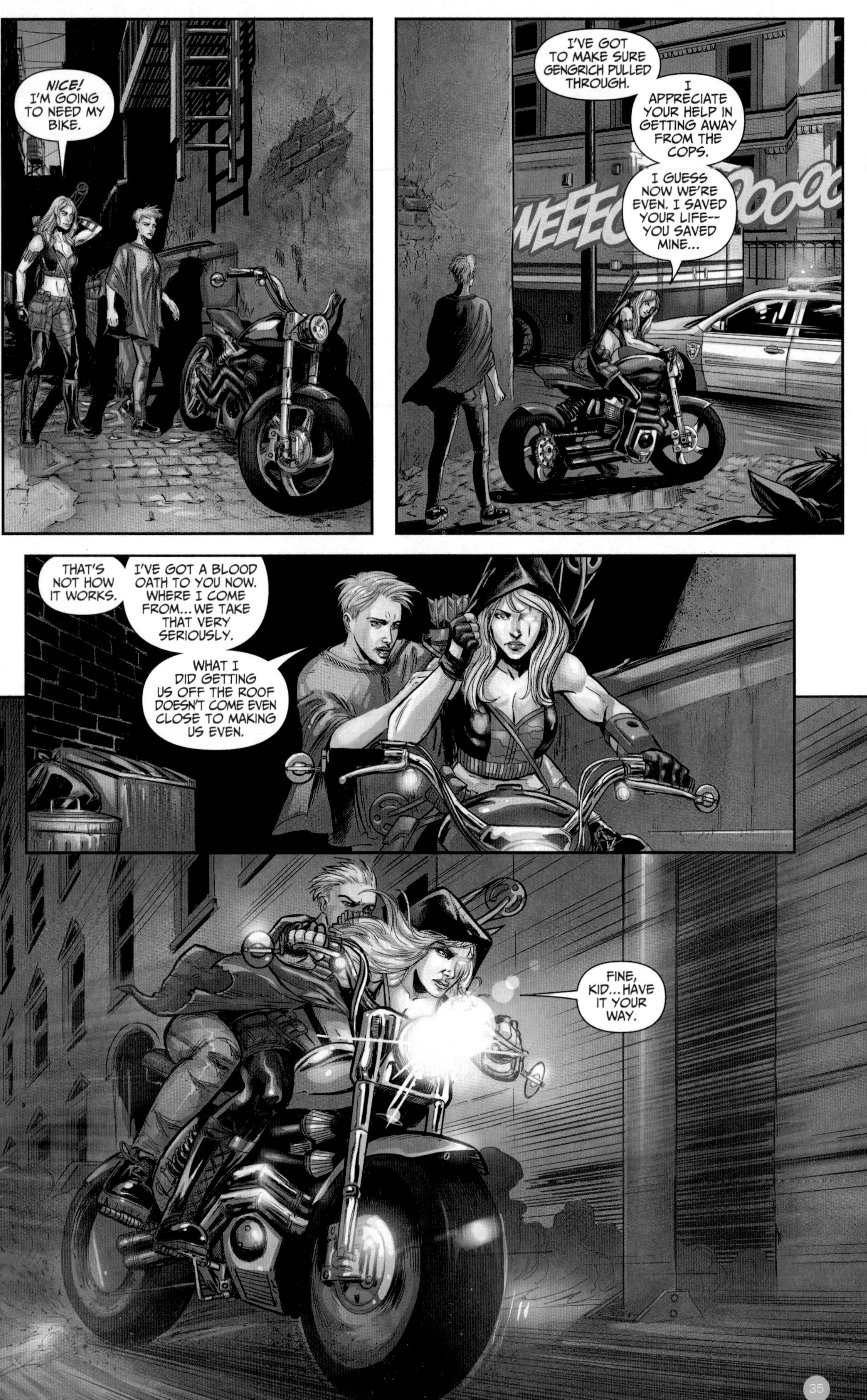
NICE! I'M GOING TO NEED MY BIKE.
I'VE GOT TO MAKE SURE GENGRICH PULLED THROUGH.
I APPRECIATE YOUR HELP IN GETTING AWAY FROM THE COPS.
I GUESS NOW WE'RE EVEN. I SAVED YOUR LIFE--YOU SAVED MINE...
THAT'S NOT HOW IT WORKS.
I'VE GOT A BLOOD OATH TO YOU NOW. WHERE I COME FROM...WE TAKE THAT VERY SERIOUSLY.
WHAT I DID GETTING US OFF THE ROOF DOESN'T COME EVEN CLOSE TO MAKING US EVEN.
FINE, KID...HAVE IT YOUR WAY.

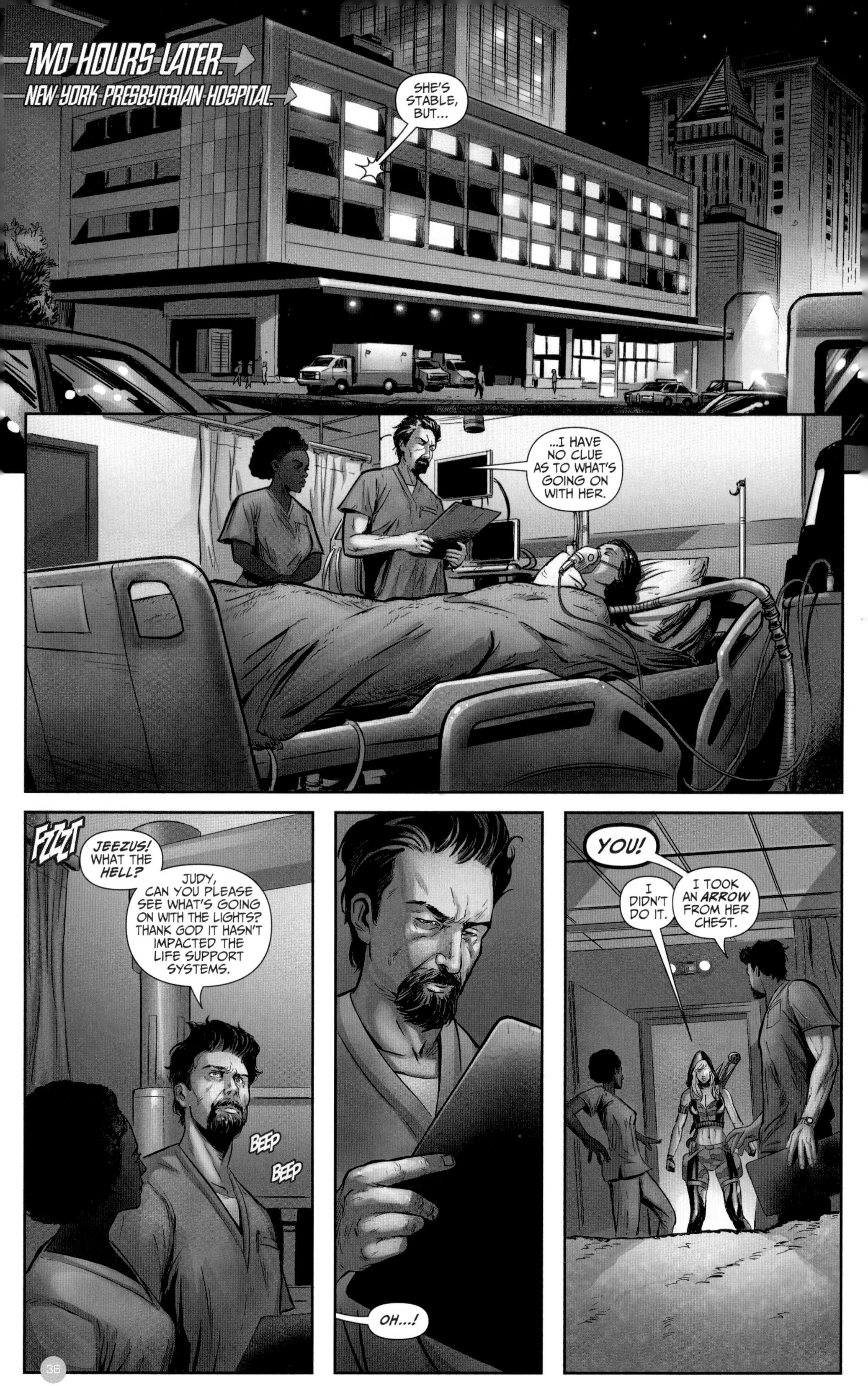

TWO HOURS LATER.
NEW YORK-PRESBYTERIAN HOSPITAL.
SHE'S STABLE, BUT...
...I HAVE NO CLUE AS TO WHAT'S GOING ON WITH HER.
FZZT
JEEZUS! WHAT THE HELL?
JUDY, CAN YOU PLEASE SEE WHAT'S GOING ON WITH THE LIGHTS? THANK GOD IT HASN'T IMPACTED THE LIFE SUPPORT SYSTEMS.
BEEP
BEEP
OH...!
YOU!
I TOOK AN ARROW FROM HER CHEST.
I DIDN'T DO IT.

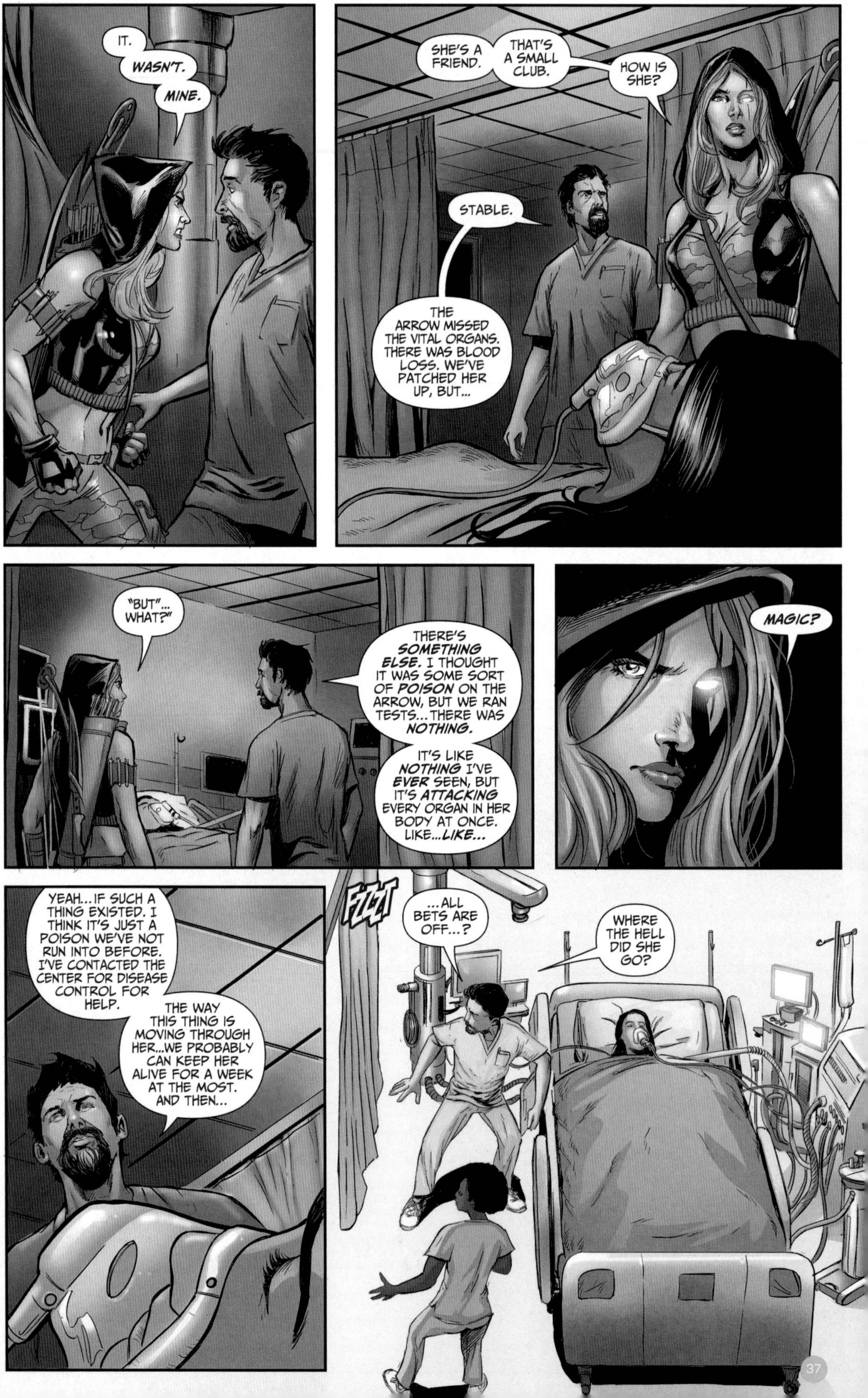
IT.
WASN'T.
MINE.
SHE'S A FRIEND.
THAT'S A SMALL CLUB.
HOW IS SHE?
STABLE.
THE ARROW MISSED THE VITAL ORGANS. THERE WAS BLOOD LOSS. WE'VE PATCHED HER UP, BUT...
"BUT"... WHAT?"
THERE'S ***SOMETHING ELSE.*** I THOUGHT IT WAS SOME SORT OF ***POISON*** ON THE ARROW, BUT WE RAN TESTS... THERE WAS ***NOTHING.***
IT'S LIKE ***NOTHING*** I'VE ***EVER*** SEEN, BUT IT'S ***ATTACKING*** EVERY ORGAN IN HER BODY AT ONCE. LIKE... ***LIKE...***
MAGIC?
YEAH... IF SUCH A THING EXISTED. I THINK IT'S JUST A POISON WE'VE NOT RUN INTO BEFORE. I'VE CONTACTED THE CENTER FOR DISEASE CONTROL FOR HELP.
THE WAY THIS THING IS MOVING THROUGH HER... WE PROBABLY CAN KEEP HER ALIVE FOR A WEEK AT THE MOST. AND THEN...
FZZZT
...ALL BETS ARE OFF...?
WHERE THE HELL DID SHE GO?

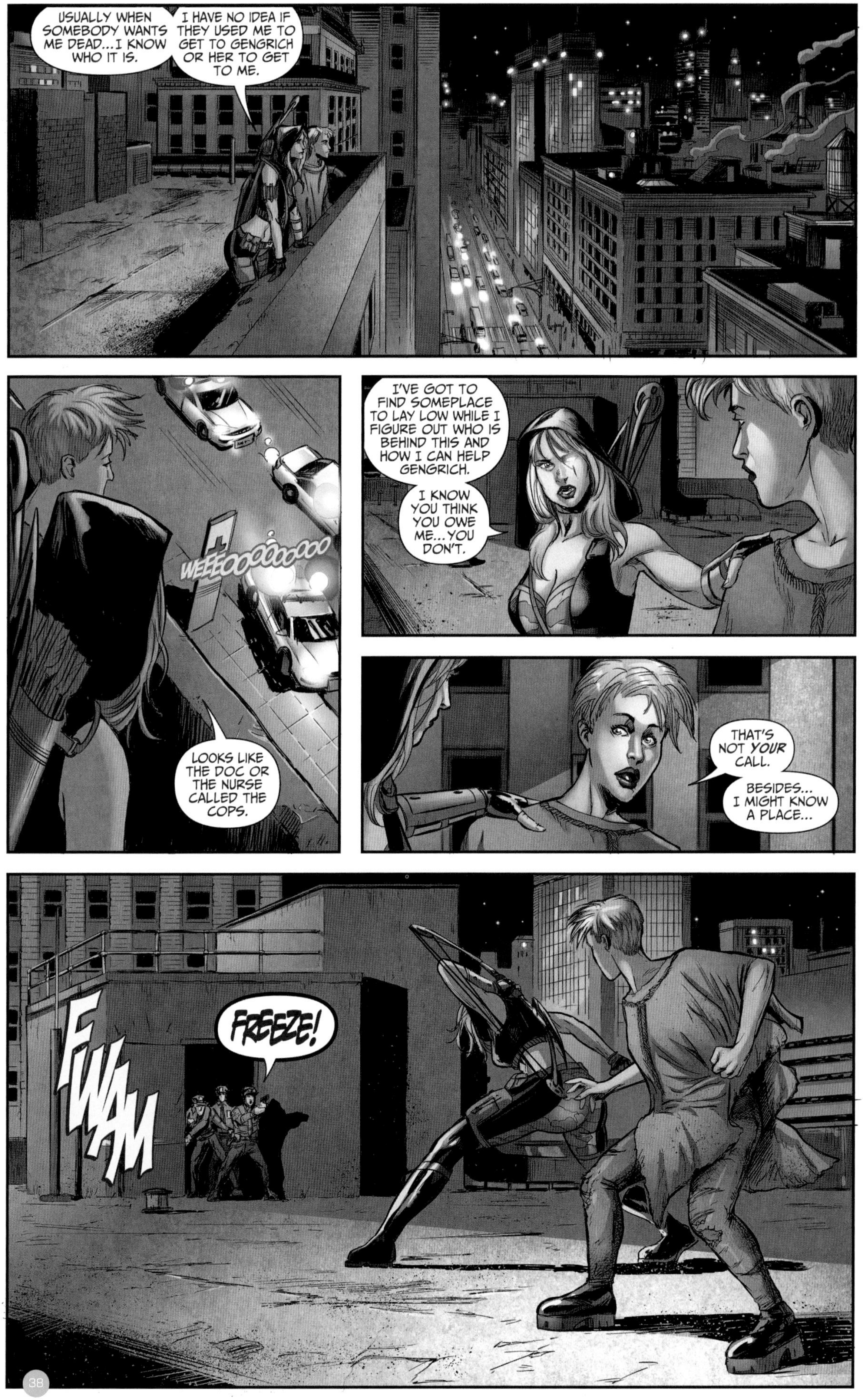
USUALLY WHEN SOMEBODY WANTS ME DEAD...I KNOW WHO IT IS.
I HAVE NO IDEA IF THEY USED ME TO GET TO GENGRICH OR HER TO GET TO ME.
WEEEOOOOOOOOOO
LOOKS LIKE THE DOC OR THE NURSE CALLED THE COPS.
I'VE GOT TO FIND SOMEPLACE TO LAY LOW WHILE I FIGURE OUT WHO IS BEHIND THIS AND HOW I CAN HELP GENGRICH.
I KNOW YOU THINK YOU OWE ME...YOU DON'T.
THAT'S NOT *YOUR* CALL.
BESIDES... I MIGHT KNOW A PLACE...
FWAM
FREEZE!

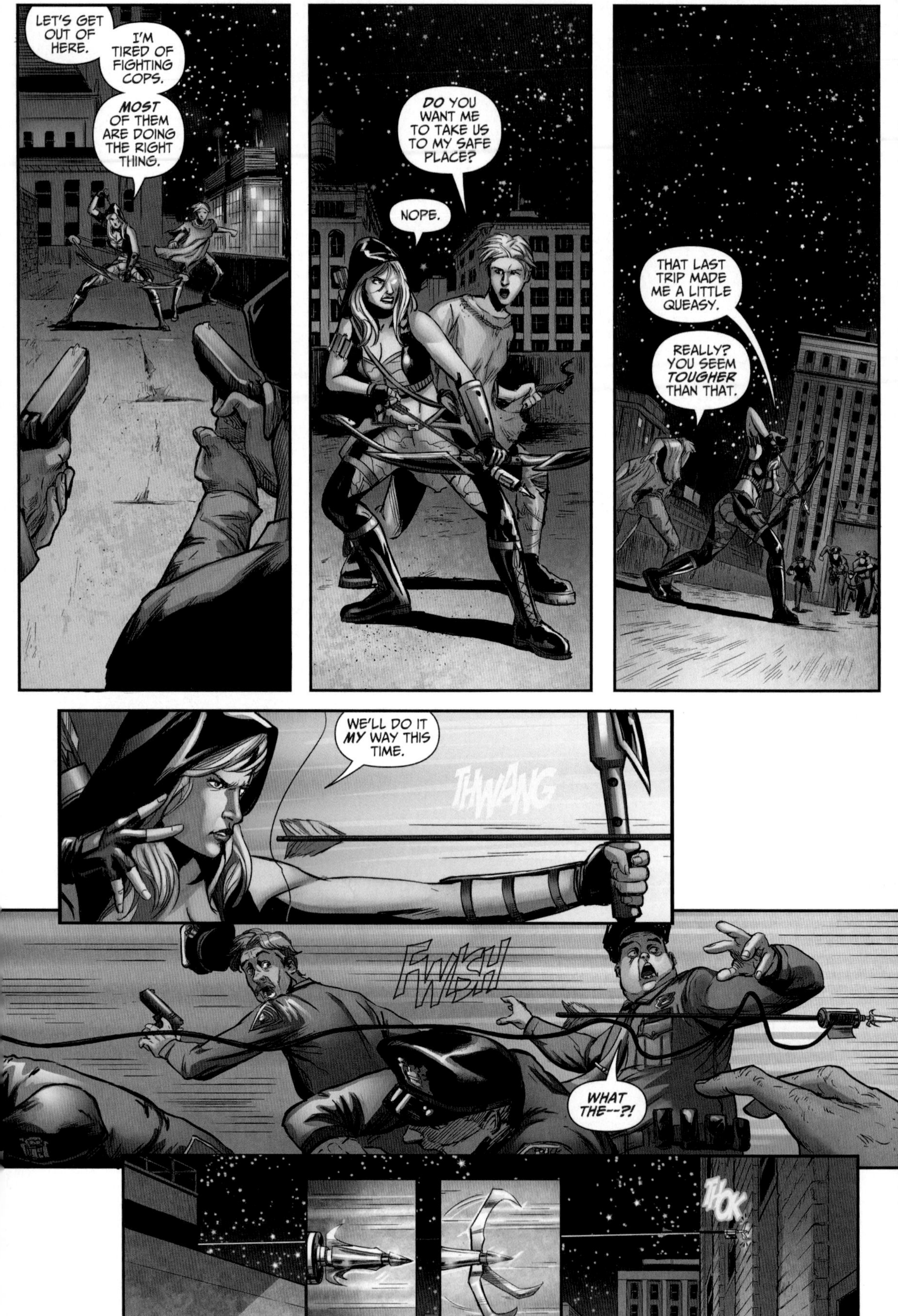
LET'S GET OUT OF HERE.
I'M TIRED OF FIGHTING COPS.
MOST OF THEM ARE DOING THE RIGHT THING.
DO YOU WANT ME TO TAKE US TO MY SAFE PLACE?
NOPE.
THAT LAST TRIP MADE ME A LITTLE QUEASY.
REALLY? YOU SEEM TOUGHER THAN THAT.
WE'LL DO IT MY WAY THIS TIME.
THWANG
FWISH
WHAT THE--?!
THOK

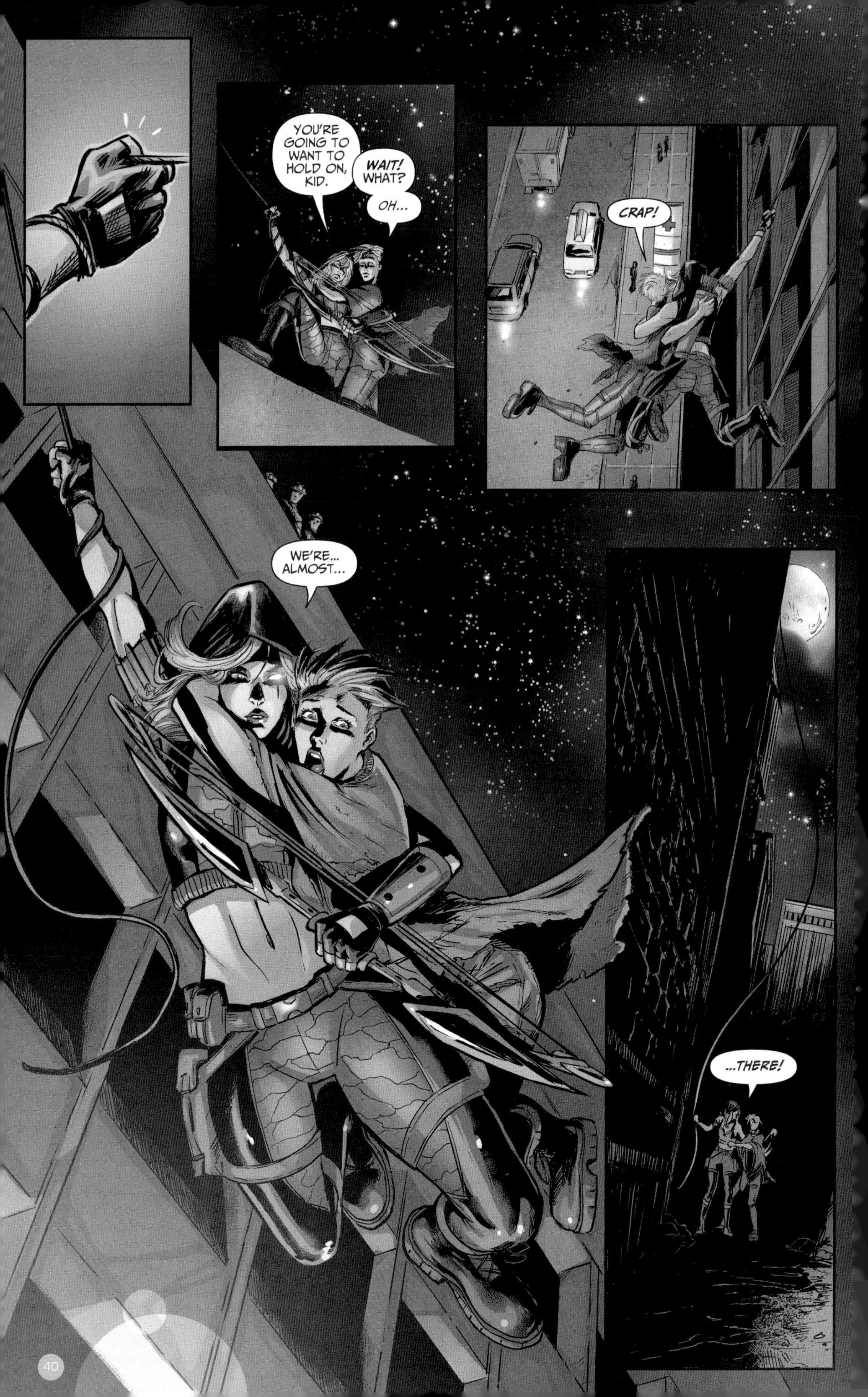

YOU'RE GOING TO WANT TO HOLD ON, KID.
WAIT! WHAT?
OH...
CRAP!
WE'RE... ALMOST...
...THERE!

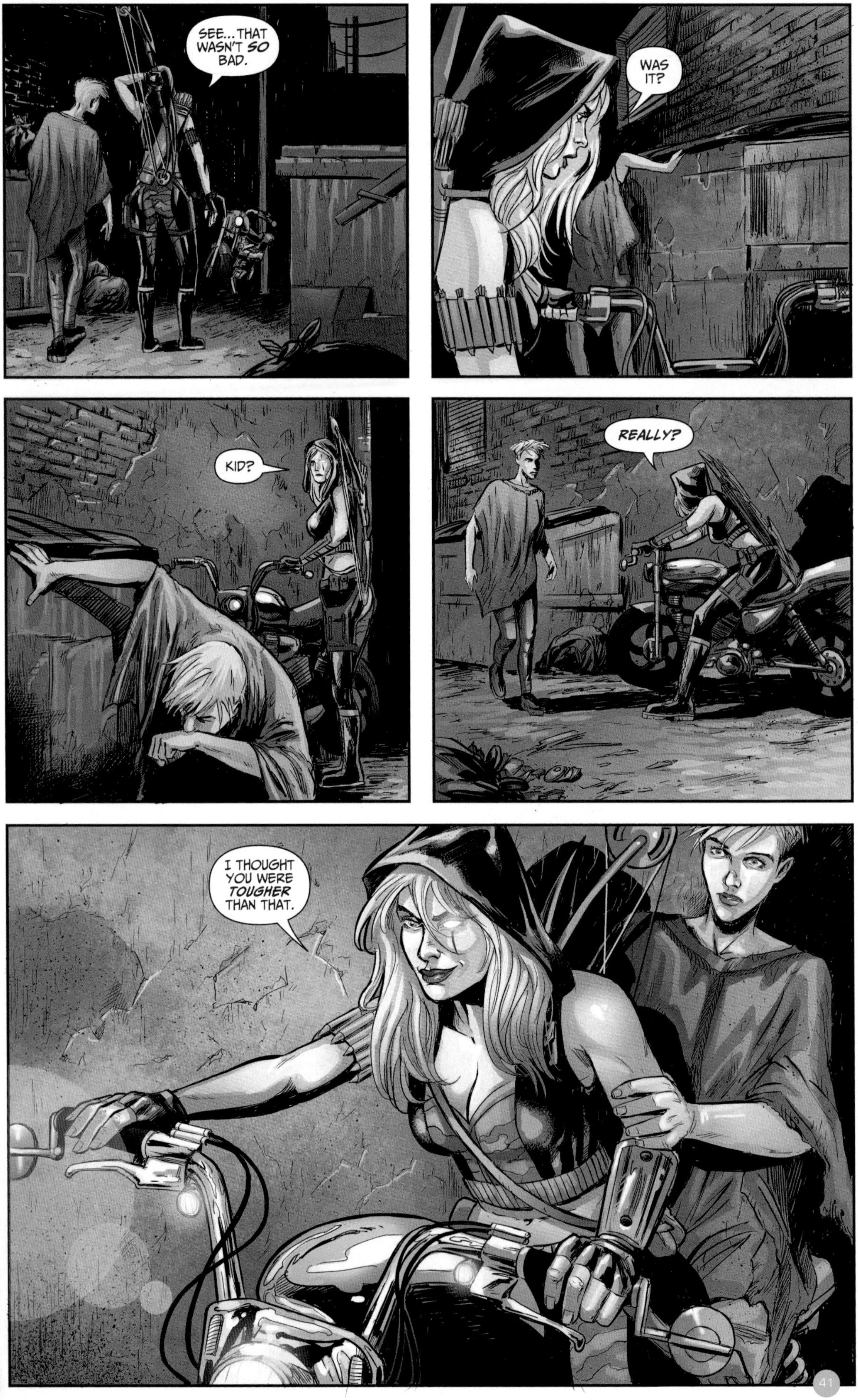
SEE... THAT WASN'T SO BAD.
WAS IT?
KID?
REALLY?
I THOUGHT YOU WERE TOUGHER THAN THAT.

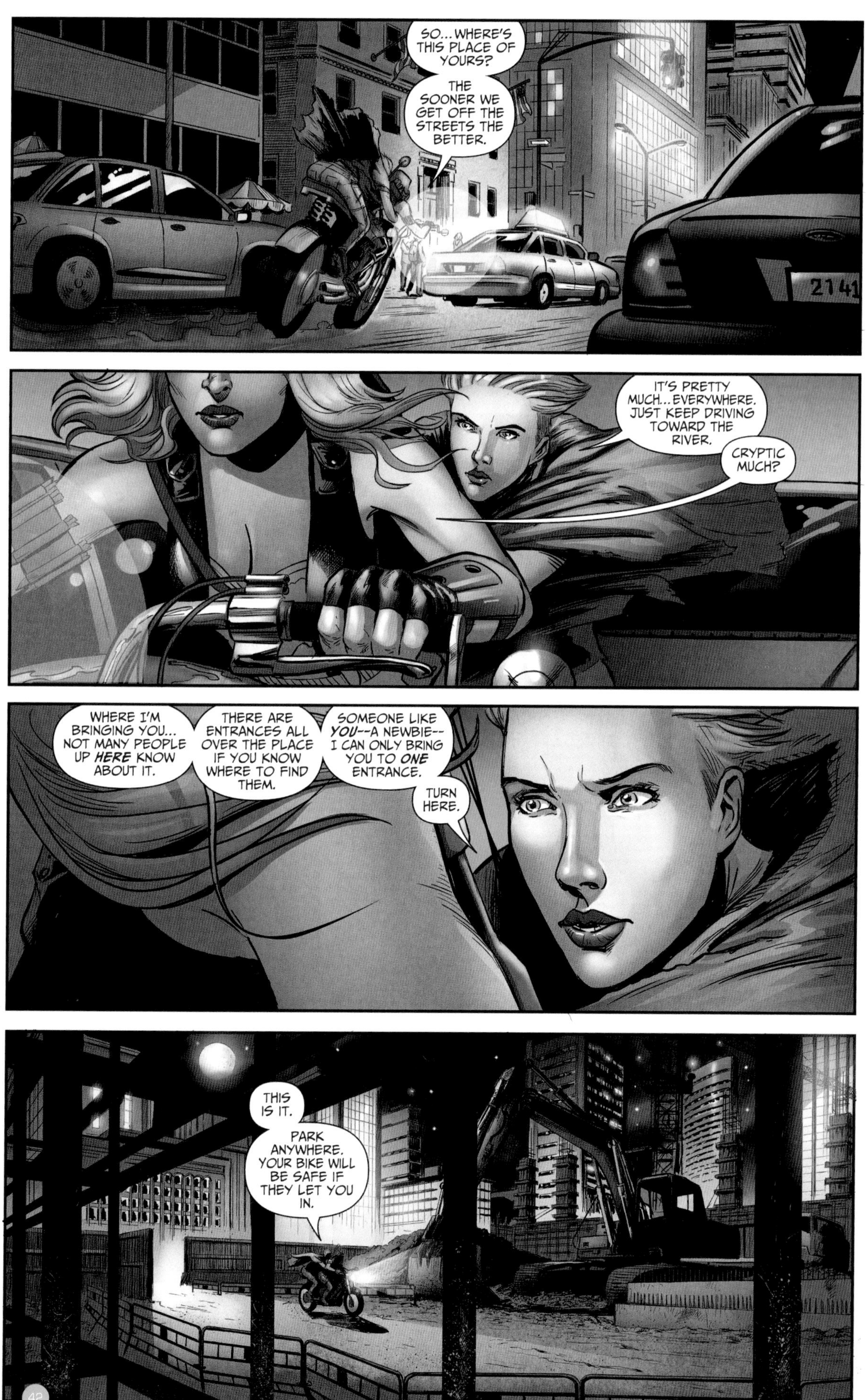
SO...WHERE'S THIS PLACE OF YOURS?
THE SOONER WE GET OFF THE STREETS THE BETTER.
2141
IT'S PRETTY MUCH...EVERYWHERE. JUST KEEP DRIVING TOWARD THE RIVER.
CRYPTIC MUCH?
WHERE I'M BRINGING YOU... NOT MANY PEOPLE UP *HERE* KNOW ABOUT IT.
THERE ARE ENTRANCES ALL OVER THE PLACE IF YOU KNOW WHERE TO FIND THEM.
SOMEONE LIKE *YOU*--A NEWBIE--I CAN ONLY BRING YOU TO *ONE* ENTRANCE.
TURN HERE.
THIS IS IT.
PARK ANYWHERE. YOUR BIKE WILL BE SAFE IF THEY LET YOU IN.

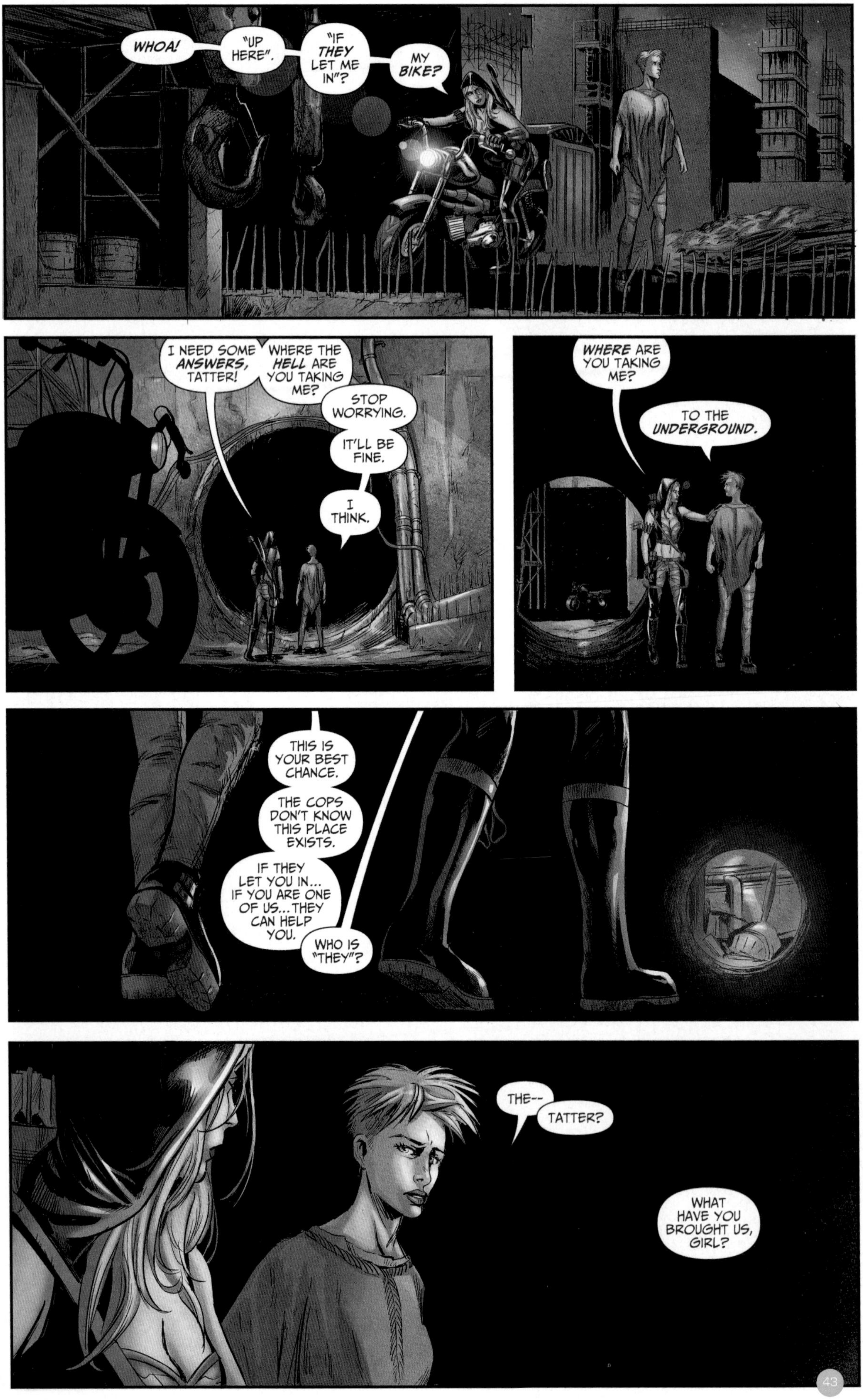
WHOA!
"UP HERE".
"IF THEY LET ME IN"?
MY BIKE?
I NEED SOME ANSWERS, TATTER!
WHERE THE HELL ARE YOU TAKING ME?
STOP WORRYING.
IT'LL BE FINE.
I THINK.
WHERE ARE YOU TAKING ME?
TO THE UNDERGROUND.
THIS IS YOUR BEST CHANCE.
THE COPS DON'T KNOW THIS PLACE EXISTS.
IF THEY LET YOU IN... IF YOU ARE ONE OF US...THEY CAN HELP YOU.
WHO IS "THEY"?
THE--
TATTER?
WHAT HAVE YOU BROUGHT US, GIRL?

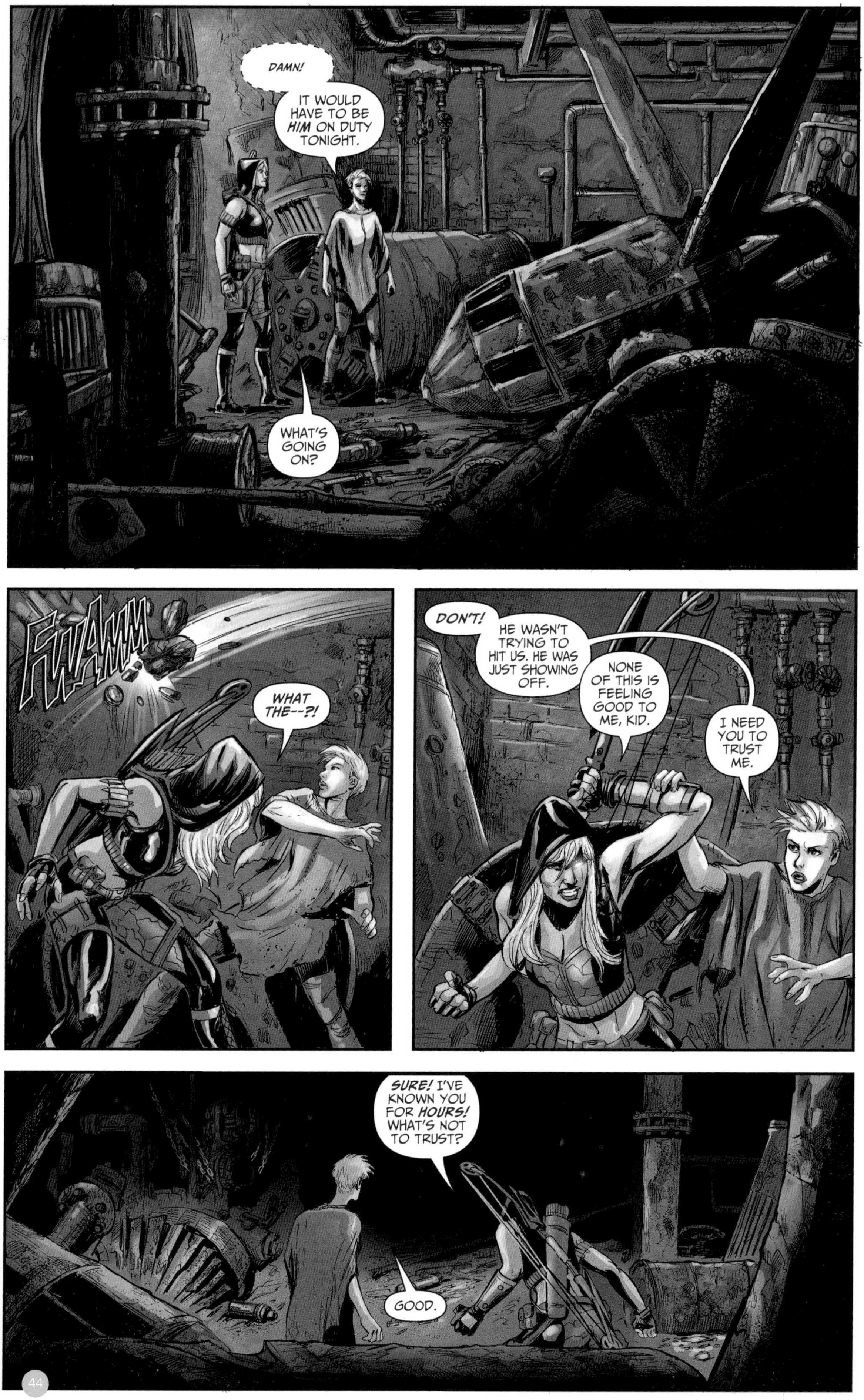
DAMN!
IT WOULD HAVE TO BE HIM ON DUTY TONIGHT.
WHAT'S GOING ON?
FWAMM
WHAT THE--?!
DON'T!
HE WASN'T TRYING TO HIT US. HE WAS JUST SHOWING OFF.
NONE OF THIS IS FEELING GOOD TO ME, KID.
I NEED YOU TO TRUST ME.
SURE! I'VE KNOWN YOU FOR HOURS! WHAT'S NOT TO TRUST?
GOOD.

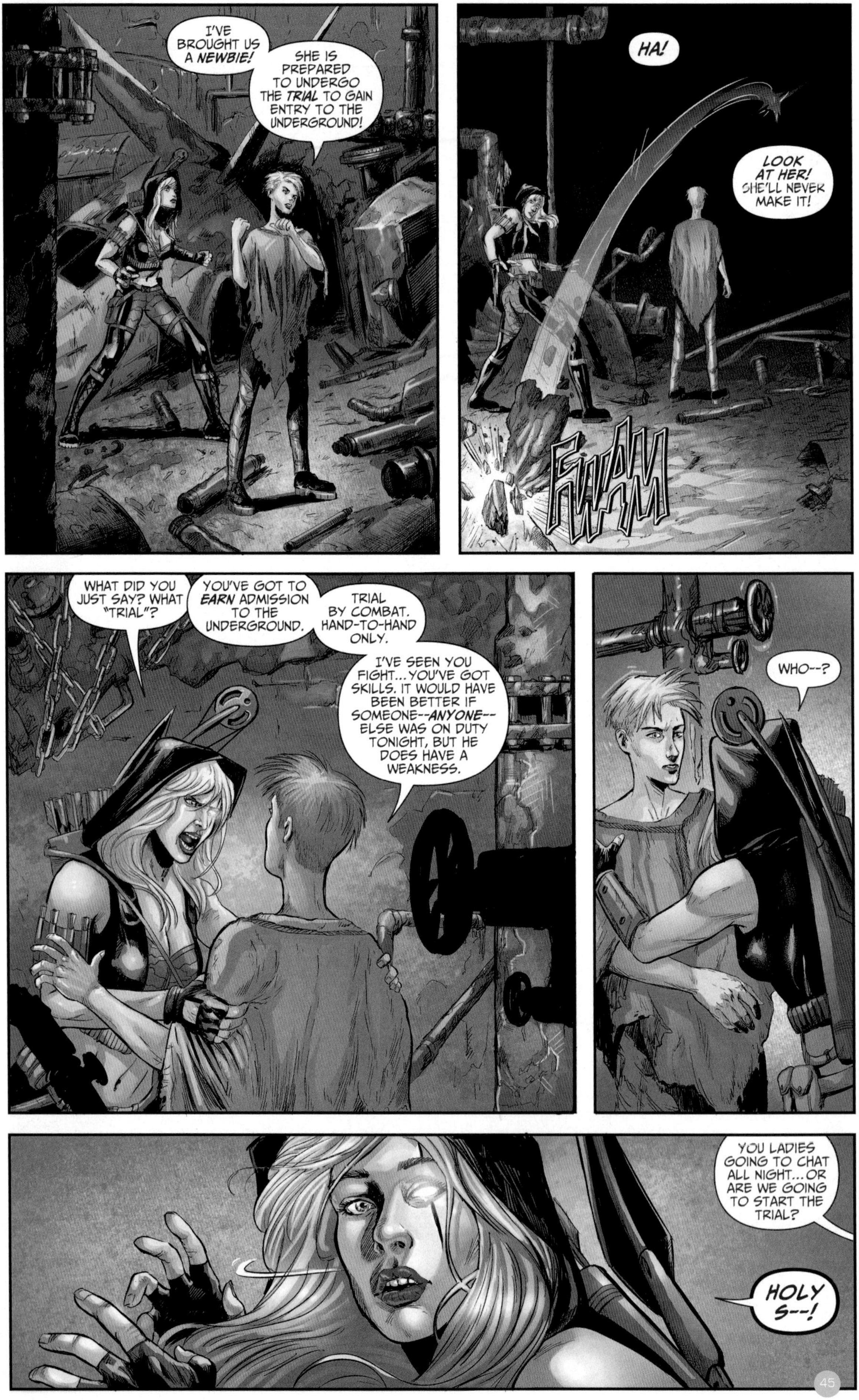
I'VE BROUGHT US A NEWBIE!
SHE IS PREPARED TO UNDERGO THE TRIAL TO GAIN ENTRY TO THE UNDERGROUND!
HA!
LOOK AT HER! SHE'LL NEVER MAKE IT!
FWAM
WHAT DID YOU JUST SAY? WHAT "TRIAL"?
YOU'VE GOT TO EARN ADMISSION TO THE UNDERGROUND.
TRIAL BY COMBAT. HAND-TO-HAND ONLY.
I'VE SEEN YOU FIGHT...YOU'VE GOT SKILLS. IT WOULD HAVE BEEN BETTER IF SOMEONE--ANYONE--ELSE WAS ON DUTY TONIGHT, BUT HE DOES HAVE A WEAKNESS.
WHO--?
YOU LADIES GOING TO CHAT ALL NIGHT...OR ARE WE GOING TO START THE TRIAL?
HOLY S--!

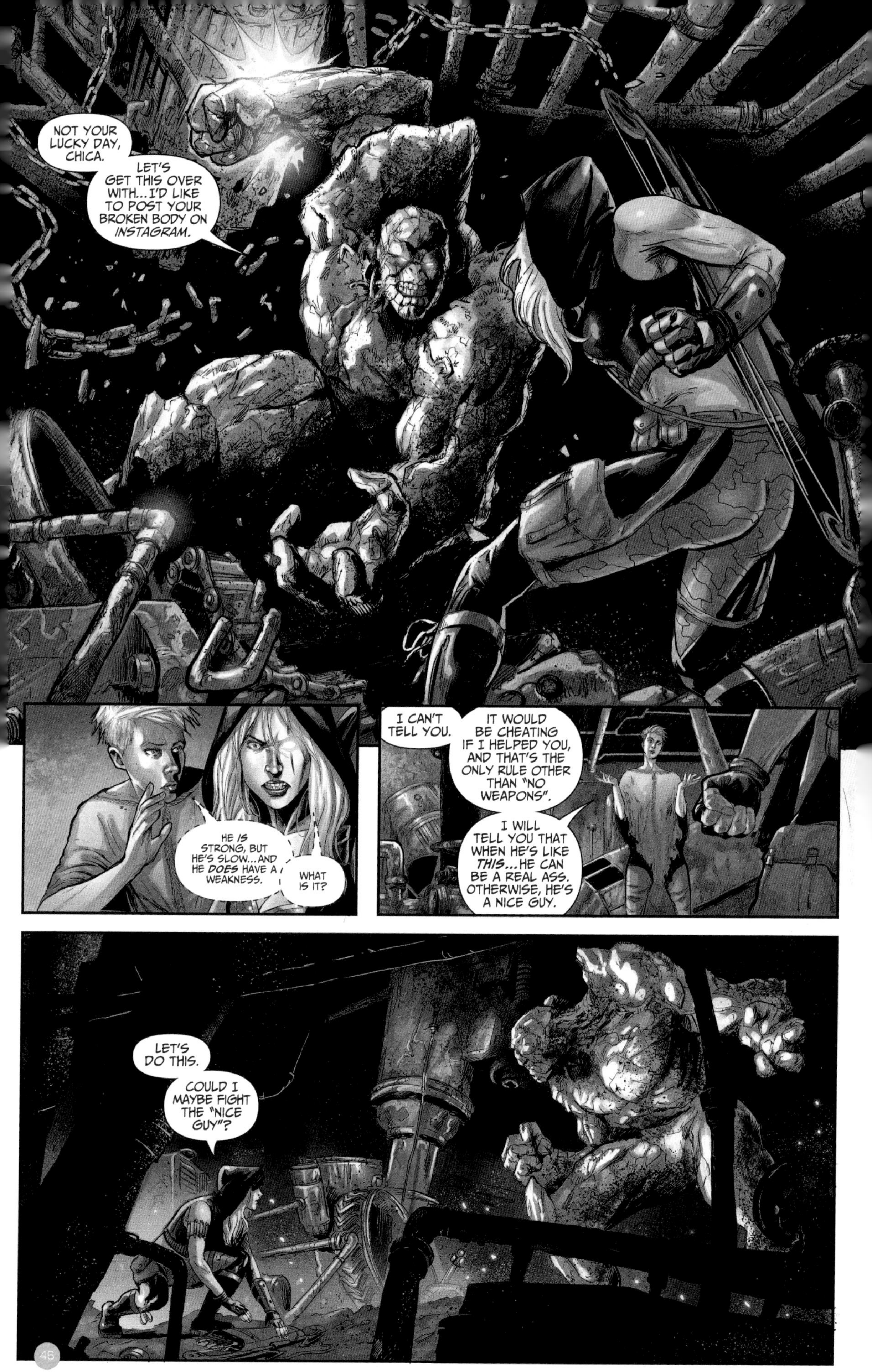
NOT YOUR LUCKY DAY, CHICA.
LET'S GET THIS OVER WITH...I'D LIKE TO POST YOUR BROKEN BODY ON *INSTAGRAM*.
HE *IS* STRONG, BUT HE'S SLOW...AND HE *DOES* HAVE A WEAKNESS.
WHAT IS IT?
I CAN'T TELL YOU.
IT WOULD BE CHEATING IF I HELPED YOU, AND THAT'S THE ONLY RULE OTHER THAN "NO WEAPONS".
I WILL TELL YOU THAT WHEN HE'S LIKE *THIS*...HE CAN BE A REAL ASS. OTHERWISE, HE'S A NICE GUY.
LET'S DO THIS.
COULD I MAYBE FIGHT THE "NICE GUY"?

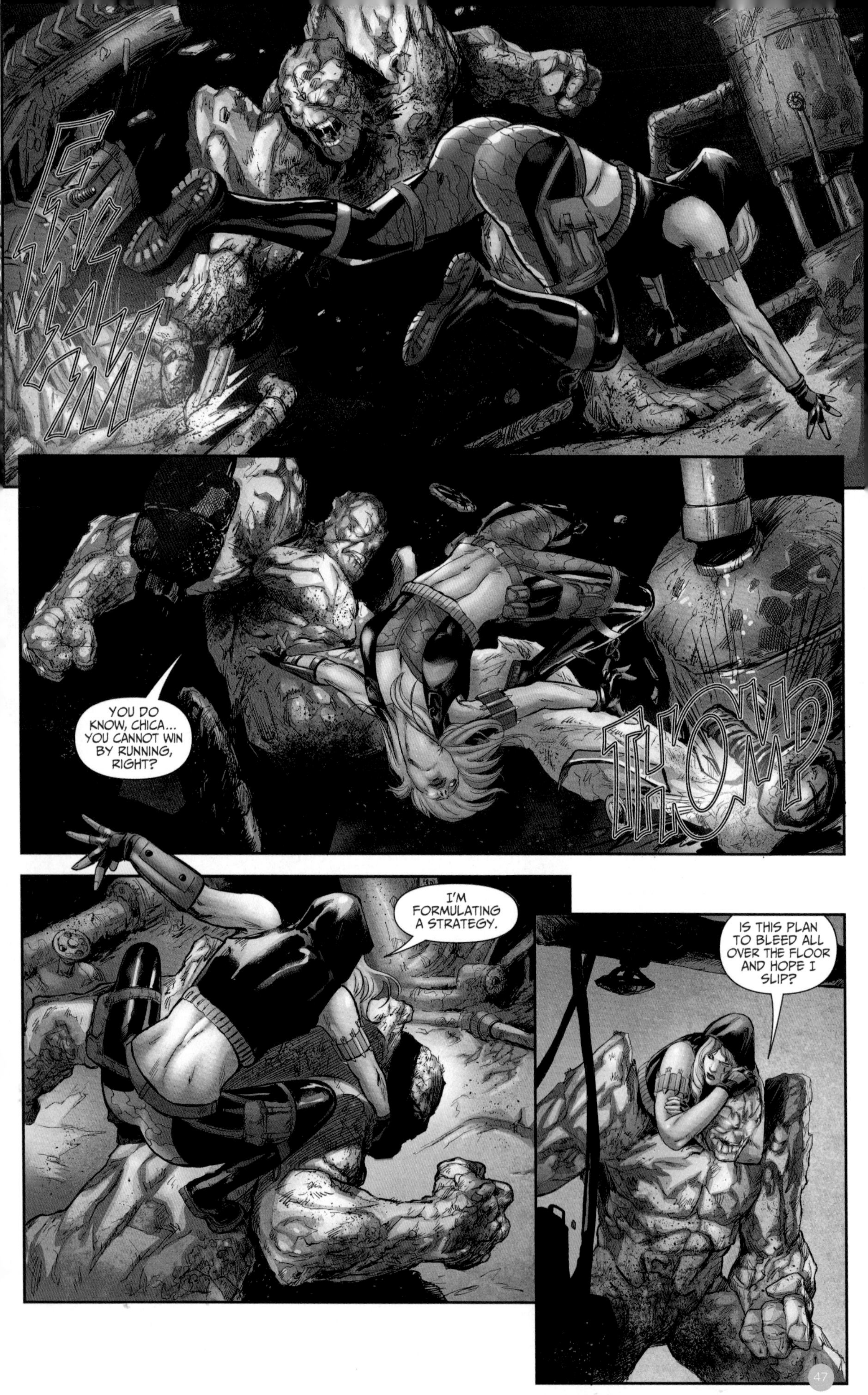
YOU DO KNOW, CHICA... YOU CANNOT WIN BY RUNNING, RIGHT?
THOMP
I'M FORMULATING A STRATEGY.
IS THIS PLAN TO BLEED ALL OVER THE FLOOR AND HOPE I SLIP?

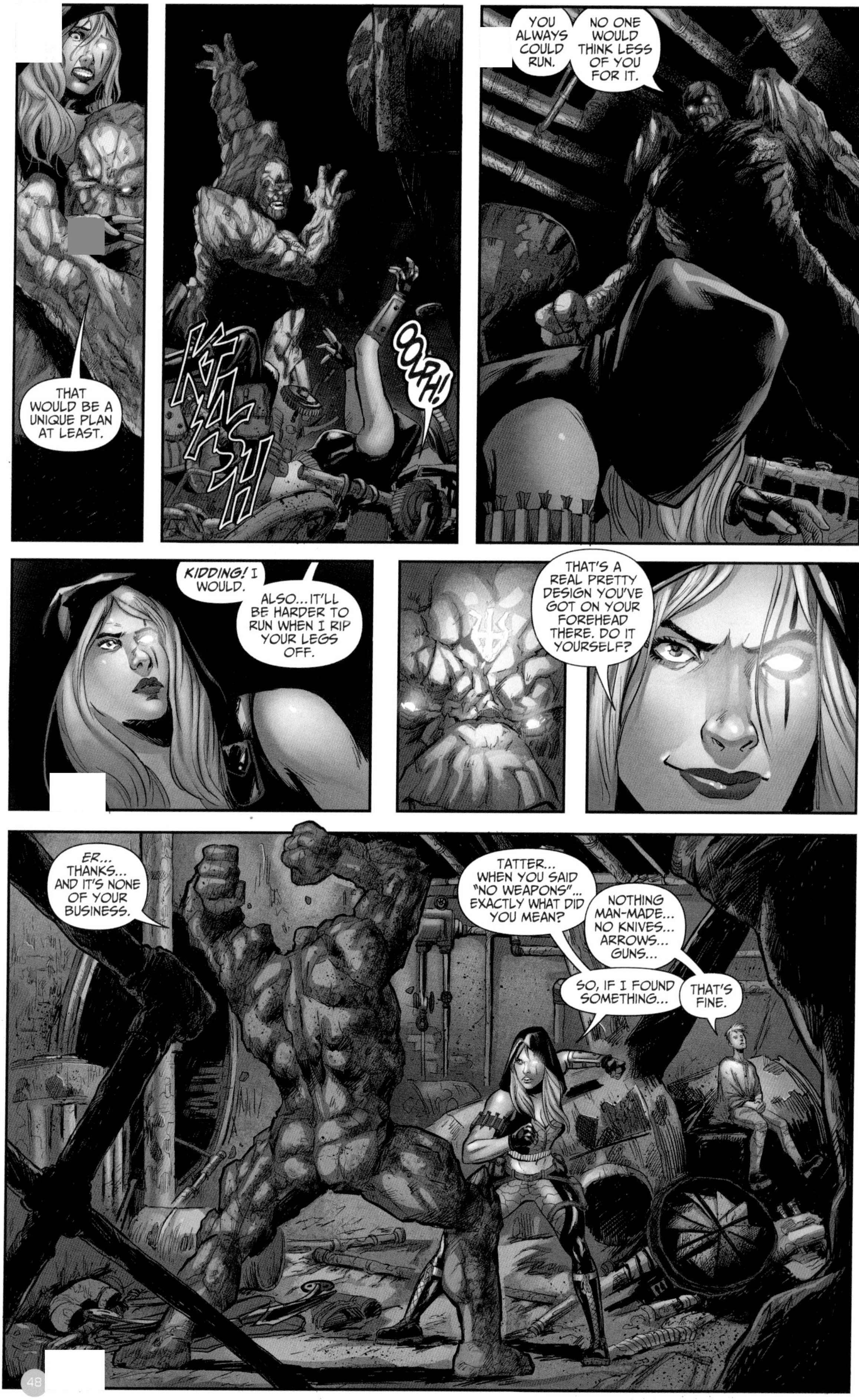
THAT WOULD BE A UNIQUE PLAN AT LEAST.
KTKASSHH
OOFH!
YOU ALWAYS COULD RUN.
NO ONE WOULD THINK LESS OF YOU FOR IT.
KIDDING! I WOULD.
ALSO...IT'LL BE HARDER TO RUN WHEN I RIP YOUR LEGS OFF.
THAT'S A REAL PRETTY DESIGN YOU'VE GOT ON YOUR FOREHEAD THERE. DO IT YOURSELF?
ER... THANKS... AND IT'S NONE OF YOUR BUSINESS.
TATTER... WHEN YOU SAID "NO WEAPONS"... EXACTLY WHAT DID YOU MEAN?
NOTHING MAN-MADE... NO KNIVES... ARROWS... GUNS...
SO, IF I FOUND SOMETHING...
THAT'S FINE.

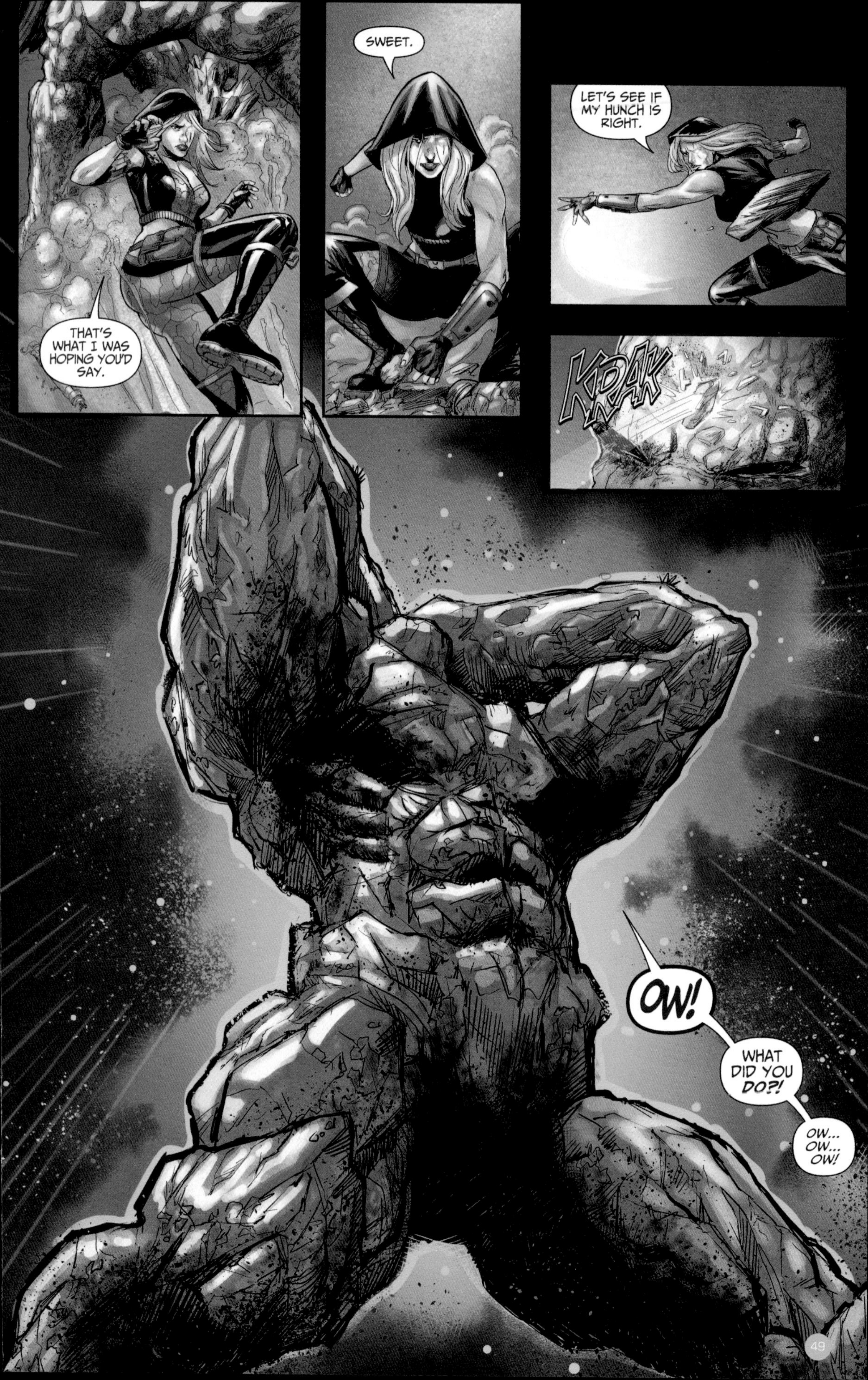
THAT'S WHAT I WAS HOPING YOU'D SAY.
SWEET.
LET'S SEE IF MY HUNCH IS RIGHT.
KRAK
OW!
WHAT DID YOU DO?!
OW... OW... OW!

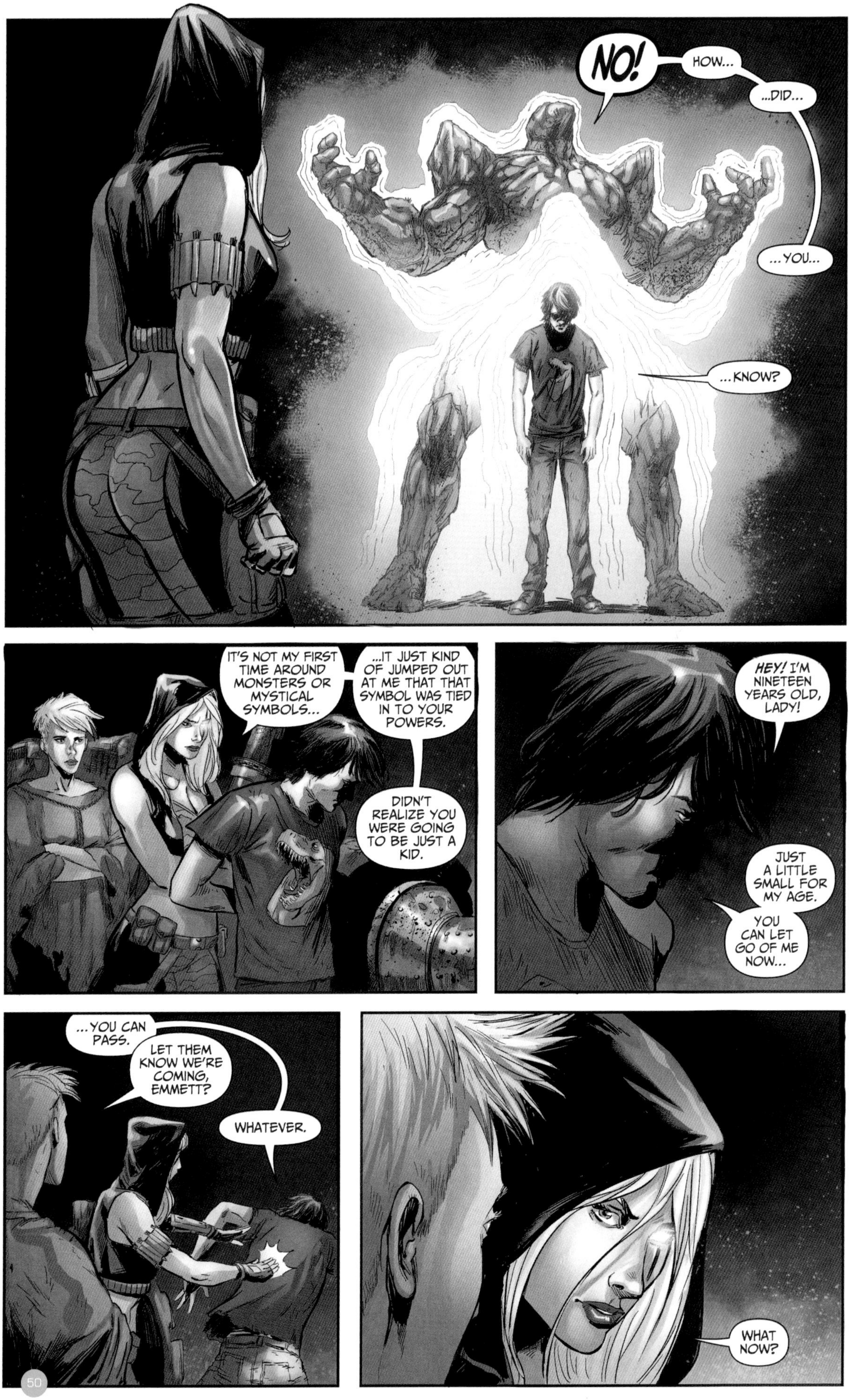
NO!
HOW...
...DID...
...YOU...
...KNOW?
IT'S NOT MY FIRST TIME AROUND MONSTERS OR MYSTICAL SYMBOLS...
...IT JUST KIND OF JUMPED OUT AT ME THAT THAT SYMBOL WAS TIED IN TO YOUR POWERS.
DIDN'T REALIZE YOU WERE GOING TO BE JUST A KID.
HEY! I'M NINETEEN YEARS OLD, LADY!
JUST A LITTLE SMALL FOR MY AGE.
YOU CAN LET GO OF ME NOW...
...YOU CAN PASS.
LET THEM KNOW WE'RE COMING, EMMETT?
WHATEVER.
WHAT NOW?

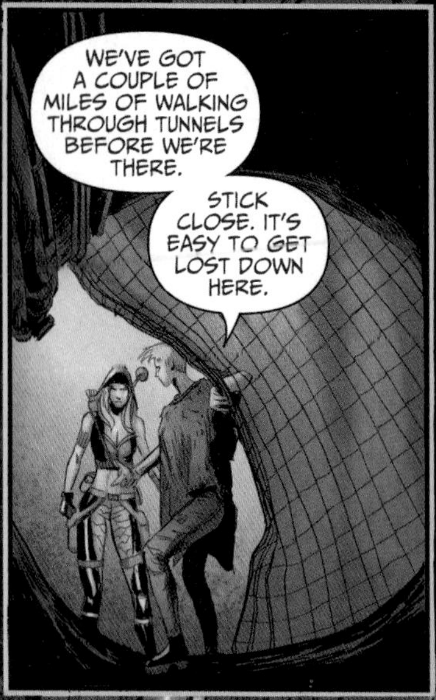
WE'VE GOT A COUPLE OF MILES OF WALKING THROUGH TUNNELS BEFORE WE'RE THERE.
STICK CLOSE. IT'S EASY TO GET LOST DOWN HERE.
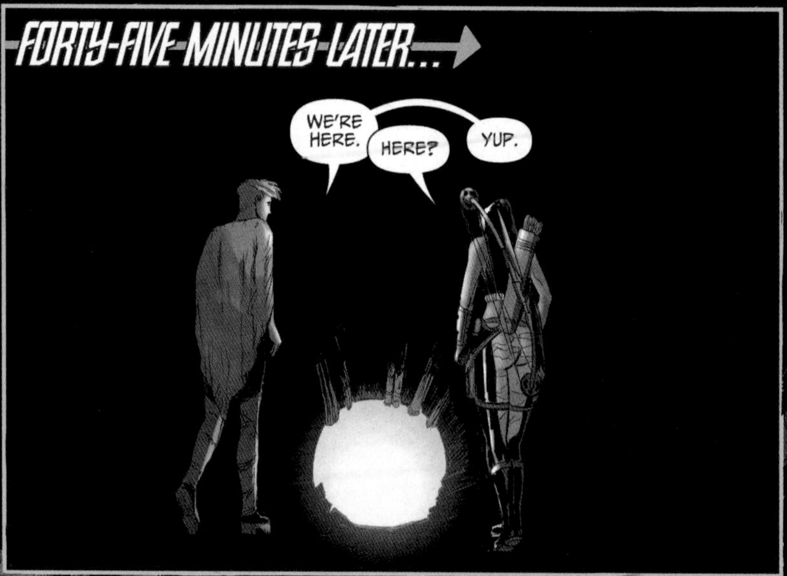
FORTY-FIVE MINUTES LATER...
WE'RE HERE.
HERE?
YUP.
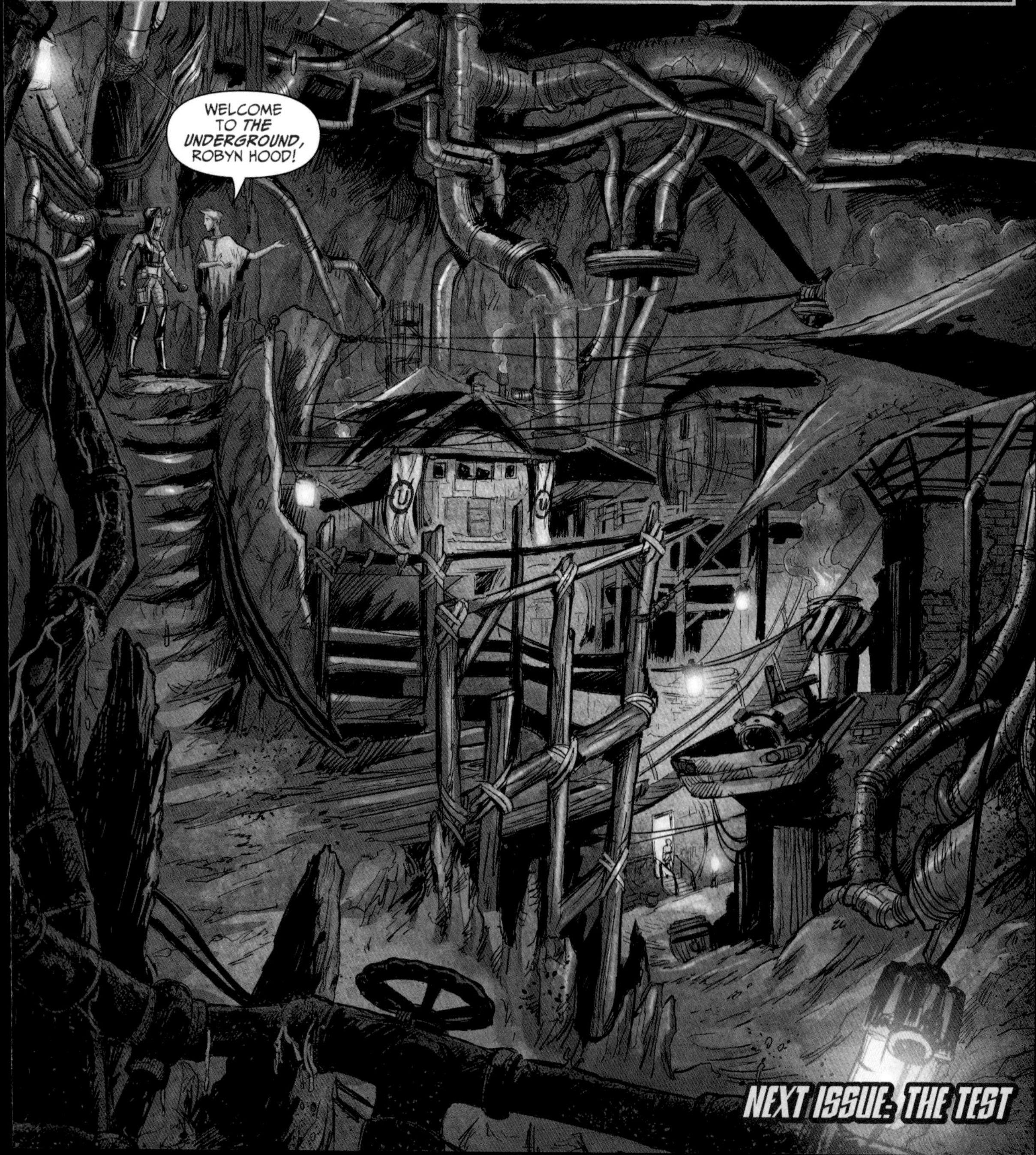
WELCOME TO *THE UNDERGROUND*, ROBYN HOOD!
NEXT ISSUE: THE TEST

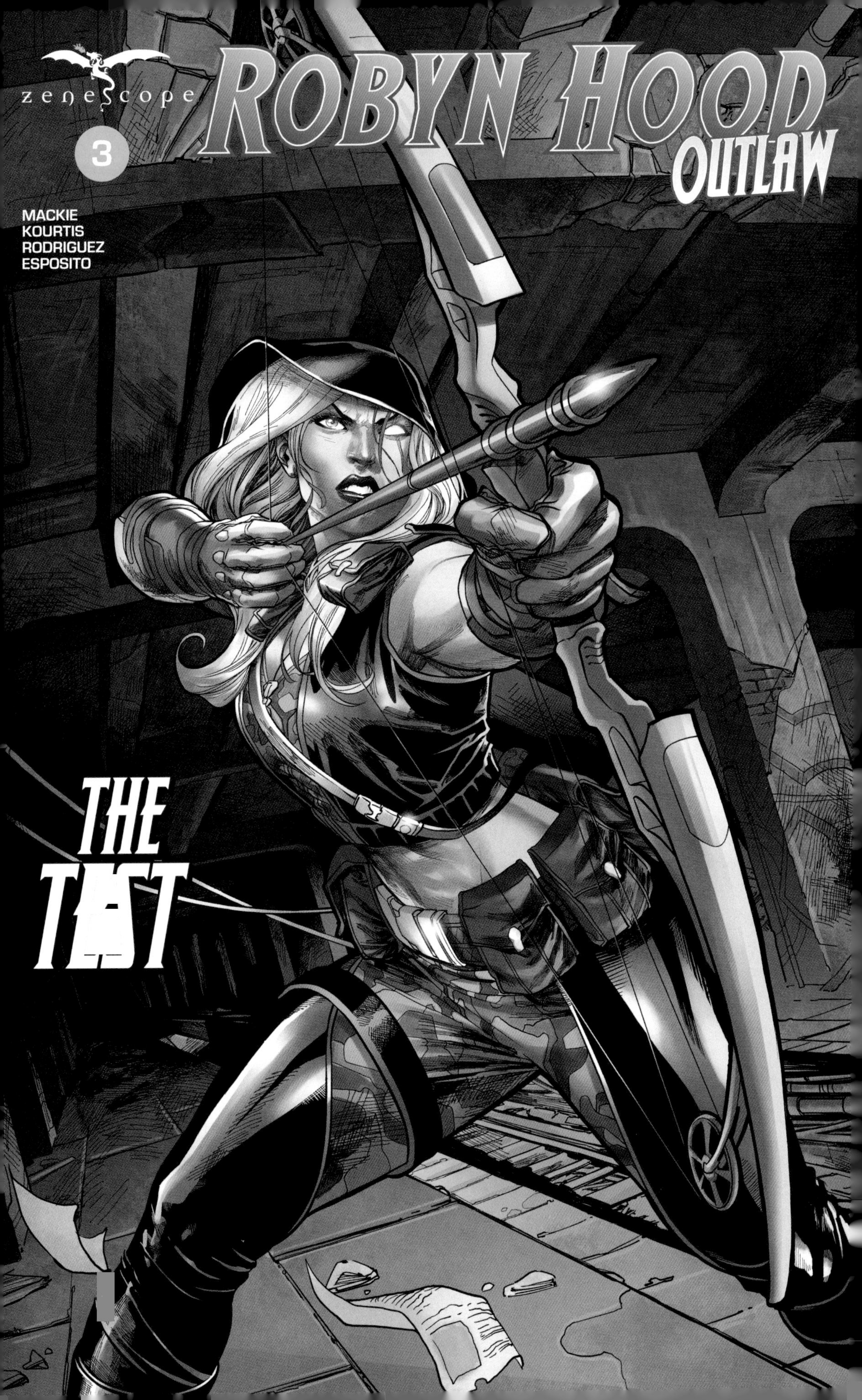
zenescope
ROBYN HOOD
OUTLAW
3
MACKIE
KOURTIS
RODRIGUEZ
ESPOSITO
THE TEST

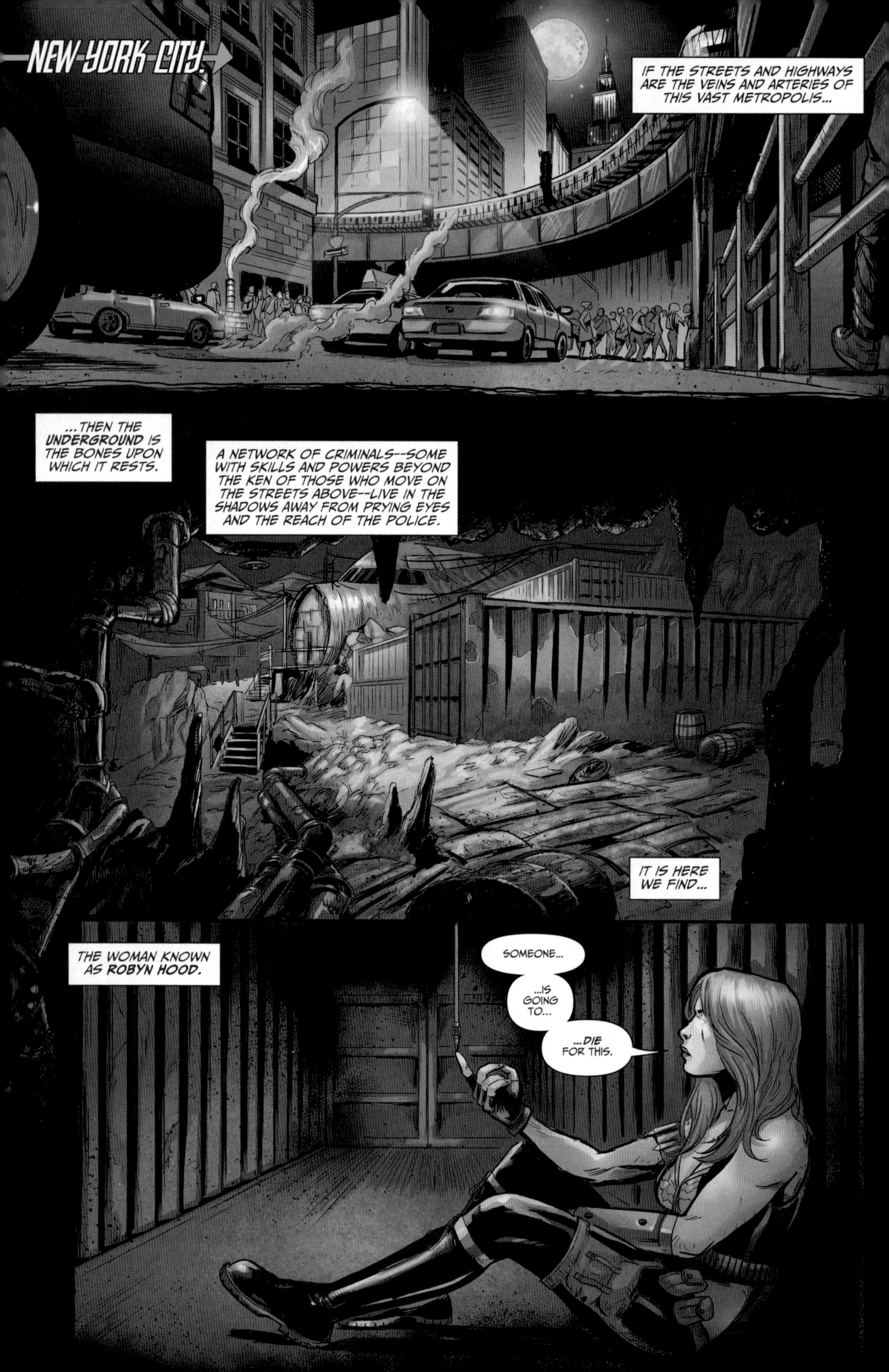
NEW YORK CITY.
IF THE STREETS AND HIGHWAYS ARE THE VEINS AND ARTERIES OF THIS VAST METROPOLIS...
...THEN THE UNDERGROUND IS THE BONES UPON WHICH IT RESTS.
A NETWORK OF CRIMINALS--SOME WITH SKILLS AND POWERS BEYOND THE KEN OF THOSE WHO MOVE ON THE STREETS ABOVE--LIVE IN THE SHADOWS AWAY FROM PRYING EYES AND THE REACH OF THE POLICE.
IT IS HERE WE FIND...
THE WOMAN KNOWN AS ROBYN HOOD.
SOMEONE...
...IS GOING TO...
...DIE FOR THIS.

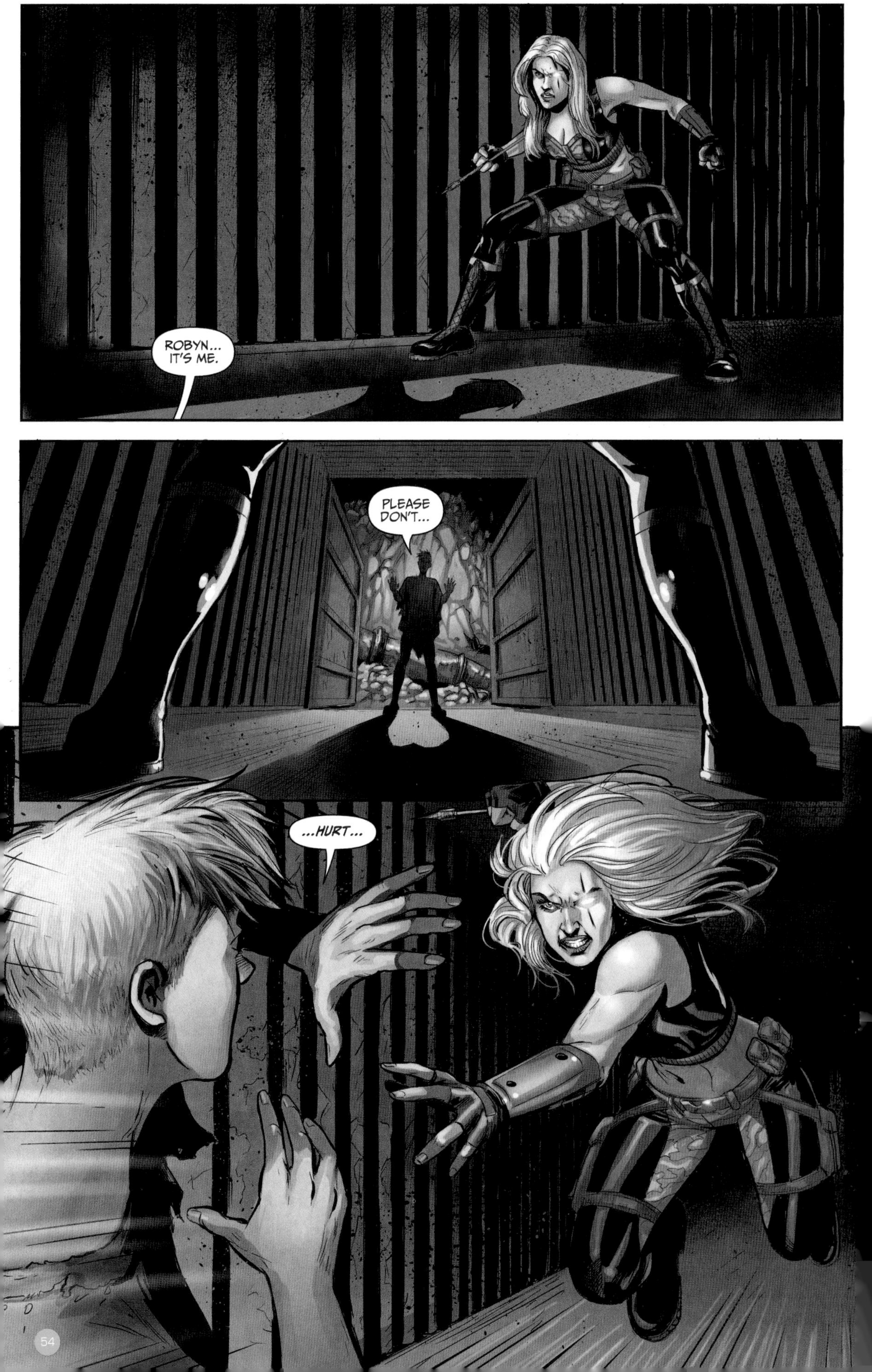
ROBYN... IT'S ME.
PLEASE DON'T...
...HURT...

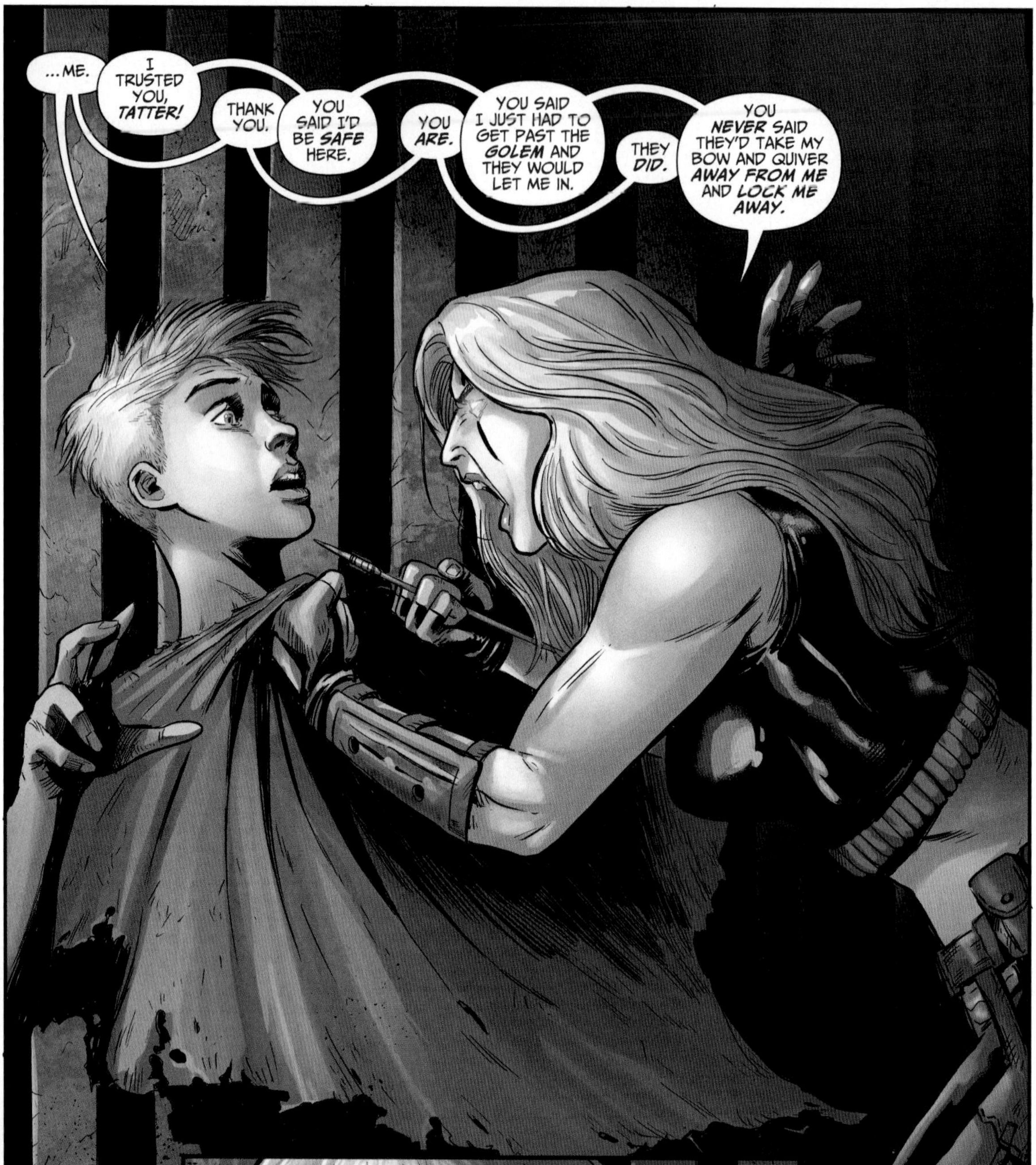

I TRUSTED YOU, TATTER!
...ME.
YOU SAID I'D BE SAFE HERE.
THANK YOU.
YOU SAID I JUST HAD TO GET PAST THE GOLEM AND THEY WOULD LET ME IN.
YOU ARE.
YOU NEVER SAID THEY'D TAKE MY BOW AND QUIVER AWAY FROM ME AND LOCK ME AWAY.
THEY DID.

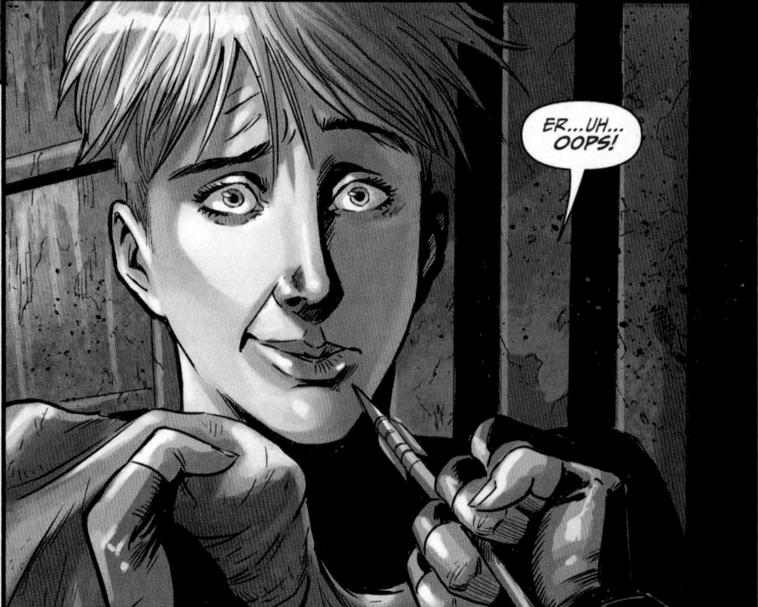

ER...UH... OOPS!

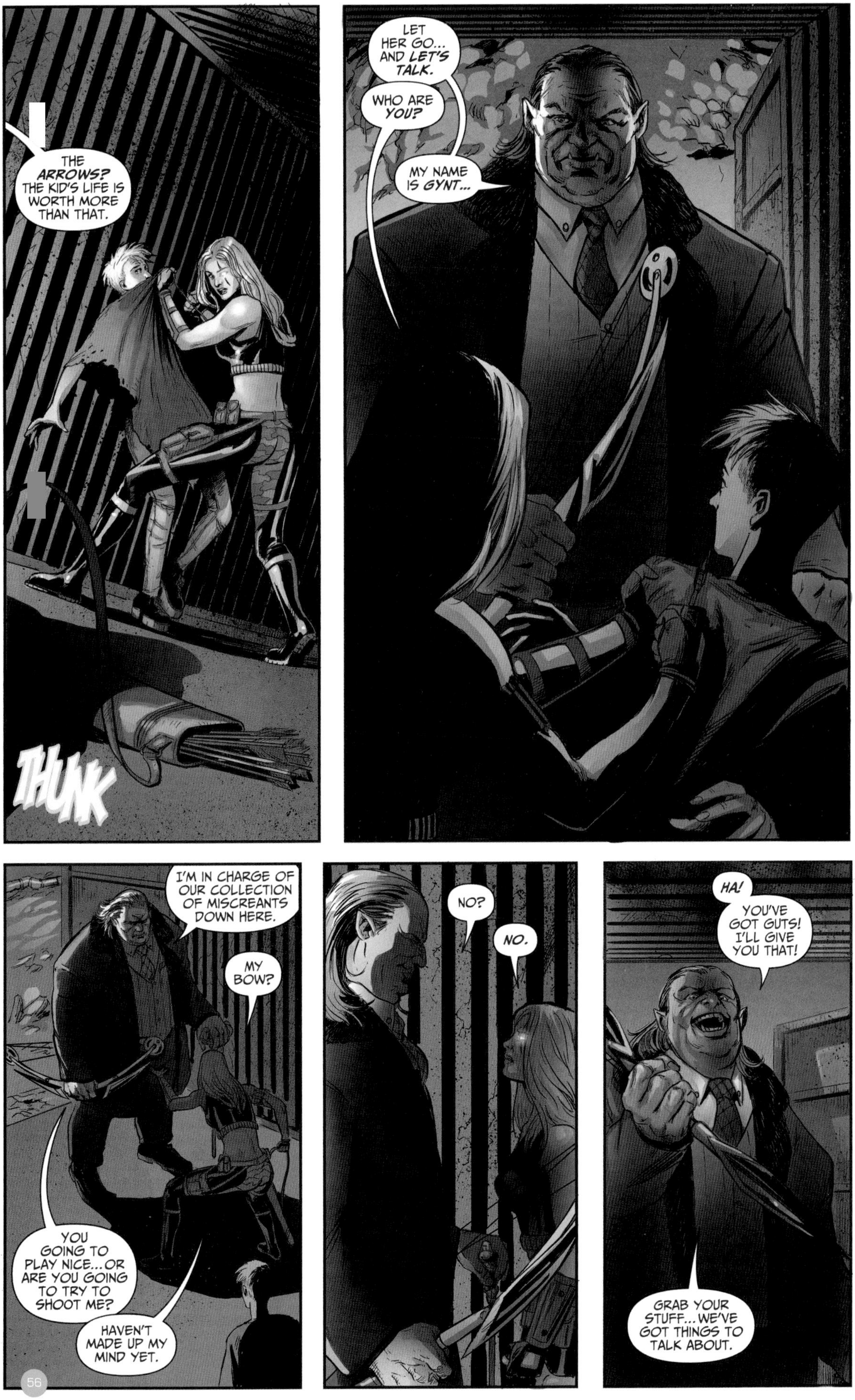
THE *ARROWS?* THE KID'S LIFE IS WORTH MORE THAN THAT.
THUNK
LET HER GO... AND *LET'S TALK.*
WHO ARE *YOU?*
MY NAME IS *GYNT...*
I'M IN CHARGE OF OUR COLLECTION OF MISCREANTS DOWN HERE.
MY BOW?
YOU GOING TO PLAY NICE...OR ARE YOU GOING TO TRY TO SHOOT ME?
HAVEN'T MADE UP MY MIND YET.
NO?
NO.
HA!
YOU'VE GOT GUTS! I'LL GIVE YOU THAT!
GRAB YOUR STUFF... WE'VE GOT THINGS TO TALK ABOUT.

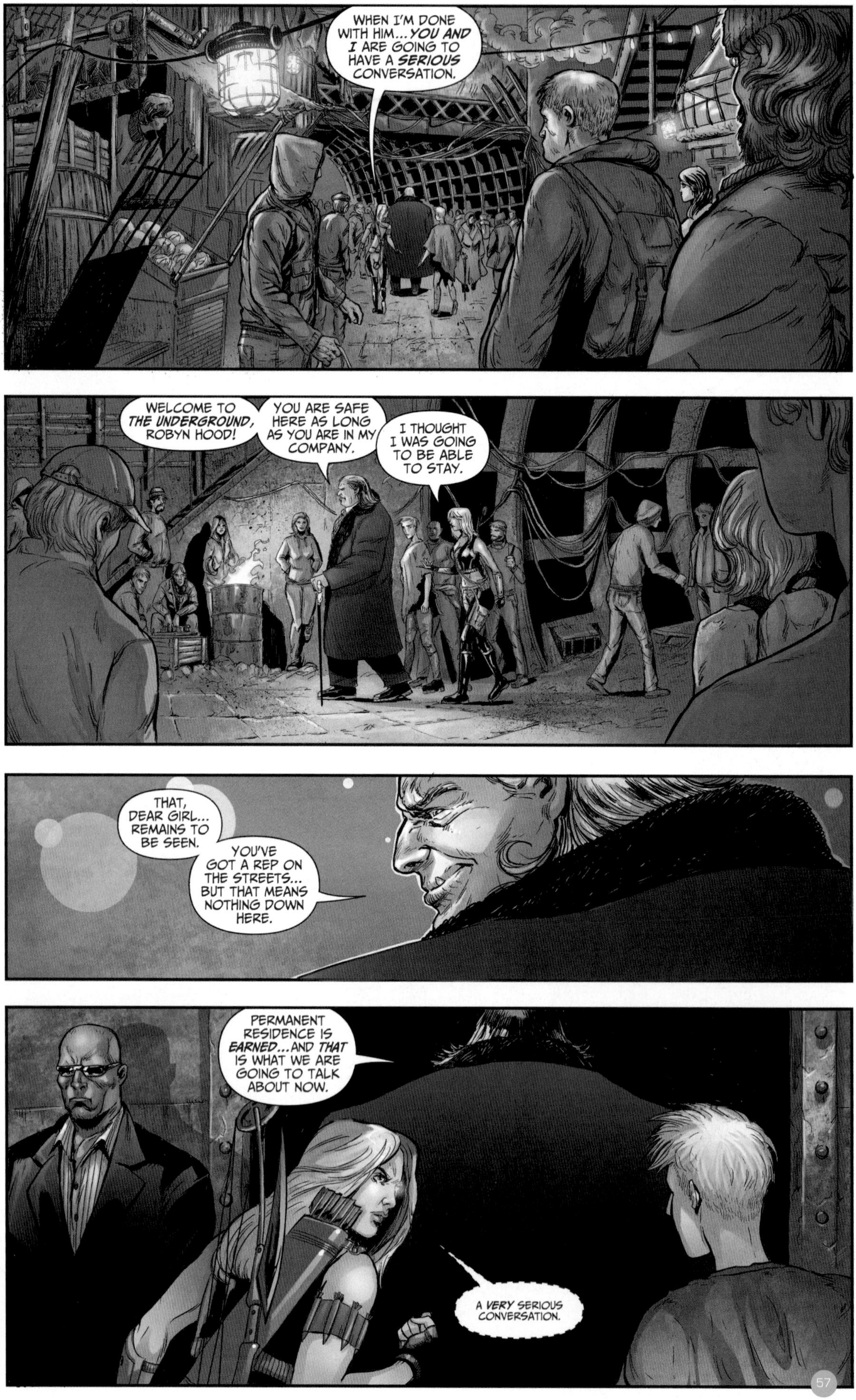
WHEN I'M DONE WITH HIM... *YOU AND I* ARE GOING TO HAVE A *SERIOUS* CONVERSATION.
WELCOME TO *THE UNDERGROUND,* ROBYN HOOD!
YOU ARE SAFE HERE AS LONG AS YOU ARE IN MY COMPANY.
I THOUGHT I WAS GOING TO BE ABLE TO STAY.
THAT, DEAR GIRL... REMAINS TO BE SEEN.
YOU'VE GOT A REP ON THE STREETS... BUT THAT MEANS NOTHING DOWN HERE.
PERMANENT RESIDENCE IS *EARNED*...AND *THAT* IS WHAT WE ARE GOING TO TALK ABOUT NOW.
A *VERY* SERIOUS CONVERSATION.

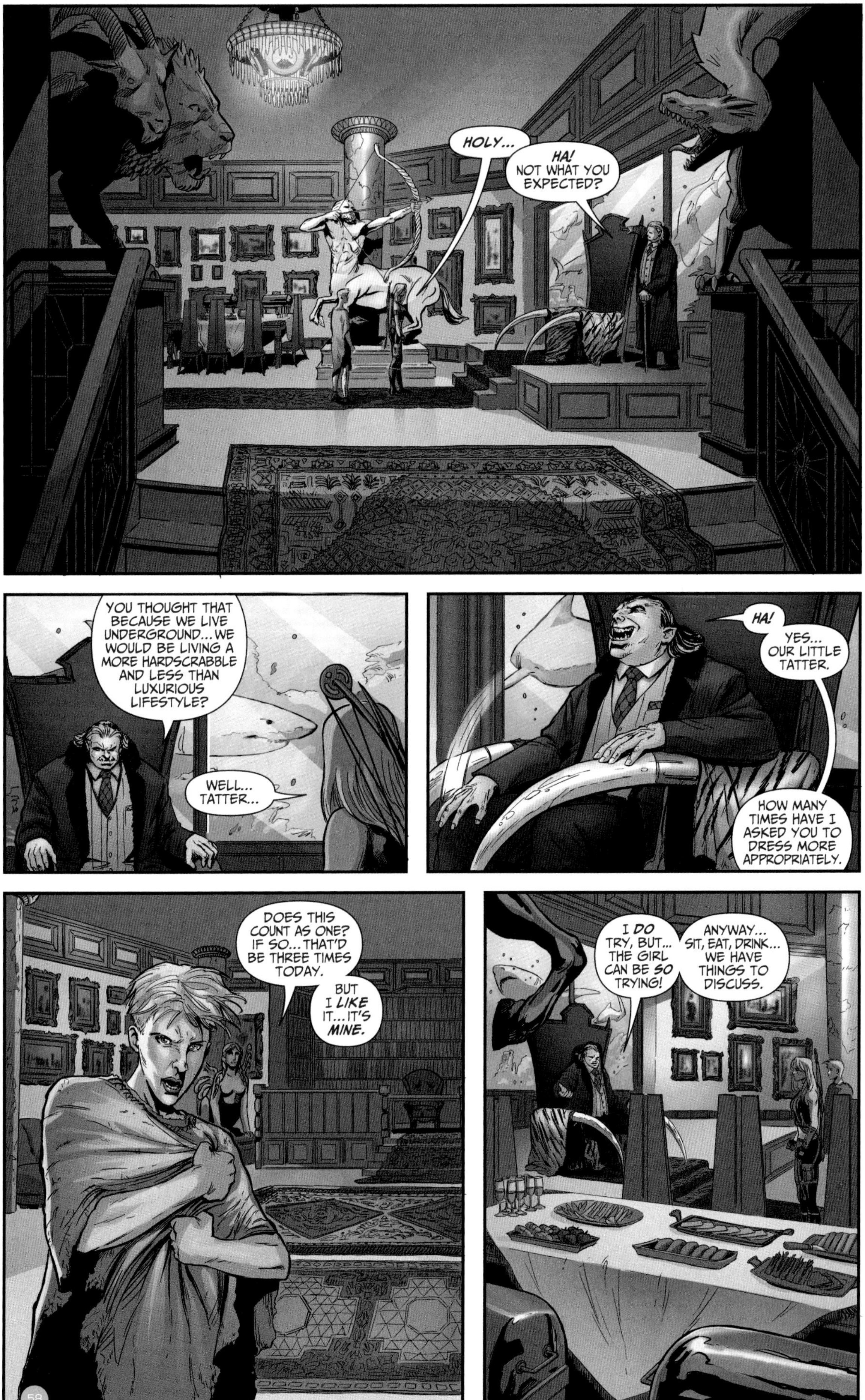
HOLY...
HA! NOT WHAT YOU EXPECTED?
YOU THOUGHT THAT BECAUSE WE LIVE UNDERGROUND...WE WOULD BE LIVING A MORE HARDSCRABBLE AND LESS THAN LUXURIOUS LIFESTYLE?
WELL... TATTER...
HA!
YES... OUR LITTLE TATTER.
HOW MANY TIMES HAVE I ASKED YOU TO DRESS MORE APPROPRIATELY.
DOES THIS COUNT AS ONE? IF SO...THAT'D BE THREE TIMES TODAY.
BUT I *LIKE* IT...IT'S ***MINE.***
I *DO* TRY, BUT... THE GIRL CAN BE *SO* TRYING!
ANYWAY... SIT, EAT, DRINK... WE HAVE THINGS TO DISCUSS.

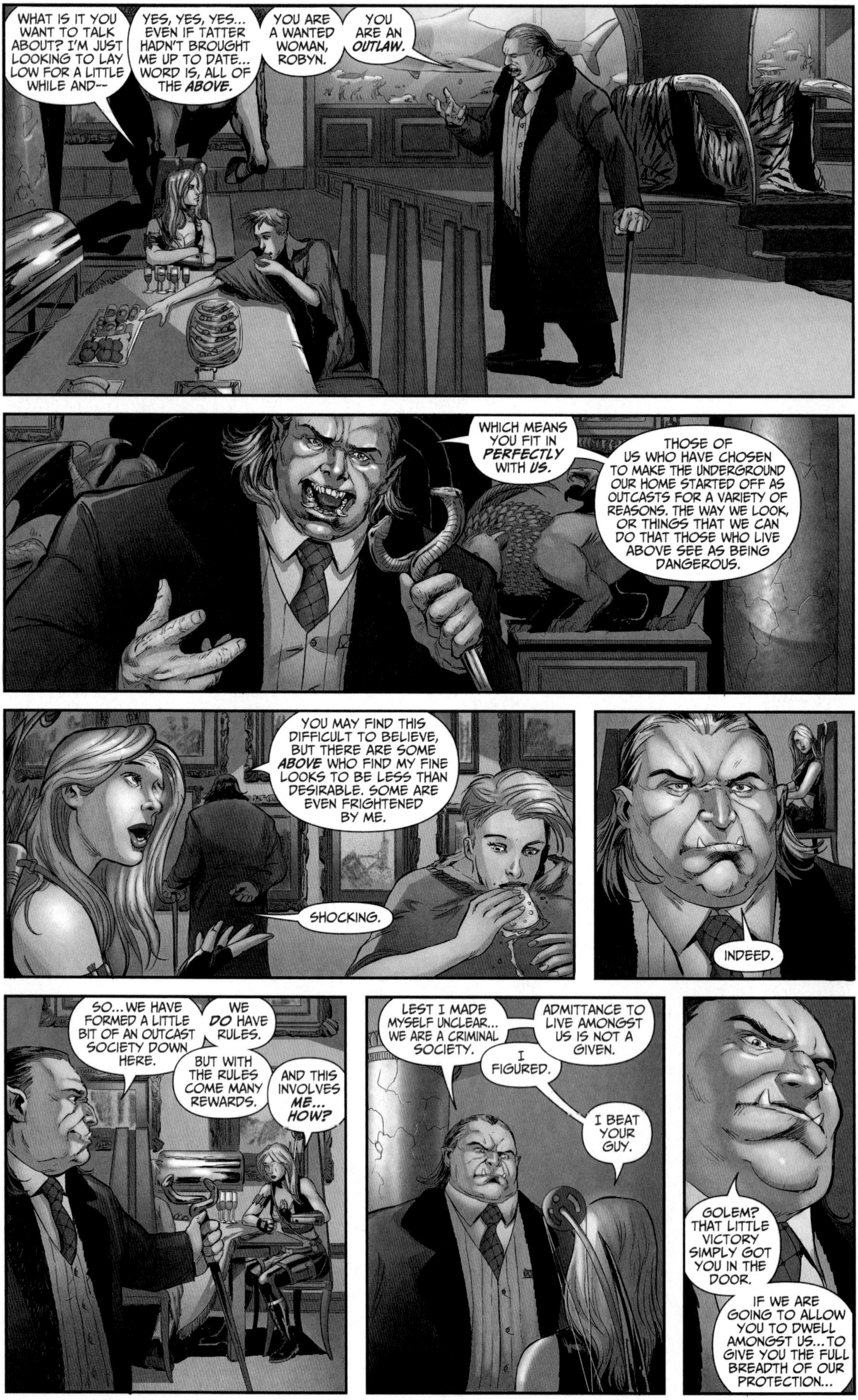
WHAT IS IT YOU WANT TO TALK ABOUT? I'M JUST LOOKING TO LAY LOW FOR A LITTLE WHILE AND--
YES, YES, YES... EVEN IF TATTER HADN'T BROUGHT ME UP TO DATE... WORD IS, ALL OF THE *ABOVE.*
YOU ARE A WANTED WOMAN, ROBYN.
YOU ARE AN *OUTLAW.*
WHICH MEANS YOU FIT IN *PERFECTLY* WITH *US.*
THOSE OF US WHO HAVE CHOSEN TO MAKE THE UNDERGROUND OUR HOME STARTED OFF AS OUTCASTS FOR A VARIETY OF REASONS. THE WAY WE LOOK, OR THINGS THAT WE CAN DO THAT THOSE WHO LIVE ABOVE SEE AS BEING DANGEROUS.
YOU MAY FIND THIS DIFFICULT TO BELIEVE, BUT THERE ARE SOME *ABOVE* WHO FIND MY FINE LOOKS TO BE LESS THAN DESIRABLE. SOME ARE EVEN FRIGHTENED BY ME.
SHOCKING.
INDEED.
SO...WE HAVE FORMED A LITTLE BIT OF AN OUTCAST SOCIETY DOWN HERE.
WE *DO* HAVE RULES.
BUT WITH THE RULES COME MANY REWARDS.
AND THIS INVOLVES *ME... HOW?*
LEST I MADE MYSELF UNCLEAR... WE ARE A CRIMINAL SOCIETY.
ADMITTANCE TO LIVE AMONGST US IS NOT A GIVEN.
I FIGURED.
I BEAT YOUR GUY.
GOLEM? THAT LITTLE VICTORY SIMPLY GOT YOU IN THE DOOR.
IF WE ARE GOING TO ALLOW YOU TO DWELL AMONGST US...TO GIVE YOU THE FULL BREADTH OF OUR PROTECTION...

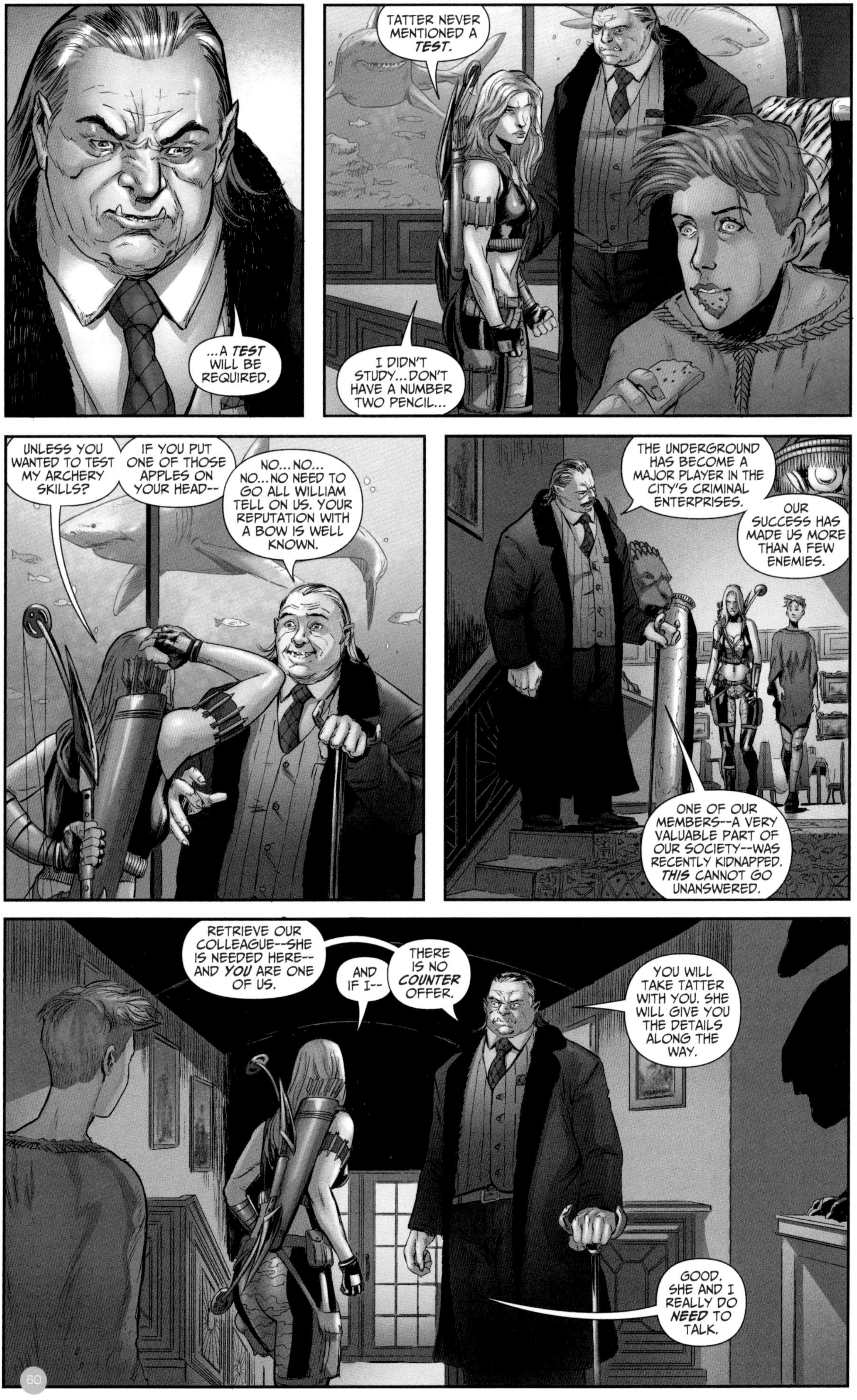
...A TEST WILL BE REQUIRED.
TATTER NEVER MENTIONED A TEST.
I DIDN'T STUDY...DON'T HAVE A NUMBER TWO PENCIL...
UNLESS YOU WANTED TO TEST MY ARCHERY SKILLS?
IF YOU PUT ONE OF THOSE APPLES ON YOUR HEAD--
NO...NO... NO...NO NEED TO GO ALL WILLIAM TELL ON US. YOUR REPUTATION WITH A BOW IS WELL KNOWN.
THE UNDERGROUND HAS BECOME A MAJOR PLAYER IN THE CITY'S CRIMINAL ENTERPRISES.
OUR SUCCESS HAS MADE US MORE THAN A FEW ENEMIES.
ONE OF OUR MEMBERS--A VERY VALUABLE PART OF OUR SOCIETY--WAS RECENTLY KIDNAPPED. THIS CANNOT GO UNANSWERED.
RETRIEVE OUR COLLEAGUE--SHE IS NEEDED HERE--AND YOU ARE ONE OF US.
AND IF I--
THERE IS NO COUNTER OFFER.
YOU WILL TAKE TATTER WITH YOU. SHE WILL GIVE YOU THE DETAILS ALONG THE WAY.
GOOD. SHE AND I REALLY DO NEED TO TALK.

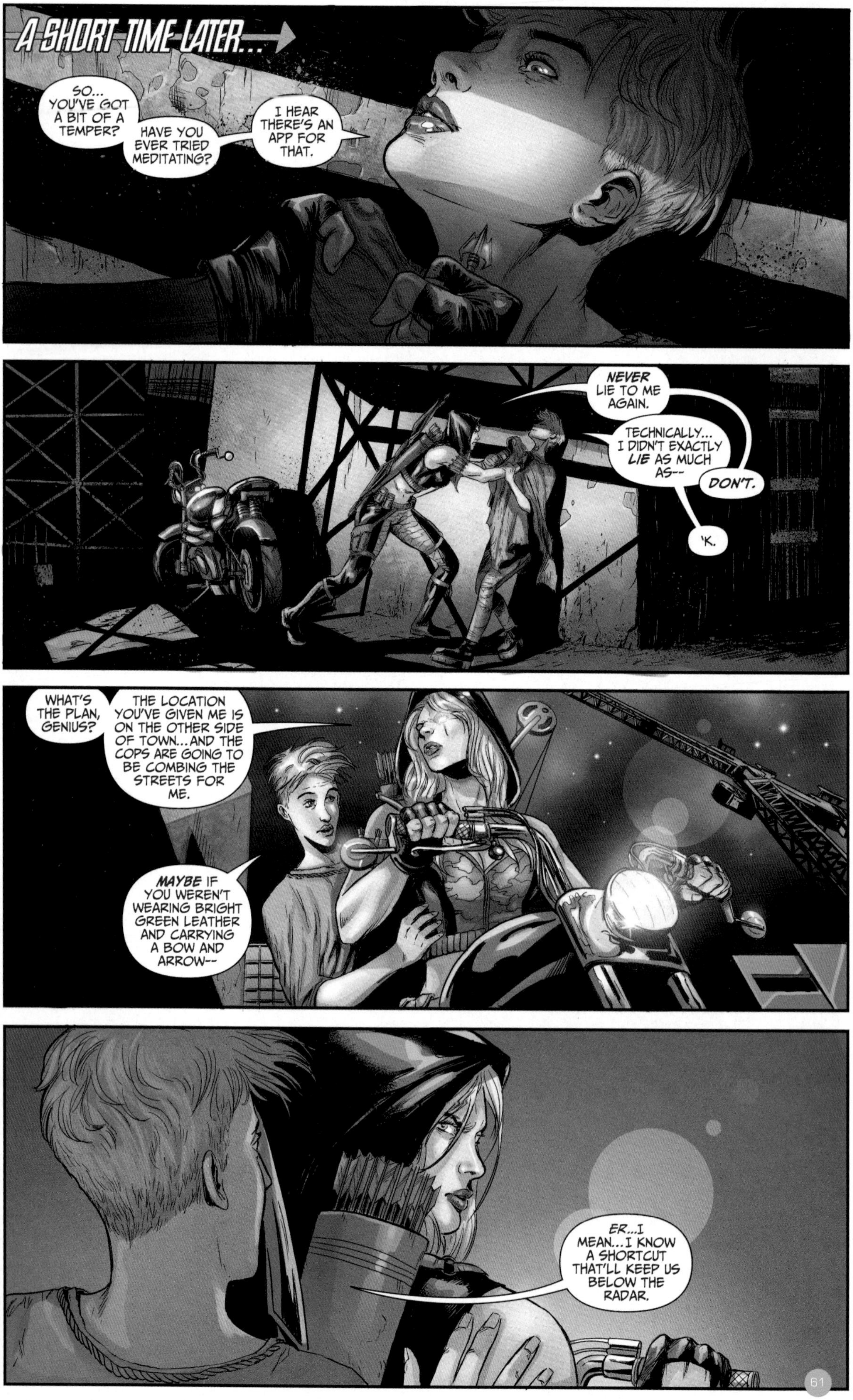
A SHORT TIME LATER...
SO... YOU'VE GOT A BIT OF A TEMPER?
HAVE YOU EVER TRIED MEDITATING?
I HEAR THERE'S AN APP FOR THAT.
NEVER LIE TO ME AGAIN.
TECHNICALLY... I DIDN'T EXACTLY LIE AS MUCH AS--
DON'T.
'K.
WHAT'S THE PLAN, GENIUS?
THE LOCATION YOU'VE GIVEN ME IS ON THE OTHER SIDE OF TOWN...AND THE COPS ARE GOING TO BE COMBING THE STREETS FOR ME.
MAYBE IF YOU WEREN'T WEARING BRIGHT GREEN LEATHER AND CARRYING A BOW AND ARROW--
ER...I MEAN...I KNOW A SHORTCUT THAT'LL KEEP US BELOW THE RADAR.

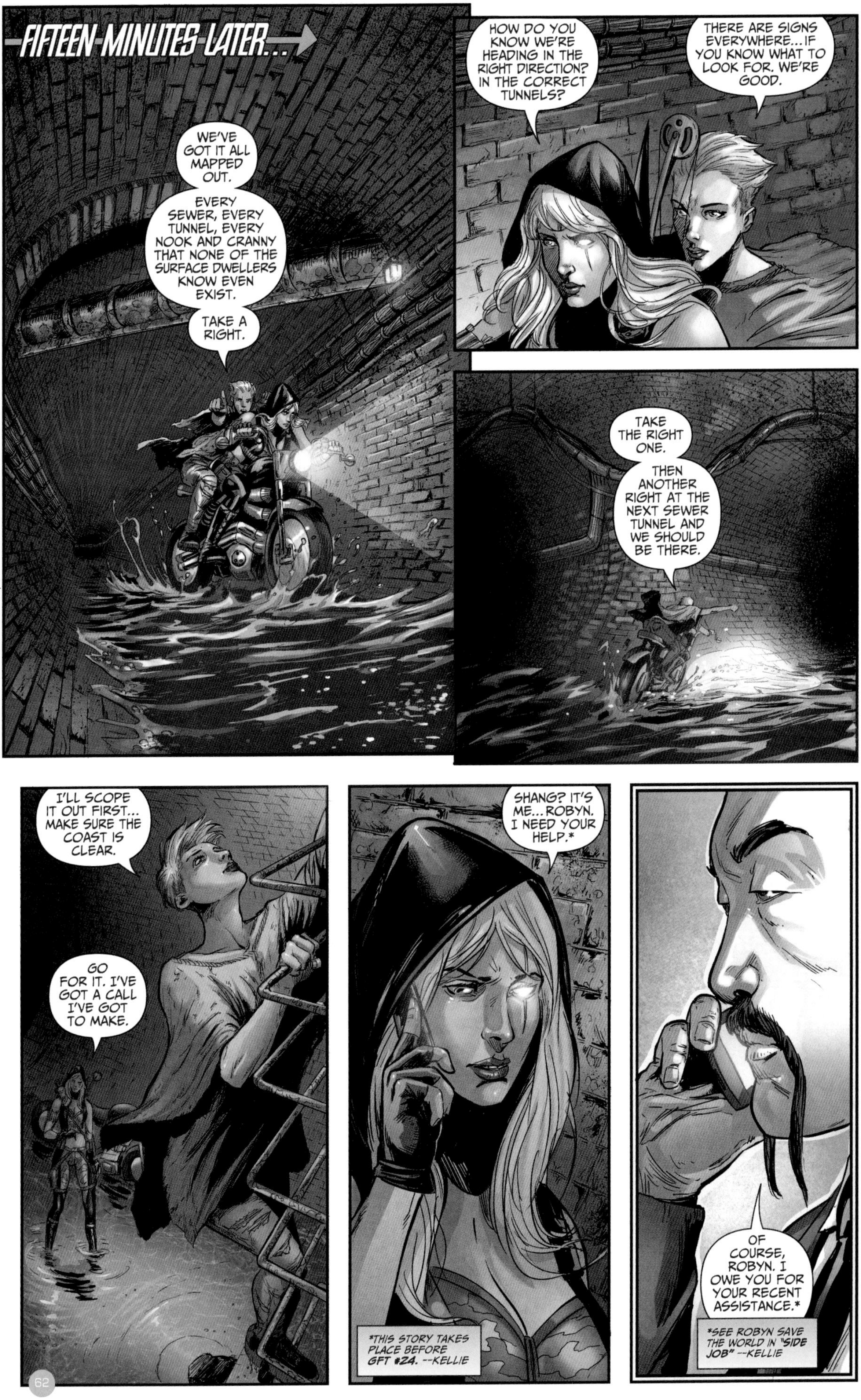
FIFTEEN MINUTES LATER...
WE'VE GOT IT ALL MAPPED OUT.
EVERY SEWER, EVERY TUNNEL, EVERY NOOK AND CRANNY THAT NONE OF THE SURFACE DWELLERS KNOW EVEN EXIST.
TAKE A RIGHT.
HOW DO YOU KNOW WE'RE HEADING IN THE RIGHT DIRECTION? IN THE CORRECT TUNNELS?
THERE ARE SIGNS EVERYWHERE... IF YOU KNOW WHAT TO LOOK FOR. WE'RE GOOD.
TAKE THE RIGHT ONE.
THEN ANOTHER RIGHT AT THE NEXT SEWER TUNNEL AND WE SHOULD BE THERE.
I'LL SCOPE IT OUT FIRST... MAKE SURE THE COAST IS CLEAR.
GO FOR IT. I'VE GOT A CALL I'VE GOT TO MAKE.
SHANG? IT'S ME... ROBYN. I NEED YOUR HELP.*
*THIS STORY TAKES PLACE BEFORE GFT #24. --KELLIE
OF COURSE, ROBYN. I OWE YOU FOR YOUR RECENT ASSISTANCE.*
*SEE ROBYN SAVE THE WORLD IN "SIDE JOB" --KELLIE

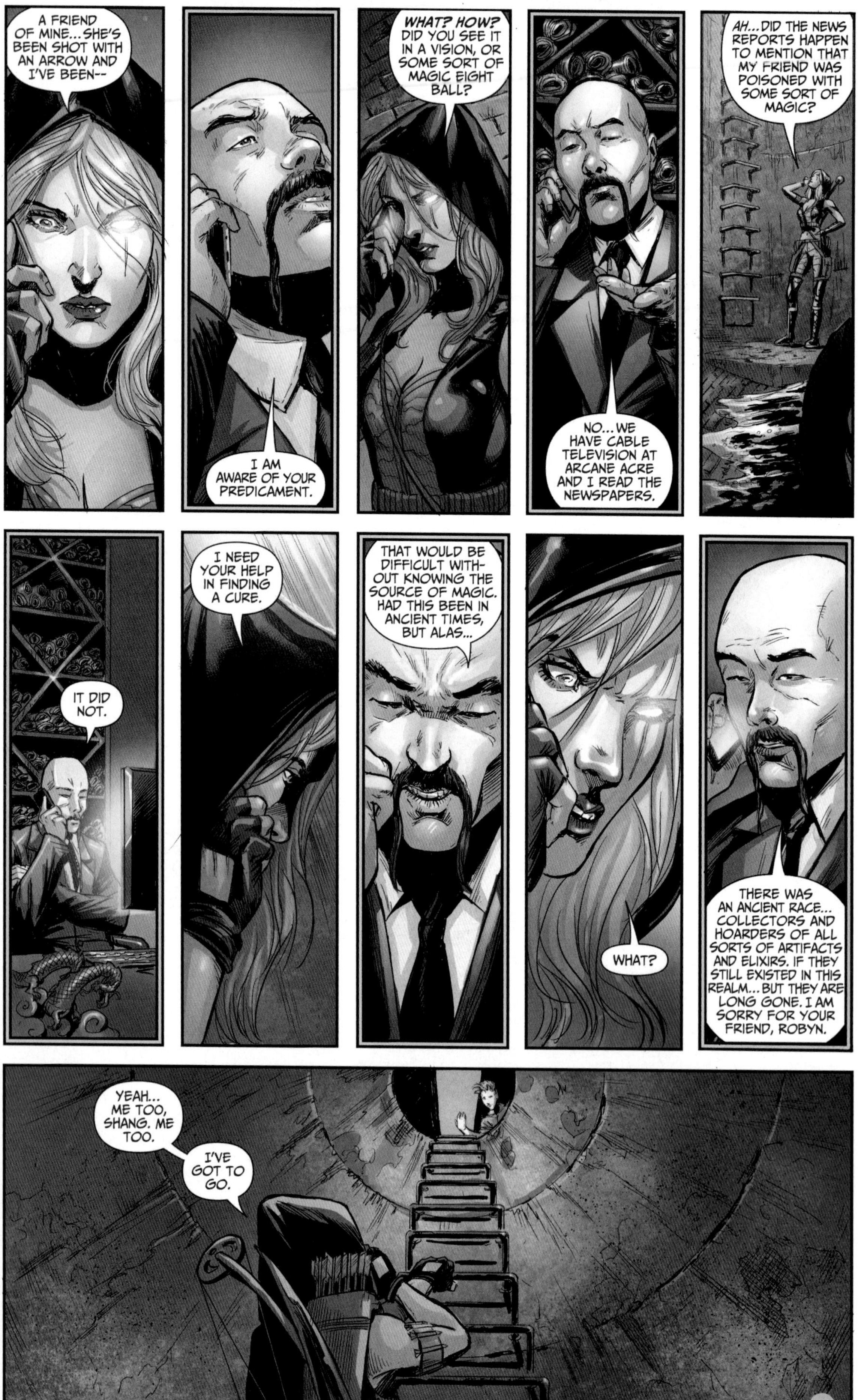
A FRIEND OF MINE...SHE'S BEEN SHOT WITH AN ARROW AND I'VE BEEN--
I AM AWARE OF YOUR PREDICAMENT.
WHAT? HOW? DID YOU SEE IT IN A VISION, OR SOME SORT OF MAGIC EIGHT BALL?
NO...WE HAVE CABLE TELEVISION AT ARCANE ACRE AND I READ THE NEWSPAPERS.
AH...DID THE NEWS REPORTS HAPPEN TO MENTION THAT MY FRIEND WAS POISONED WITH SOME SORT OF MAGIC?
IT DID NOT.
I NEED YOUR HELP IN FINDING A CURE.
THAT WOULD BE DIFFICULT WITHOUT KNOWING THE SOURCE OF MAGIC. HAD THIS BEEN IN ANCIENT TIMES, BUT ALAS...
WHAT?
THERE WAS AN ANCIENT RACE... COLLECTORS AND HOARDERS OF ALL SORTS OF ARTIFACTS AND ELIXIRS. IF THEY STILL EXISTED IN THIS REALM...BUT THEY ARE LONG GONE. I AM SORRY FOR YOUR FRIEND, ROBYN.
YEAH... ME TOO, SHANG. ME TOO.
I'VE GOT TO GO.

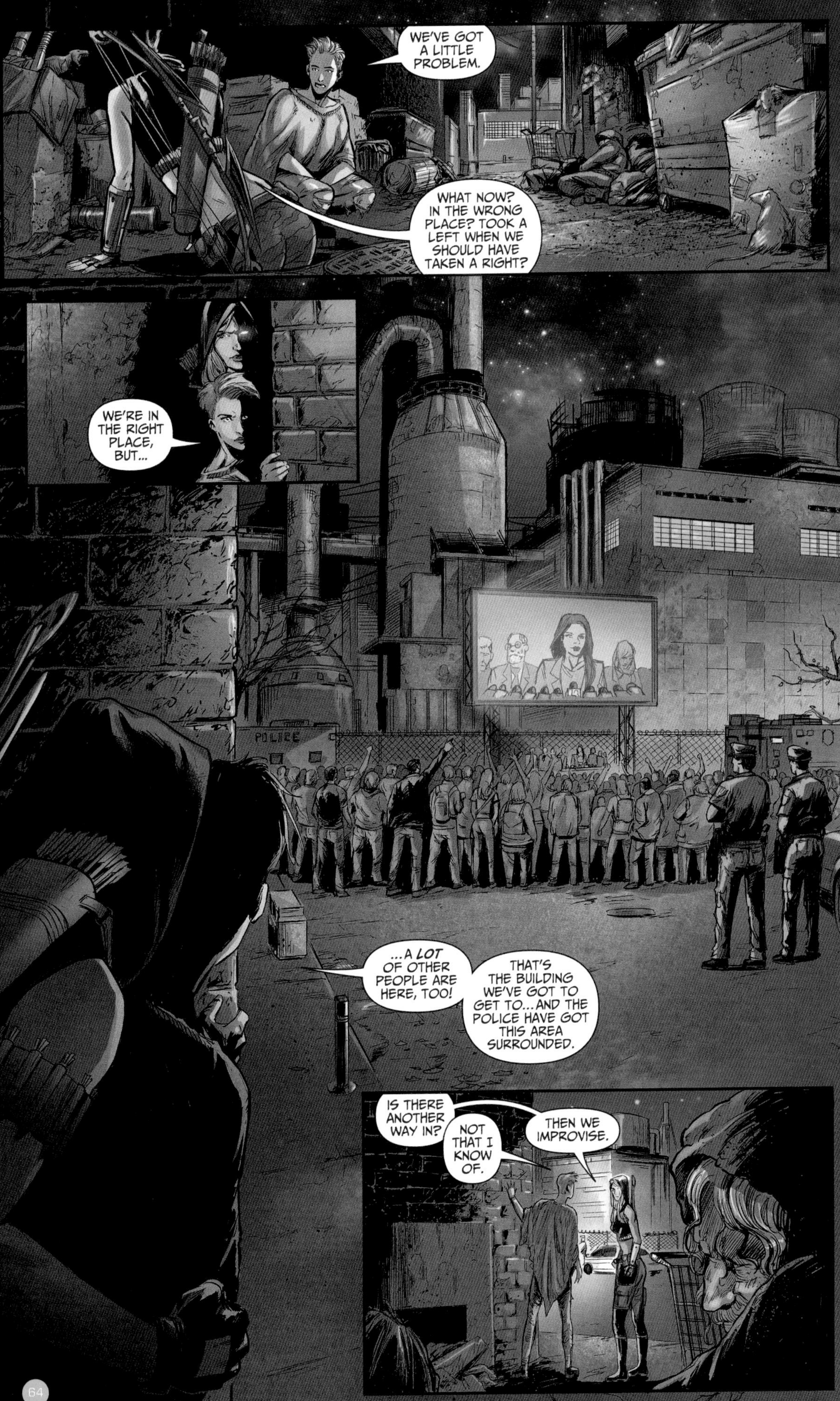
WE'VE GOT A LITTLE PROBLEM.
WHAT NOW? IN THE WRONG PLACE? TOOK A LEFT WHEN WE SHOULD HAVE TAKEN A RIGHT?
WE'RE IN THE RIGHT PLACE, BUT...
POLICE
...A *LOT* OF OTHER PEOPLE ARE HERE, TOO!
THAT'S THE BUILDING WE'VE GOT TO GET TO...AND THE POLICE HAVE GOT THIS AREA SURROUNDED.
IS THERE ANOTHER WAY IN?
NOT THAT I KNOW OF.
THEN WE IMPROVISE.

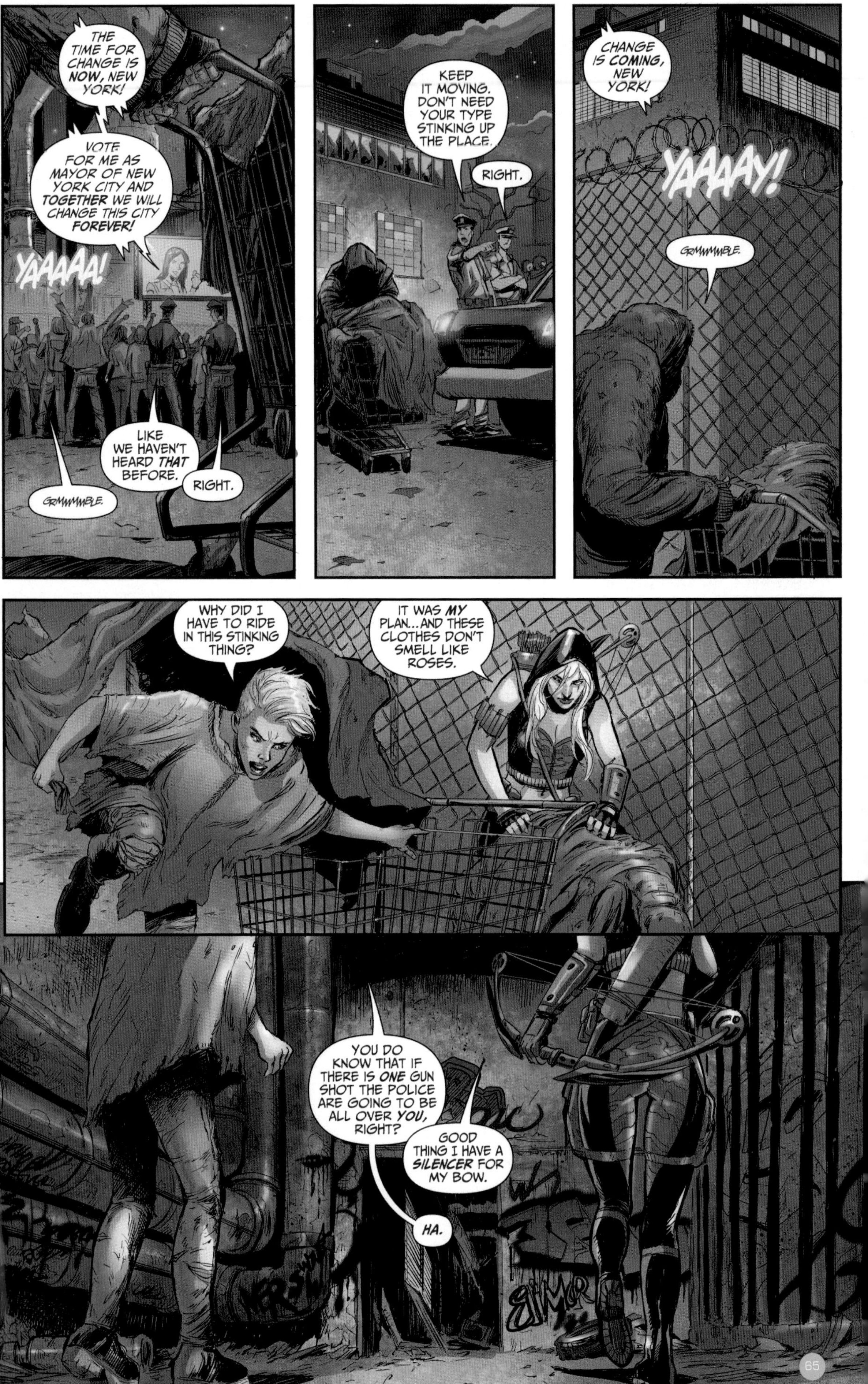
THE TIME FOR CHANGE IS NOW, NEW YORK!
VOTE FOR ME AS MAYOR OF NEW YORK CITY AND TOGETHER WE WILL CHANGE THIS CITY FOREVER!
YAAAAA!
LIKE WE HAVEN'T HEARD THAT BEFORE.
RIGHT.
GRMMMMBLE.
KEEP IT MOVING. DON'T NEED YOUR TYPE STINKING UP THE PLACE.
RIGHT.
CHANGE IS COMING, NEW YORK!
YAAAAY!
GRMMMMBLE.
WHY DID I HAVE TO RIDE IN THIS STINKING THING?
IT WAS MY PLAN...AND THESE CLOTHES DON'T SMELL LIKE ROSES.
YOU DO KNOW THAT IF THERE IS ONE GUN SHOT THE POLICE ARE GOING TO BE ALL OVER YOU, RIGHT?
GOOD THING I HAVE A SILENCER FOR MY BOW.
HA.

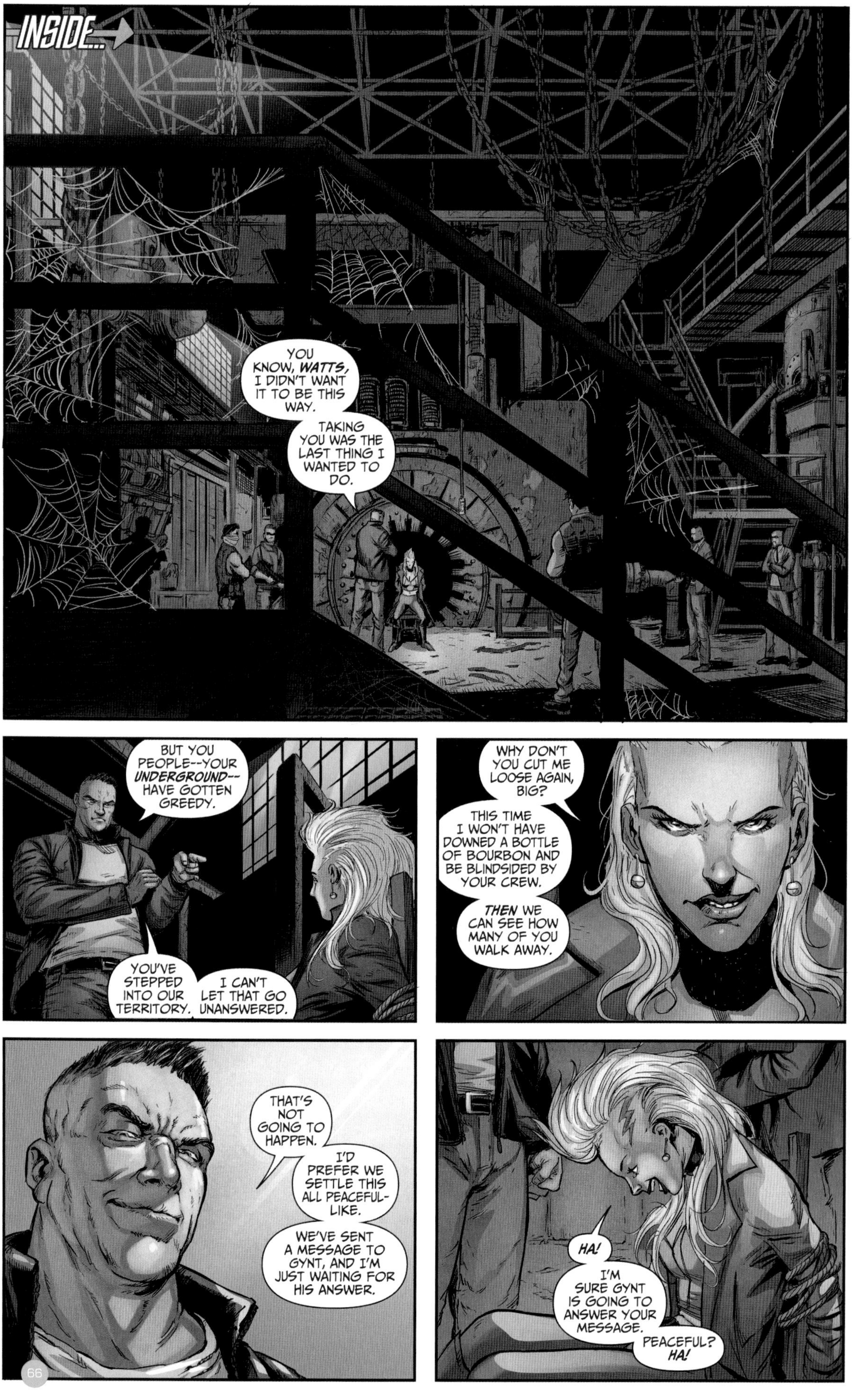
INSIDE...
YOU KNOW, WATTS, I DIDN'T WANT IT TO BE THIS WAY.
TAKING YOU WAS THE LAST THING I WANTED TO DO.
BUT YOU PEOPLE--YOUR UNDERGROUND--HAVE GOTTEN GREEDY.
YOU'VE STEPPED INTO OUR TERRITORY.
I CAN'T LET THAT GO UNANSWERED.
WHY DON'T YOU CUT ME LOOSE AGAIN, BIG?
THIS TIME I WON'T HAVE DOWNED A BOTTLE OF BOURBON AND BE BLINDSIDED BY YOUR CREW.
THEN WE CAN SEE HOW MANY OF YOU WALK AWAY.
THAT'S NOT GOING TO HAPPEN.
I'D PREFER WE SETTLE THIS ALL PEACEFUL-LIKE.
WE'VE SENT A MESSAGE TO GYNT, AND I'M JUST WAITING FOR HIS ANSWER.
HA!
I'M SURE GYNT IS GOING TO ANSWER YOUR MESSAGE.
PEACEFUL? HA!

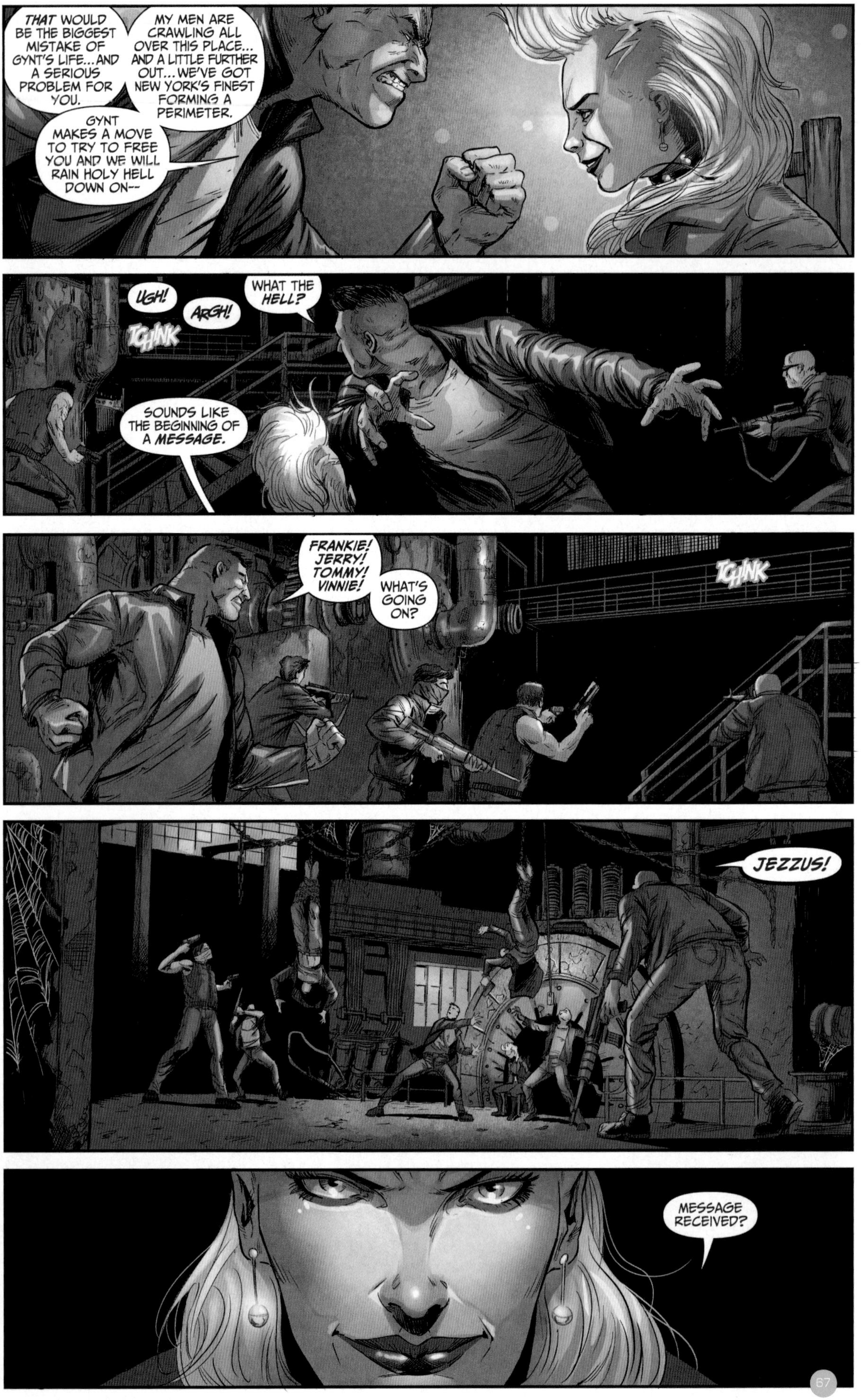
THAT WOULD BE THE BIGGEST MISTAKE OF GYNT'S LIFE...AND A SERIOUS PROBLEM FOR YOU.
MY MEN ARE CRAWLING ALL OVER THIS PLACE... AND A LITTLE FURTHER OUT...WE'VE GOT NEW YORK'S FINEST FORMING A PERIMETER.
GYNT MAKES A MOVE TO TRY TO FREE YOU AND WE WILL RAIN HOLY HELL DOWN ON--
UGH!
ARGH!
TCHINK
WHAT THE HELL?
SOUNDS LIKE THE BEGINNING OF A MESSAGE.
FRANKIE! JERRY! TOMMY! VINNIE!
WHAT'S GOING ON?
TCHINK
JEZZUS!
MESSAGE RECEIVED?

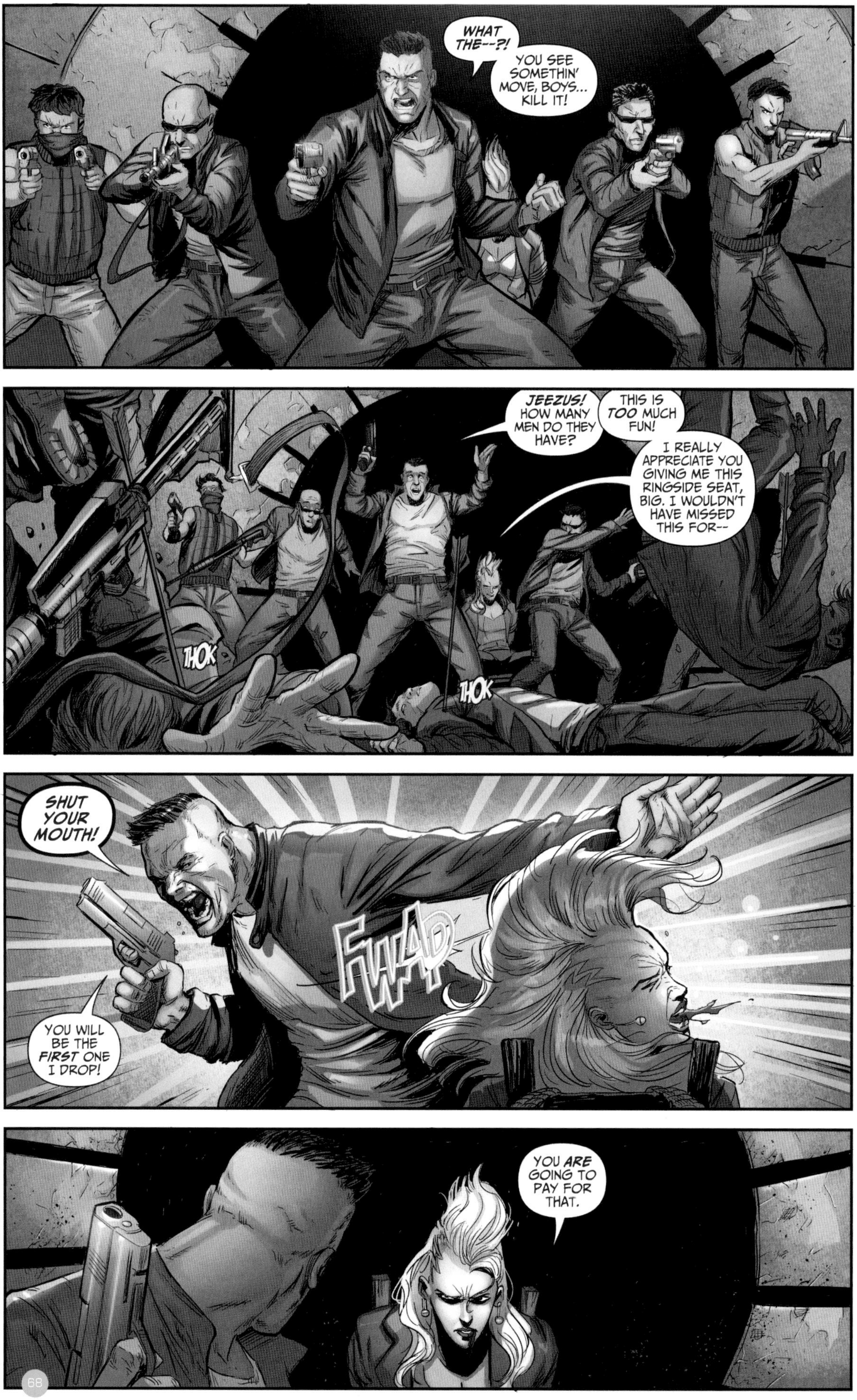
WHAT THE--?!
YOU SEE SOMETHIN' MOVE, BOYS... KILL IT!
JEEZUS! HOW MANY MEN DO THEY HAVE?
THIS IS TOO MUCH FUN!
I REALLY APPRECIATE YOU GIVING ME THIS RINGSIDE SEAT, BIG. I WOULDN'T HAVE MISSED THIS FOR--
THOK
THOK
SHUT YOUR MOUTH!
FWAP
YOU WILL BE THE FIRST ONE I DROP!
YOU ARE GOING TO PAY FOR THAT.

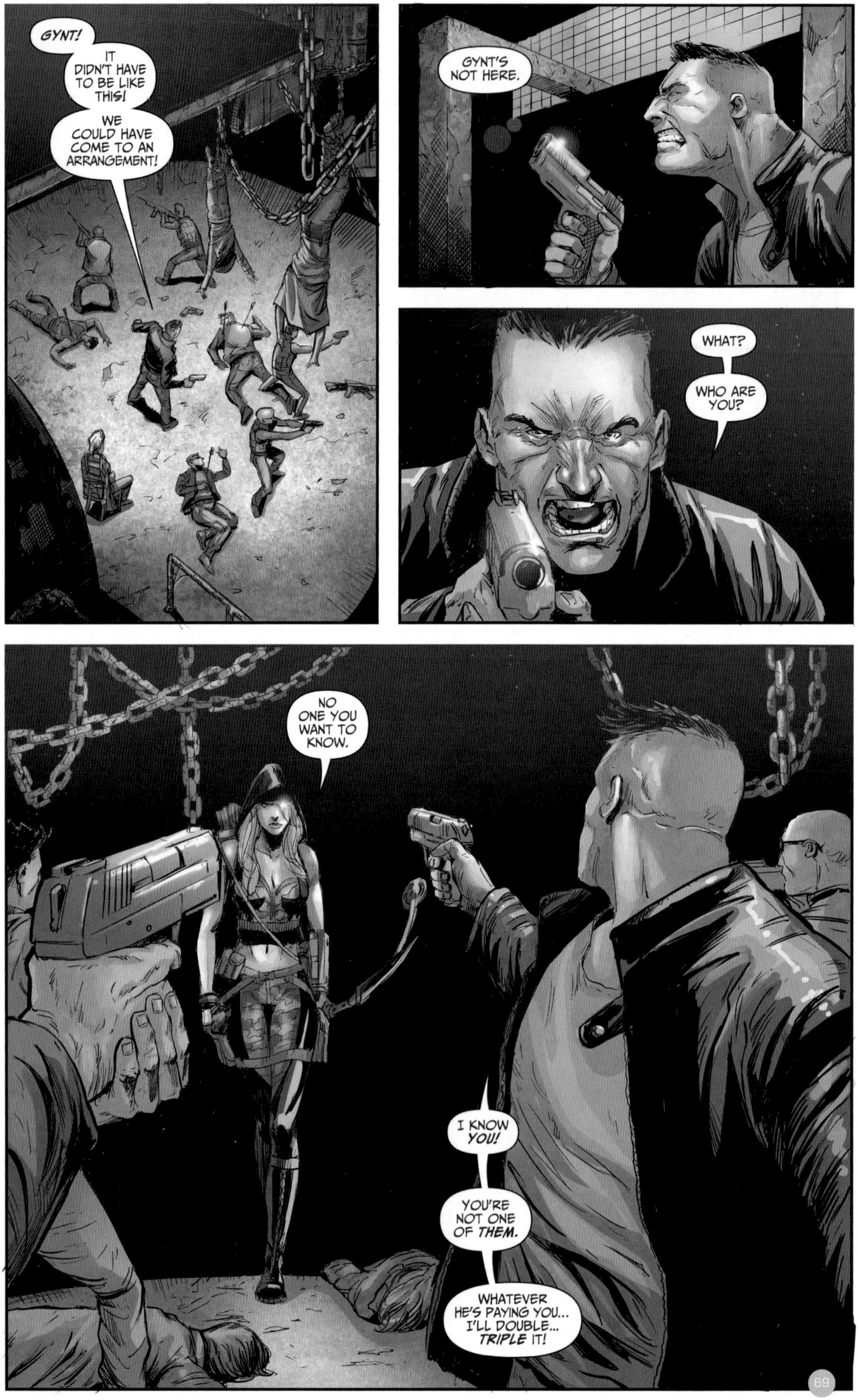
GYNT!
IT DIDN'T HAVE TO BE LIKE THIS!
WE COULD HAVE COME TO AN ARRANGEMENT!
GYNT'S NOT HERE.
WHAT?
WHO ARE YOU?
NO ONE YOU WANT TO KNOW.
I KNOW YOU!
YOU'RE NOT ONE OF THEM.
WHATEVER HE'S PAYING YOU... I'LL DOUBLE... TRIPLE IT!

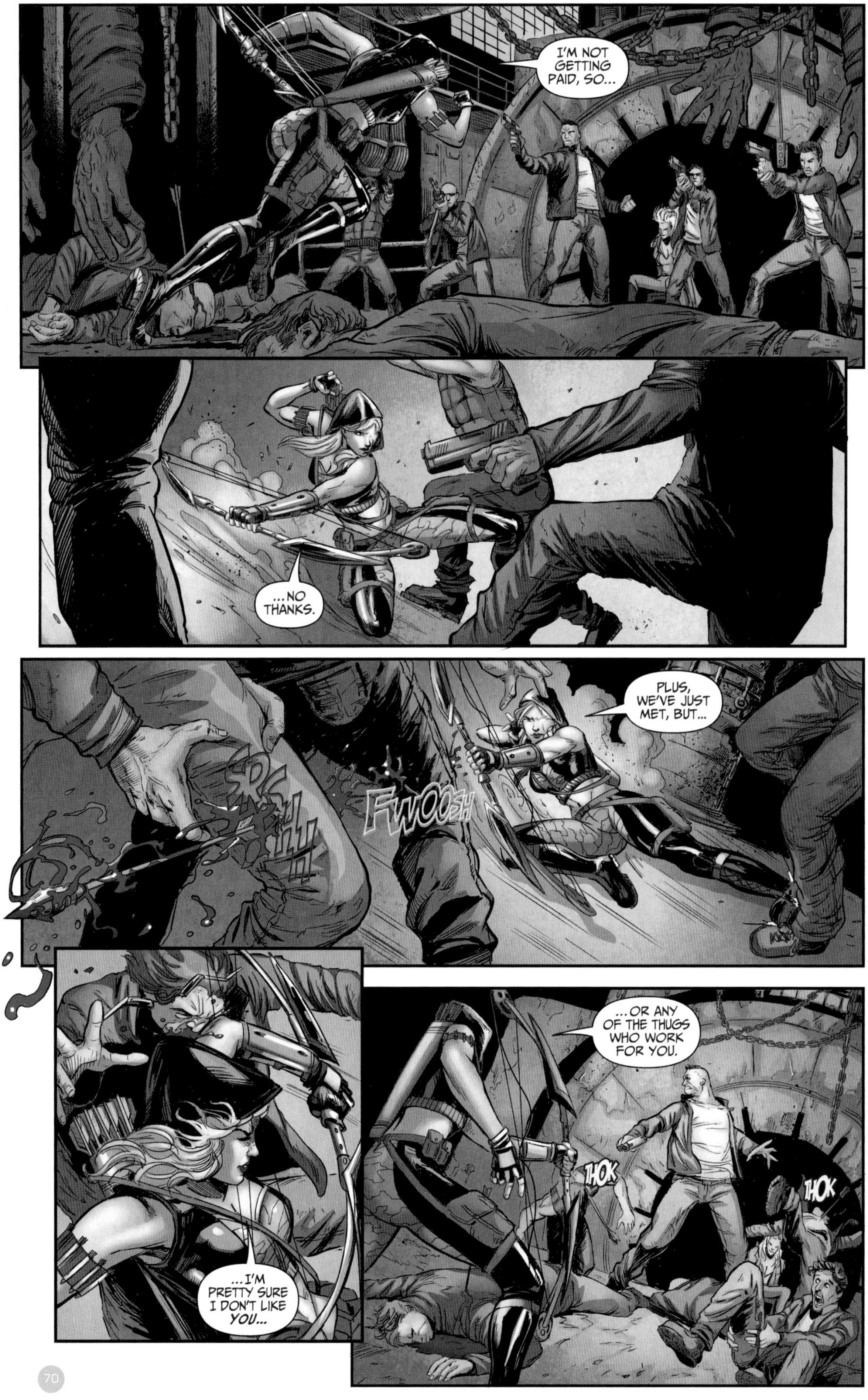
I'M NOT GETTING PAID, SO...
...NO THANKS.
PLUS, WE'VE JUST MET, BUT...
FWOOSH
...I'M PRETTY SURE I DON'T LIKE YOU...
...OR ANY OF THE THUGS WHO WORK FOR YOU.
THOK
THOK

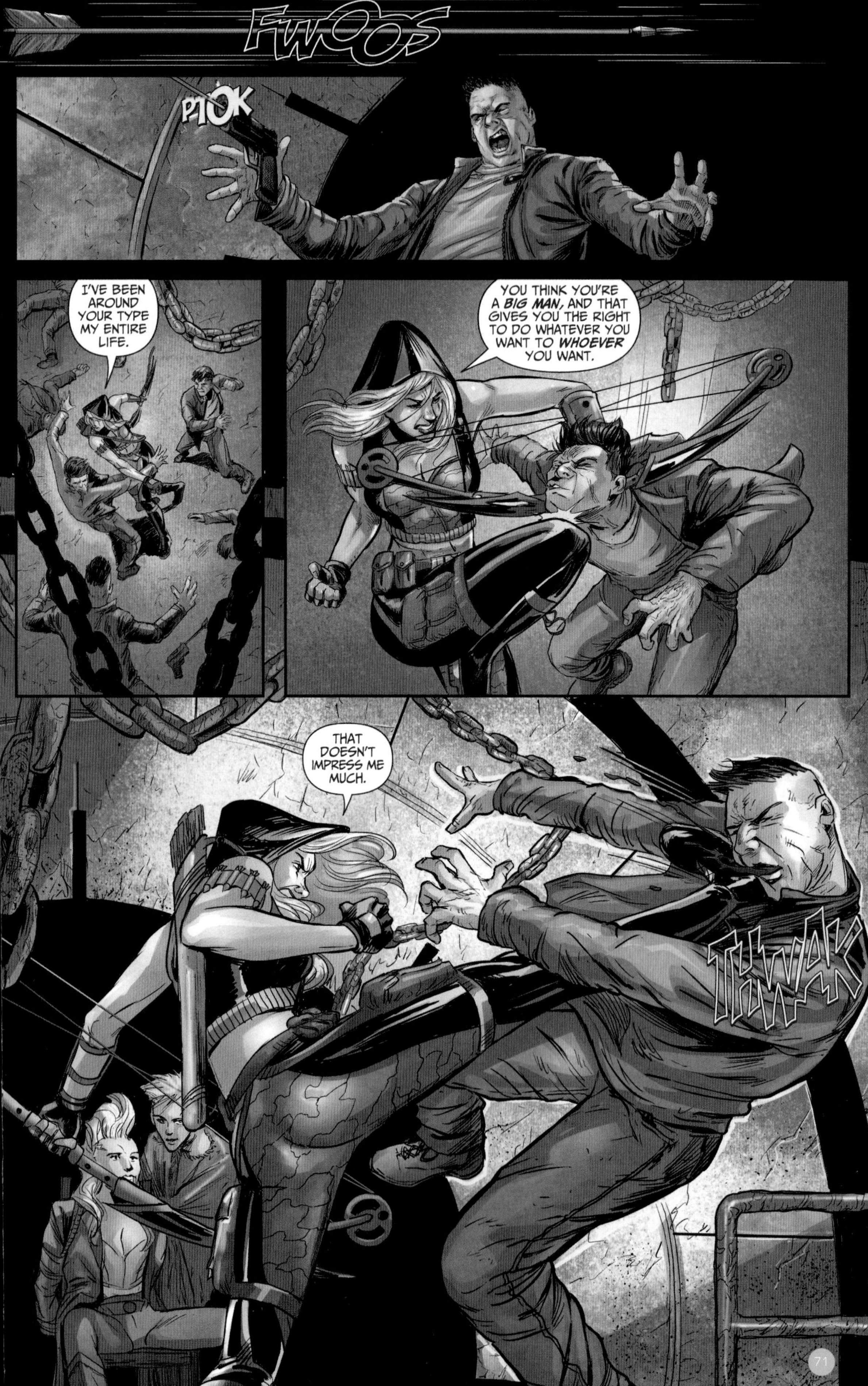
FWOOOS
PTOK
I'VE BEEN AROUND YOUR TYPE MY ENTIRE LIFE.
YOU THINK YOU'RE A **BIG MAN,** AND THAT GIVES YOU THE RIGHT TO DO WHATEVER YOU WANT TO **WHOEVER** YOU WANT.
THAT DOESN'T IMPRESS ME MUCH.
THWAK

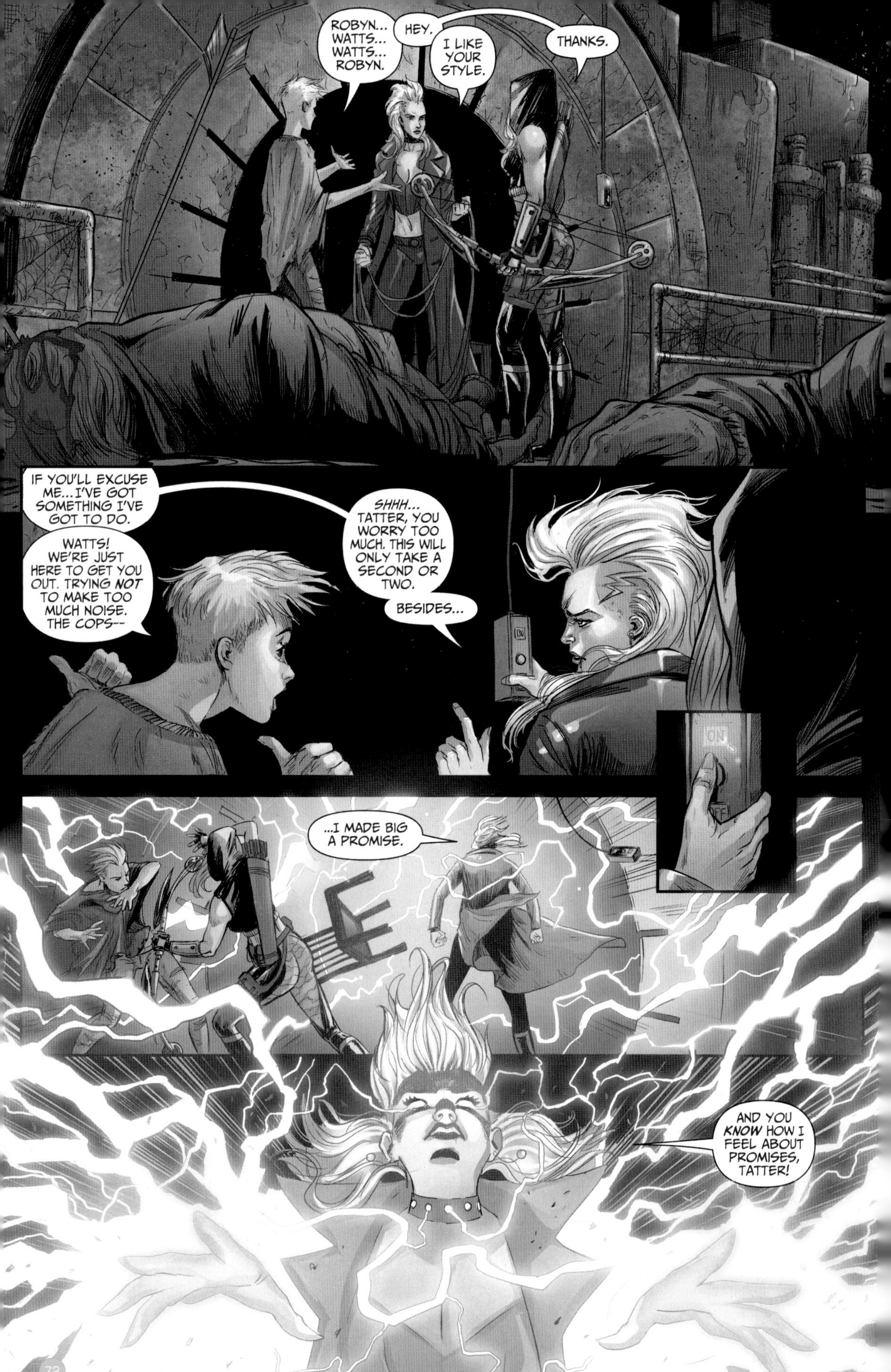
ROBYN... WATTS... WATTS... ROBYN.
HEY.
I LIKE YOUR STYLE.
THANKS.
IF YOU'LL EXCUSE ME... I'VE GOT SOMETHING I'VE GOT TO DO.
WATTS! WE'RE JUST HERE TO GET YOU OUT. TRYING *NOT* TO MAKE TOO MUCH NOISE. THE COPS--
SHHH... TATTER, YOU WORRY TOO MUCH. THIS WILL ONLY TAKE A SECOND OR TWO.
BESIDES...
ON
...I MADE BIG A PROMISE.
AND YOU *KNOW* HOW I FEEL ABOUT PROMISES, TATTER!

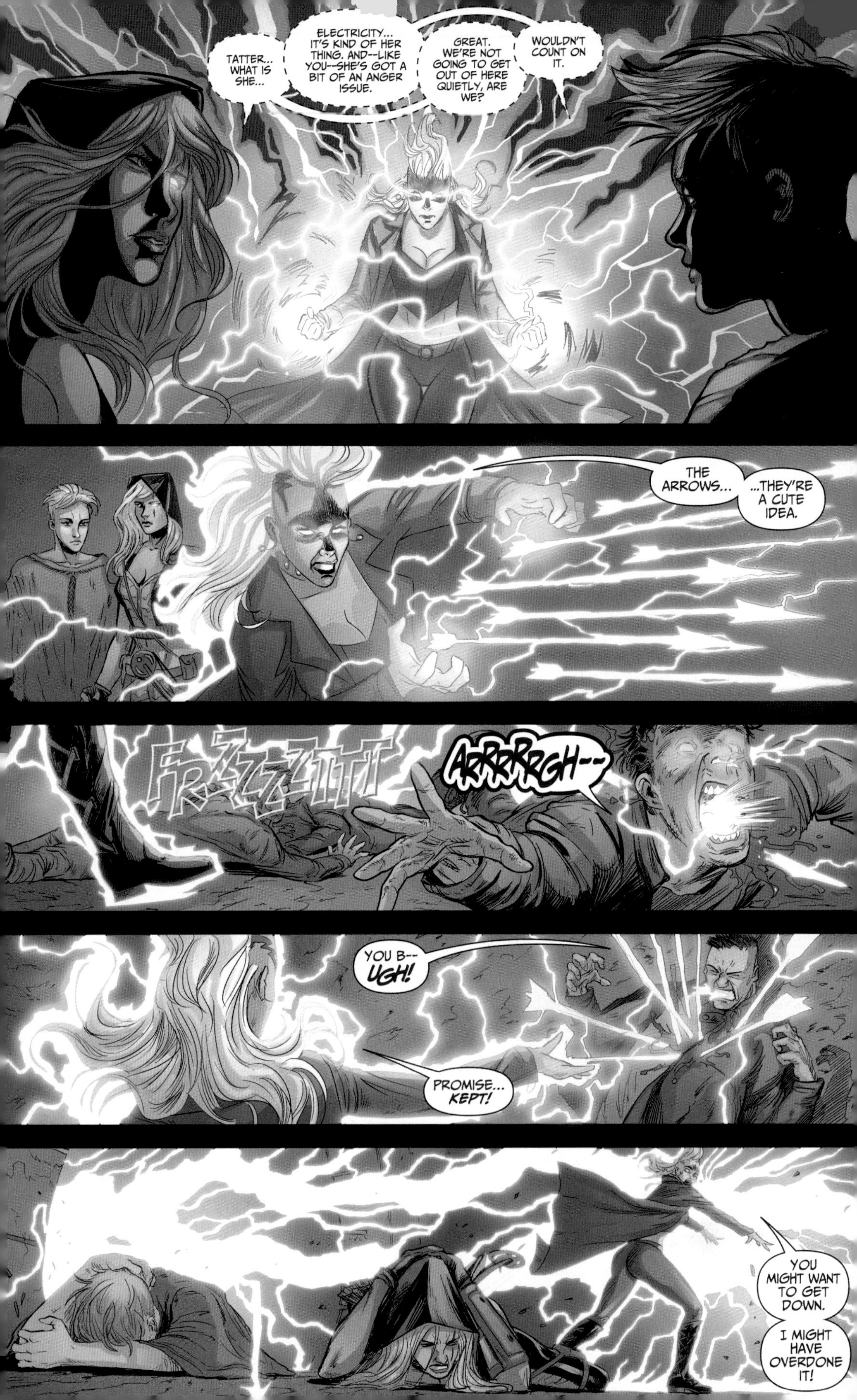
TATTER... WHAT IS SHE...
ELECTRICITY... IT'S KIND OF HER THING. AND--LIKE YOU--SHE'S GOT A BIT OF AN ANGER ISSUE.
GREAT. WE'RE NOT GOING TO GET OUT OF HERE QUIETLY, ARE WE?
WOULDN'T COUNT ON IT.
THE ARROWS...
...THEY'RE A CUTE IDEA.
FRZZZZTTT
ARRRRRGH--
YOU B--
UGH!
PROMISE... KEPT!
YOU MIGHT WANT TO GET DOWN.
I MIGHT HAVE OVERDONE IT!

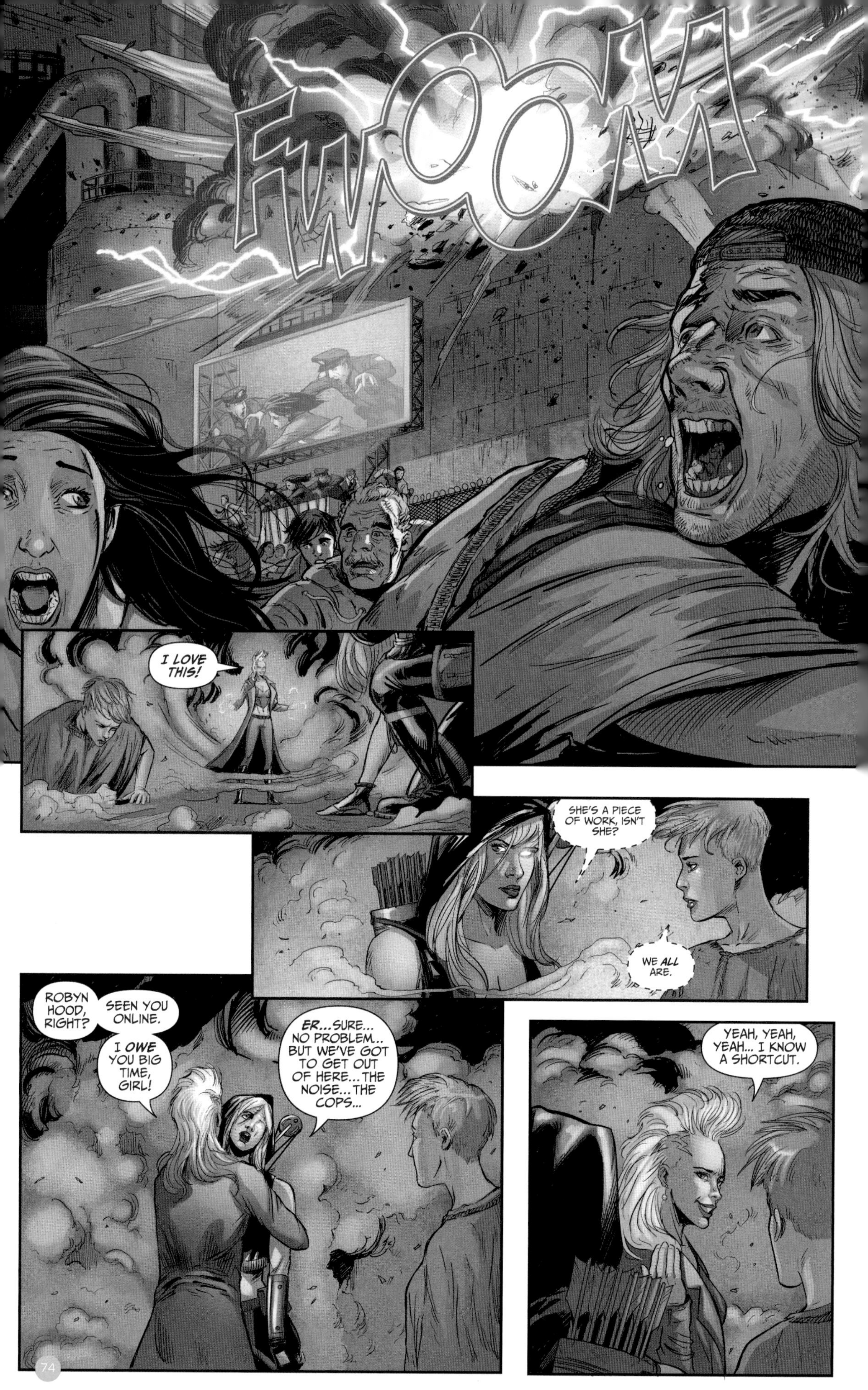
FWOOM
I LOVE THIS!
SHE'S A PIECE OF WORK, ISN'T SHE?
WE ALL ARE.
ROBYN HOOD, RIGHT?
SEEN YOU ONLINE.
I OWE YOU BIG TIME, GIRL!
ER...SURE... NO PROBLEM... BUT WE'VE GOT TO GET OUT OF HERE...THE NOISE...THE COPS...
YEAH, YEAH, YEAH... I KNOW A SHORTCUT.

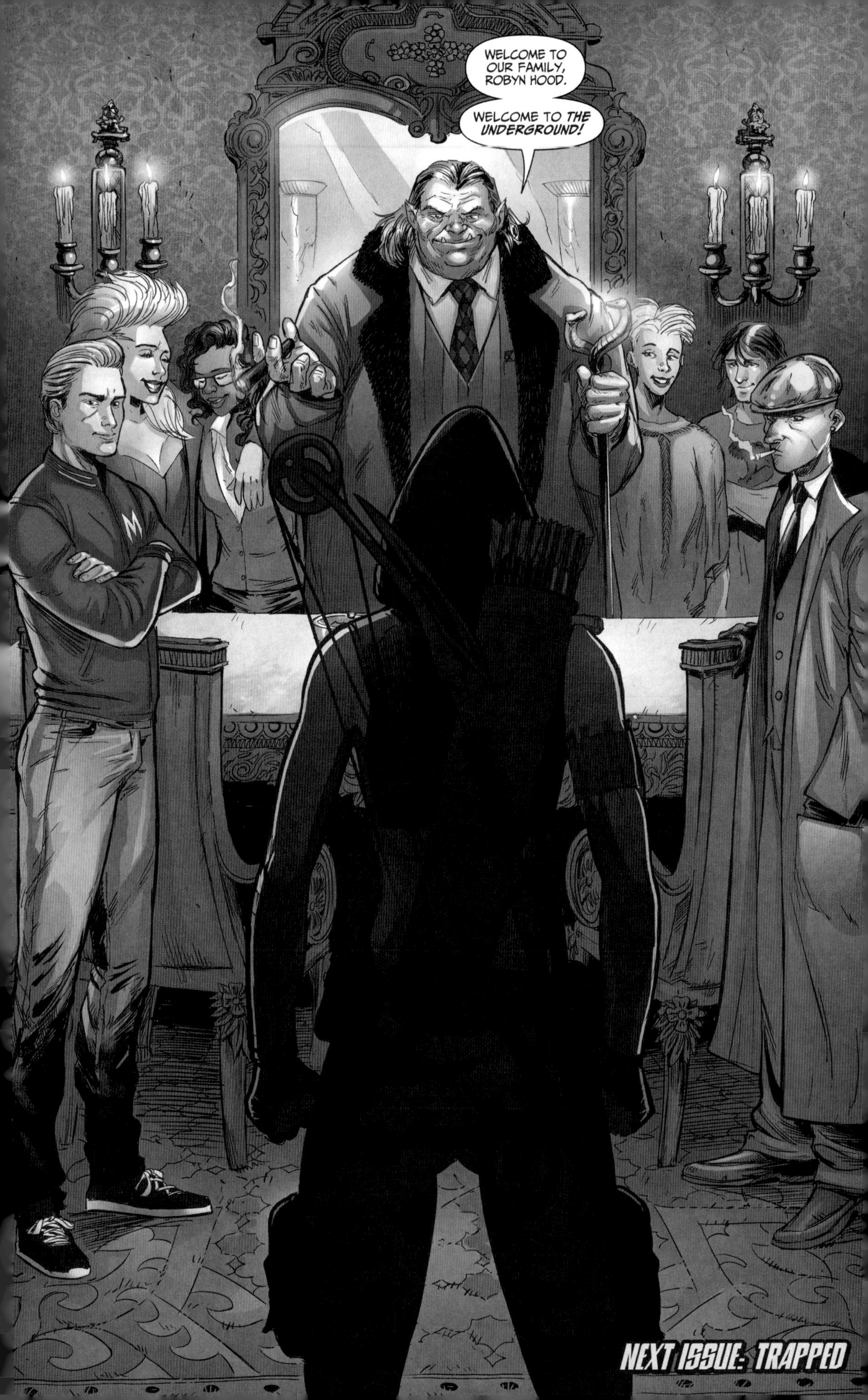
WELCOME TO OUR FAMILY, ROBYN HOOD.
WELCOME TO *THE UNDERGROUND!*
NEXT ISSUE: TRAPPED

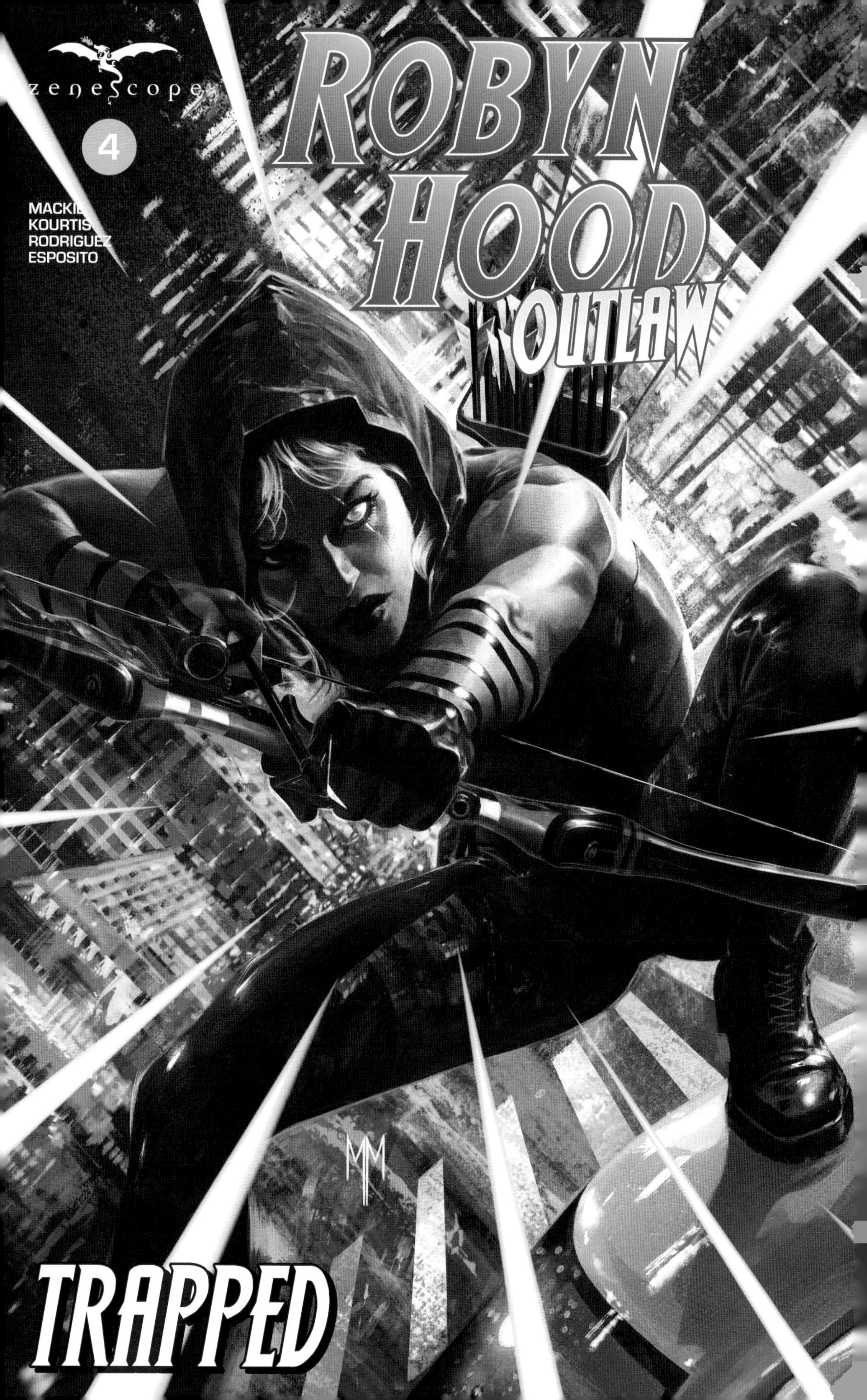
zenescope
4
ROBYN HOOD
OUTLAW
MACKIE
KOURTIS
RODRIGUEZ
ESPOSITO
TRAPPED

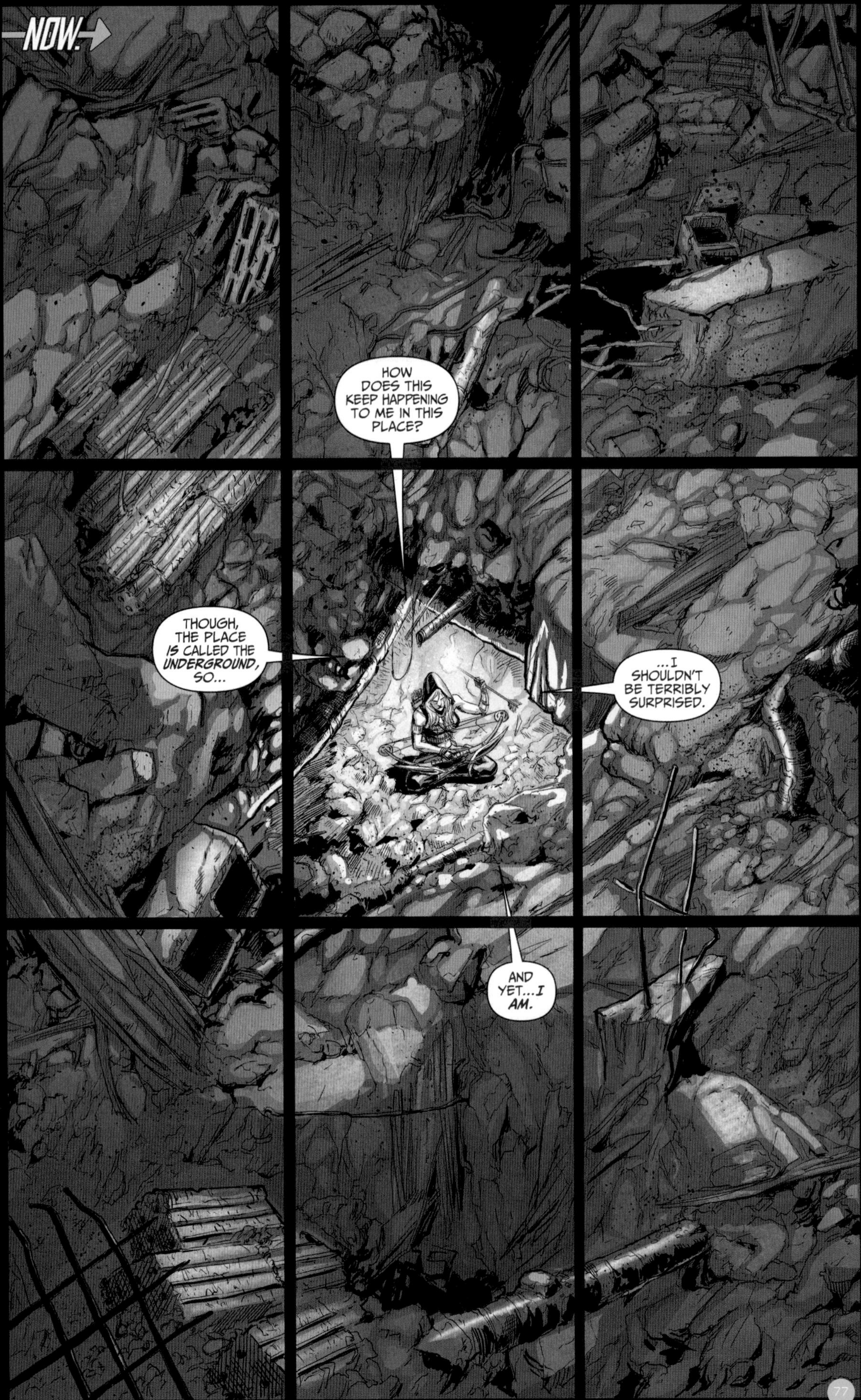
NOW.
HOW DOES THIS KEEP HAPPENING TO ME IN THIS PLACE?
THOUGH, THE PLACE *IS* CALLED THE *UNDERGROUND*, SO...
...I SHOULDN'T BE TERRIBLY SURPRISED.
AND YET...I *AM*.

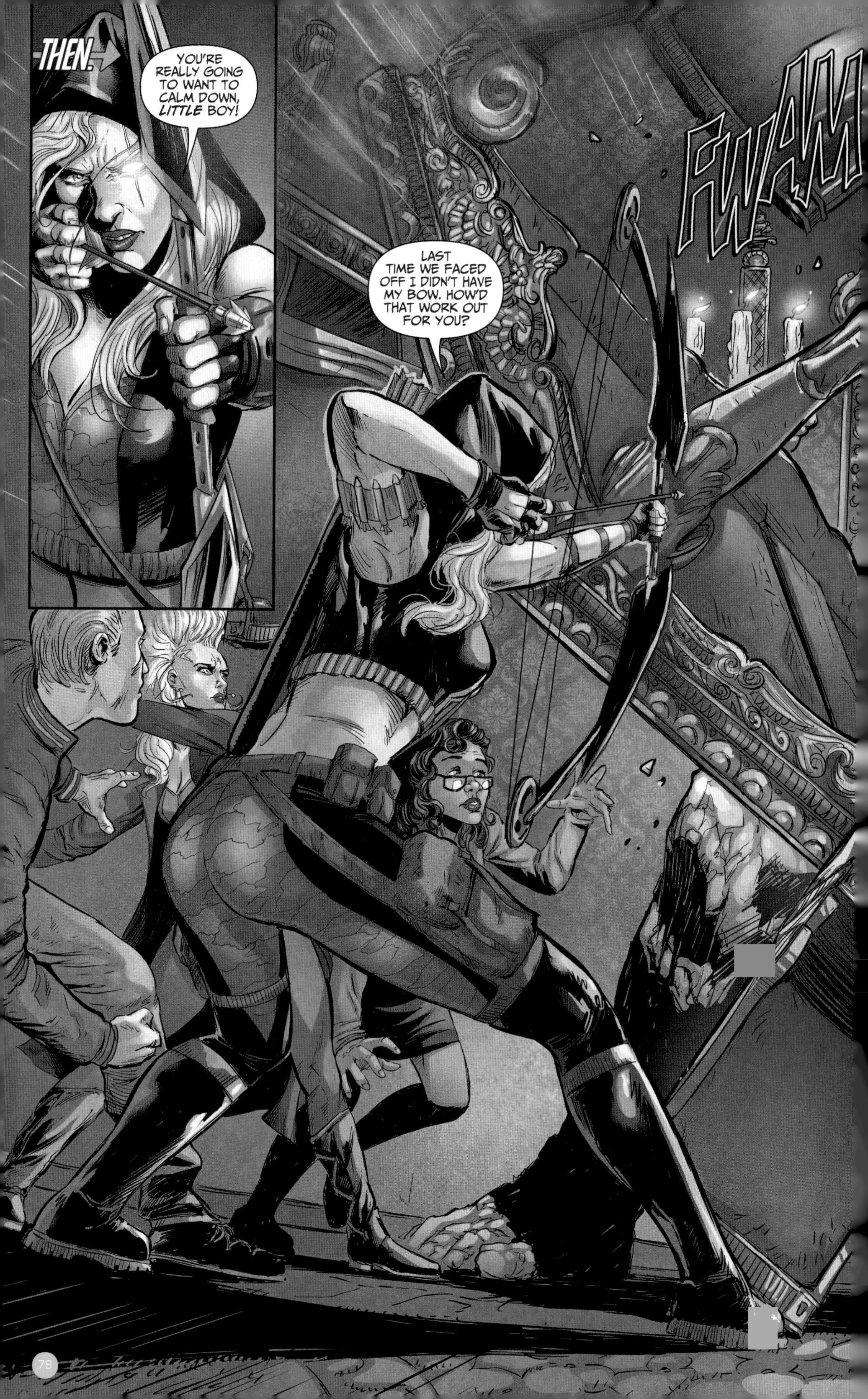
THEN.
YOU'RE REALLY GOING TO WANT TO CALM DOWN, *LITTLE* BOY!
FWAM
LAST TIME WE FACED OFF I DIDN'T HAVE MY BOW. HOW'D THAT WORK OUT FOR YOU?

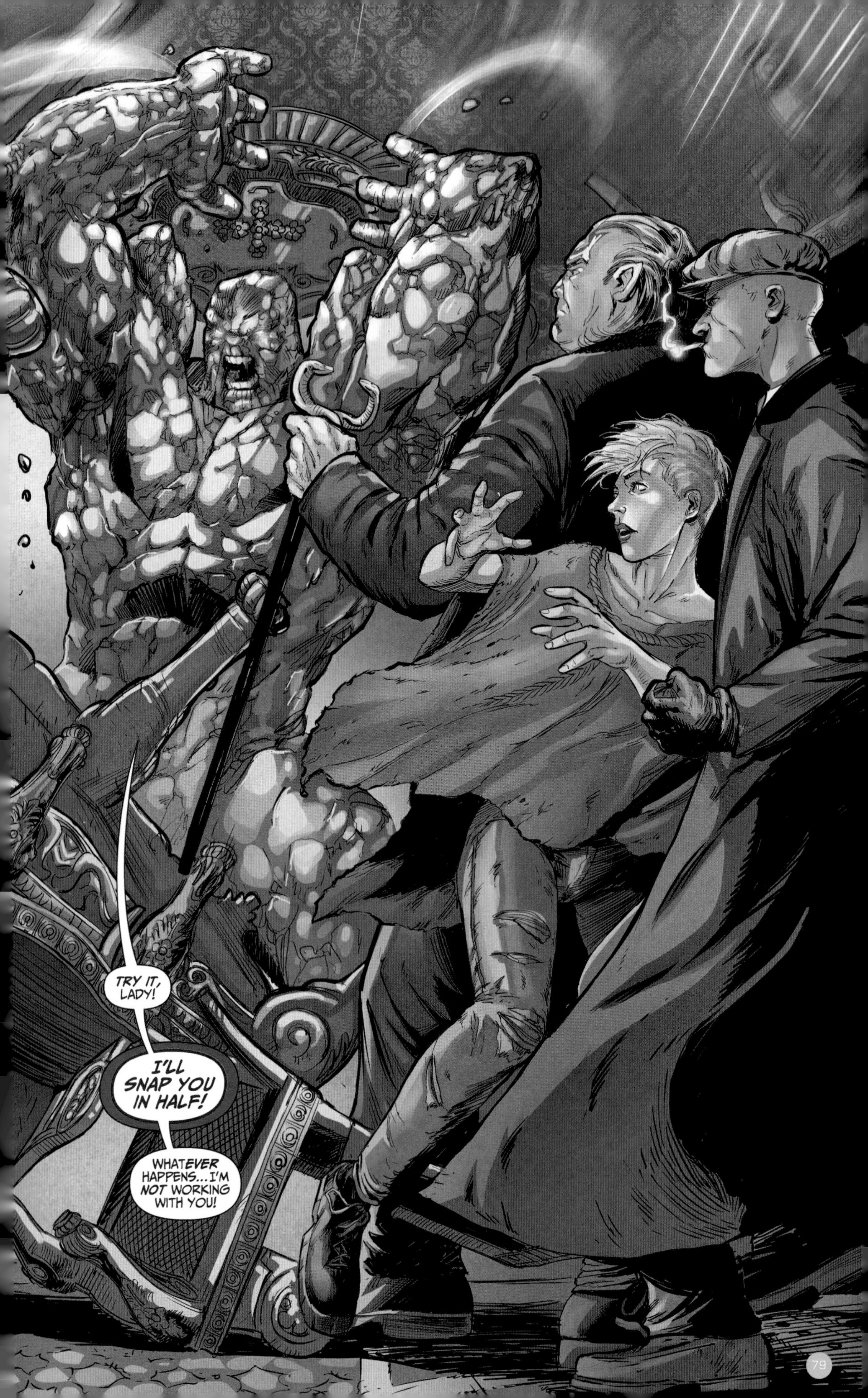
TRY IT, LADY!
I'LL SNAP YOU IN HALF!
WHATEVER HAPPENS... I'M NOT WORKING WITH YOU!

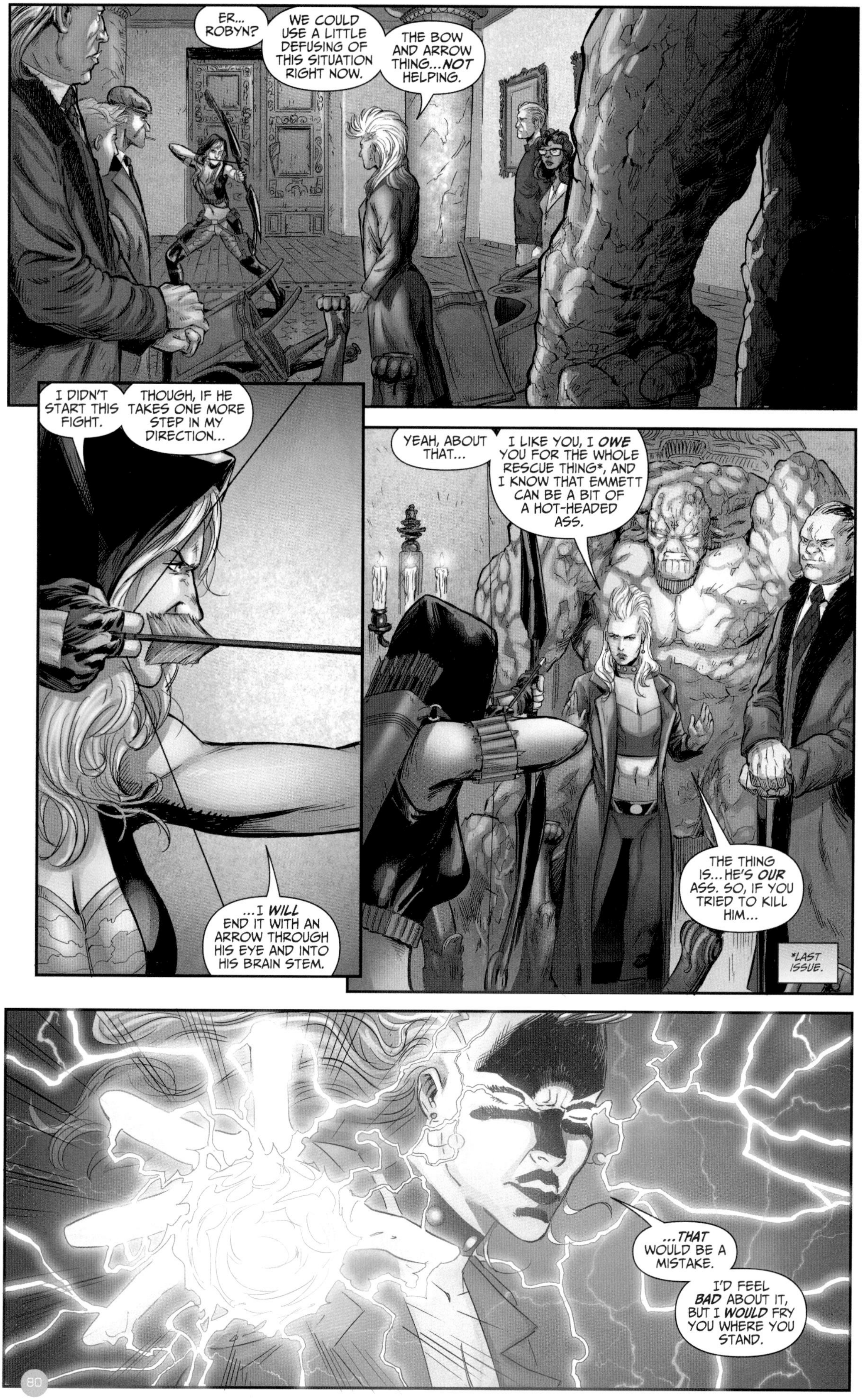
ER... ROBYN?
WE COULD USE A LITTLE DEFUSING OF THIS SITUATION RIGHT NOW.
THE BOW AND ARROW THING...NOT HELPING.
I DIDN'T START THIS FIGHT.
THOUGH, IF HE TAKES ONE MORE STEP IN MY DIRECTION...
...I WILL END IT WITH AN ARROW THROUGH HIS EYE AND INTO HIS BRAIN STEM.
YEAH, ABOUT THAT...
I LIKE YOU, I OWE YOU FOR THE WHOLE RESCUE THING*, AND I KNOW THAT EMMETT CAN BE A BIT OF A HOT-HEADED ASS.
THE THING IS...HE'S OUR ASS. SO, IF YOU TRIED TO KILL HIM...
*LAST ISSUE.
...THAT WOULD BE A MISTAKE.
I'D FEEL BAD ABOUT IT, BUT I WOULD FRY YOU WHERE YOU STAND.

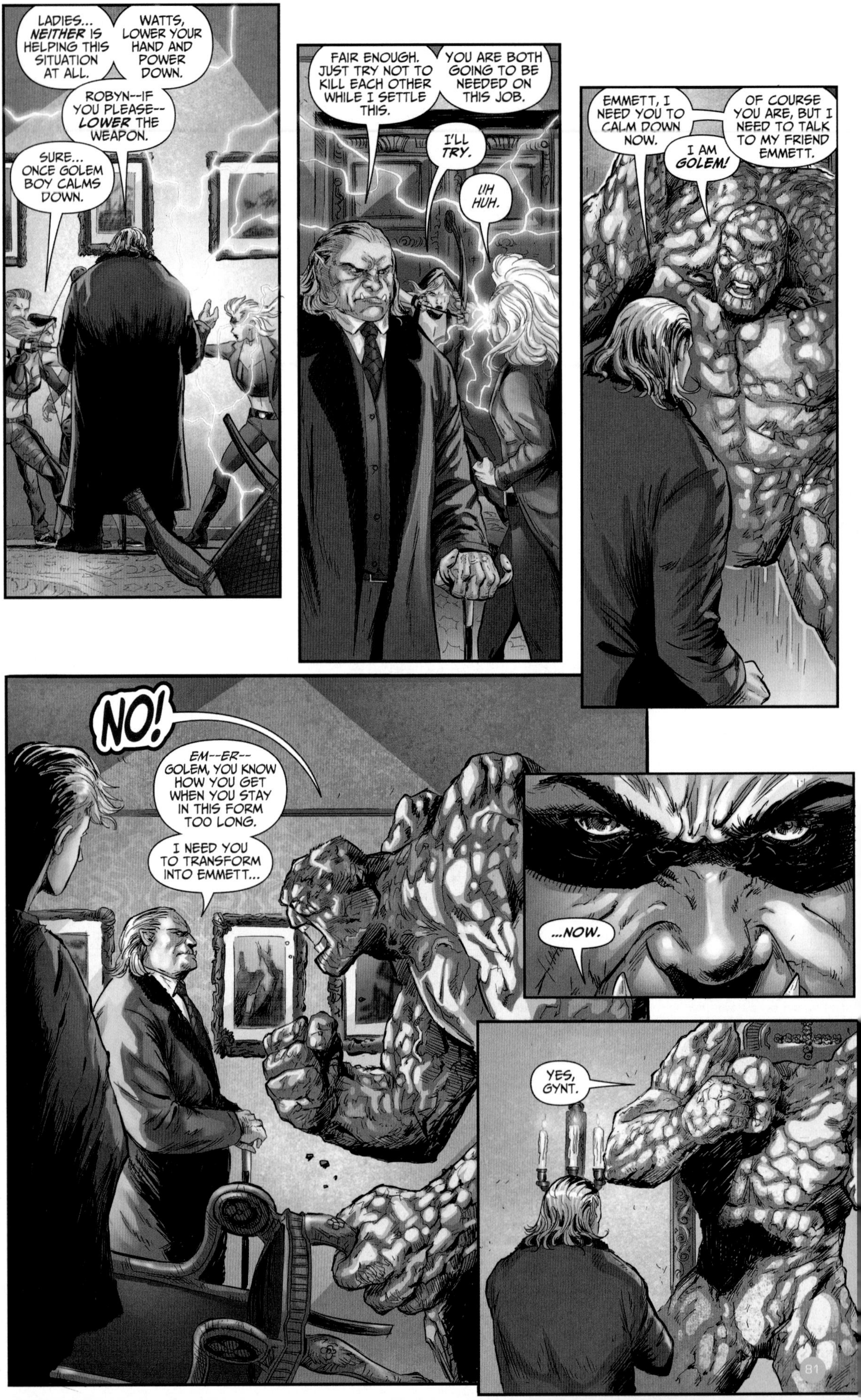
LADIES... NEITHER IS HELPING THIS SITUATION AT ALL.
WATTS, LOWER YOUR HAND AND POWER DOWN.
ROBYN--IF YOU PLEASE--LOWER THE WEAPON.
SURE... ONCE GOLEM BOY CALMS DOWN.
FAIR ENOUGH. JUST TRY NOT TO KILL EACH OTHER WHILE I SETTLE THIS.
YOU ARE BOTH GOING TO BE NEEDED ON THIS JOB.
I'LL TRY.
UH HUH.
EMMETT, I NEED YOU TO CALM DOWN NOW.
OF COURSE YOU ARE, BUT I NEED TO TALK TO MY FRIEND EMMETT.
I AM GOLEM!
NO!
EM--ER--GOLEM, YOU KNOW HOW YOU GET WHEN YOU STAY IN THIS FORM TOO LONG.
I NEED YOU TO TRANSFORM INTO EMMETT...
...NOW.
YES, GYNT.

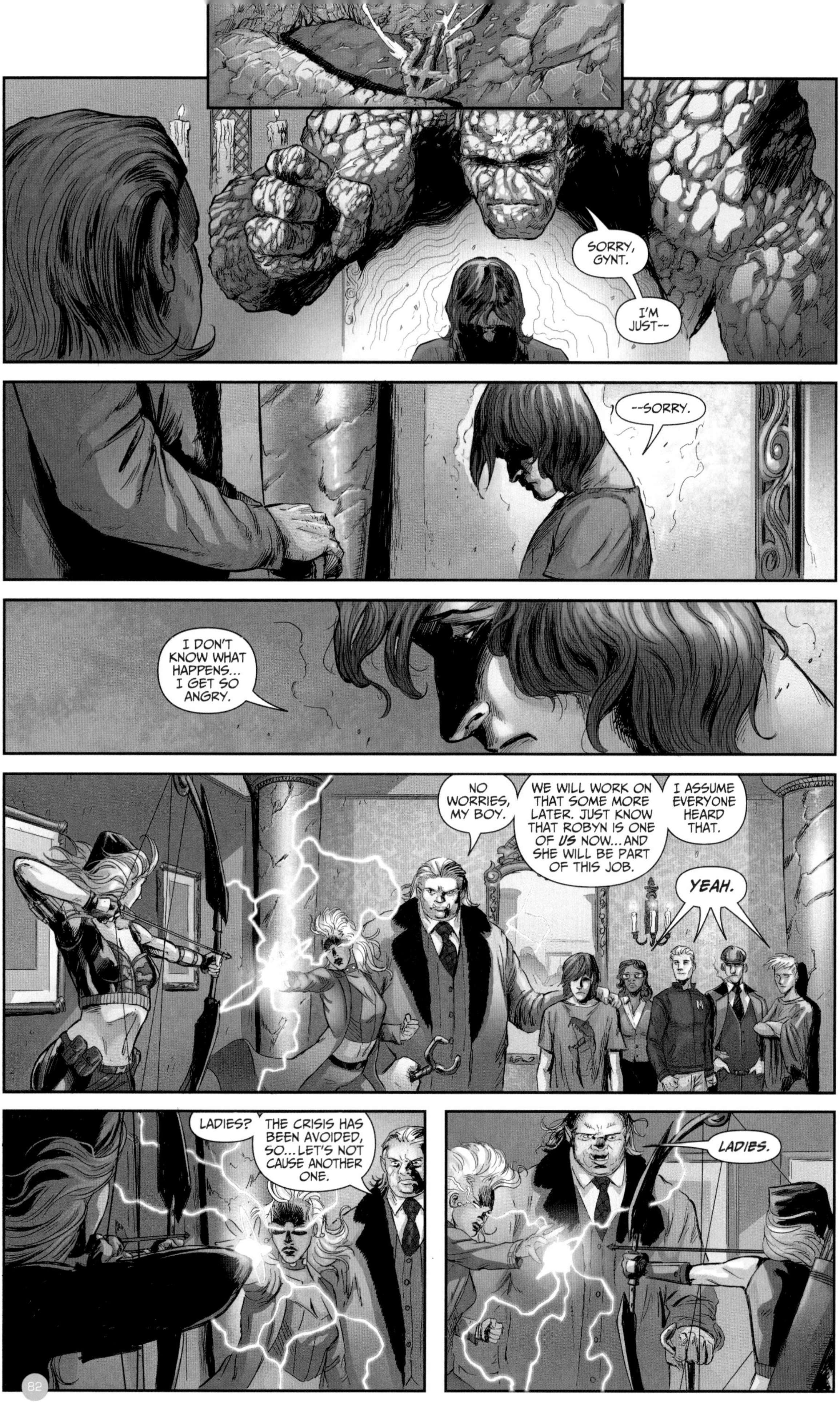
SORRY, GYNT.
I'M JUST--
--SORRY.
I DON'T KNOW WHAT HAPPENS... I GET SO ANGRY.
NO WORRIES, MY BOY.
WE WILL WORK ON THAT SOME MORE LATER. JUST KNOW THAT ROBYN IS ONE OF US NOW...AND SHE WILL BE PART OF THIS JOB.
I ASSUME EVERYONE HEARD THAT.
YEAH.
LADIES?
THE CRISIS HAS BEEN AVOIDED, SO...LET'S NOT CAUSE ANOTHER ONE.
LADIES.

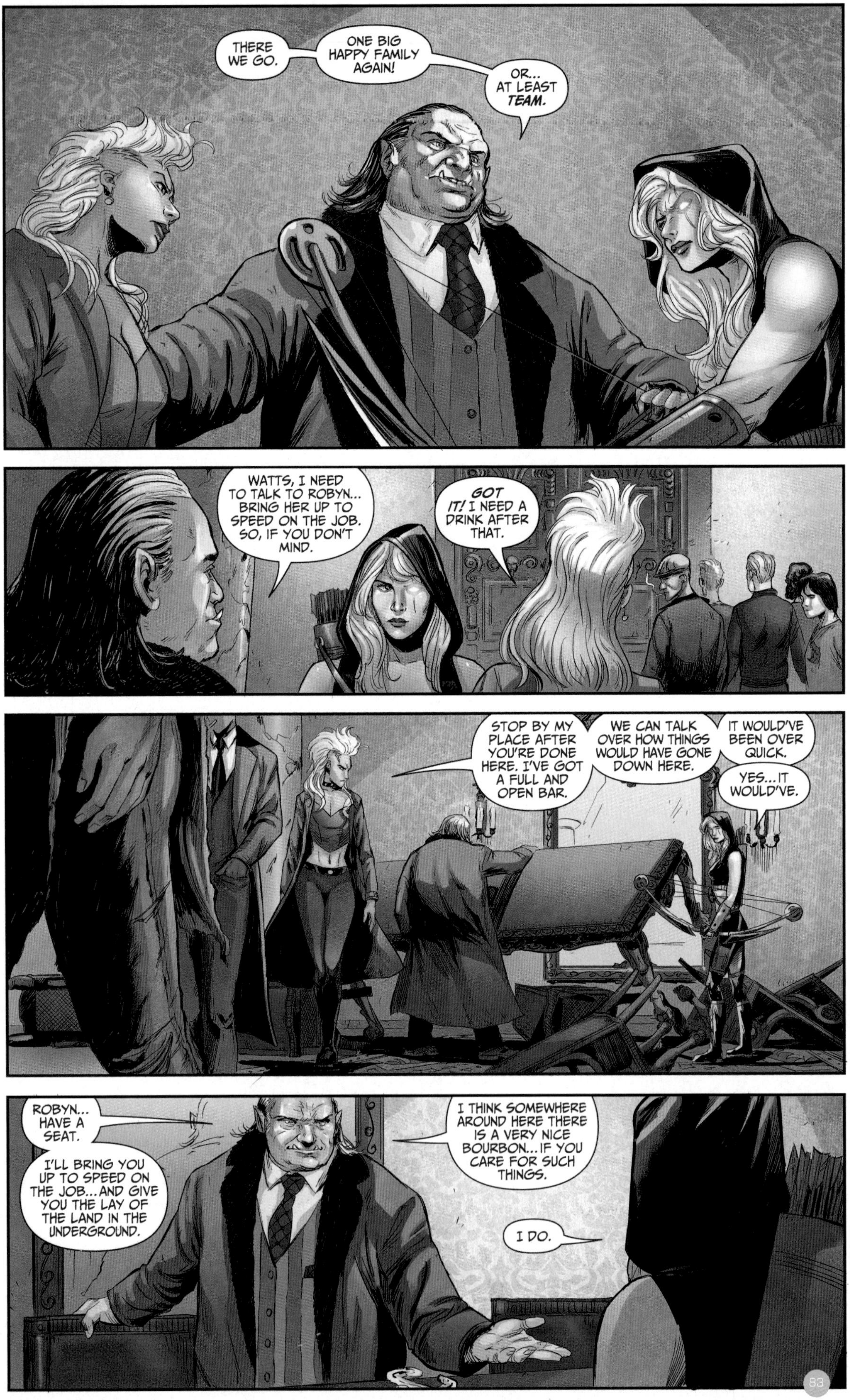
THERE WE GO.
ONE BIG HAPPY FAMILY AGAIN!
OR... AT LEAST TEAM.
WATTS, I NEED TO TALK TO ROBYN... BRING HER UP TO SPEED ON THE JOB. SO, IF YOU DON'T MIND.
GOT IT! I NEED A DRINK AFTER THAT.
STOP BY MY PLACE AFTER YOU'RE DONE HERE. I'VE GOT A FULL AND OPEN BAR.
WE CAN TALK OVER HOW THINGS WOULD HAVE GONE DOWN HERE.
IT WOULD'VE BEEN OVER QUICK.
YES...IT WOULD'VE.
ROBYN... HAVE A SEAT.
I'LL BRING YOU UP TO SPEED ON THE JOB...AND GIVE YOU THE LAY OF THE LAND IN THE UNDERGROUND.
I THINK SOMEWHERE AROUND HERE THERE IS A VERY NICE BOURBON...IF YOU CARE FOR SUCH THINGS.
I DO.

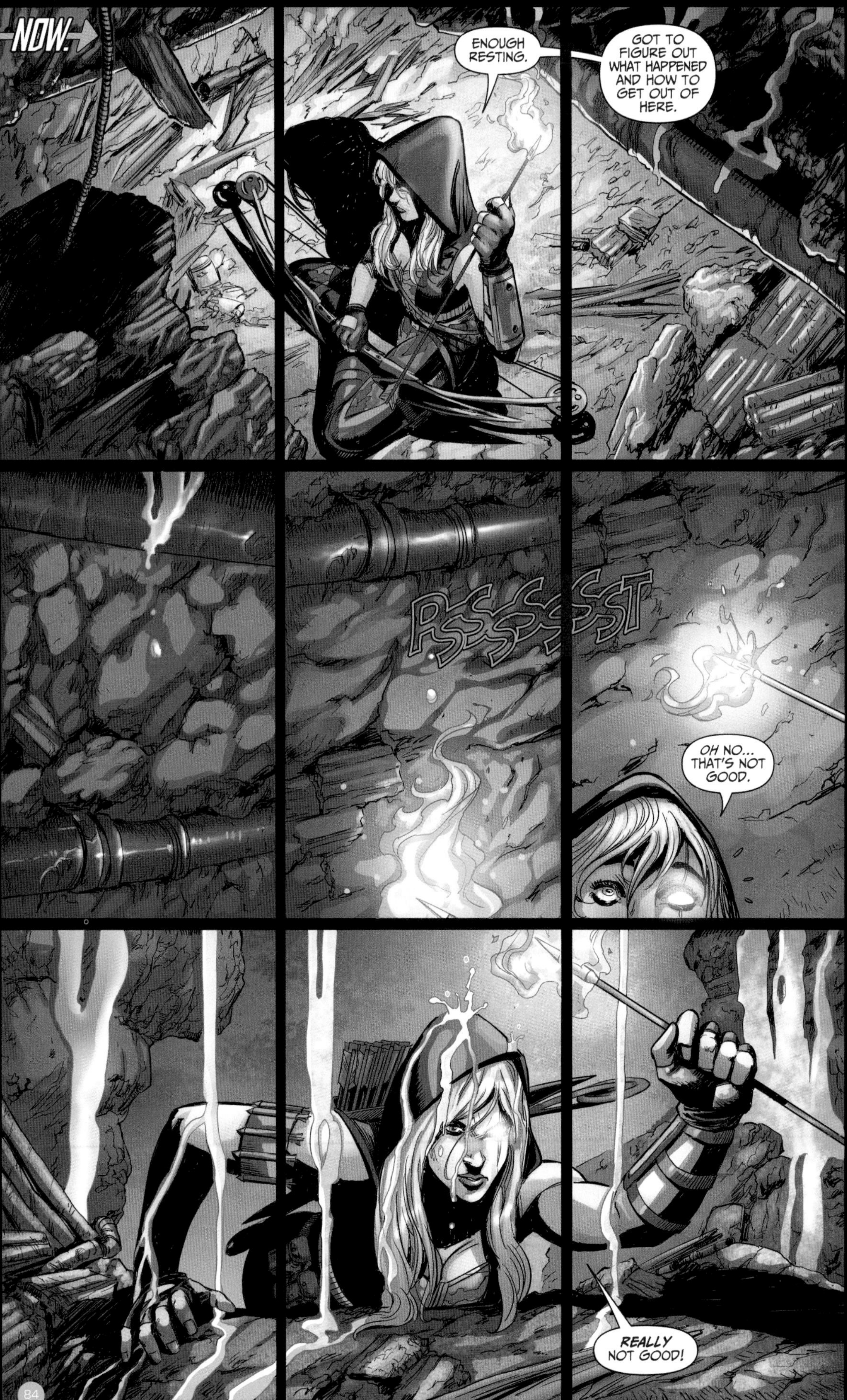
NOW.
ENOUGH RESTING.
GOT TO FIGURE OUT WHAT HAPPENED AND HOW TO GET OUT OF HERE.
PSSSSSST
OH NO... THAT'S NOT GOOD.
REALLY NOT GOOD!

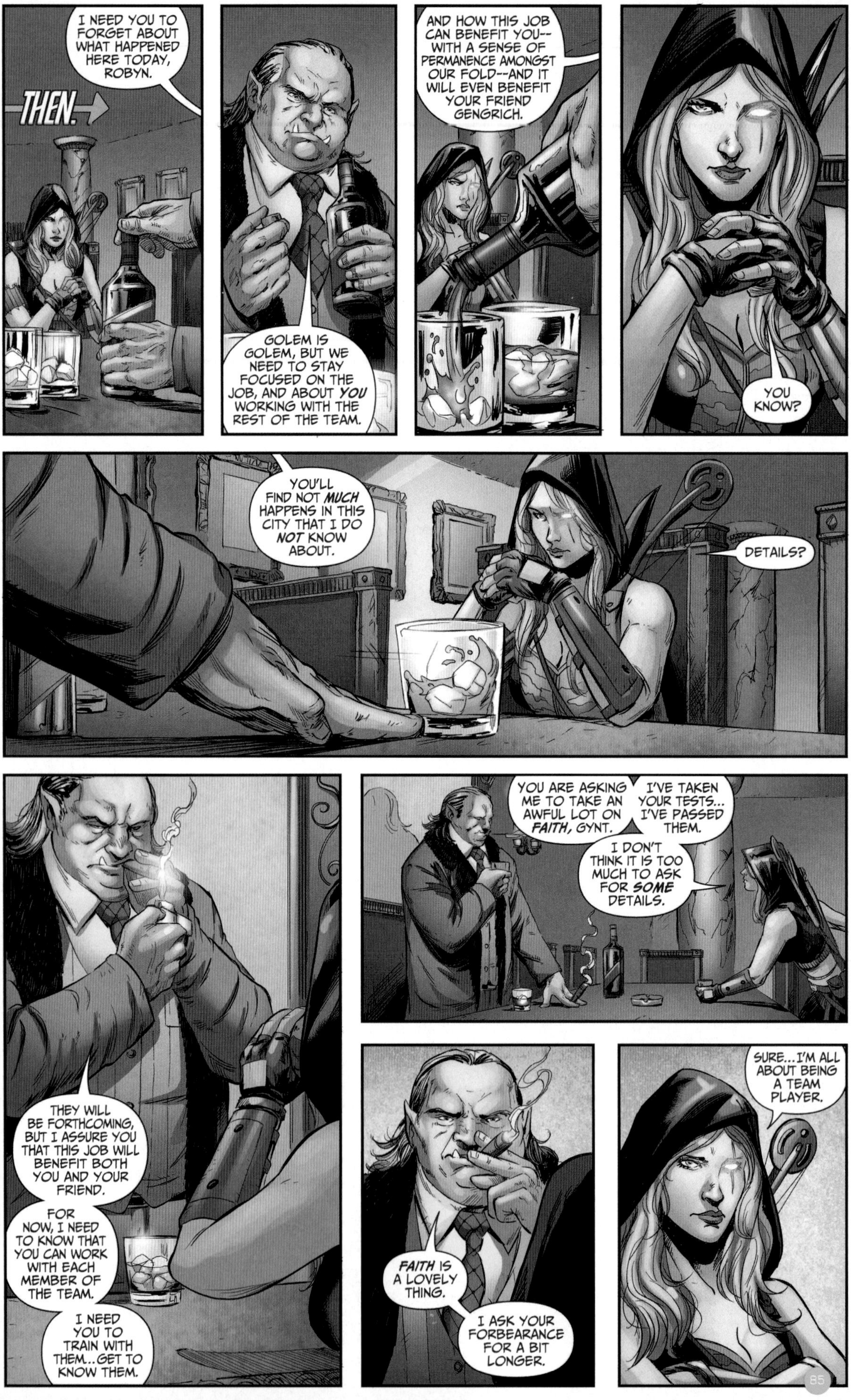
I NEED YOU TO FORGET ABOUT WHAT HAPPENED HERE TODAY, ROBYN.
THEN.
GOLEM IS GOLEM, BUT WE NEED TO STAY FOCUSED ON THE JOB, AND ABOUT *YOU* WORKING WITH THE REST OF THE TEAM.
AND HOW THIS JOB CAN BENEFIT YOU-- WITH A SENSE OF PERMANENCE AMONGST OUR FOLD--AND IT WILL EVEN BENEFIT YOUR FRIEND GENGRICH.
YOU KNOW?
YOU'LL FIND NOT *MUCH* HAPPENS IN THIS CITY THAT I DO *NOT* KNOW ABOUT.
DETAILS?
THEY WILL BE FORTHCOMING, BUT I ASSURE YOU THAT THIS JOB WILL BENEFIT BOTH YOU AND YOUR FRIEND.
FOR NOW, I NEED TO KNOW THAT YOU CAN WORK WITH EACH MEMBER OF THE TEAM.
I NEED YOU TO TRAIN WITH THEM...GET TO KNOW THEM.
YOU ARE ASKING ME TO TAKE AN AWFUL LOT ON *FAITH,* GYNT.
I'VE TAKEN YOUR TESTS... I'VE PASSED THEM.
I DON'T THINK IT IS TOO MUCH TO ASK FOR *SOME* DETAILS.
FAITH IS A LOVELY THING.
I ASK YOUR FORBEARANCE FOR A BIT LONGER.
SURE...I'M ALL ABOUT BEING A TEAM PLAYER.

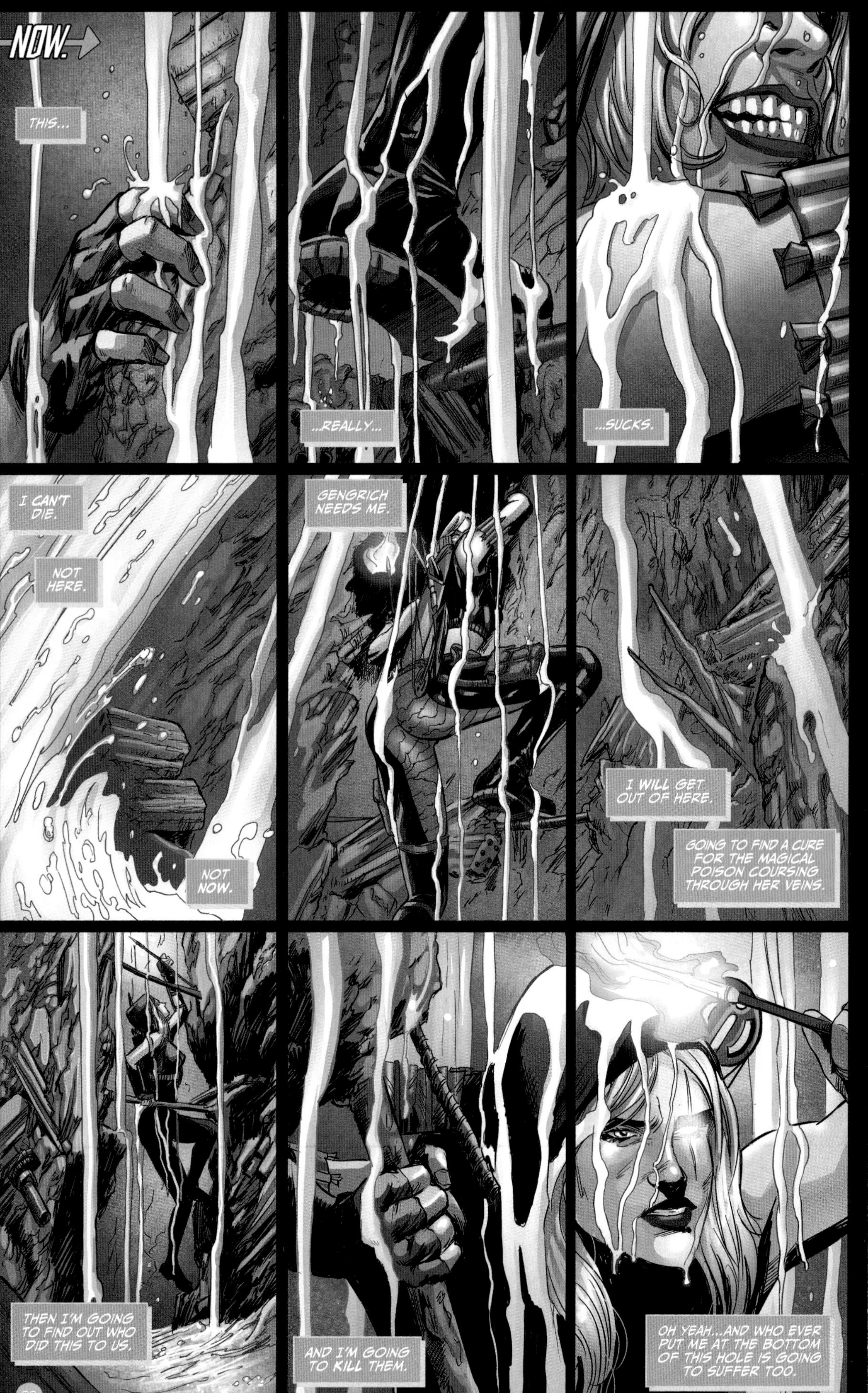
NOW.
THIS...
...REALLY...
...SUCKS.
I CAN'T DIE.
NOT HERE.
NOT NOW.
GENGRICH NEEDS ME.
I WILL GET OUT OF HERE.
GOING TO FIND A CURE FOR THE MAGICAL POISON COURSING THROUGH HER VEINS.
THEN I'M GOING TO FIND OUT WHO DID THIS TO US.
AND I'M GOING TO KILL THEM.
OH YEAH...AND WHO EVER PUT ME AT THE BOTTOM OF THIS HOLE IS GOING TO SUFFER TOO.

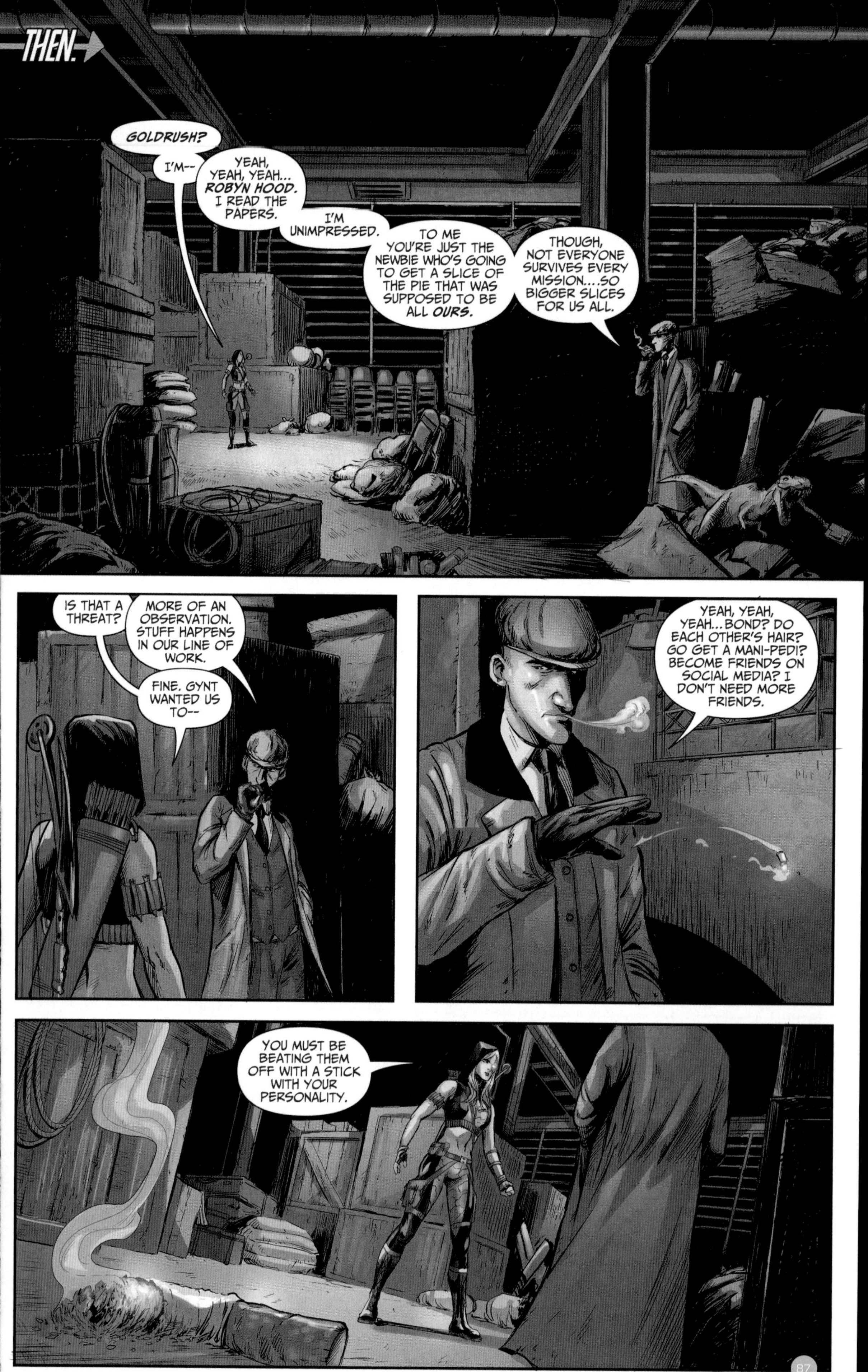
THEN.
GOLDRUSH?
I'M--
YEAH, YEAH, YEAH... ROBYN HOOD. I READ THE PAPERS.
I'M UNIMPRESSED.
TO ME YOU'RE JUST THE NEWBIE WHO'S GOING TO GET A SLICE OF THE PIE THAT WAS SUPPOSED TO BE ALL OURS.
THOUGH, NOT EVERYONE SURVIVES EVERY MISSION....SO BIGGER SLICES FOR US ALL.
IS THAT A THREAT?
MORE OF AN OBSERVATION. STUFF HAPPENS IN OUR LINE OF WORK.
FINE. GYNT WANTED US TO--
YEAH, YEAH, YEAH...BOND? DO EACH OTHER'S HAIR? GO GET A MANI-PEDI? BECOME FRIENDS ON SOCIAL MEDIA? I DON'T NEED MORE FRIENDS.
YOU MUST BE BEATING THEM OFF WITH A STICK WITH YOUR PERSONALITY.

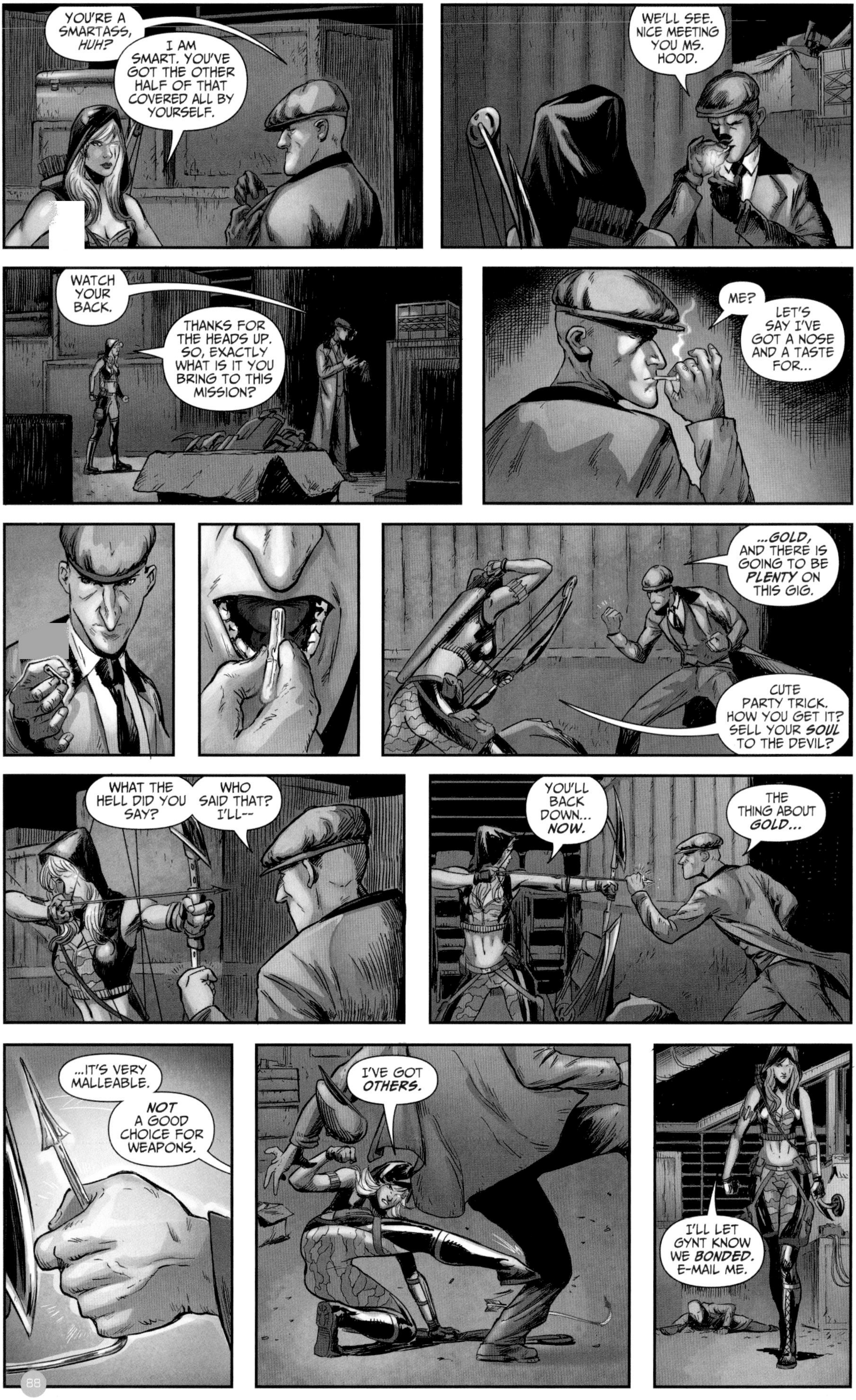
YOU'RE A SMARTASS, *HUH?*
I AM SMART. YOU'VE GOT THE OTHER HALF OF THAT COVERED ALL BY YOURSELF.
WE'LL SEE. NICE MEETING YOU MS. HOOD.
WATCH YOUR BACK.
THANKS FOR THE HEADS UP. SO, EXACTLY WHAT IS IT YOU BRING TO THIS MISSION?
ME?
LET'S SAY I'VE GOT A NOSE AND A TASTE FOR...
...GOLD, AND THERE IS GOING TO BE ***PLENTY*** ON THIS GIG.
CUTE PARTY TRICK. HOW YOU GET IT? SELL YOUR ***SOUL*** TO THE DEVIL?
WHAT THE HELL DID YOU SAY?
WHO SAID THAT? I'LL--
YOU'LL BACK DOWN... ***NOW.***
THE THING ABOUT ***GOLD...***
...IT'S VERY MALLEABLE.
NOT A GOOD CHOICE FOR WEAPONS.
I'VE GOT ***OTHERS.***
I'LL LET GYNT KNOW WE ***BONDED.*** E-MAIL ME.

GENGRICH.

REVENGE.

GENGRICH.

SHE'S ONE OF THE FEW FRIENDS I'VE GOT.

NO ONE DOWN HERE WOULD HAVE MY BACK LIKE SHE DOES.

I...

...WON'T...

...FAIL--

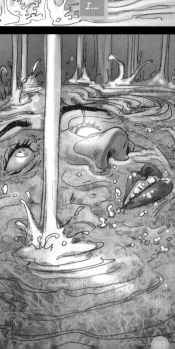

B9

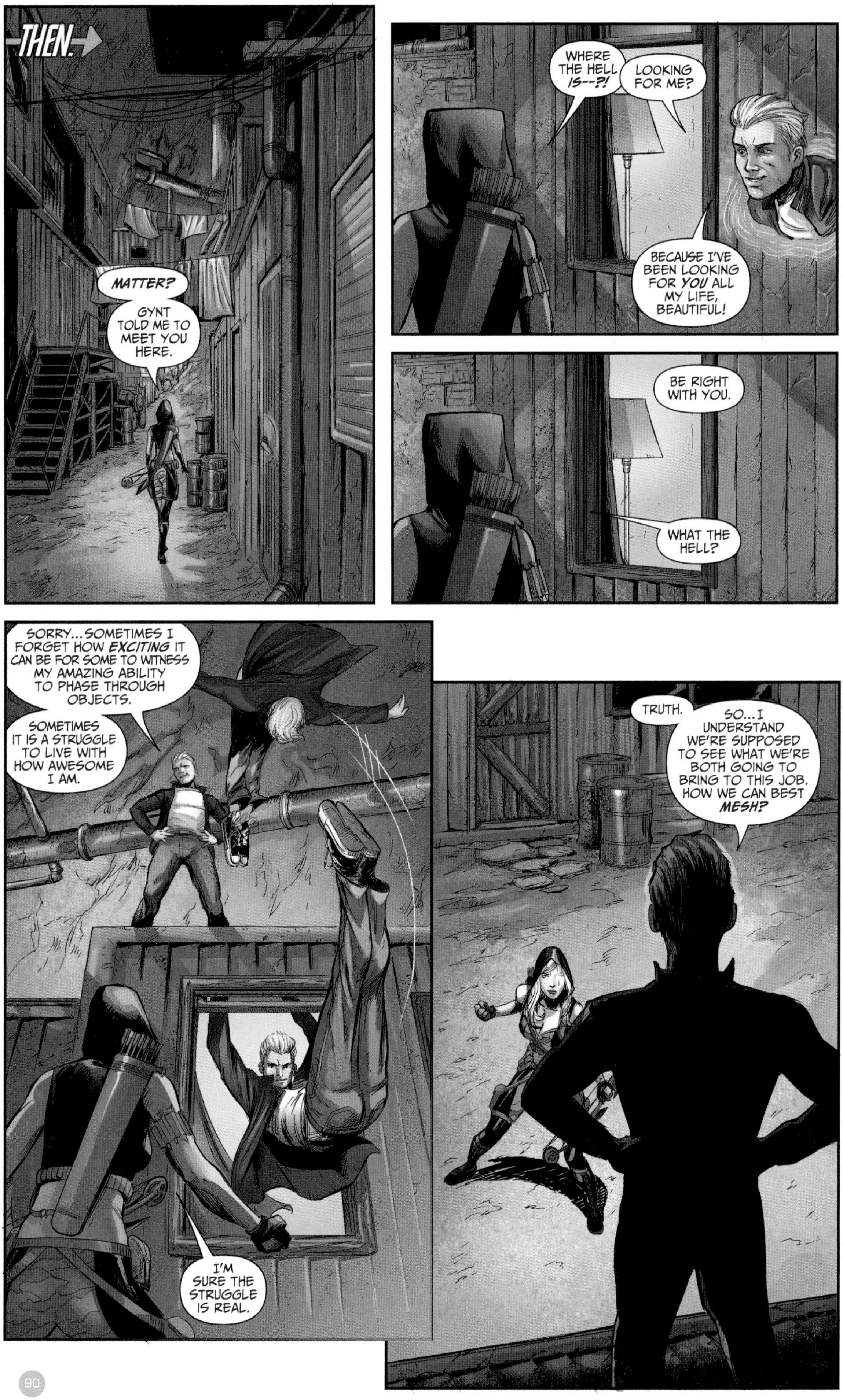
THEN.
MATTER?
GYNT TOLD ME TO MEET YOU HERE.
WHERE THE HELL IS--?!
LOOKING FOR ME?
BECAUSE I'VE BEEN LOOKING FOR YOU ALL MY LIFE, BEAUTIFUL!
BE RIGHT WITH YOU.
WHAT THE HELL?
SORRY... SOMETIMES I FORGET HOW EXCITING IT CAN BE FOR SOME TO WITNESS MY AMAZING ABILITY TO PHASE THROUGH OBJECTS.
SOMETIMES IT IS A STRUGGLE TO LIVE WITH HOW AWESOME I AM.
I'M SURE THE STRUGGLE IS REAL.
TRUTH.
SO... I UNDERSTAND WE'RE SUPPOSED TO SEE WHAT WE'RE BOTH GOING TO BRING TO THIS JOB. HOW WE CAN BEST MESH?

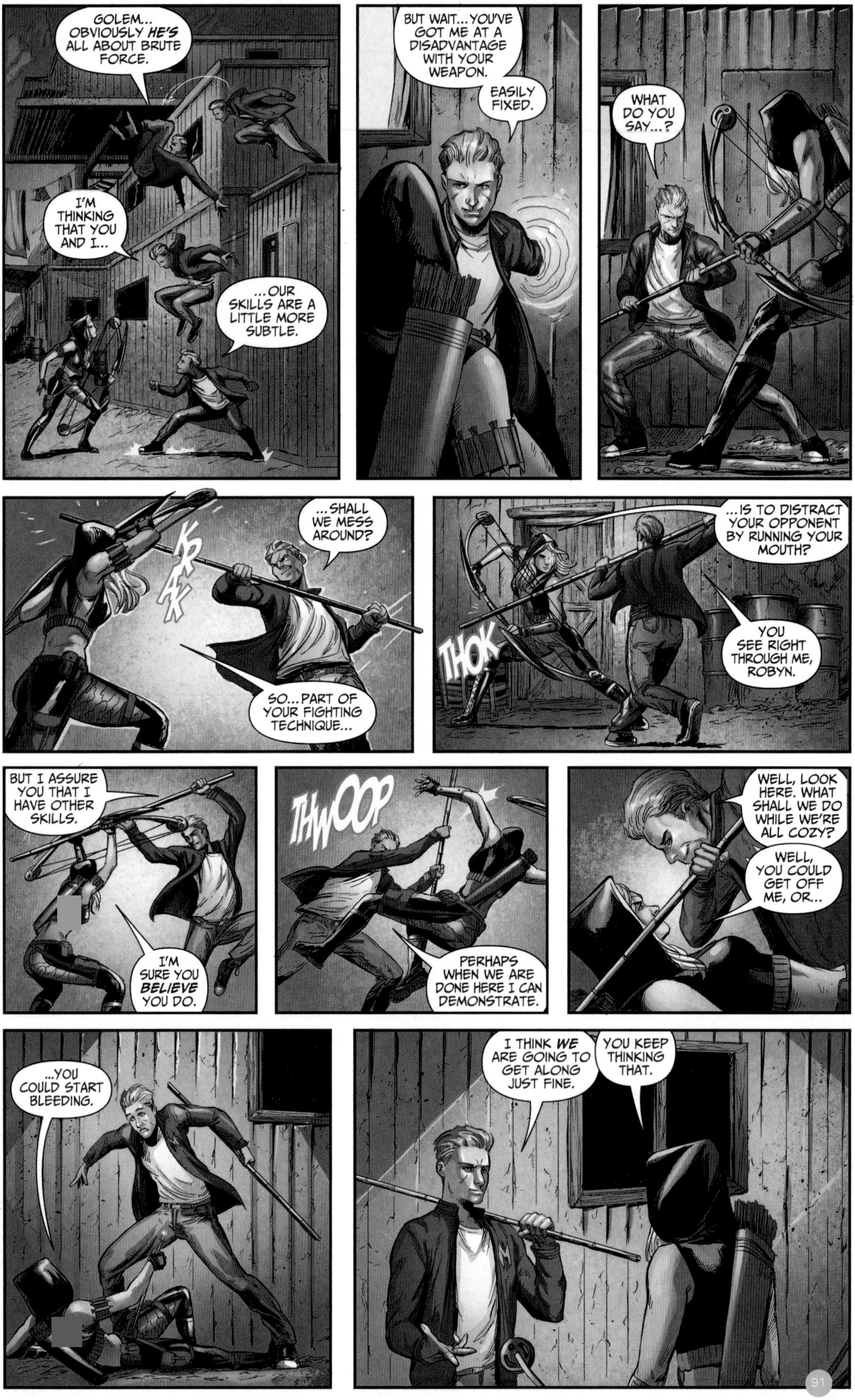
GOLEM... OBVIOUSLY HE'S ALL ABOUT BRUTE FORCE.
I'M THINKING THAT YOU AND I...
...OUR SKILLS ARE A LITTLE MORE SUBTLE.
BUT WAIT...YOU'VE GOT ME AT A DISADVANTAGE WITH YOUR WEAPON.
EASILY FIXED.
WHAT DO YOU SAY...?
...SHALL WE MESS AROUND?
KRAK
SO...PART OF YOUR FIGHTING TECHNIQUE...
...IS TO DISTRACT YOUR OPPONENT BY RUNNING YOUR MOUTH?
THOK
YOU SEE RIGHT THROUGH ME, ROBYN.
BUT I ASSURE YOU THAT I HAVE OTHER SKILLS.
I'M SURE YOU BELIEVE YOU DO.
THWOOP
PERHAPS WHEN WE ARE DONE HERE I CAN DEMONSTRATE.
WELL, LOOK HERE. WHAT SHALL WE DO WHILE WE'RE ALL COZY?
WELL, YOU COULD GET OFF ME, OR...
...YOU COULD START BLEEDING.
I THINK WE ARE GOING TO GET ALONG JUST FINE.
YOU KEEP THINKING THAT.

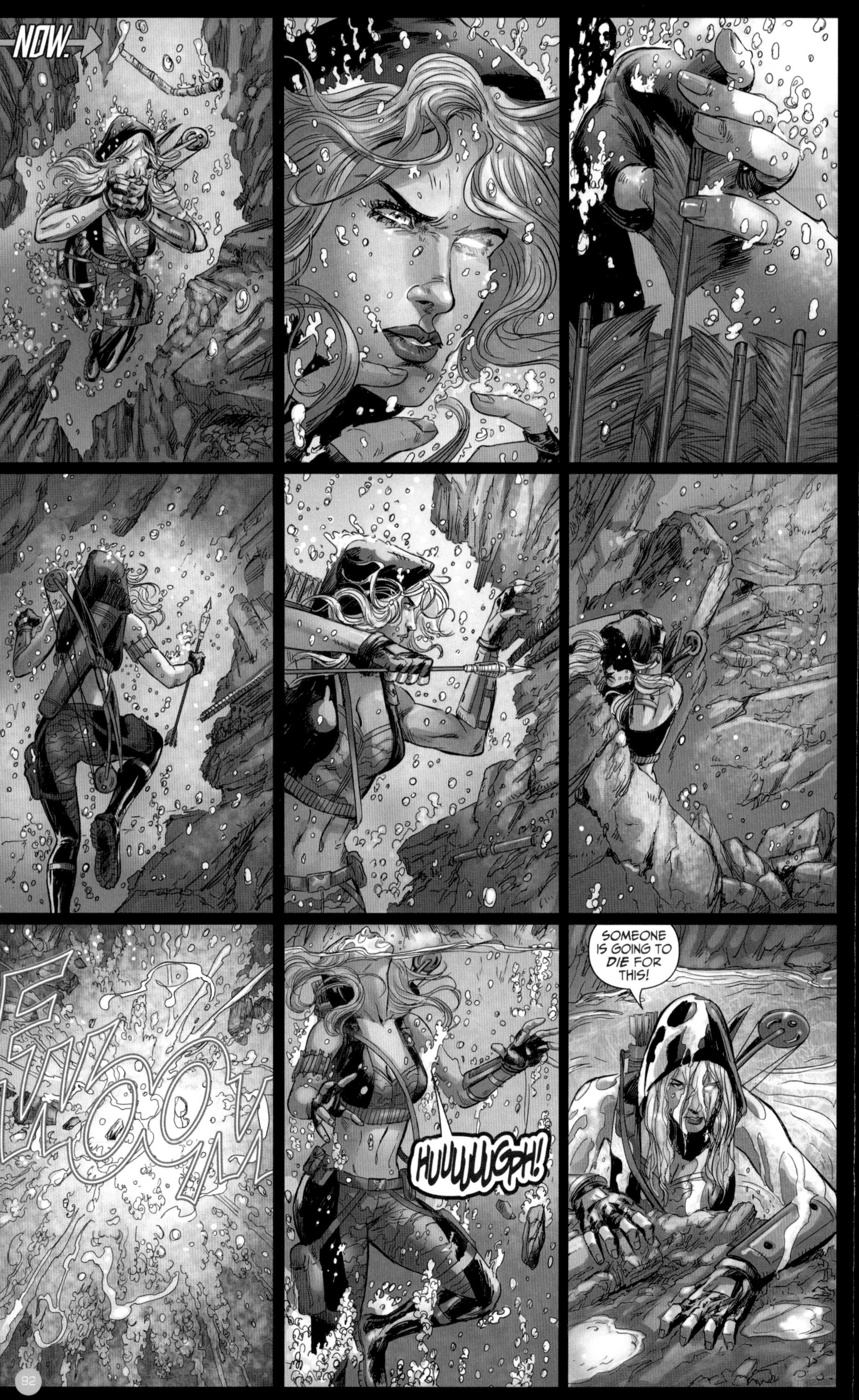
NOW.
HUUUUGPH!
SOMEONE IS GOING TO DIE FOR THIS!

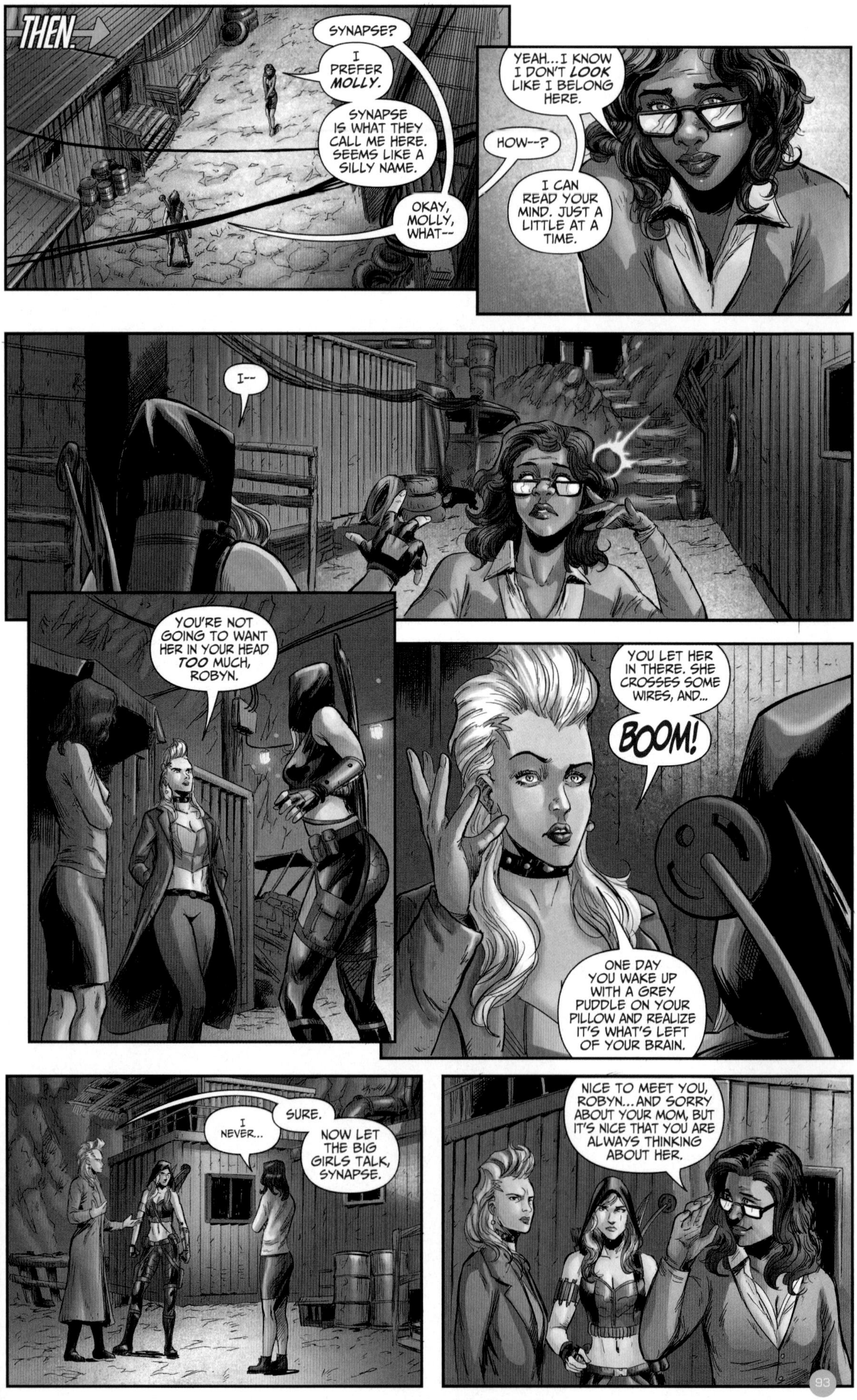
THEN.
SYNAPSE?
I PREFER MOLLY.
SYNAPSE IS WHAT THEY CALL ME HERE. SEEMS LIKE A SILLY NAME.
OKAY, MOLLY, WHAT--
YEAH...I KNOW I DON'T LOOK LIKE I BELONG HERE.
HOW--?
I CAN READ YOUR MIND. JUST A LITTLE AT A TIME.
I--
YOU'RE NOT GOING TO WANT HER IN YOUR HEAD TOO MUCH, ROBYN.
YOU LET HER IN THERE. SHE CROSSES SOME WIRES, AND...
BOOM!
ONE DAY YOU WAKE UP WITH A GREY PUDDLE ON YOUR PILLOW AND REALIZE IT'S WHAT'S LEFT OF YOUR BRAIN.
I NEVER...
SURE.
NOW LET THE BIG GIRLS TALK, SYNAPSE.
NICE TO MEET YOU, ROBYN...AND SORRY ABOUT YOUR MOM, BUT IT'S NICE THAT YOU ARE ALWAYS THINKING ABOUT HER.

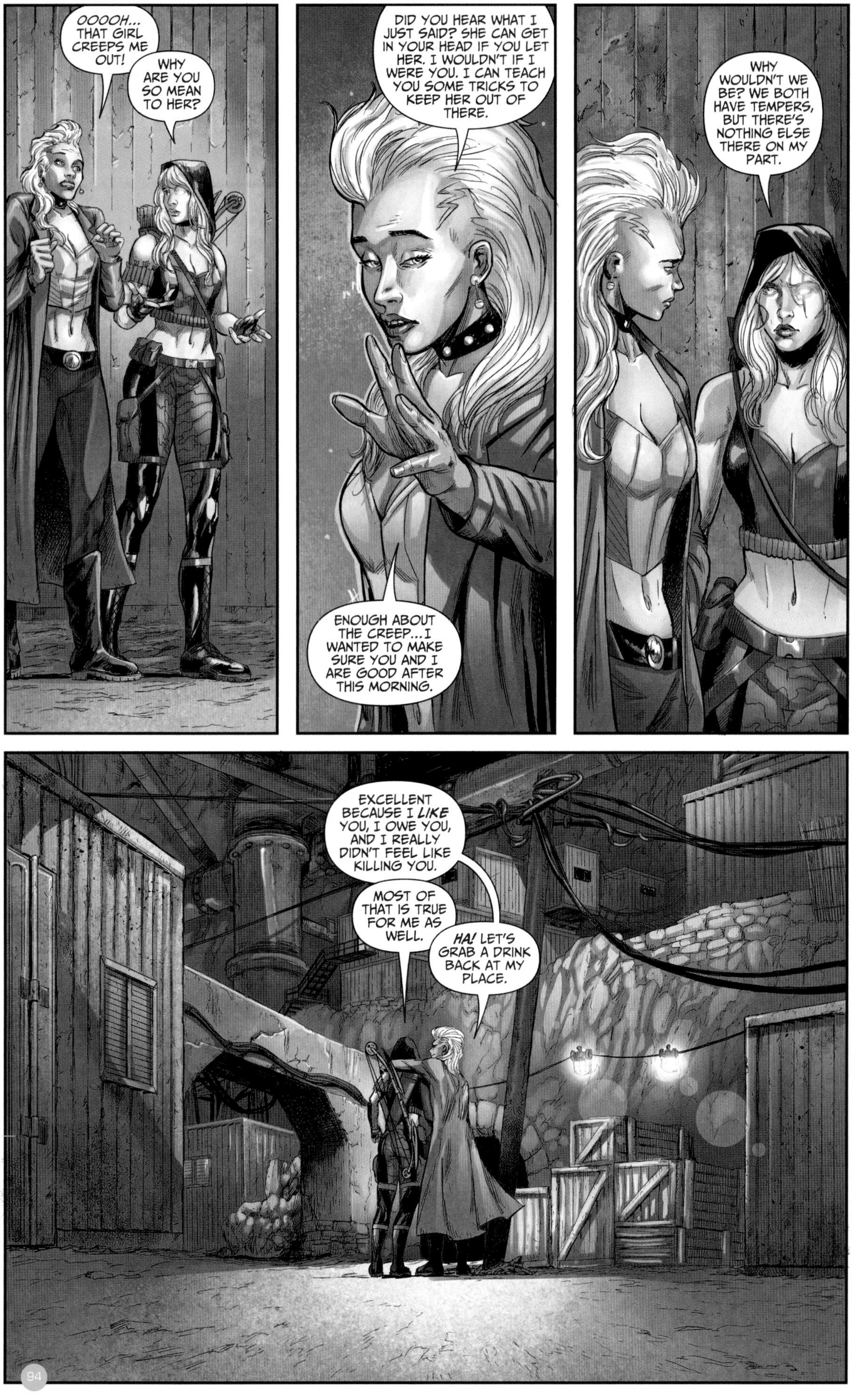
OOOOH... THAT GIRL CREEPS ME OUT!
WHY ARE YOU SO MEAN TO HER?
DID YOU HEAR WHAT I JUST SAID? SHE CAN GET IN YOUR HEAD IF YOU LET HER. I WOULDN'T IF I WERE YOU. I CAN TEACH YOU SOME TRICKS TO KEEP HER OUT OF THERE.
ENOUGH ABOUT THE CREEP...I WANTED TO MAKE SURE YOU AND I ARE GOOD AFTER THIS MORNING.
WHY WOULDN'T WE BE? WE BOTH HAVE TEMPERS, BUT THERE'S NOTHING ELSE THERE ON MY PART.
EXCELLENT BECAUSE I *LIKE* YOU, I OWE YOU, AND I REALLY DIDN'T FEEL LIKE KILLING YOU.
MOST OF THAT IS TRUE FOR ME AS WELL.
HA! LET'S GRAB A DRINK BACK AT MY PLACE.

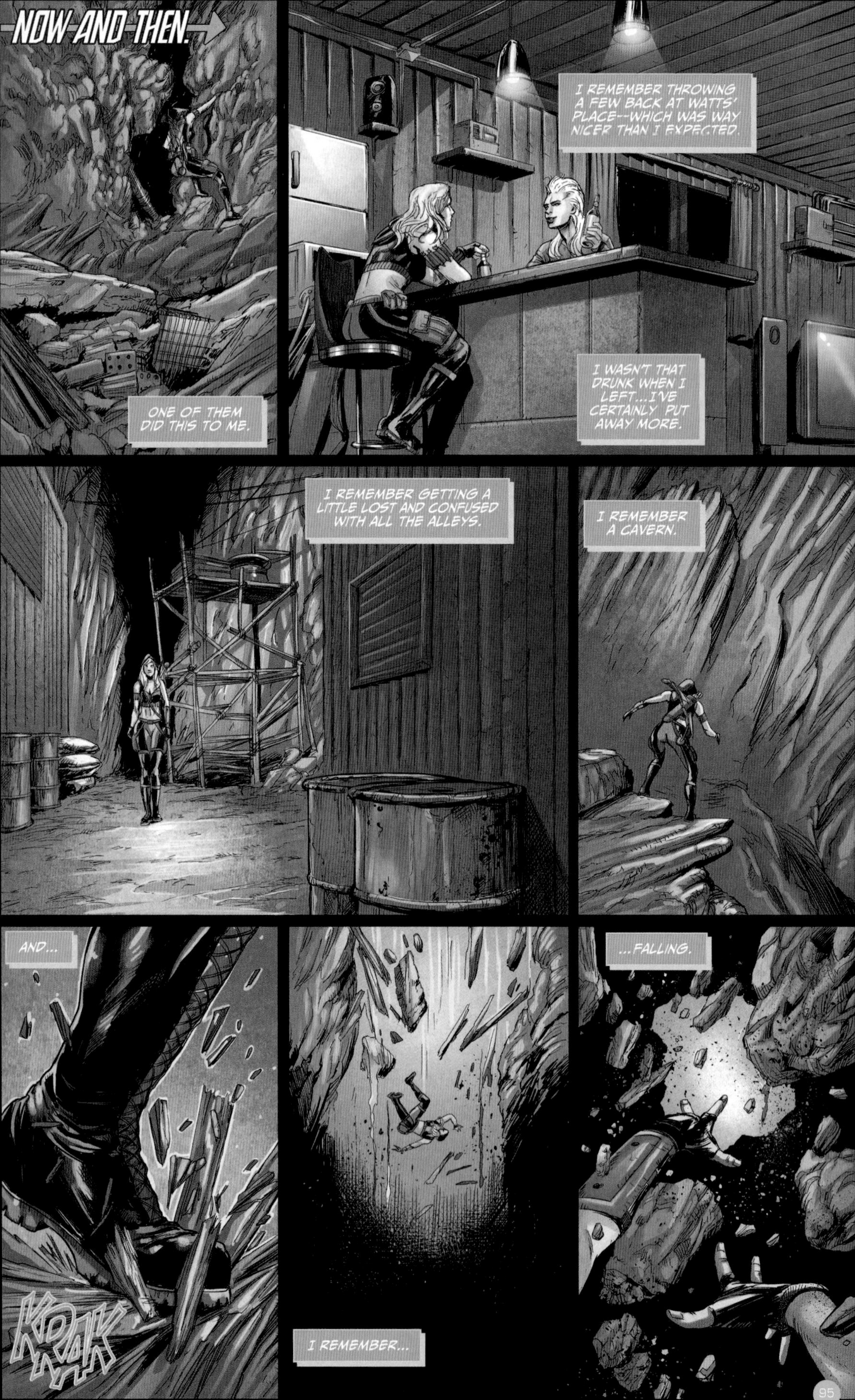
NOW AND THEN.
ONE OF THEM DID THIS TO ME.
I REMEMBER THROWING A FEW BACK AT WATTS' PLACE--WHICH WAS WAY NICER THAN I EXPECTED.
I WASN'T THAT DRUNK WHEN I LEFT...I'VE CERTAINLY PUT AWAY MORE.
I REMEMBER GETTING A LITTLE LOST AND CONFUSED WITH ALL THE ALLEYS.
I REMEMBER A CAVERN.
AND...
KRAK
I REMEMBER...
...FALLING.

WAS THIS ALL MY FAULT?

CRAP.

I CAN *SEE* THAT'S THE WAY OUT, BUT...

...THERE IS NO WAY I CAN DIG MY WAY THROUGH THE REST OF THE RUBBLE BLOCKING--

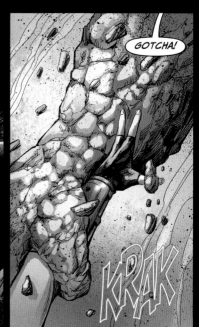

GOTCHA!

KRAK

TATTER? GOLEM? WHAT? WHY? HOW?

DANGER

ABSOLUTELY KEEP OUT OR **DIE**

I WAS GETTING WORRIED WHEN I COULDN'T FIND YOU ANYWHERE.

I GOT EMMETT TO HELP ME. IT WAS *HIS IDEA TO LOOK IN HERE!* THIS REALLY WAS THE LAST PLACE WE EXPECTED TO FIND YOU.

DIDN'T YOU SEE THE SIGNS?

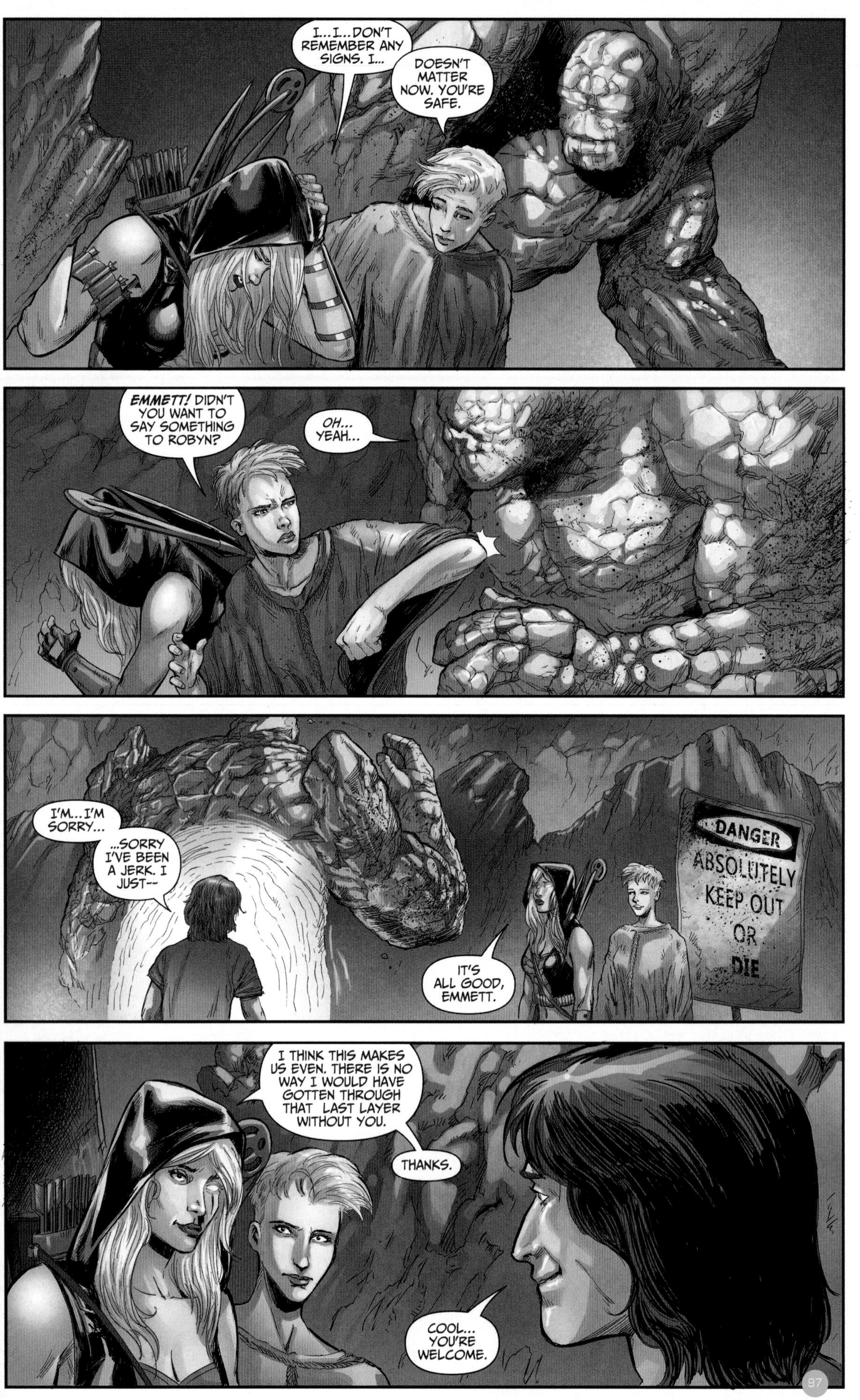

I...I...DON'T REMEMBER ANY SIGNS. I...
DOESN'T MATTER NOW. YOU'RE SAFE.
EMMETT! DIDN'T YOU WANT TO SAY SOMETHING TO ROBYN?
OH... YEAH...
I'M...I'M SORRY...
...SORRY I'VE BEEN A JERK. I JUST--
DANGER
ABSOLUTELY KEEP OUT OR DIE
IT'S ALL GOOD, EMMETT.
I THINK THIS MAKES US EVEN. THERE IS NO WAY I WOULD HAVE GOTTEN THROUGH THAT LAST LAYER WITHOUT YOU.
THANKS.
COOL... YOU'RE WELCOME.

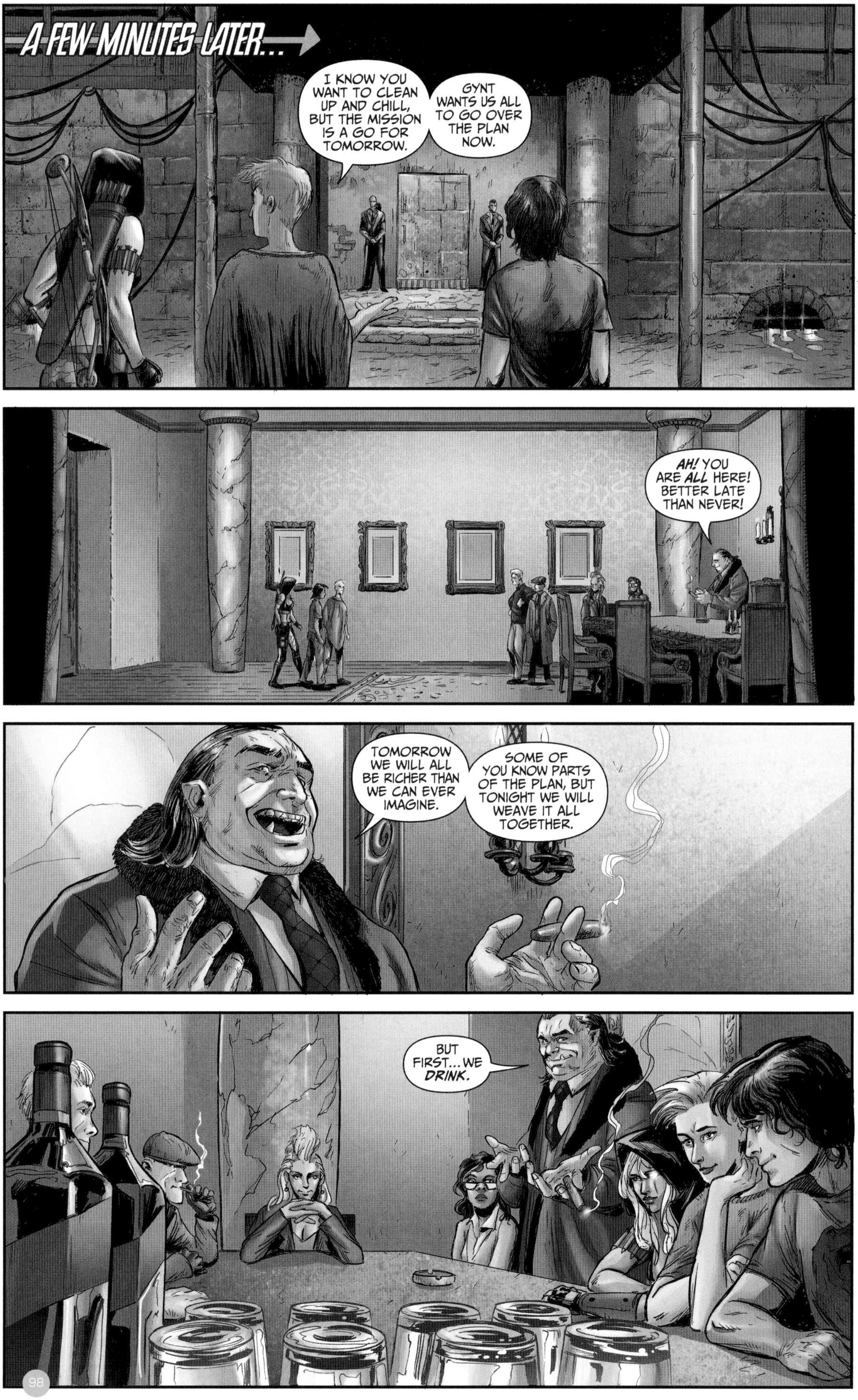
A FEW MINUTES LATER...
I KNOW YOU WANT TO CLEAN UP AND CHILL, BUT THE MISSION IS A GO FOR TOMORROW.
GYNT WANTS US ALL TO GO OVER THE PLAN NOW.
AH! YOU ARE ***ALL*** HERE! BETTER LATE THAN NEVER!
TOMORROW WE WILL ALL BE RICHER THAN WE CAN EVER IMAGINE.
SOME OF YOU KNOW PARTS OF THE PLAN, BUT TONIGHT WE WILL WEAVE IT ALL TOGETHER.
BUT FIRST... WE ***DRINK.***

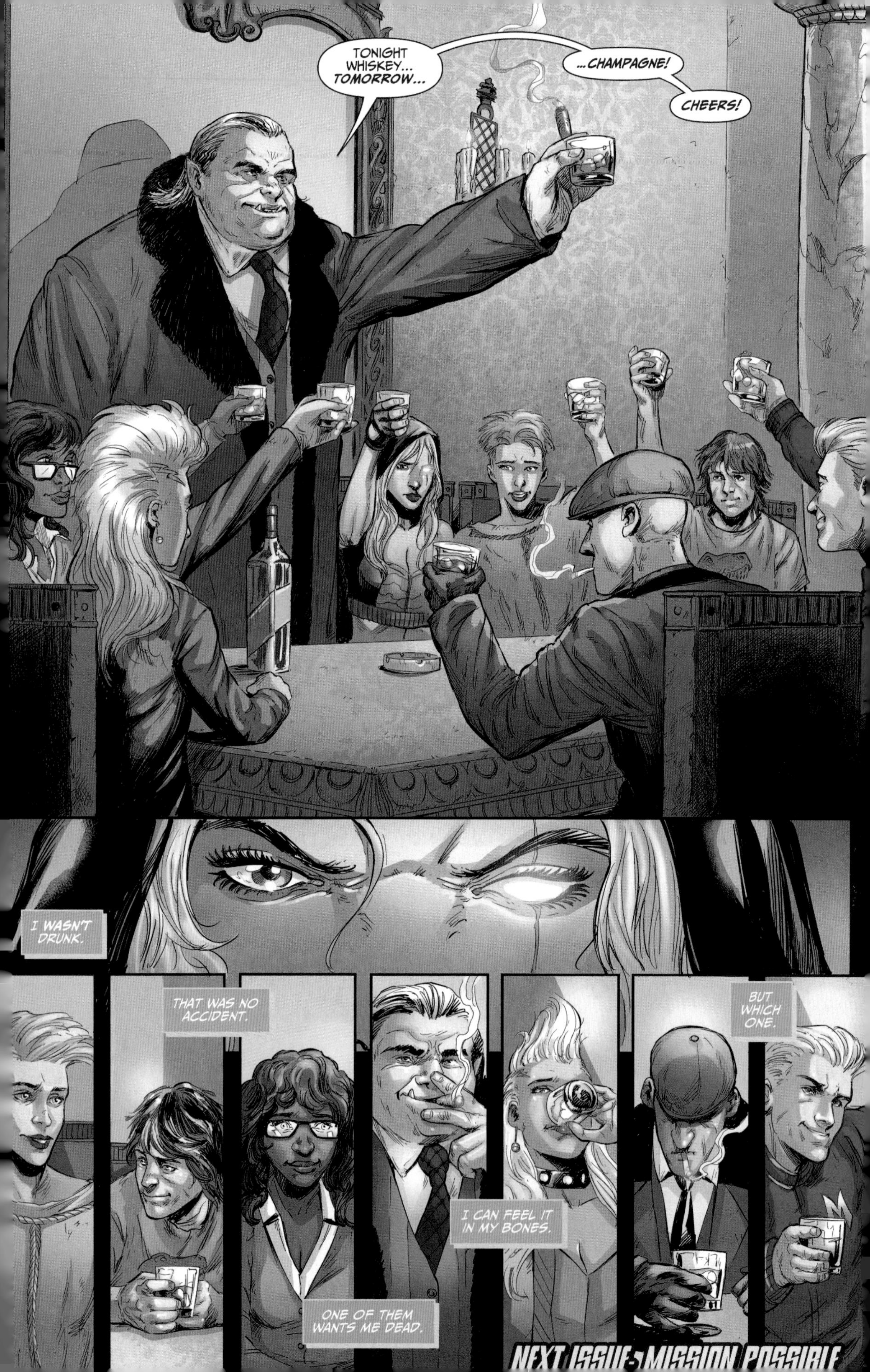
TONIGHT WHISKEY... TOMORROW...
...CHAMPAGNE!
CHEERS!
I WASN'T DRUNK.
THAT WAS NO ACCIDENT.
ONE OF THEM WANTS ME DEAD.
I CAN FEEL IT IN MY BONES.
BUT WHICH ONE.
NEXT ISSUE: MISSION POSSIBLE

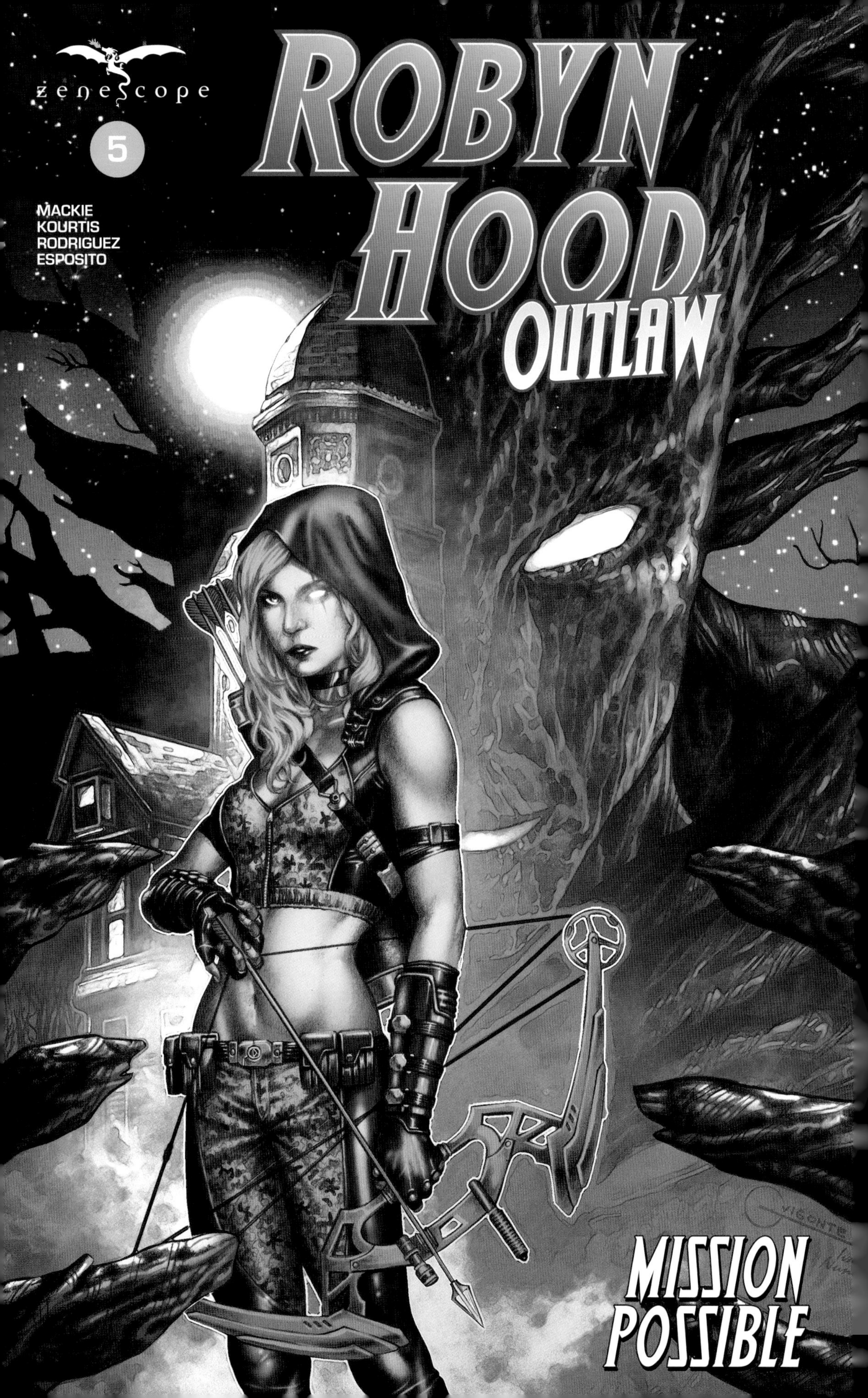

zenescope
5
MACKIE
KOURTIS
RODRIGUEZ
ESPOSITO
ROBYN HOOD
OUTLAW
MISSION POSSIBLE

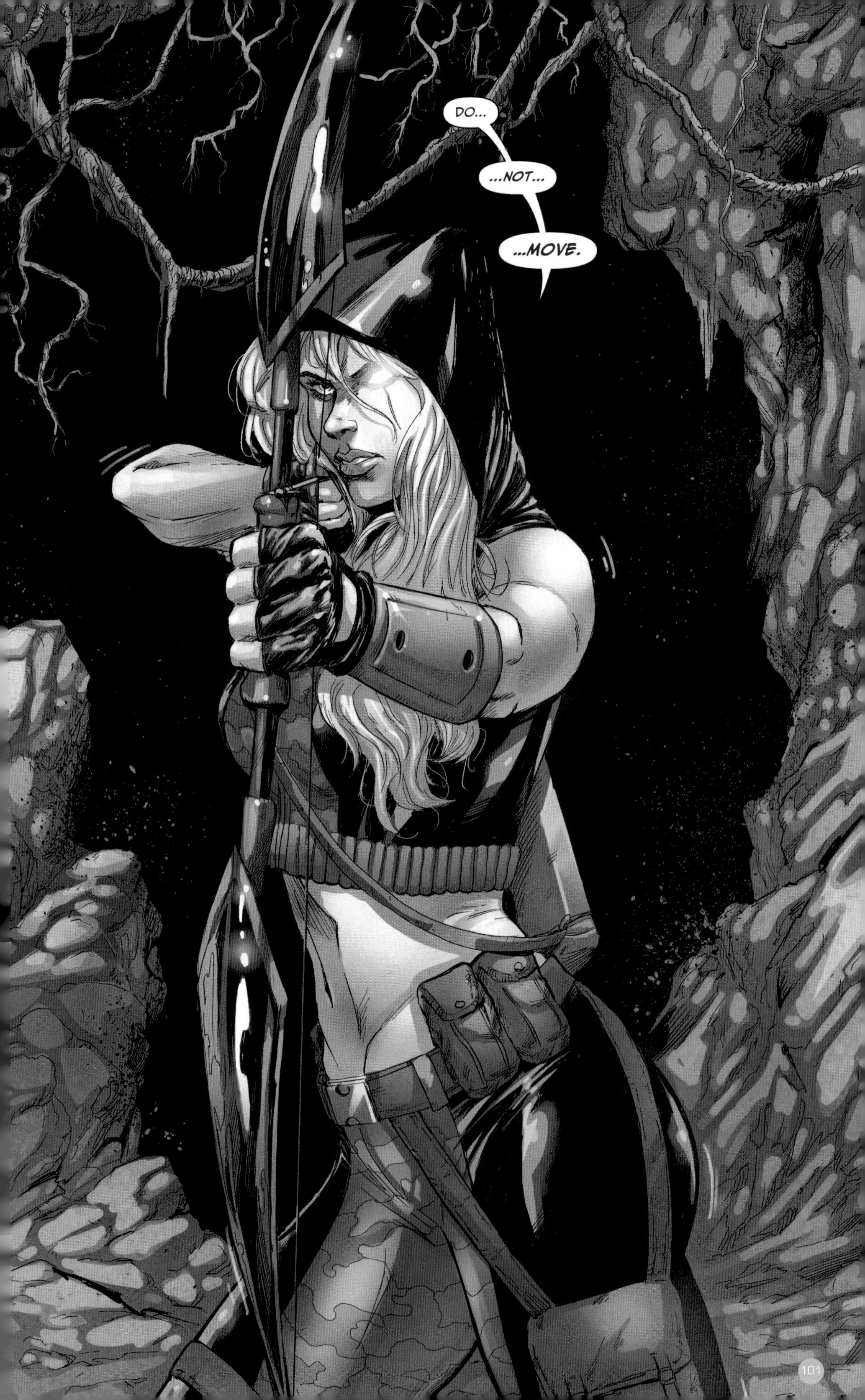
DO...
...NOT...
...MOVE.

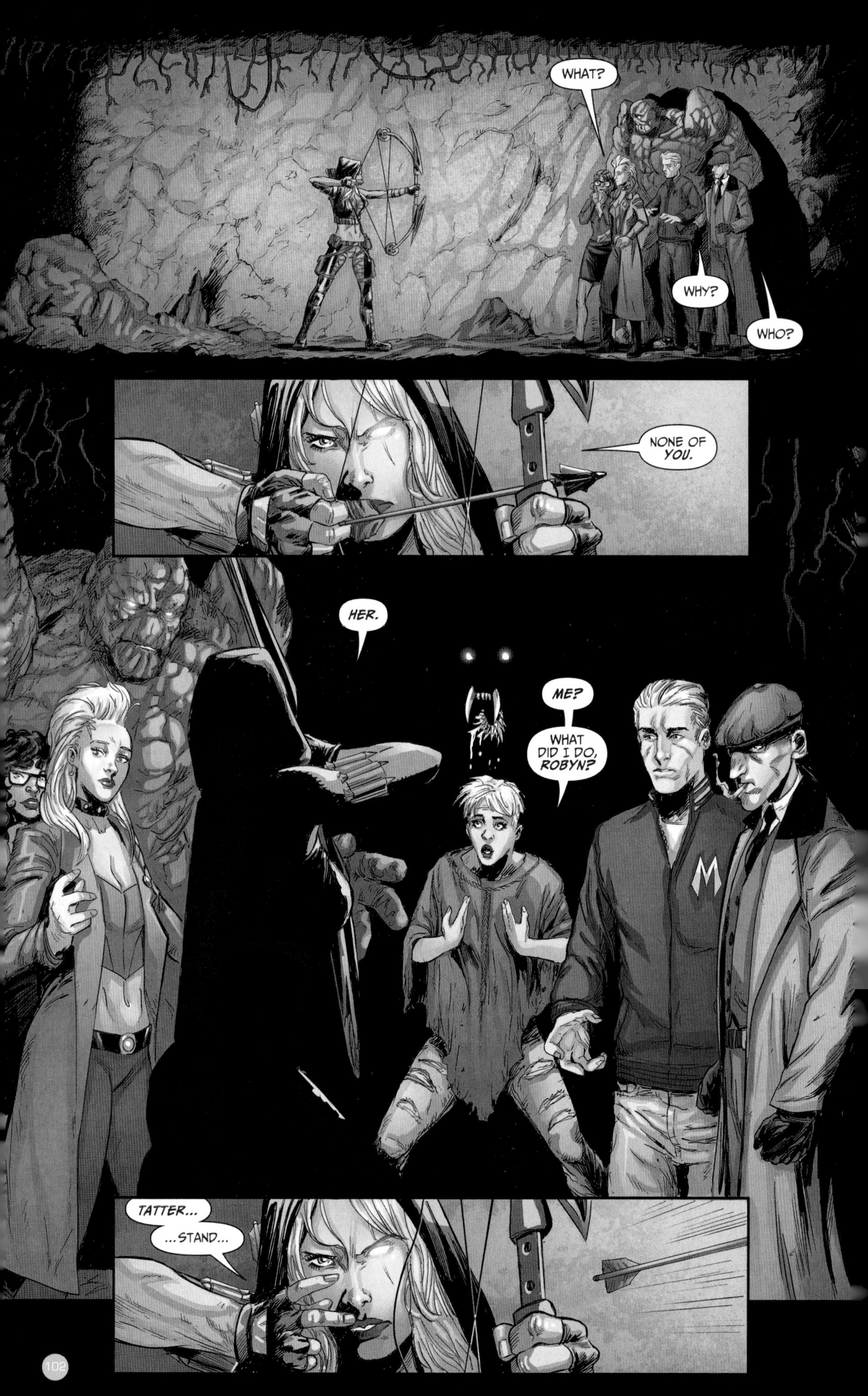
WHAT?
WHY?
WHO?
NONE OF YOU.
HER.
ME?
WHAT DID I DO, ROBYN?
TATTER...
...STAND...

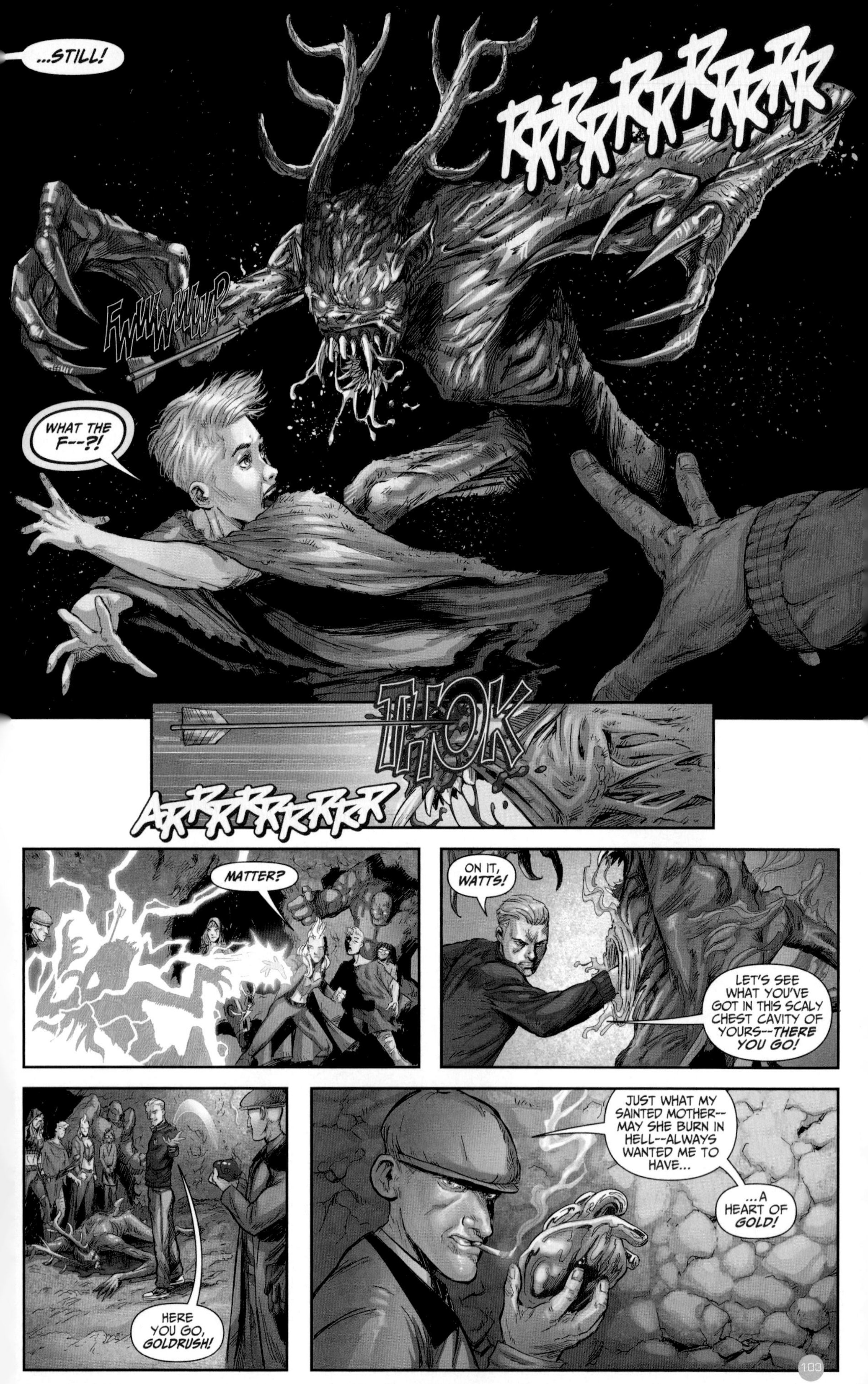
...STILL!
RRRRRRRRRRRR
FWWWWWWP
WHAT THE F--?!
THOK
ARRRRRRRRRR
MATTER?
ON IT, WATTS!
LET'S SEE WHAT YOU'VE GOT IN THIS SCALY CHEST CAVITY OF YOURS--THERE YOU GO!
HERE YOU GO, GOLDRUSH!
JUST WHAT MY SAINTED MOTHER--MAY SHE BURN IN HELL--ALWAYS WANTED ME TO HAVE...
...A HEART OF GOLD!

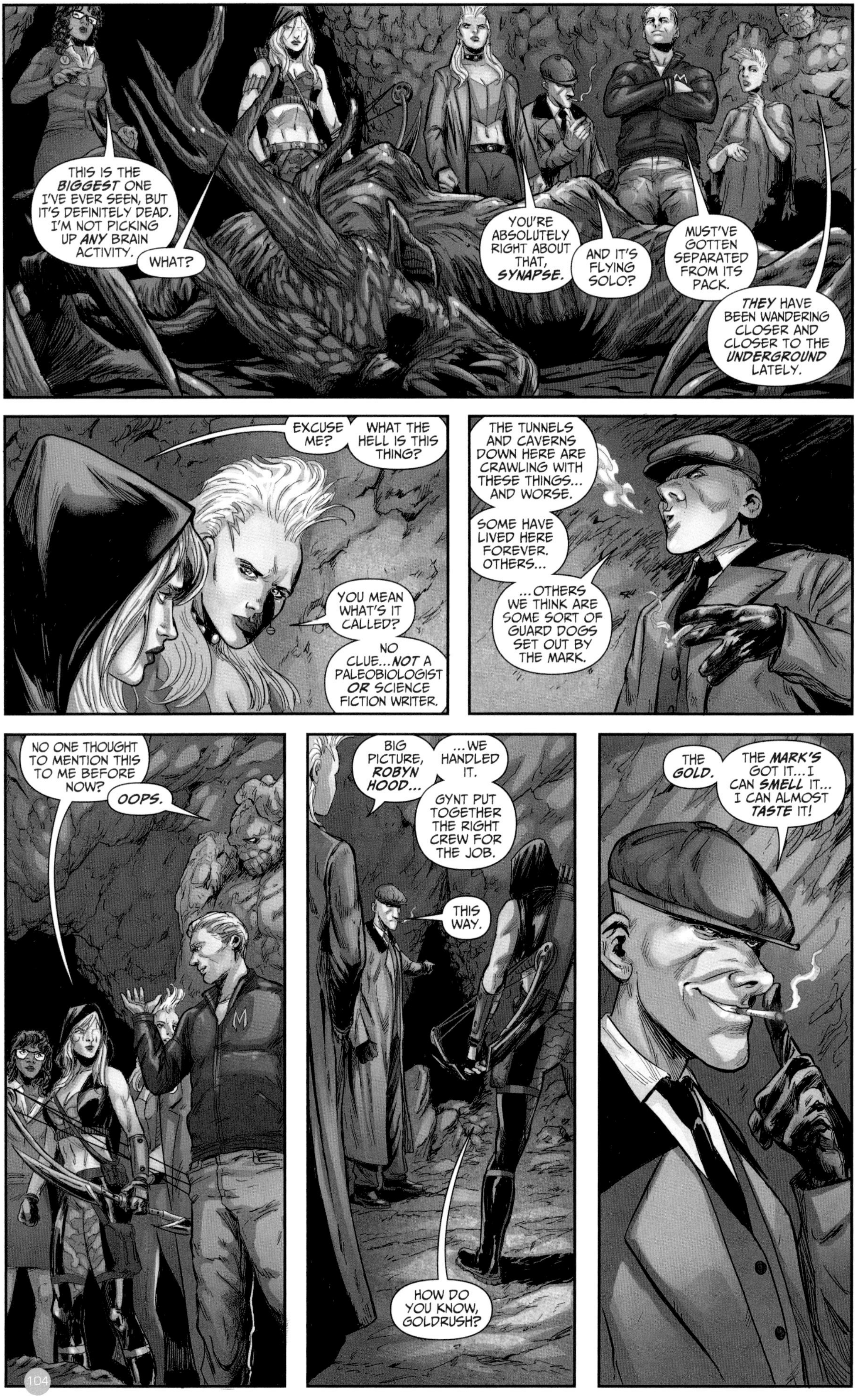
THIS IS THE ***BIGGEST*** ONE I'VE EVER SEEN, BUT IT'S DEFINITELY DEAD. I'M NOT PICKING UP ***ANY*** BRAIN ACTIVITY.
WHAT?
YOU'RE ABSOLUTELY RIGHT ABOUT THAT, ***SYNAPSE.***
AND IT'S FLYING SOLO?
MUST'VE GOTTEN SEPARATED FROM ITS PACK.
THEY HAVE BEEN WANDERING CLOSER AND CLOSER TO THE ***UNDERGROUND*** LATELY.
EXCUSE ME?
WHAT THE HELL IS THIS THING?
YOU MEAN WHAT'S IT CALLED?
NO CLUE...***NOT*** A PALEOBIOLOGIST ***OR*** SCIENCE FICTION WRITER.
THE TUNNELS AND CAVERNS DOWN HERE ARE CRAWLING WITH THESE THINGS... AND WORSE.
SOME HAVE LIVED HERE FOREVER. OTHERS...
...OTHERS WE THINK ARE SOME SORT OF GUARD DOGS SET OUT BY THE MARK.
NO ONE THOUGHT TO MENTION THIS TO ME BEFORE NOW?
OOPS.
BIG PICTURE, ***ROBYN HOOD...***
...WE HANDLED IT.
GYNT PUT TOGETHER THE RIGHT CREW FOR THE JOB.
THIS WAY.
HOW DO YOU KNOW, GOLDRUSH?
THE ***GOLD.***
THE ***MARK'S*** GOT IT...I CAN ***SMELL*** IT... I CAN ALMOST ***TASTE*** IT!

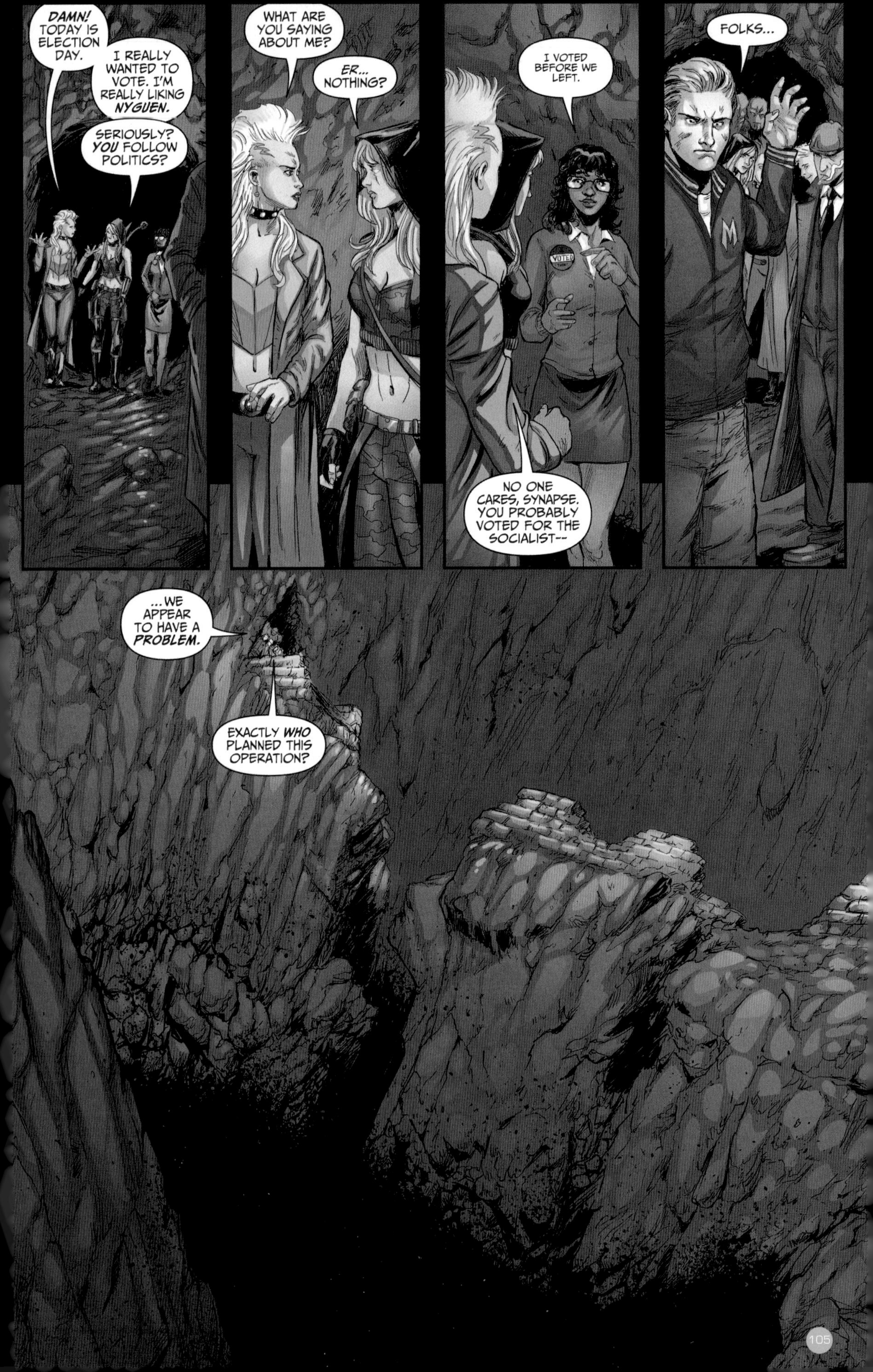
DAMN! TODAY IS ELECTION DAY.
I REALLY WANTED TO VOTE. I'M REALLY LIKING NYGUEN.
SERIOUSLY? YOU FOLLOW POLITICS?
WHAT ARE YOU SAYING ABOUT ME?
ER... NOTHING?
I VOTED BEFORE WE LEFT.
NO ONE CARES, SYNAPSE. YOU PROBABLY VOTED FOR THE SOCIALIST--
VOTED
FOLKS...
...WE APPEAR TO HAVE A PROBLEM.
EXACTLY WHO PLANNED THIS OPERATION?

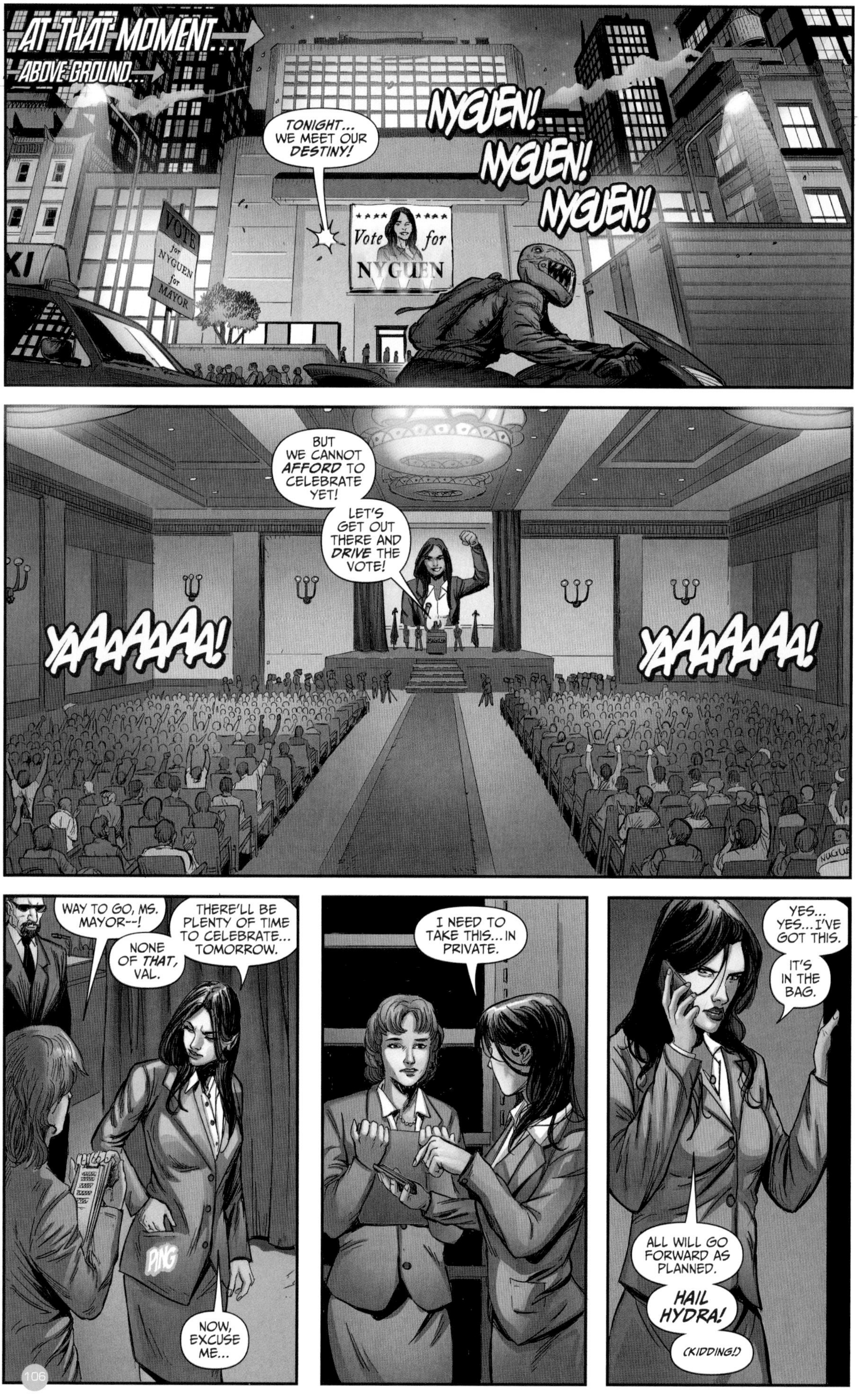
AT THAT MOMENT...
ABOVE GROUND...
TONIGHT... WE MEET OUR DESTINY!
NYGUEN! NYGUEN! NYGUEN!
VOTE for NYGUEN for MAYOR
Vote for NYGUEN
BUT WE CANNOT AFFORD TO CELEBRATE YET!
LET'S GET OUT THERE AND DRIVE THE VOTE!
YAAAAAAA!
YAAAAAAA!
WAY TO GO, MS. MAYOR--!
NONE OF THAT, VAL.
THERE'LL BE PLENTY OF TIME TO CELEBRATE... TOMORROW.
PING
NOW, EXCUSE ME...
I NEED TO TAKE THIS... IN PRIVATE.
YES... YES... I'VE GOT THIS.
IT'S IN THE BAG.
ALL WILL GO FORWARD AS PLANNED.
HAIL HYDRA!
(KIDDING!)

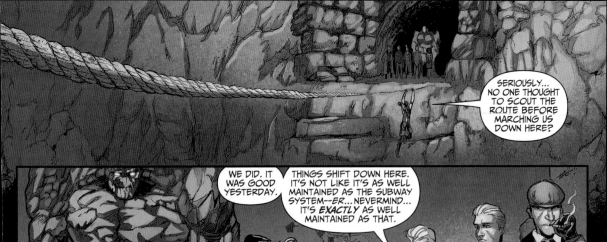

SERIOUSLY... NO ONE THOUGHT TO SCOUT THE ROUTE BEFORE MARCHING US DOWN HERE?

WE DID. IT WAS GOOD YESTERDAY.

THINGS SHIFT DOWN HERE. IT'S NOT LIKE IT'S AS WELL MAINTAINED AS THE SUBWAY SYSTEM--*ER*...NEVERMIND... IT'S *EXACTLY* AS WELL MAINTAINED AS THAT.

THOUGH IT DOES EXPLAIN WHY THE *WAR-DOG* GOT STRANDED ON THE OTHER SIDE. IT'S NOT LIKE THEM TO BE SEPARATED FROM THE *PACK.*

I THOUGHT YOU SAID THEY HAD NO NAME?

JUST MADE IT UP.

MAYBE I *WILL* GO FOR THAT DEGREE IN PALEOBIOLOGY AFTER ALL.

THIS IS THE TUNNEL WE WANT.

THE SMELL OF THE GOLD IS TICKLING MY SINUSES.

TATTER...DID WATTS JUST SAY "THE *PACK*"? HOW MANY OF THOSE THINGS DO YOU CONSIDER A PACK?

DEPENDS. I HEAR BREEDING SEASON WAS PRETTY STRONG THIS YEAR.

CRAP.

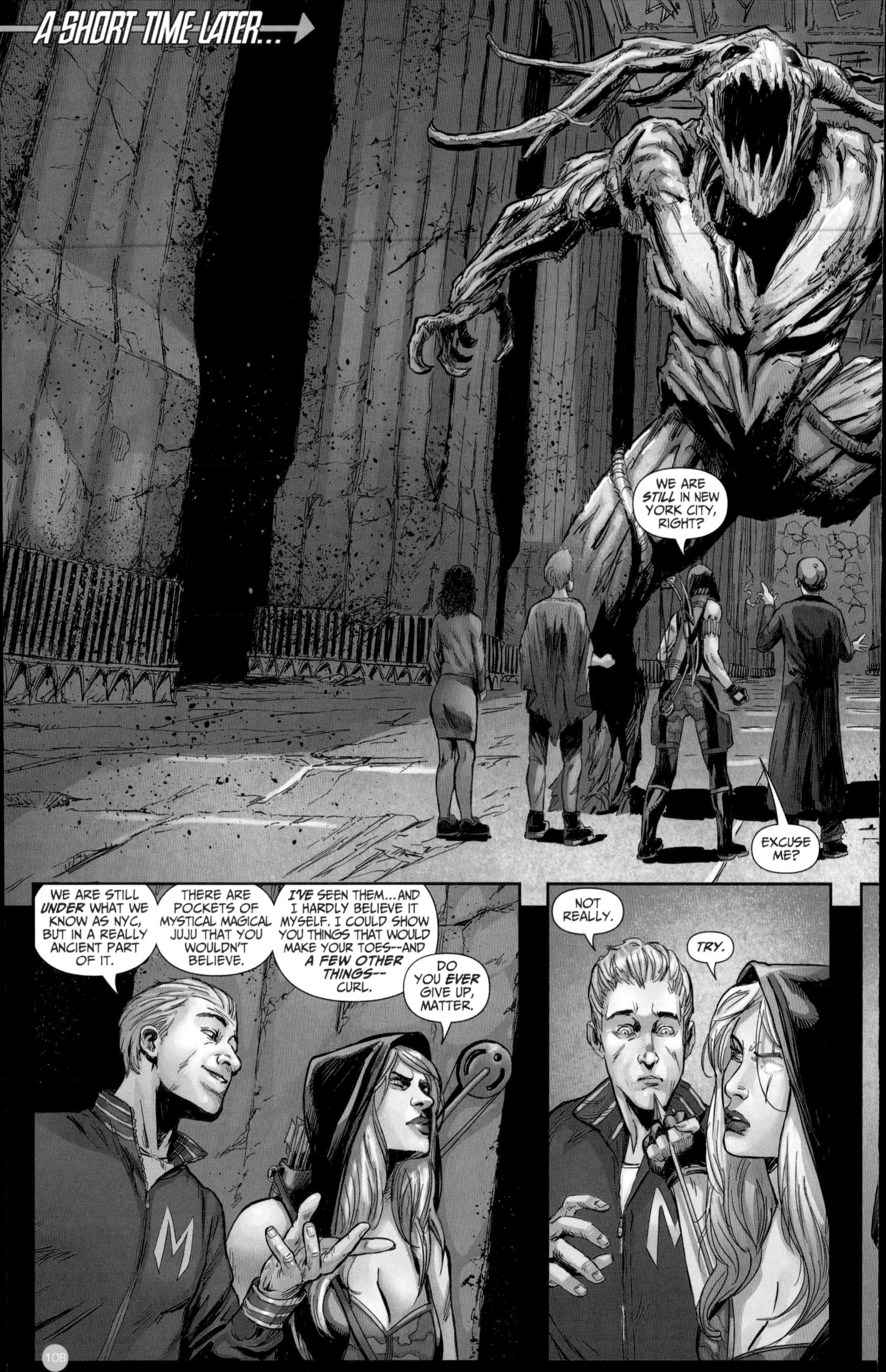
A SHORT TIME LATER...
WE ARE STILL IN NEW YORK CITY, RIGHT?
EXCUSE ME?
WE ARE STILL UNDER WHAT WE KNOW AS NYC, BUT IN A REALLY ANCIENT PART OF IT.
THERE ARE POCKETS OF MYSTICAL MAGICAL JUJU THAT YOU WOULDN'T BELIEVE.
I'VE SEEN THEM...AND I HARDLY BELIEVE IT MYSELF. I COULD SHOW YOU THINGS THAT WOULD MAKE YOUR TOES--AND A FEW OTHER THINGS-- CURL.
DO YOU EVER GIVE UP, MATTER.
NOT REALLY.
TRY.

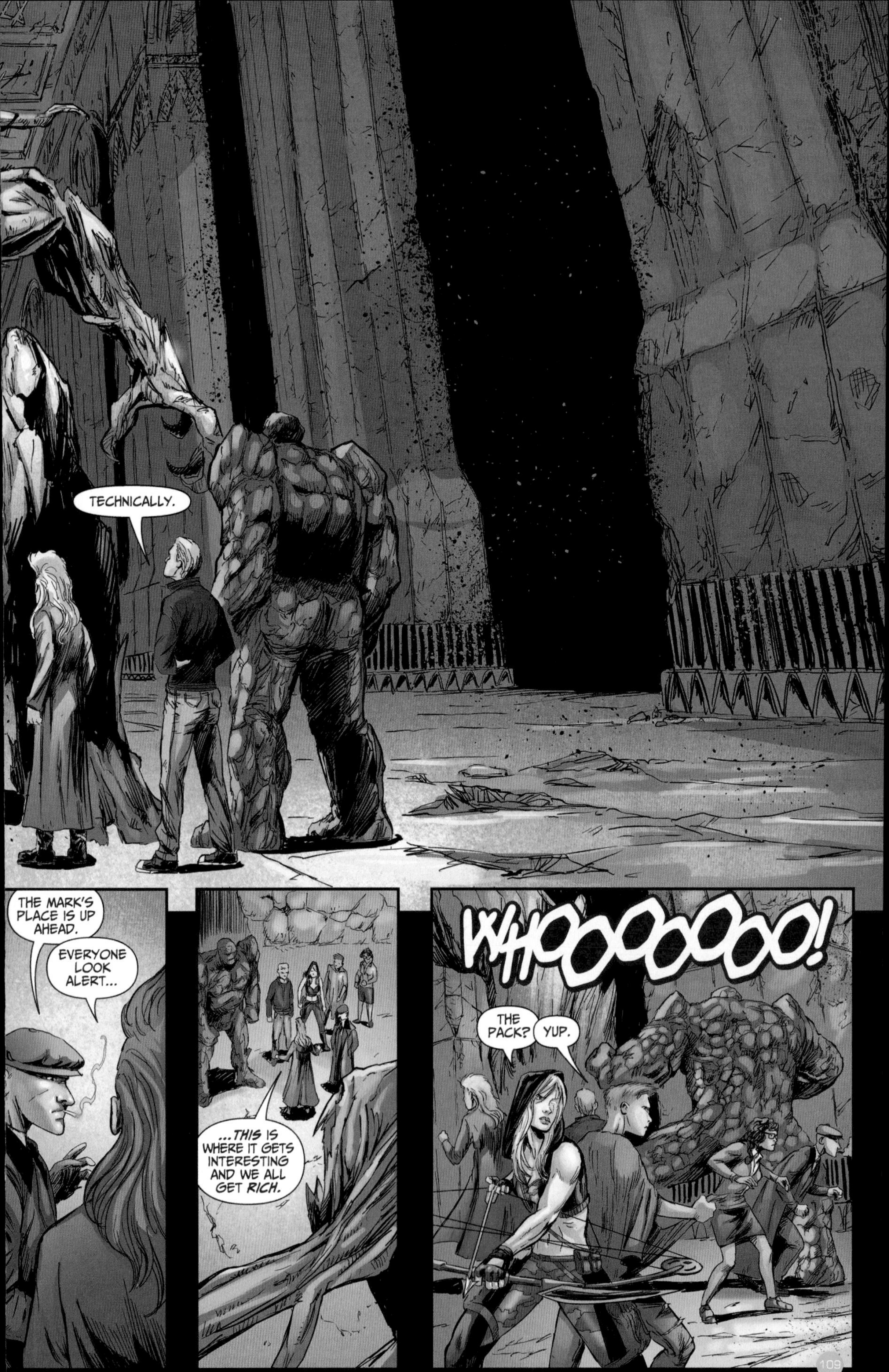

TECHNICALLY.
THE MARK'S PLACE IS UP AHEAD.
EVERYONE LOOK ALERT...
...THIS IS WHERE IT GETS INTERESTING AND WE ALL GET RICH.
WHOOOOOOOO!
THE PACK?
YUP.

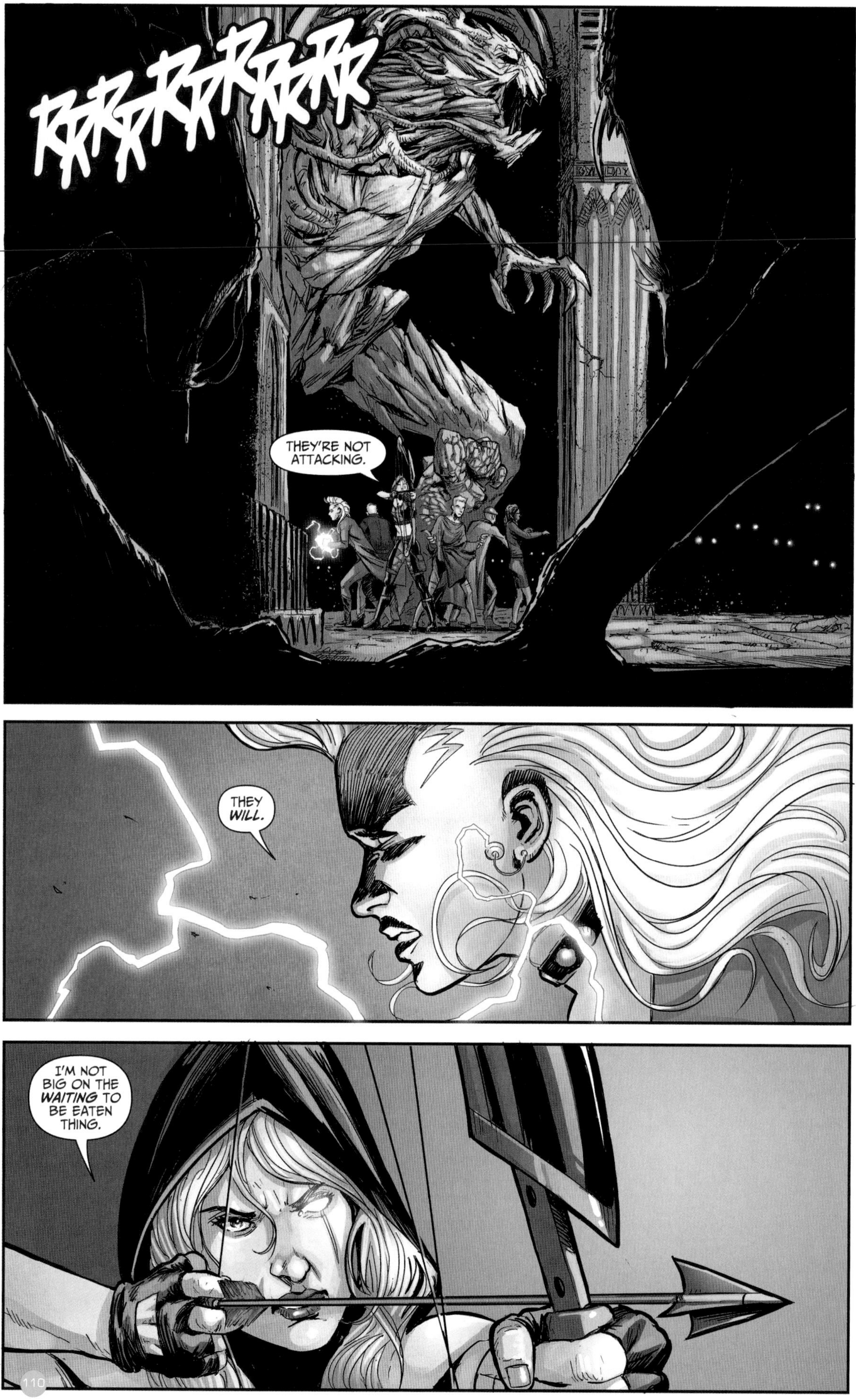
RRRRRRRRRRR
THEY'RE NOT ATTACKING.
THEY WILL.
I'M NOT BIG ON THE WAITING TO BE EATEN THING.

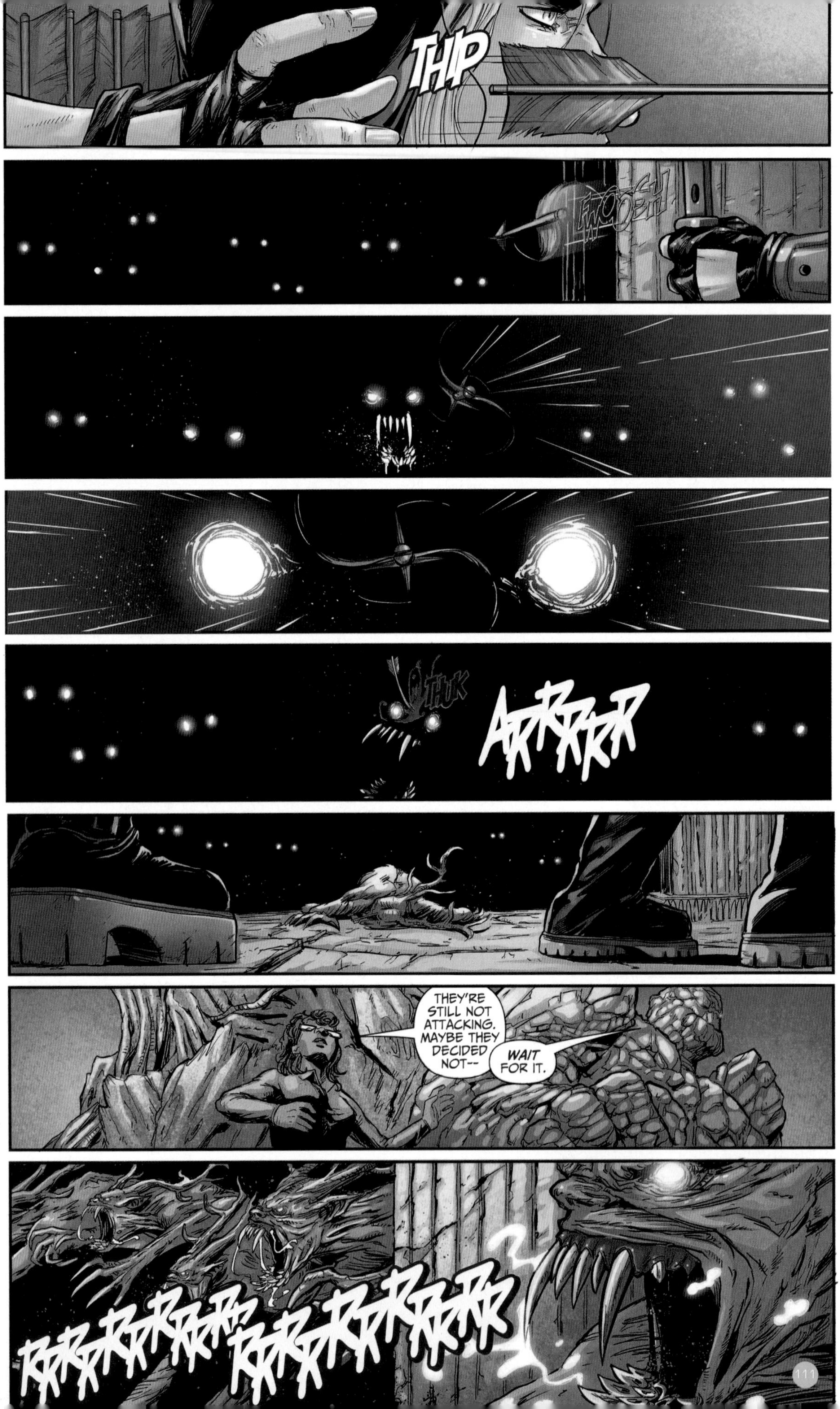
THIP
THUK
THEY'RE STILL NOT ATTACKING. MAYBE THEY DECIDED NOT--
WAIT FOR IT.

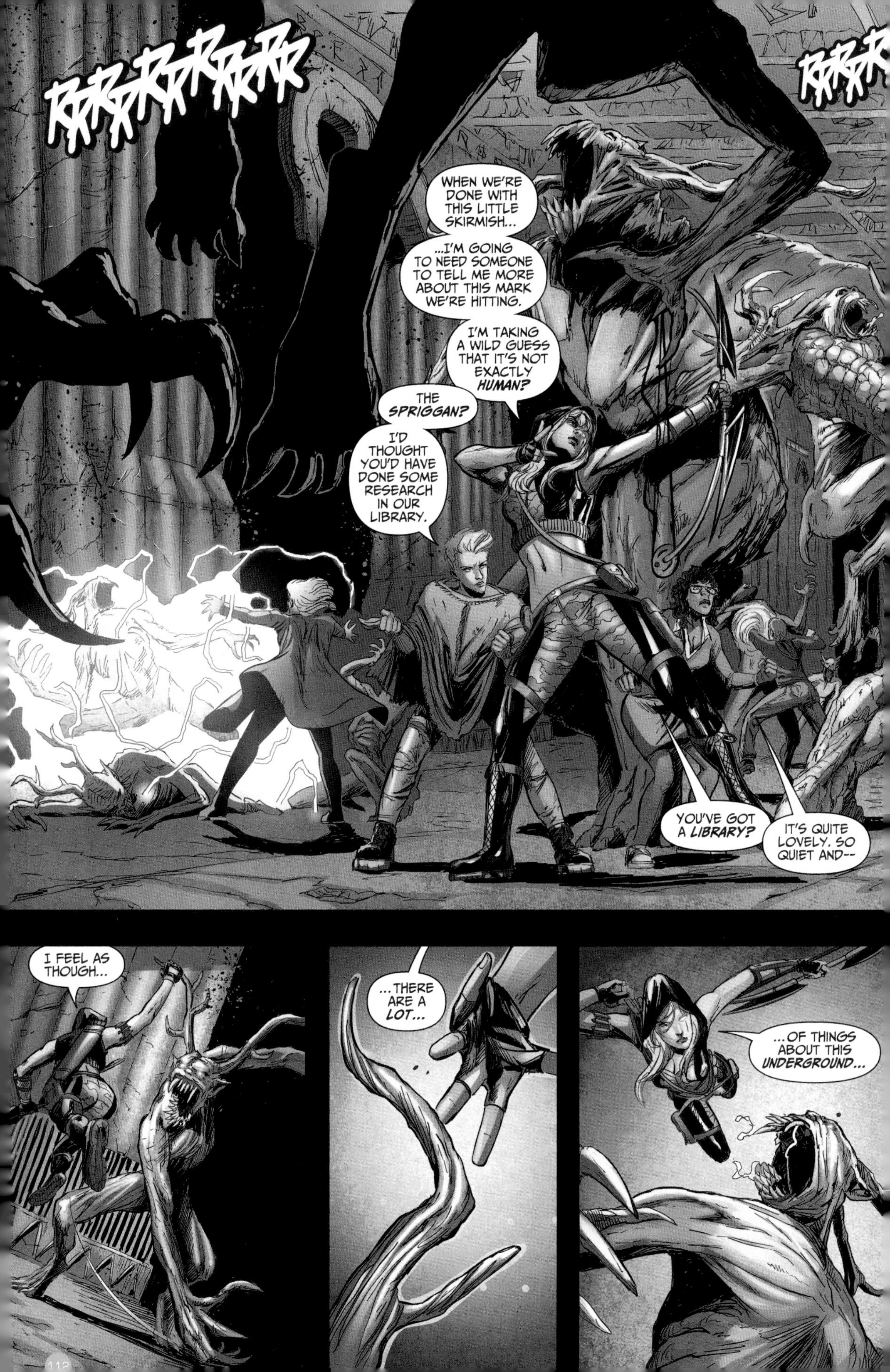
WHEN WE'RE DONE WITH THIS LITTLE SKIRMISH...
...I'M GOING TO NEED SOMEONE TO TELL ME MORE ABOUT THIS MARK WE'RE HITTING.
I'M TAKING A WILD GUESS THAT IT'S NOT EXACTLY *HUMAN?*
THE *SPRIGGAN?*
I'D THOUGHT YOU'D HAVE DONE SOME RESEARCH IN OUR LIBRARY.
YOU'VE GOT A *LIBRARY?*
IT'S QUITE LOVELY. SO QUIET AND--
I FEEL AS THOUGH...
...THERE ARE A *LOT*...
...OF THINGS ABOUT THIS *UNDERGROUND*...

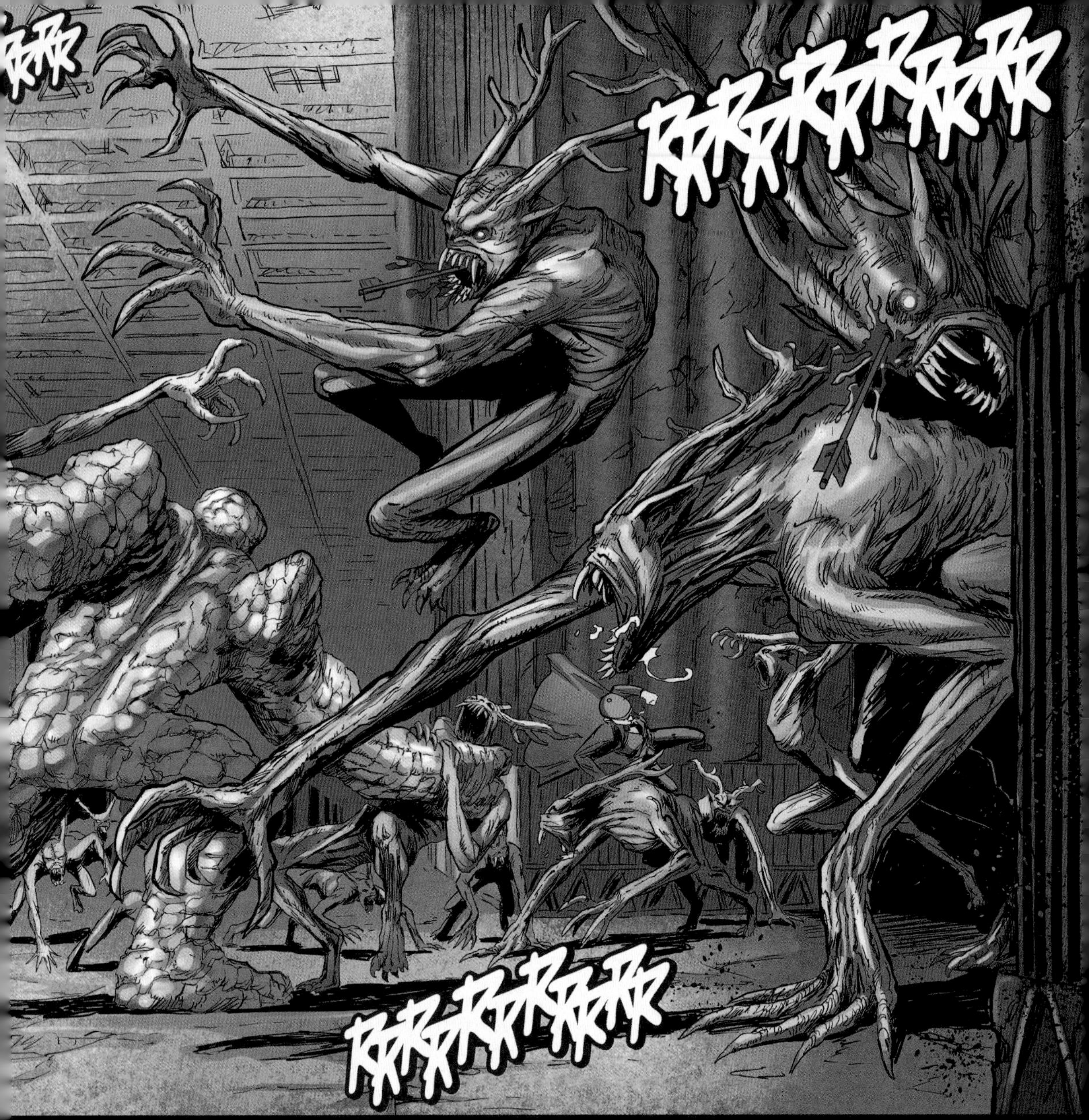
RRR
RRRRRRRRRRR
RRRRRRRRRRR

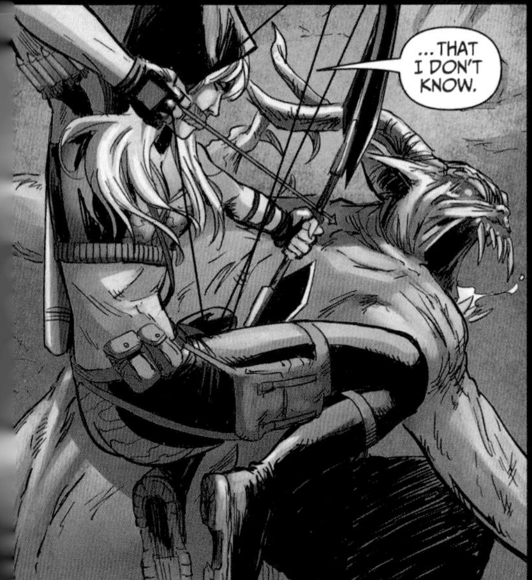
...THAT I DON'T KNOW.

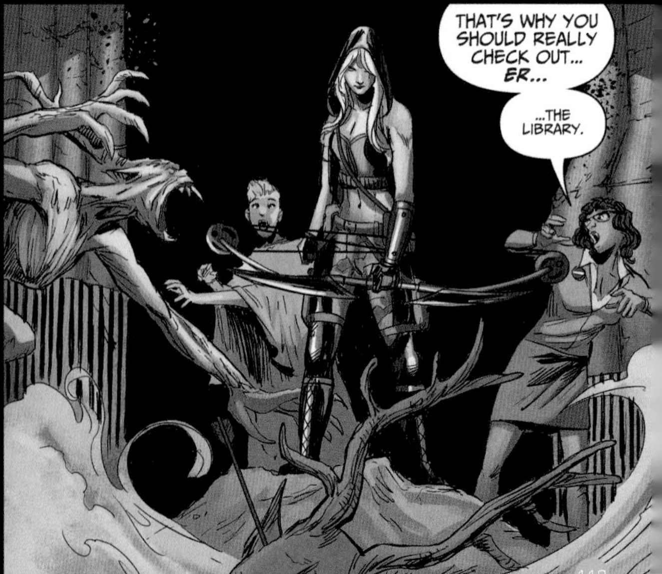
THAT'S WHY YOU SHOULD REALLY CHECK OUT... *ER...*
...THE LIBRARY.

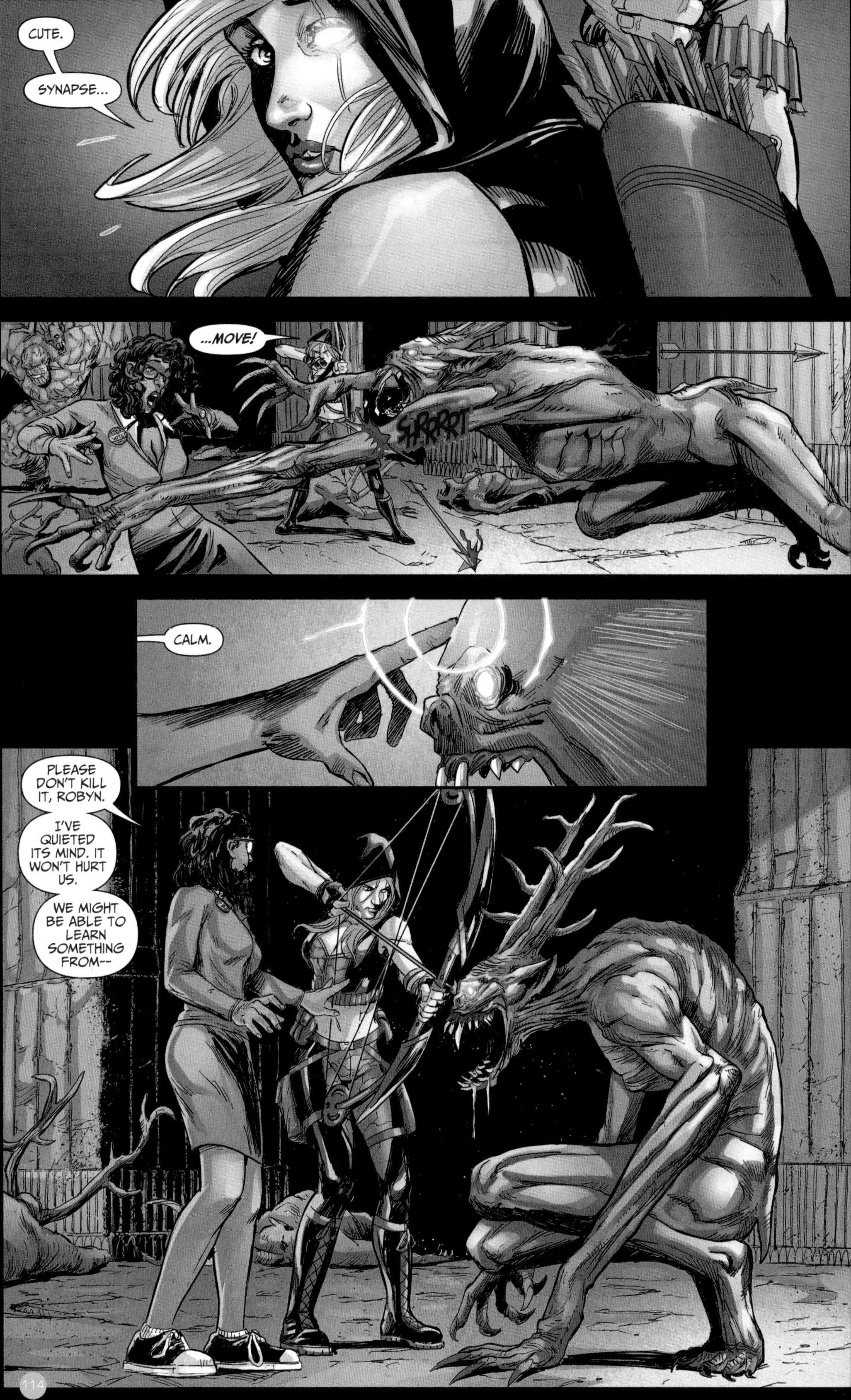
CUTE.
SYNAPSE...
...MOVE!
SHRRRT!
CALM.
PLEASE DON'T KILL IT, ROBYN.
I'VE QUIETED ITS MIND. IT WON'T HURT US.
WE MIGHT BE ABLE TO LEARN SOMETHING FROM--

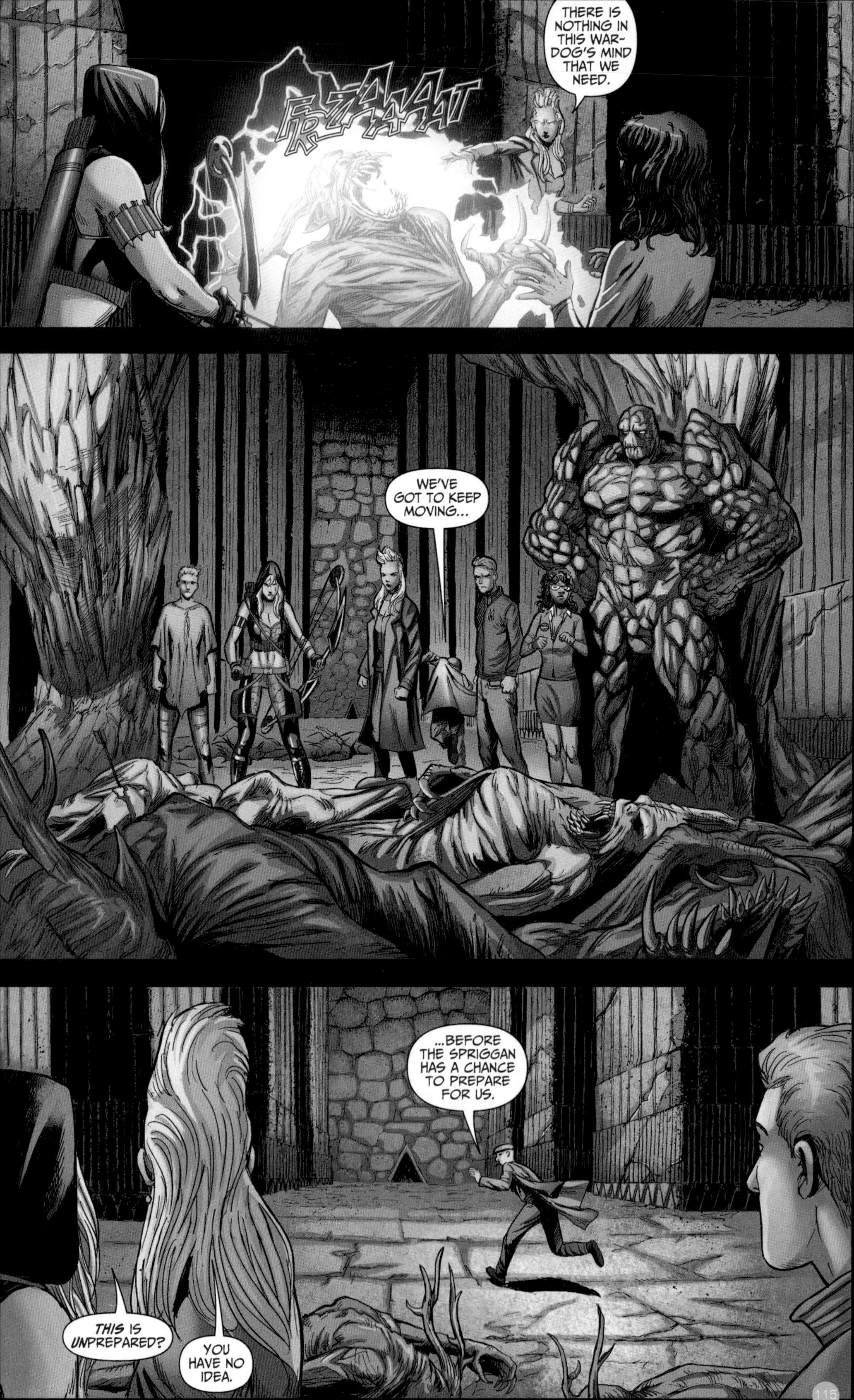
FRZZAAAAT
THERE IS NOTHING IN THIS WAR-DOG'S MIND THAT WE NEED.
WE'VE GOT TO KEEP MOVING...
...BEFORE THE SPRIGGAN HAS A CHANCE TO PREPARE FOR US.
THIS IS UNPREPARED?
YOU HAVE NO IDEA.

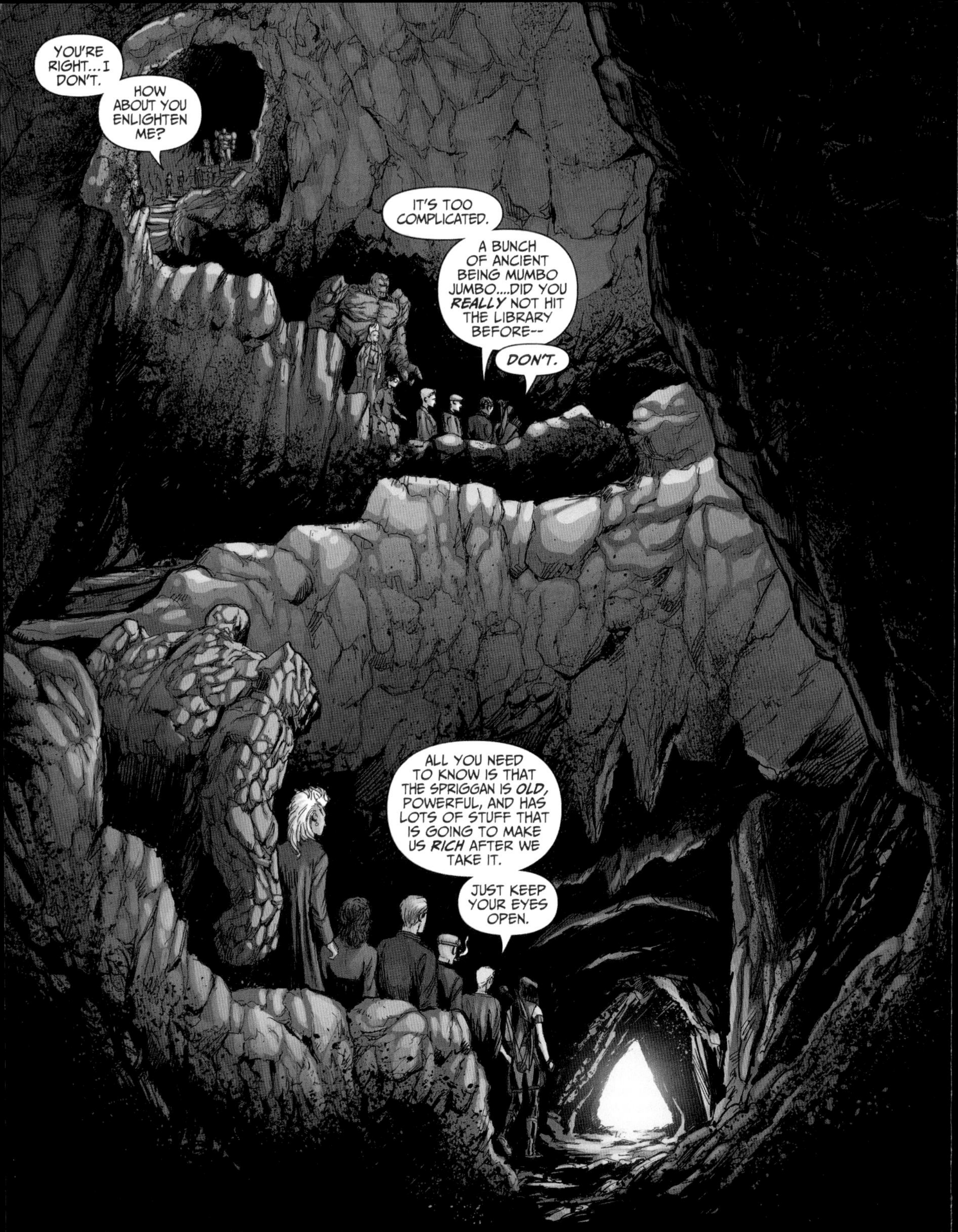
YOU'RE RIGHT... I DON'T.
HOW ABOUT YOU ENLIGHTEN ME?
IT'S TOO COMPLICATED.
A BUNCH OF ANCIENT BEING MUMBO JUMBO....DID YOU *REALLY* NOT HIT THE LIBRARY BEFORE--
DON'T.
ALL YOU NEED TO KNOW IS THAT THE SPRIGGAN IS *OLD*, POWERFUL, AND HAS LOTS OF STUFF THAT IS GOING TO MAKE US *RICH* AFTER WE TAKE IT.
JUST KEEP YOUR EYES OPEN.

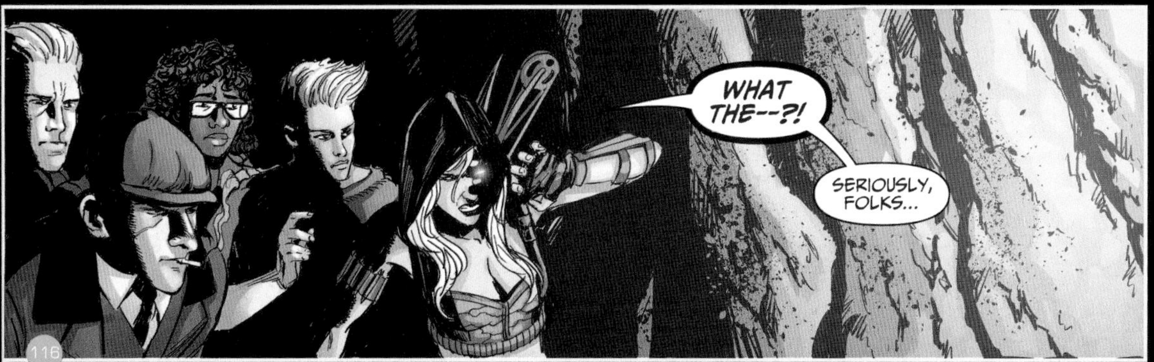
WHAT THE--?!
SERIOUSLY, FOLKS...

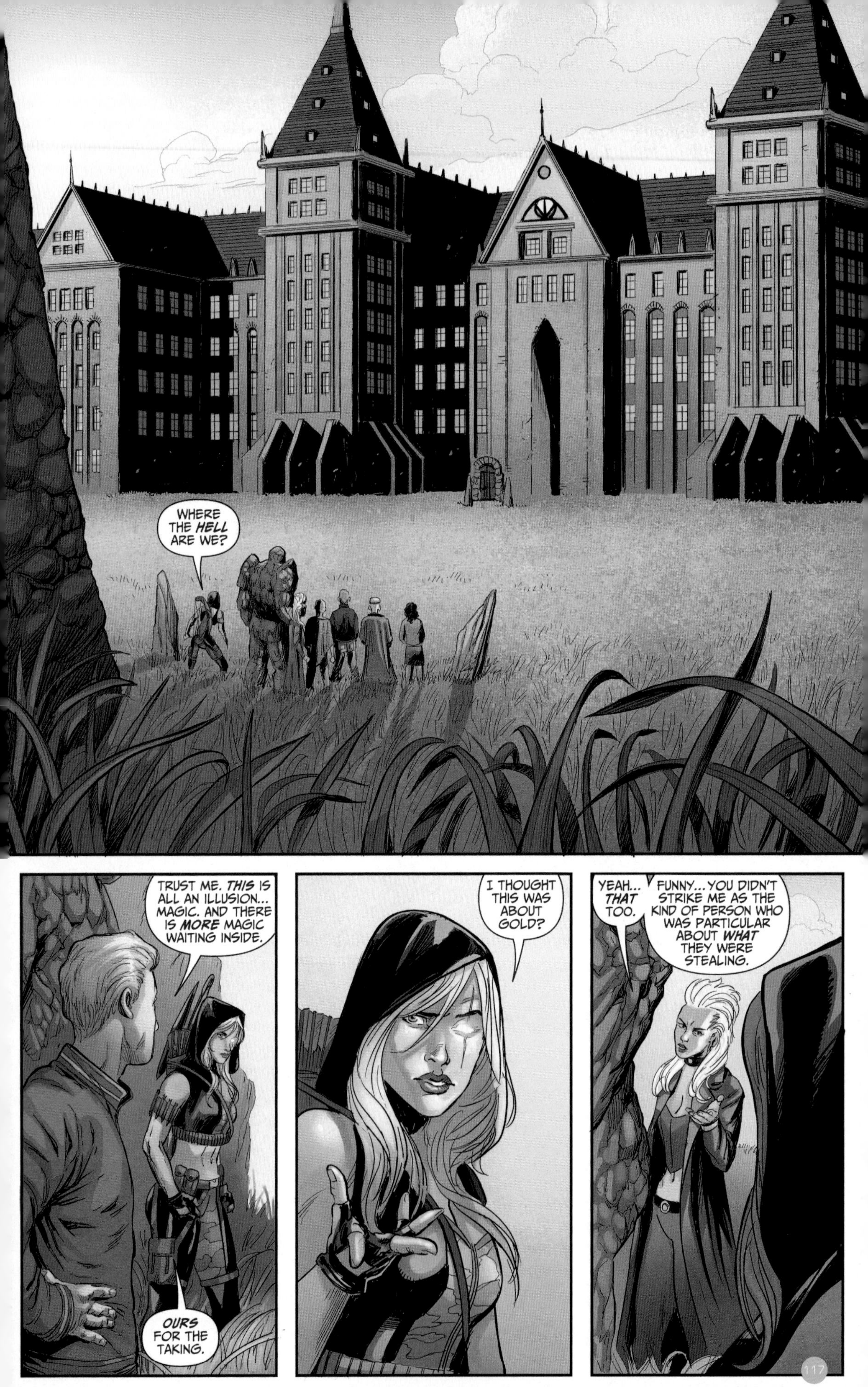
WHERE THE ***HELL*** ARE WE?
TRUST ME. ***THIS*** IS ALL AN ILLUSION... MAGIC. AND THERE IS ***MORE*** MAGIC WAITING INSIDE.
OURS FOR THE TAKING.
I THOUGHT THIS WAS ABOUT GOLD?
YEAH... ***THAT*** TOO.
FUNNY... YOU DIDN'T STRIKE ME AS THE KIND OF PERSON WHO WAS PARTICULAR ABOUT ***WHAT*** THEY WERE STEALING.

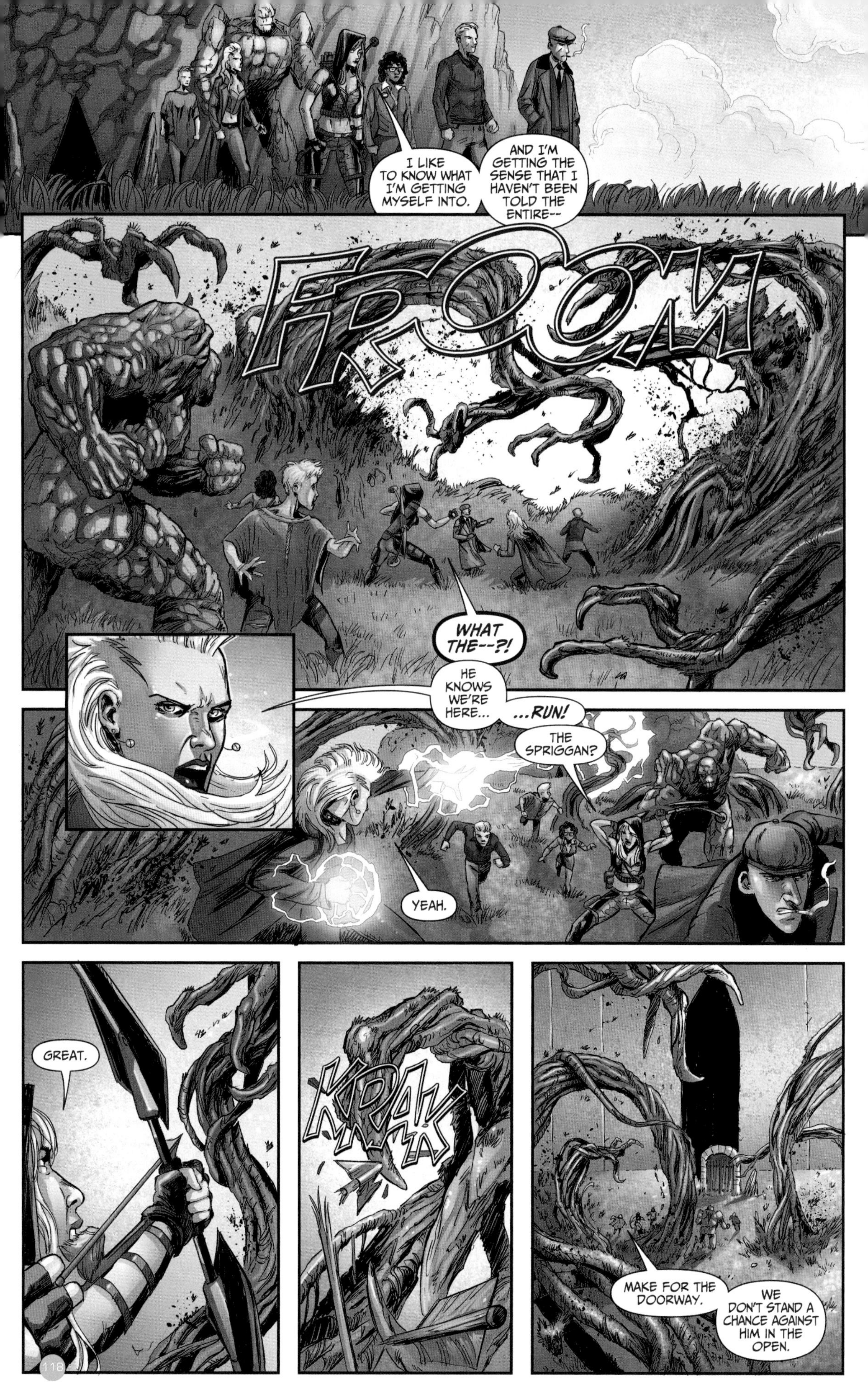

I LIKE TO KNOW WHAT I'M GETTING MYSELF INTO.
AND I'M GETTING THE SENSE THAT I HAVEN'T BEEN TOLD THE ENTIRE--
FROOM
WHAT THE--?!
HE KNOWS WE'RE HERE...
...RUN!
THE SPRIGGAN?
YEAH.
GREAT.
MAKE FOR THE DOORWAY.
WE DON'T STAND A CHANCE AGAINST HIM IN THE OPEN.

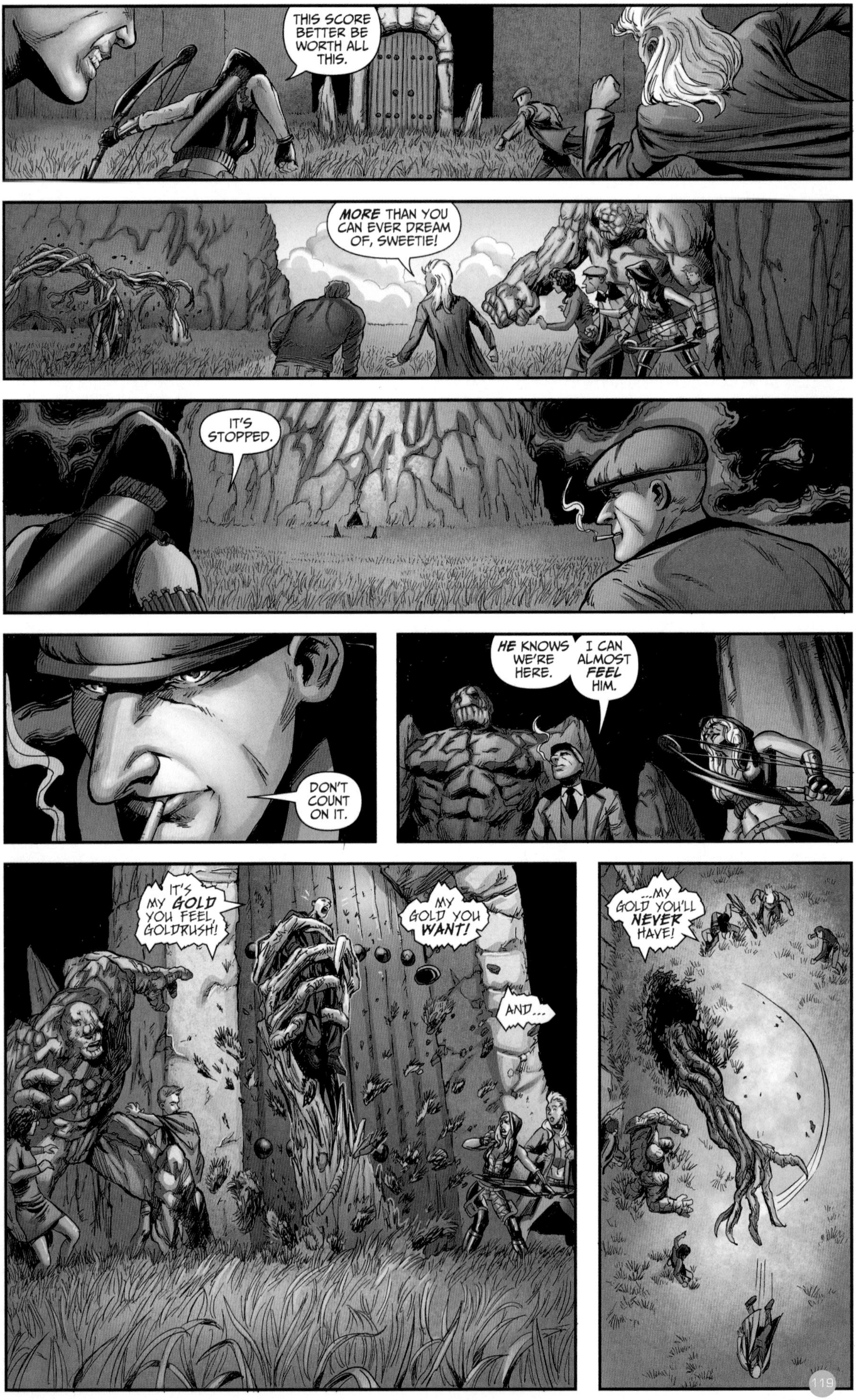
THIS SCORE BETTER BE WORTH ALL THIS.
MORE THAN YOU CAN EVER DREAM OF, SWEETIE!
IT'S STOPPED.
DON'T COUNT ON IT.
HE KNOWS WE'RE HERE.
I CAN ALMOST FEEL HIM.
IT'S MY GOLD YOU FEEL, GOLDRUSH!
MY GOLD YOU WANT!
AND...
...MY GOLD YOU'LL NEVER HAVE!

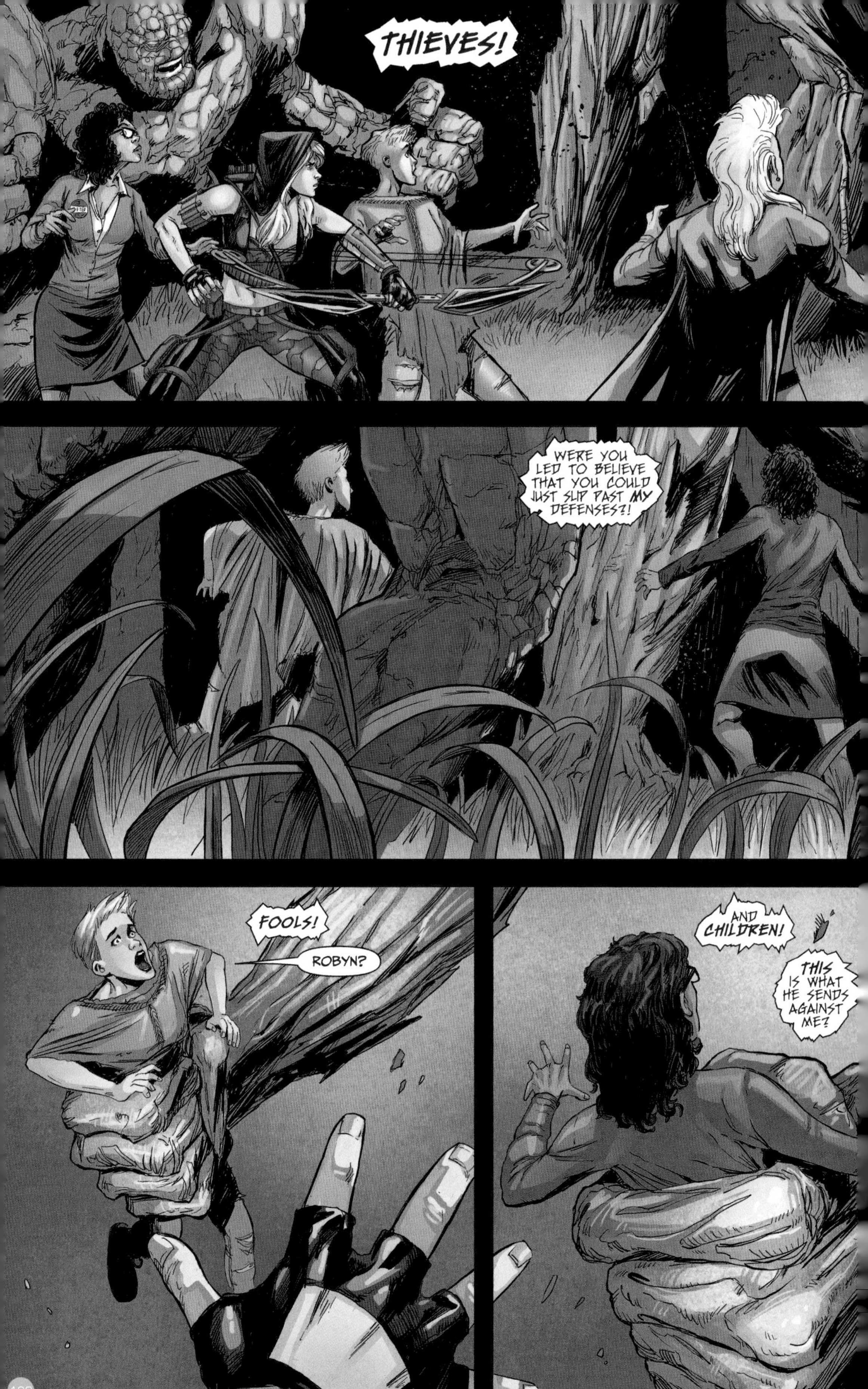
THIEVES!
WERE YOU LED TO BELIEVE THAT YOU COULD JUST SLIP PAST MY DEFENSES?!
FOOLS!
ROBYN?
AND CHILDREN!
THIS IS WHAT HE SENDS AGAINST ME?

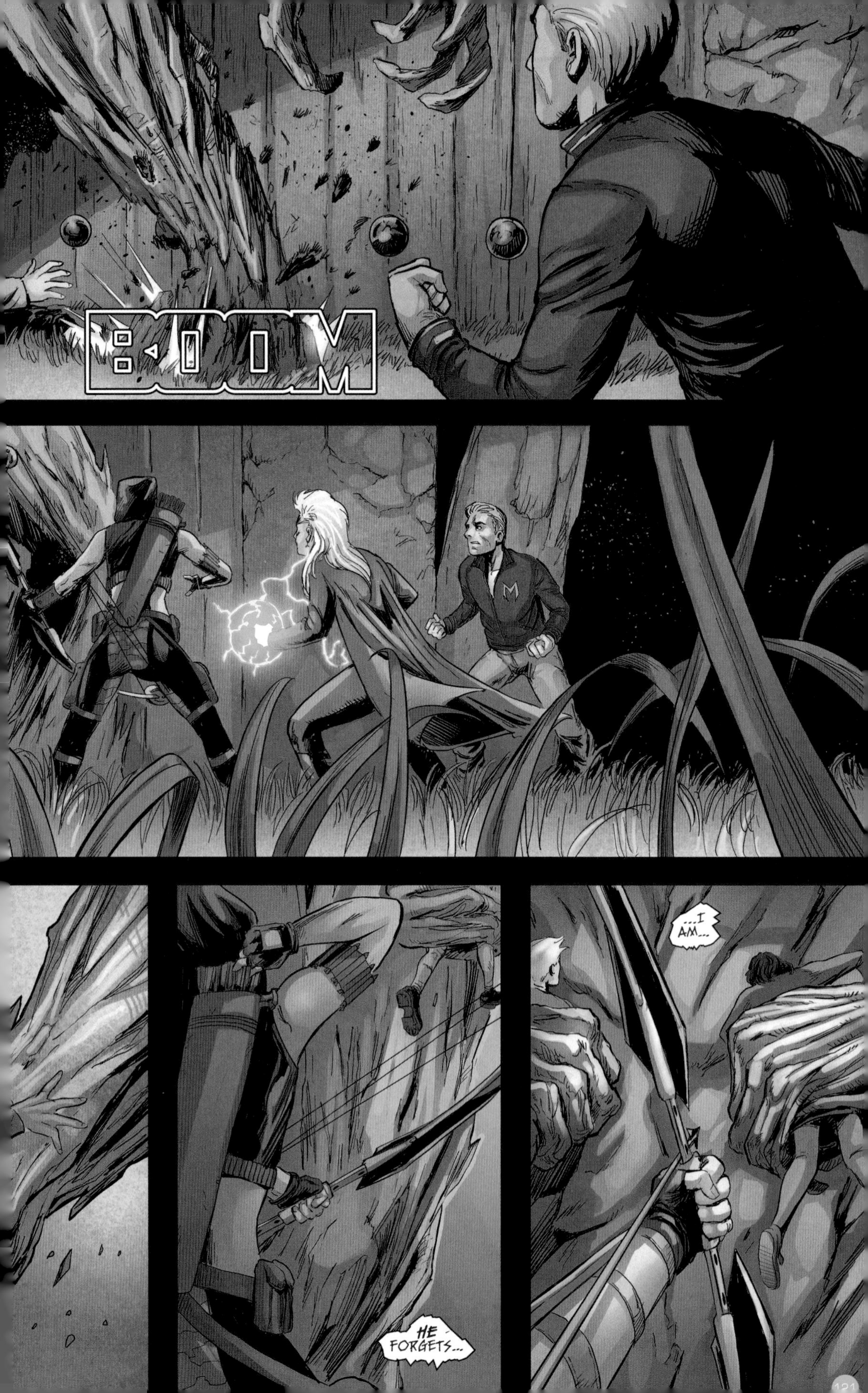
BOOM
HE FORGETS...
...I AM...

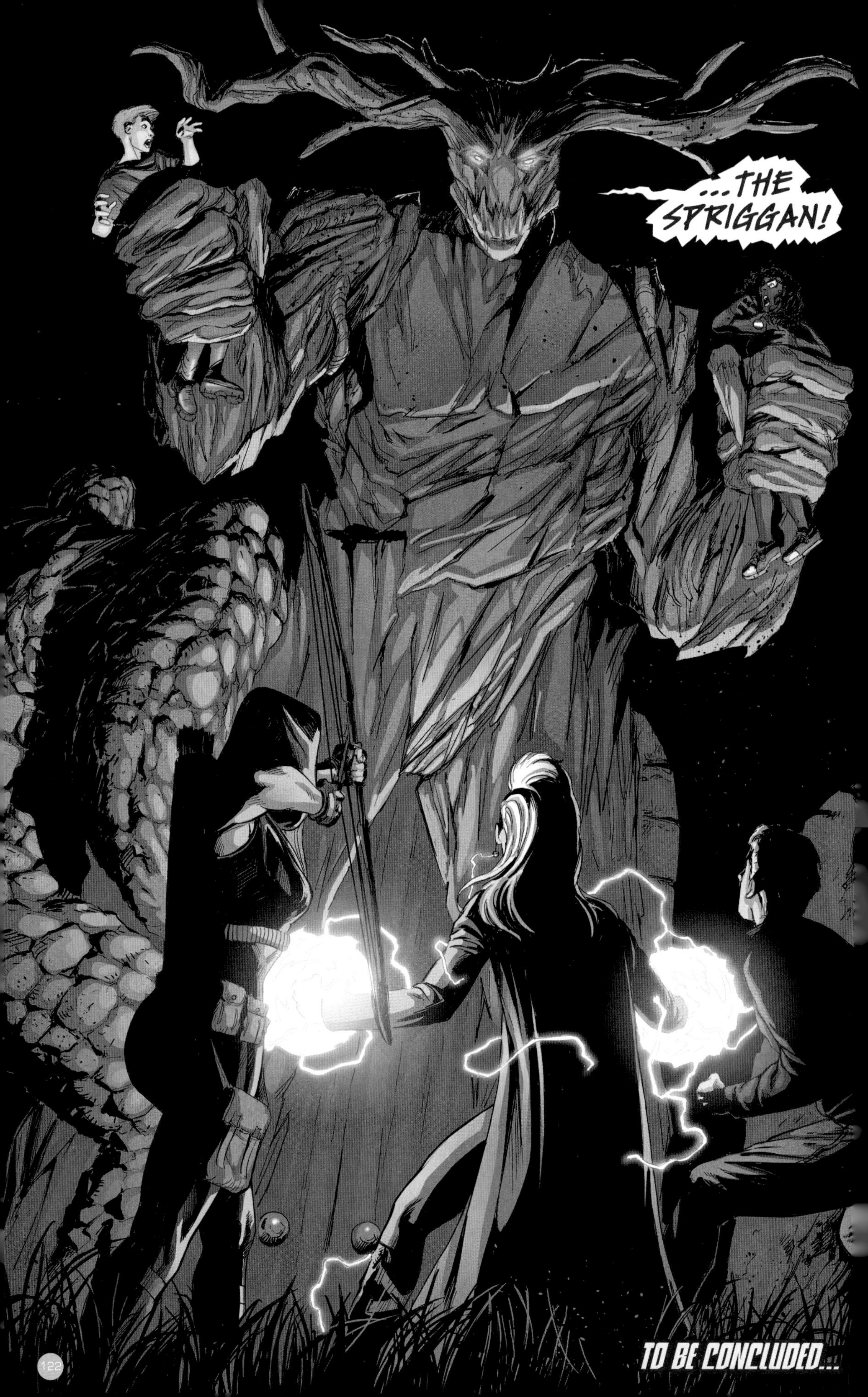
...THE SPRIGGAN!
TO BE CONCLUDED...

ROBYN HOOD

HOOD

OUTLAW

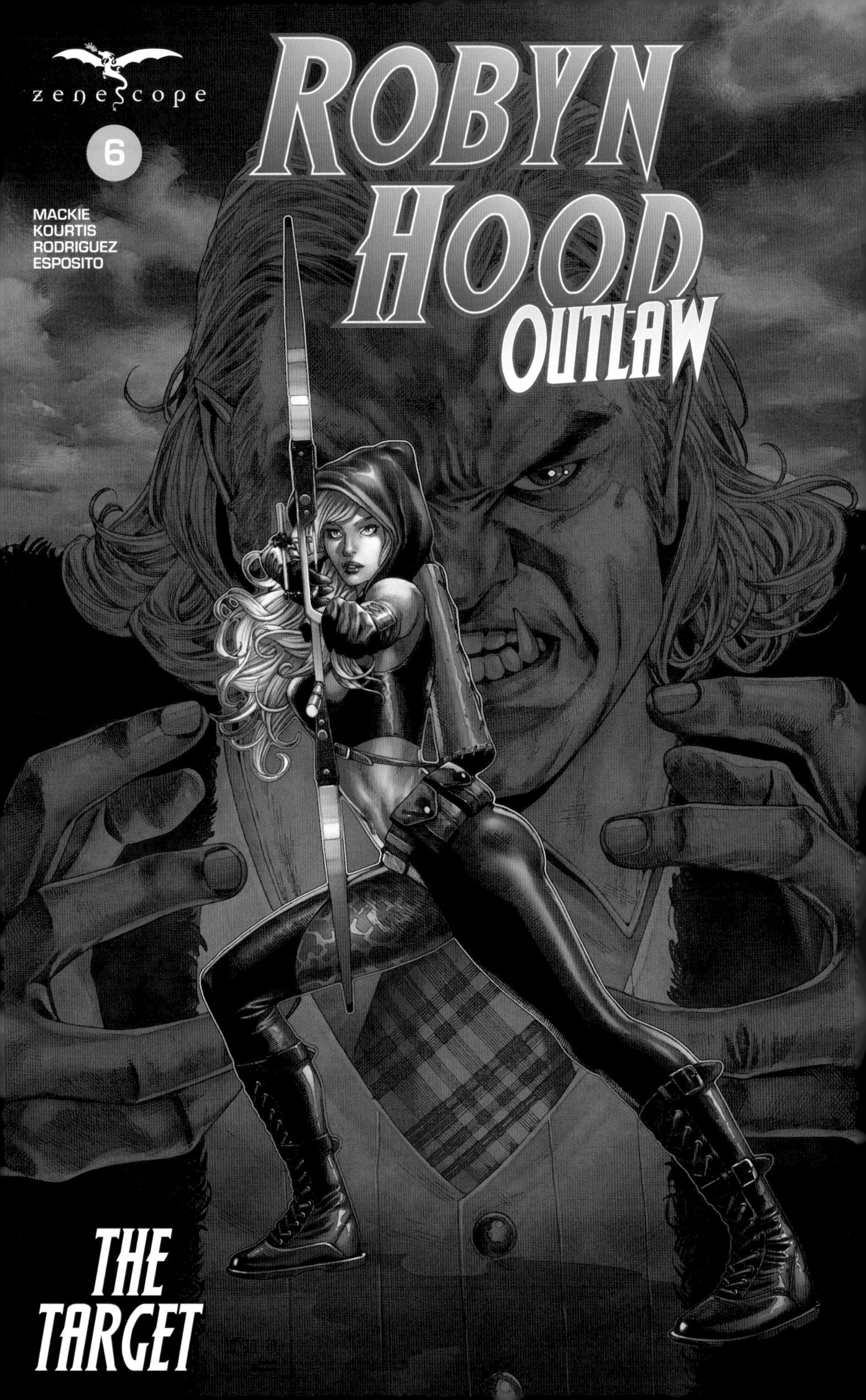
zenescope
6
MACKIE
KOURTIS
RODRIGUEZ
ESPOSITO
ROBYN HOOD
OUTLAW
THE TARGET

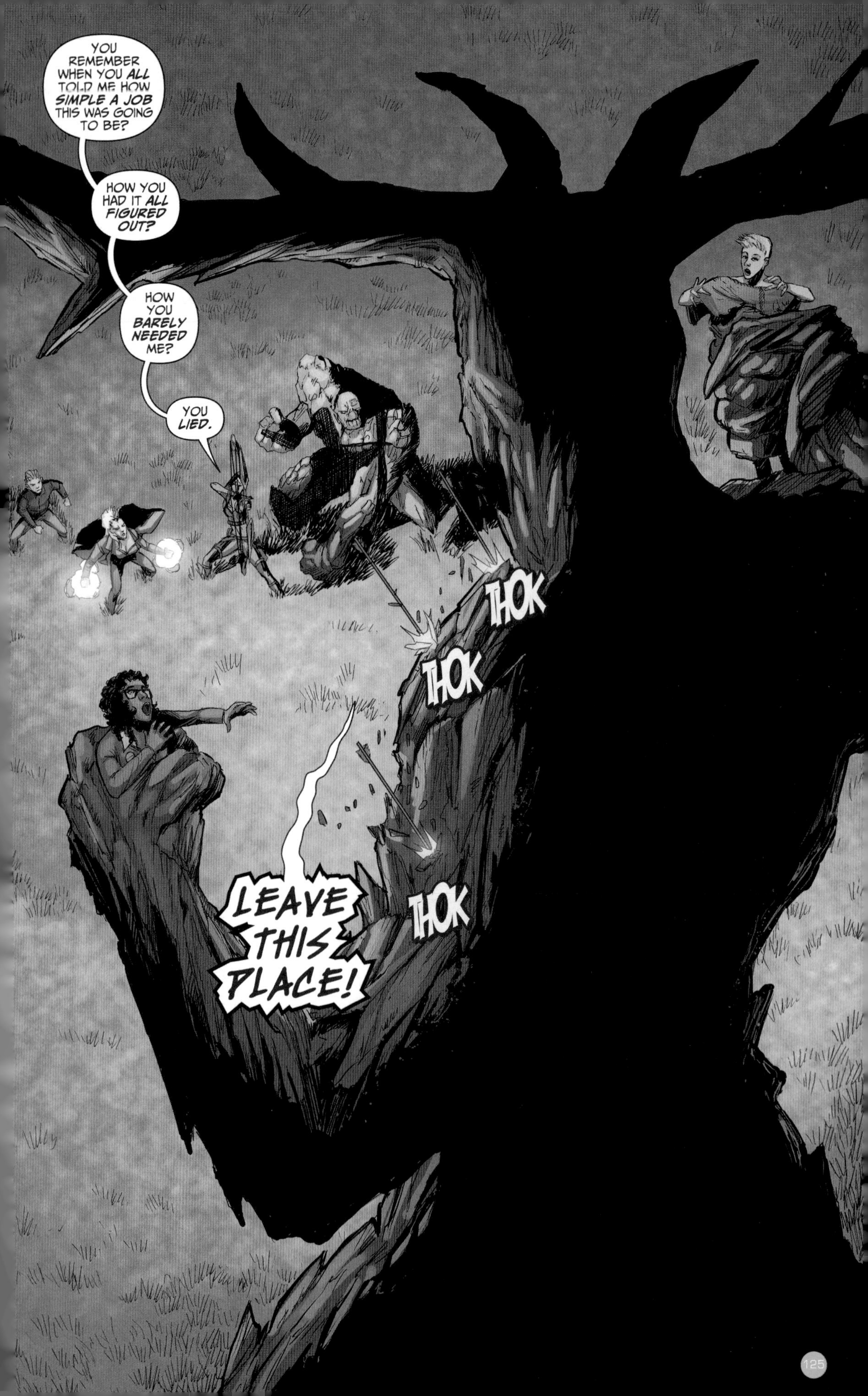
YOU REMEMBER WHEN YOU ALL TOLD ME HOW SIMPLE A JOB THIS WAS GOING TO BE?
HOW YOU HAD IT ALL FIGURED OUT?
HOW YOU BARELY NEEDED ME?
YOU LIED.
THOK
THOK
LEAVE THIS PLACE!
THOK

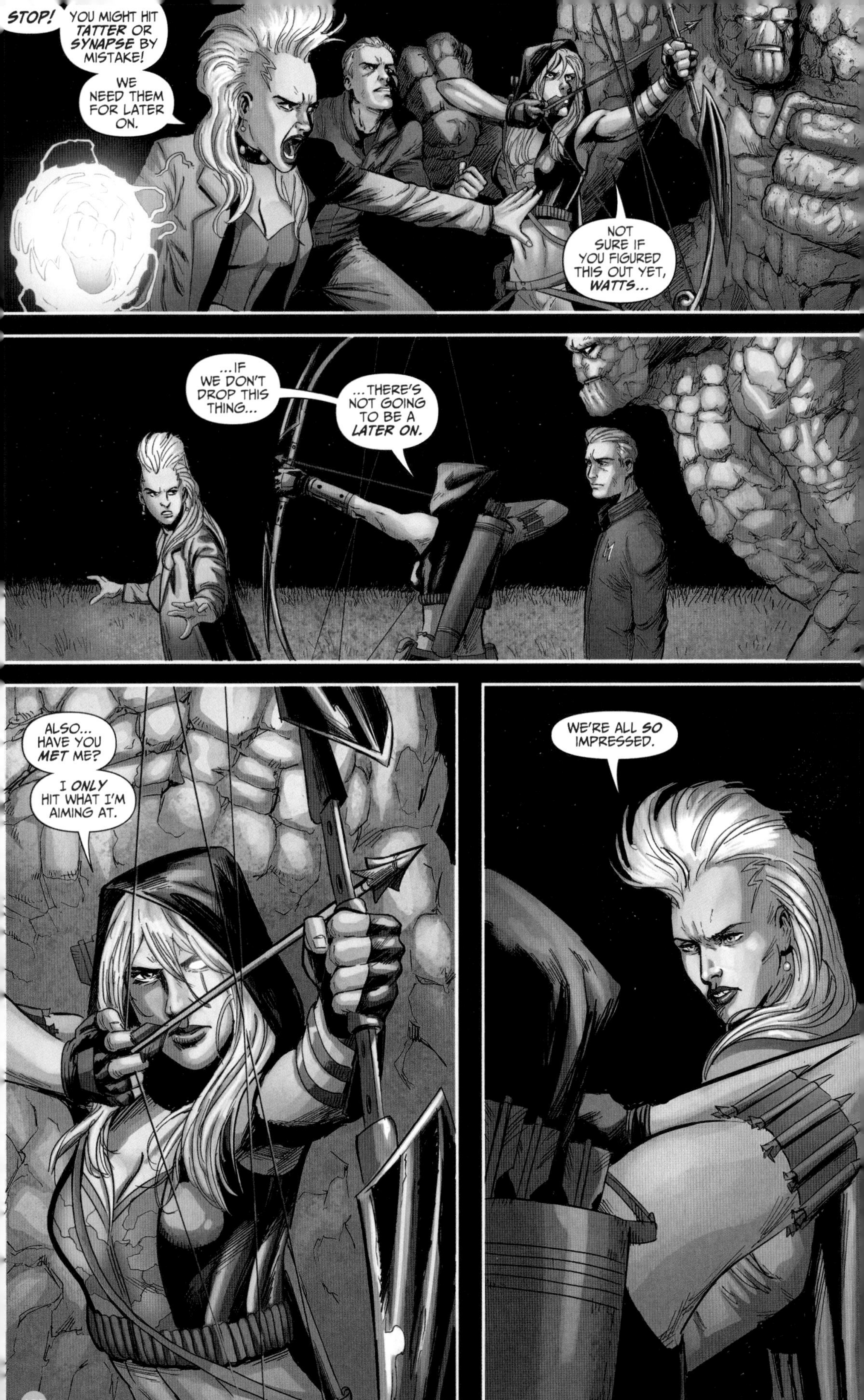
STOP!
YOU MIGHT HIT TATTER OR SYNAPSE BY MISTAKE!
WE NEED THEM FOR LATER ON.
NOT SURE IF YOU FIGURED THIS OUT YET, WATTS...
...IF WE DON'T DROP THIS THING...
...THERE'S NOT GOING TO BE A LATER ON.
ALSO... HAVE YOU MET ME?
I ONLY HIT WHAT I'M AIMING AT.
WE'RE ALL SO IMPRESSED.

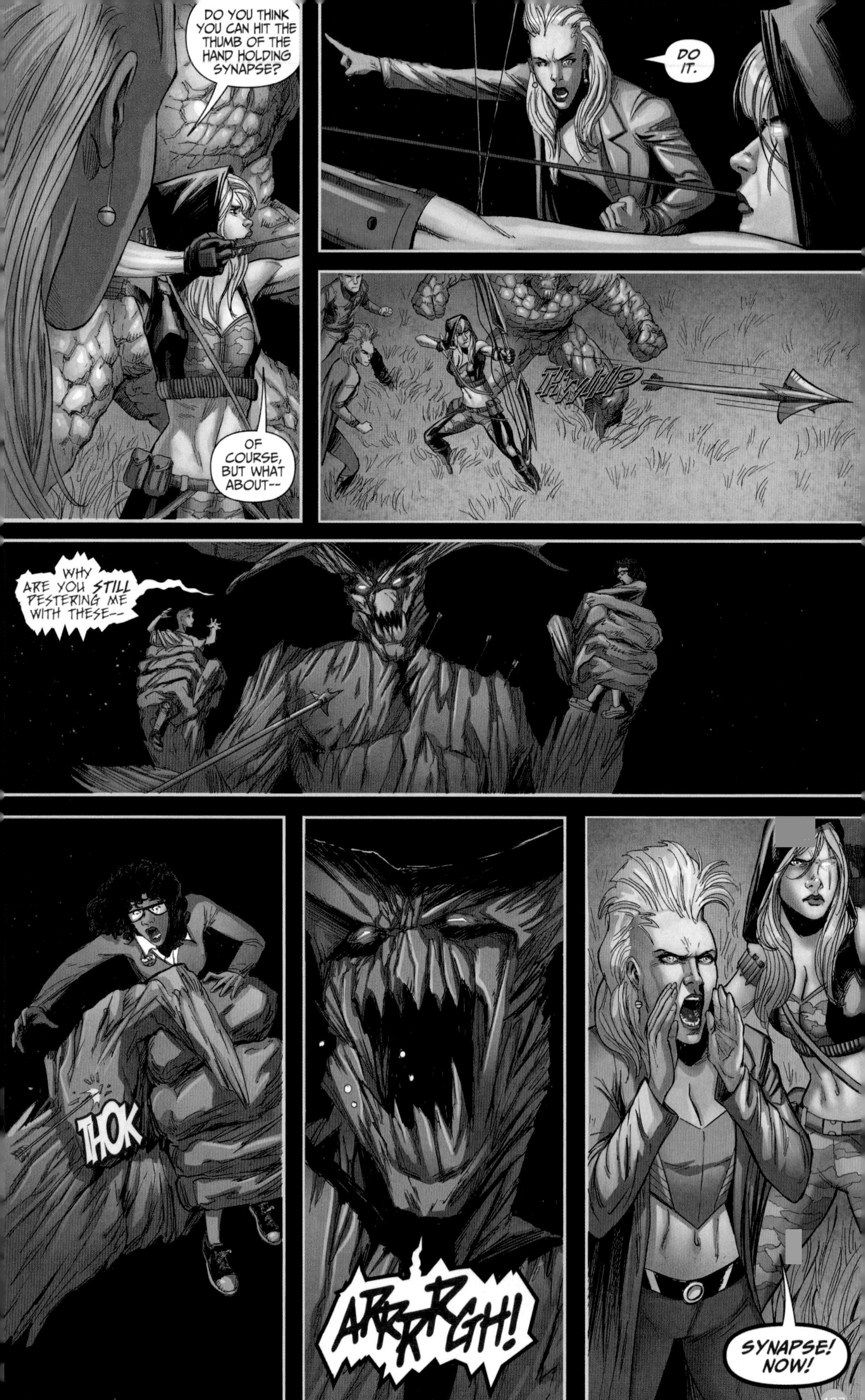
DO YOU THINK YOU CAN HIT THE THUMB OF THE HAND HOLDING SYNAPSE?
OF COURSE, BUT WHAT ABOUT--
DO IT.
THWUP
WHY ARE YOU STILL PESTERING ME WITH THESE--
THOK
ARRRRRGH!
SYNAPSE! NOW!

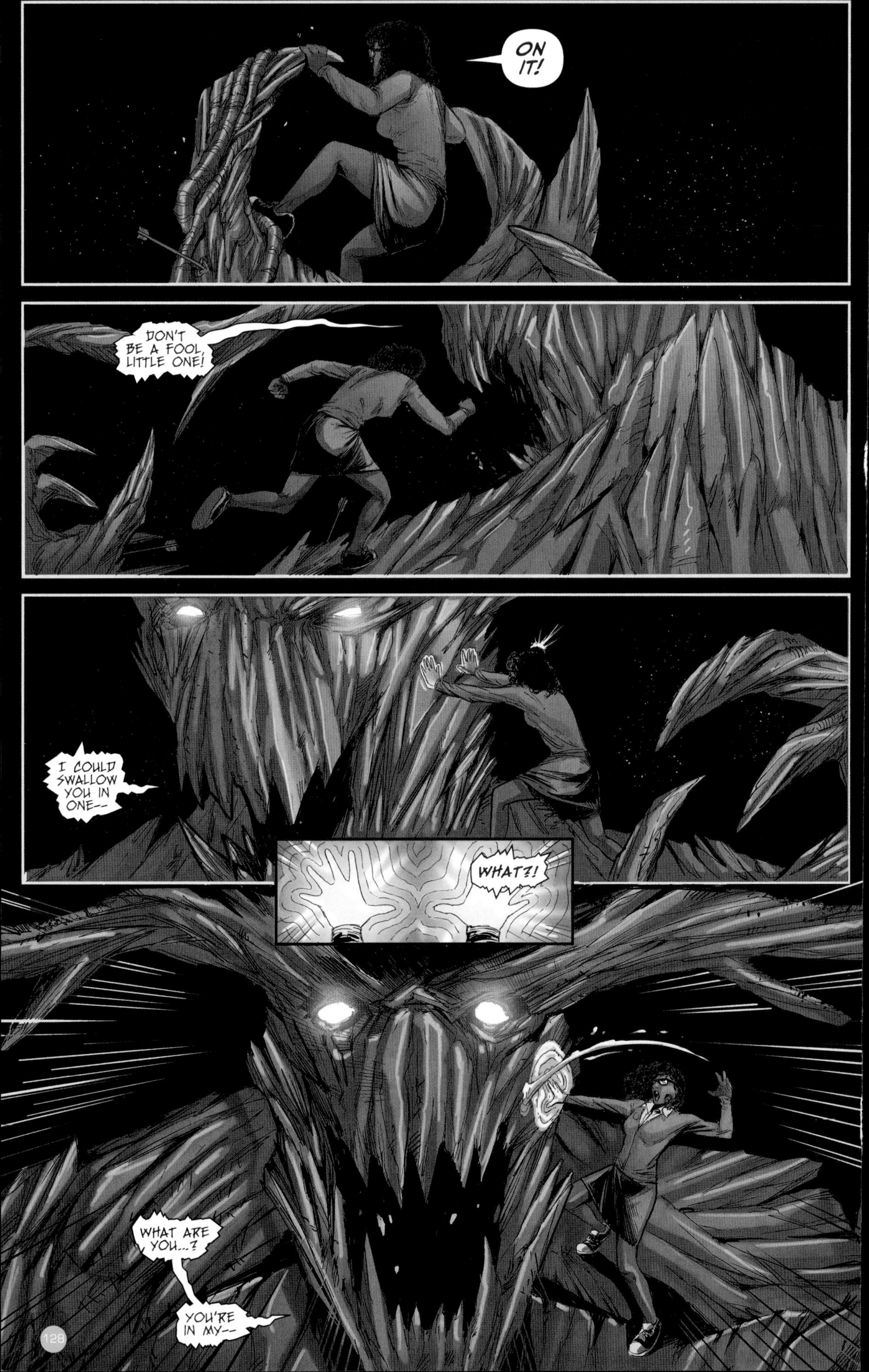
ON IT!
DON'T BE A FOOL, LITTLE ONE!
I COULD SWALLOW YOU IN ONE--
WHAT?!
WHAT ARE YOU...?
YOU'RE IN MY--

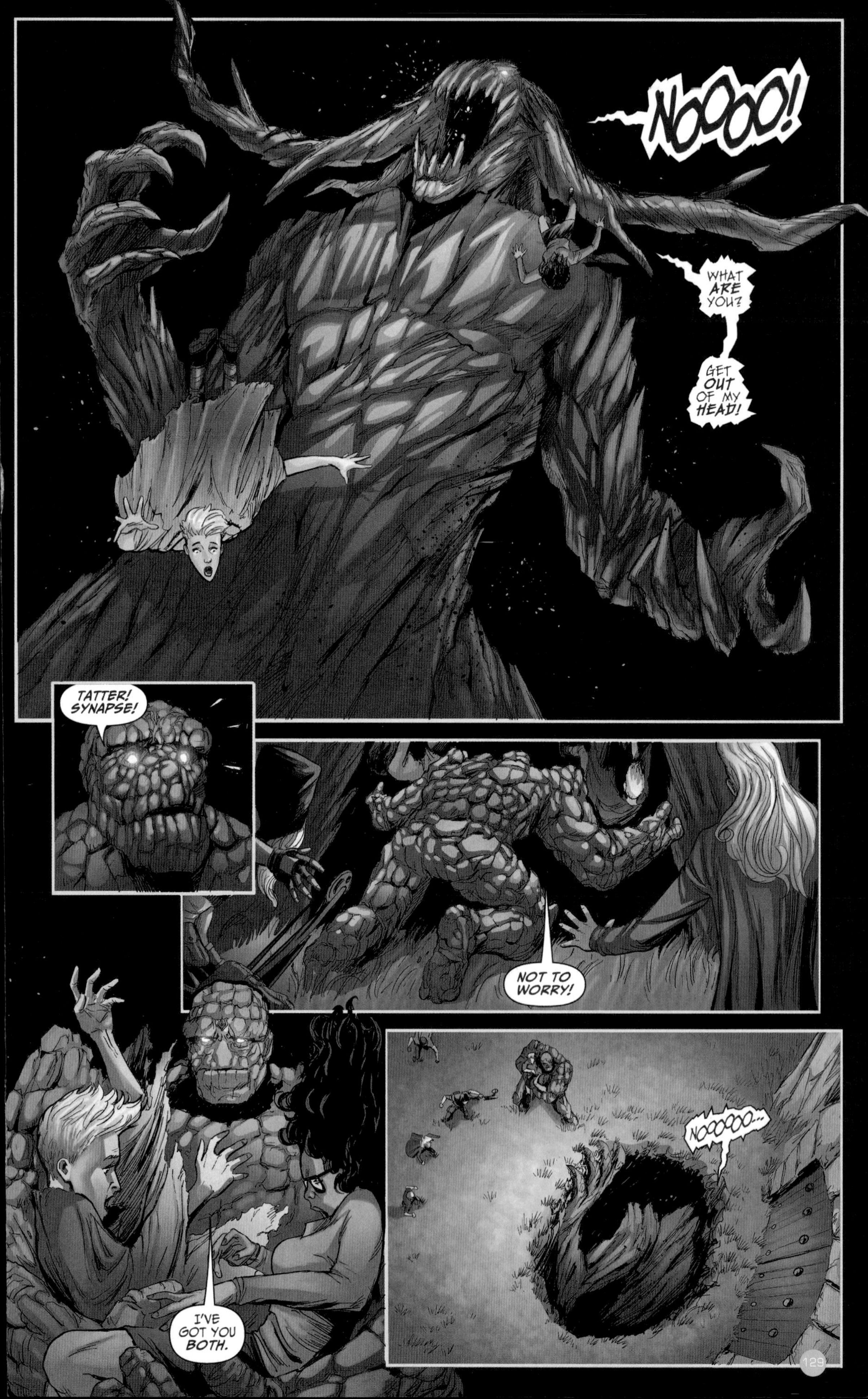
NOOOO!
WHAT ARE YOU?
GET OUT OF MY HEAD!
TATTER! SYNAPSE!
NOT TO WORRY!
I'VE GOT YOU BOTH.
NOOOOO...

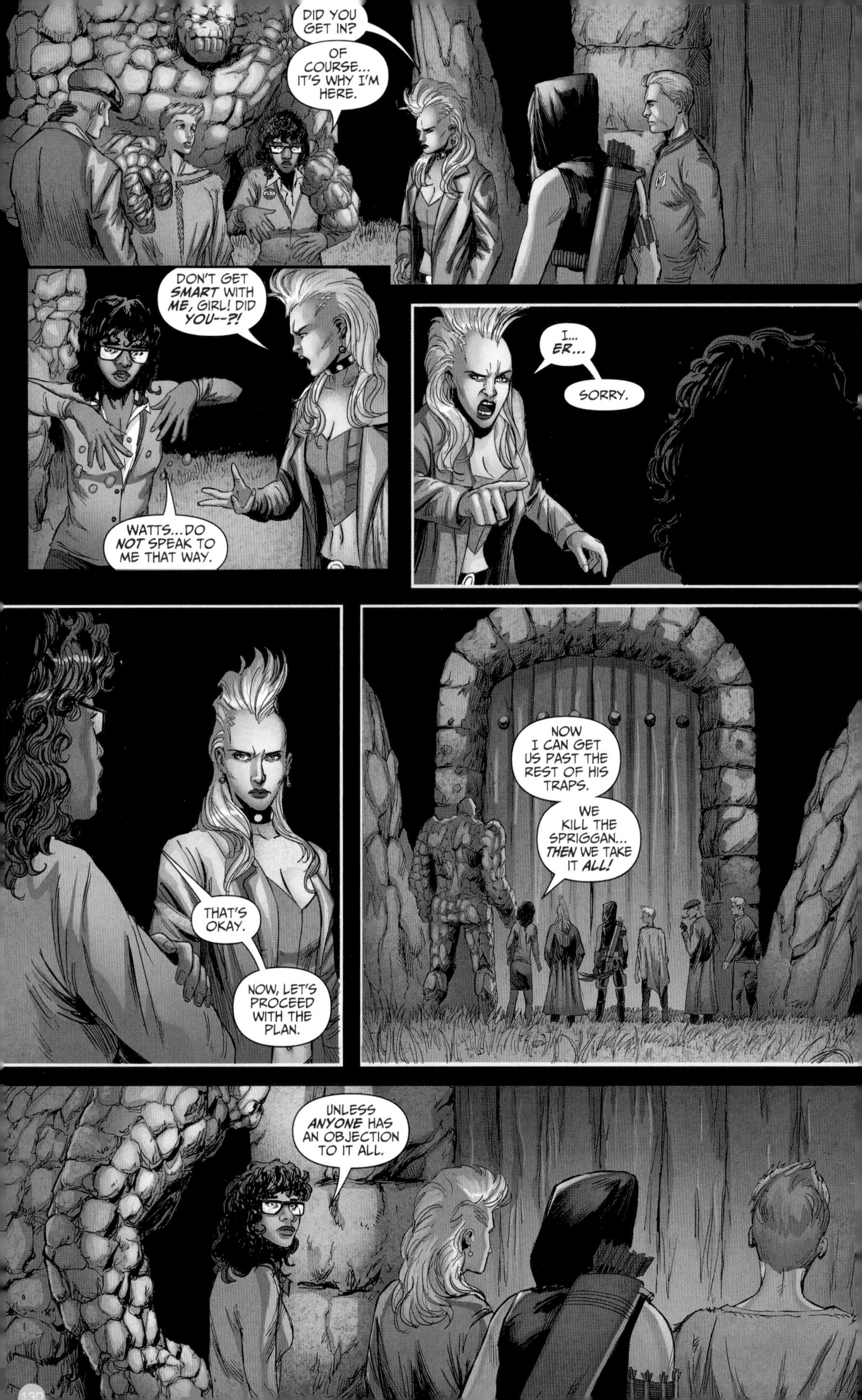
DID YOU GET IN?
OF COURSE... IT'S WHY I'M HERE.
DON'T GET *SMART* WITH *ME*, GIRL! DID *YOU--?!*
WATTS...DO *NOT* SPEAK TO ME THAT WAY.
I... *ER...*
SORRY.
THAT'S OKAY.
NOW, LET'S PROCEED WITH THE PLAN.
NOW I CAN GET US PAST THE REST OF HIS TRAPS.
WE KILL THE SPRIGGAN... *THEN* WE TAKE IT *ALL!*
UNLESS *ANYONE* HAS AN OBJECTION TO IT ALL.

NYGUEN!

THANK YOU!

IT LOOKS LIKE WE *DID* IT!

AND AS *MAYOR* OF THIS BEAUTIFUL CITY, I AM GOING TO SEE TO IT THAT A NEW AGE IS HERALDED IN!

I WILL BE BACK WHEN THE FINAL VOTES ARE TALLIED!

NYGUEN!

NYGUEN!

GET ME THE INTERIM POLICE COMMISSIONER...

...WE ARE ABOUT TO START MAKING BIG CHANGES IN THIS CITY.

NOW, LEAVE ME.

I MUST REPORT IN.

MASTER...

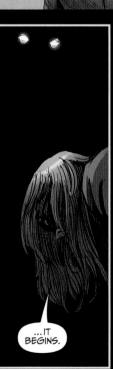

...IT BEGINS.

THE NEW AGE!

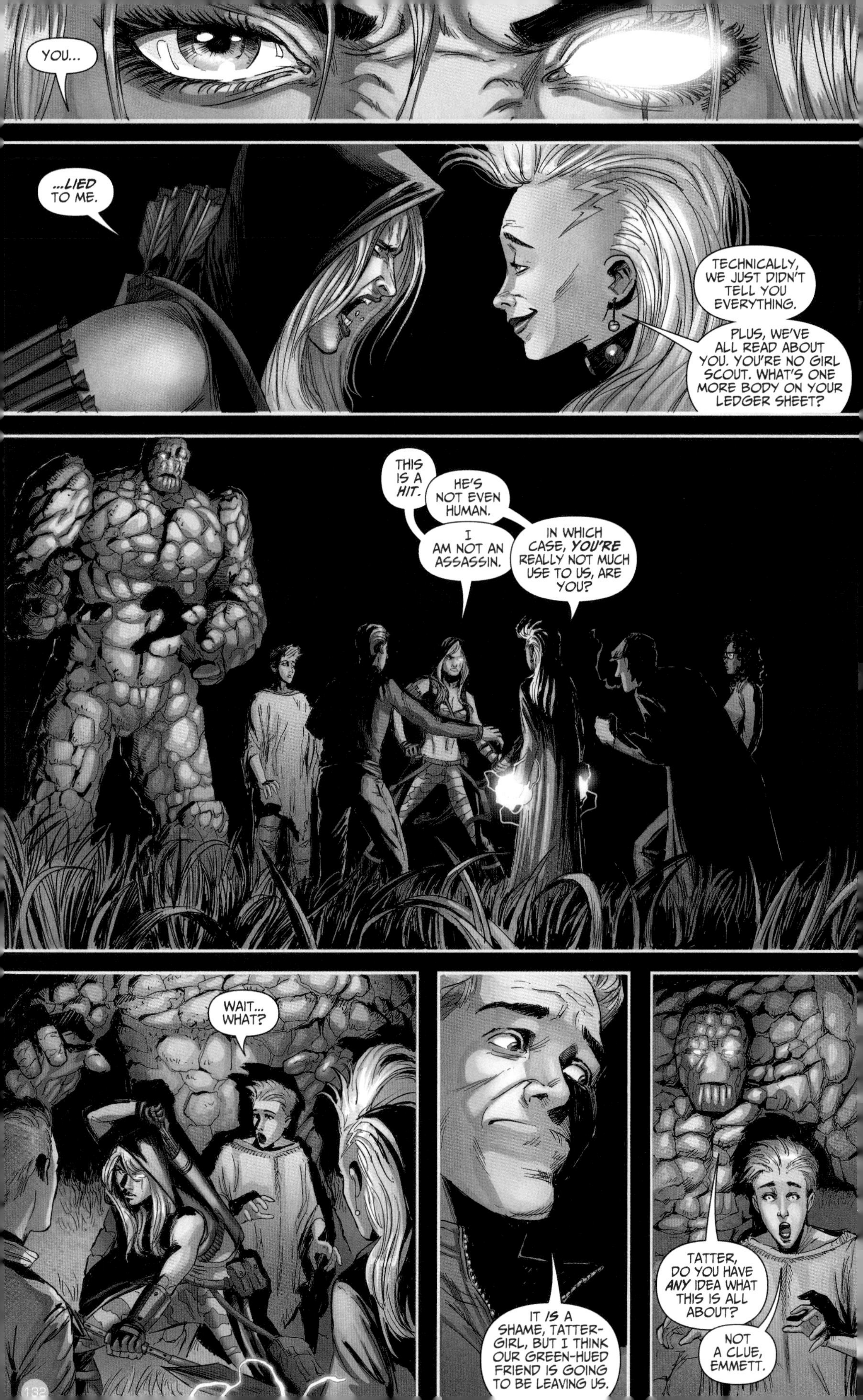
YOU...
...LIED TO ME.
TECHNICALLY, WE JUST DIDN'T TELL YOU EVERYTHING.
PLUS, WE'VE ALL READ ABOUT YOU. YOU'RE NO GIRL SCOUT. WHAT'S ONE MORE BODY ON YOUR LEDGER SHEET?
THIS IS A *HIT*.
HE'S NOT EVEN HUMAN.
I AM NOT AN ASSASSIN.
IN WHICH CASE, ***YOU'RE*** REALLY NOT MUCH USE TO US, ARE YOU?
WAIT... WHAT?
IT *IS* A SHAME, TATTER-GIRL, BUT I THINK OUR GREEN-HUED FRIEND IS GOING TO BE LEAVING US.
TATTER, DO YOU HAVE *ANY* IDEA WHAT THIS IS ALL ABOUT?
NOT A CLUE, EMMETT.

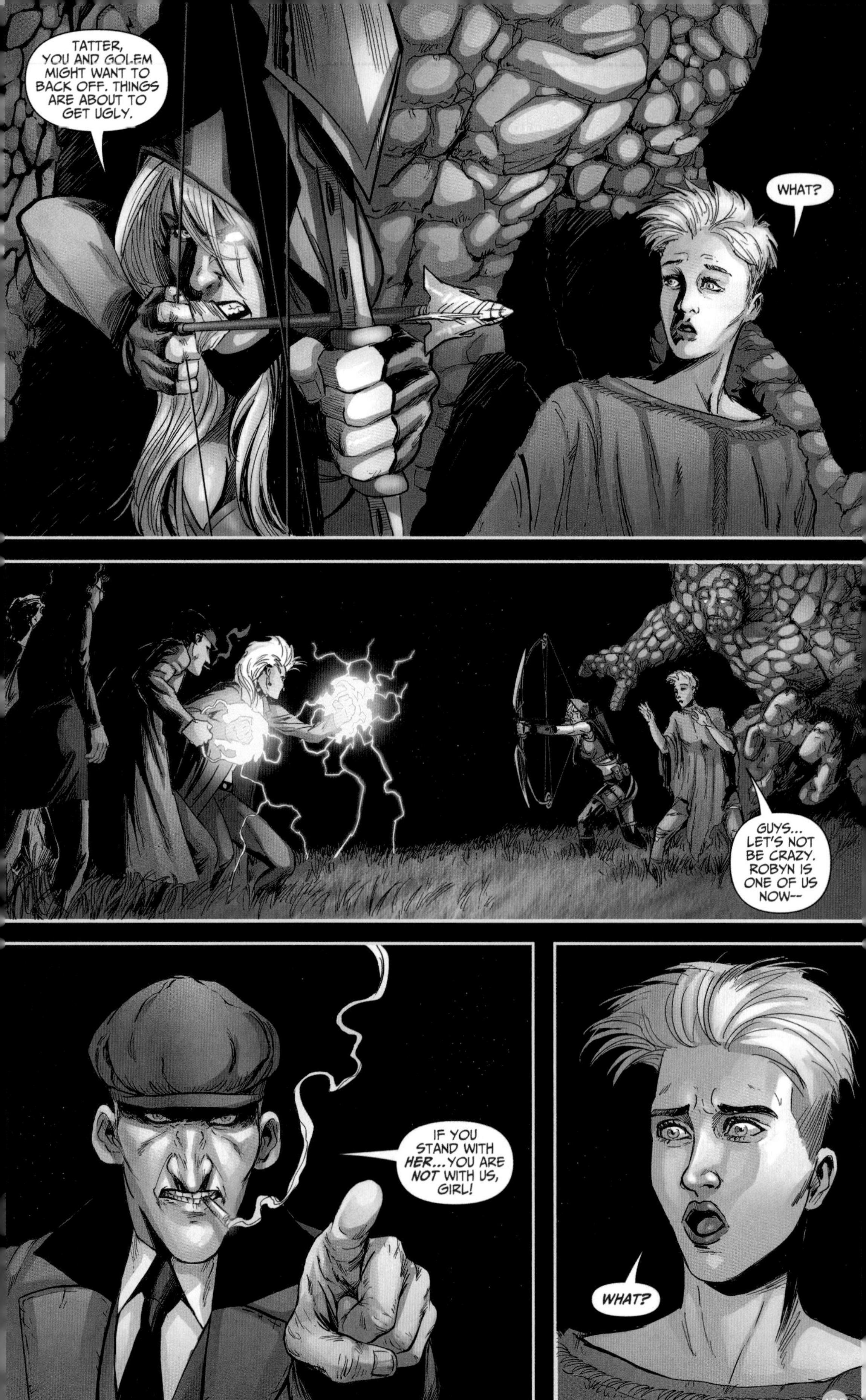
TATTER, YOU AND GOLEM MIGHT WANT TO BACK OFF. THINGS ARE ABOUT TO GET UGLY.
WHAT?
GUYS... LET'S NOT BE CRAZY. ROBYN IS ONE OF US NOW--
IF YOU STAND WITH *HER*...YOU ARE *NOT* WITH US, GIRL!
WHAT?

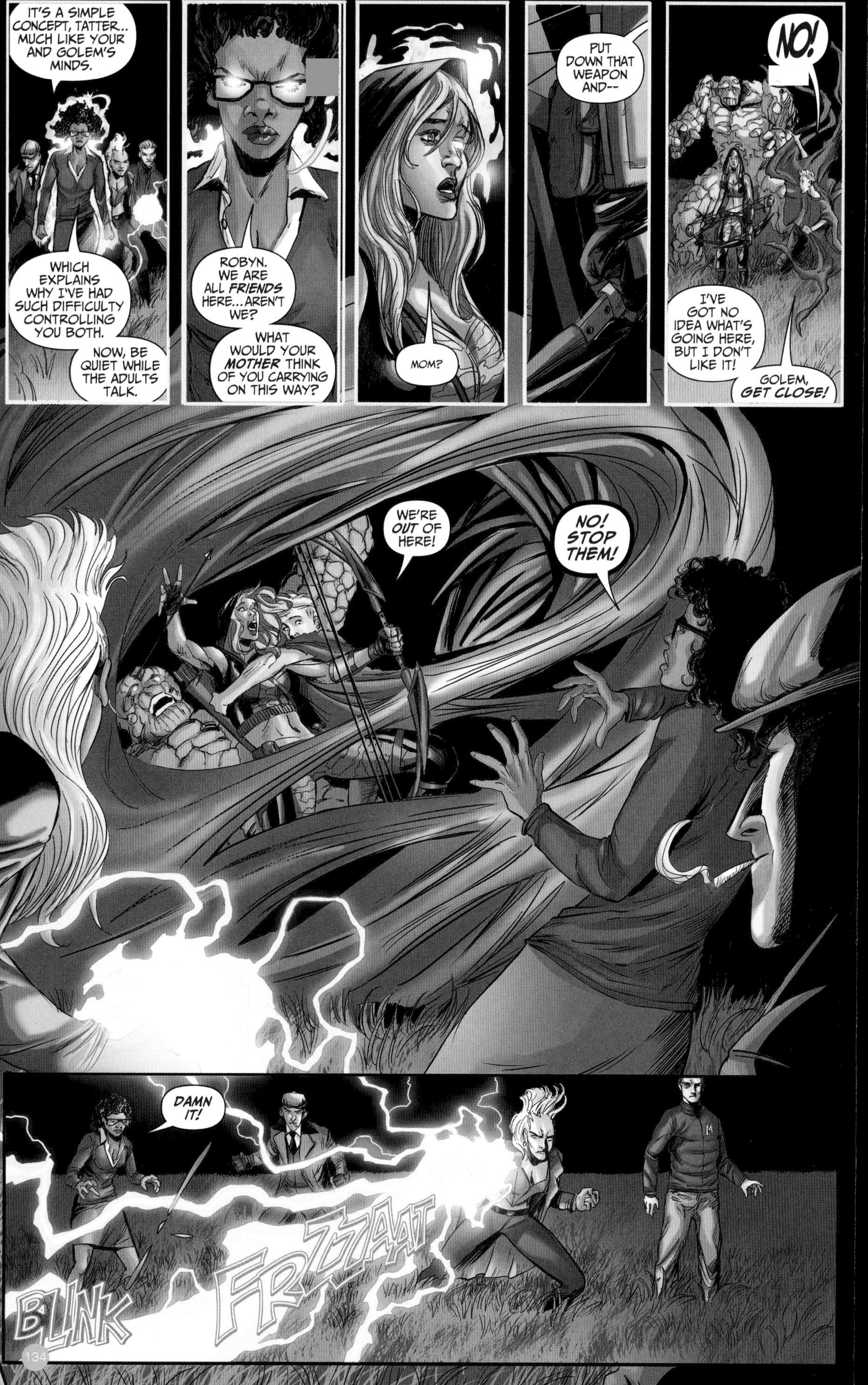

IT'S A SIMPLE CONCEPT, TATTER.. MUCH LIKE YOUR AND GOLEM'S MINDS.
WHICH EXPLAINS WHY I'VE HAD SUCH DIFFICULTY CONTROLLING YOU BOTH.
NOW, BE QUIET WHILE THE ADULTS TALK.
ROBYN. WE ARE ALL **FRIENDS** HERE... AREN'T WE?
WHAT WOULD YOUR **MOTHER** THINK OF YOU CARRYING ON THIS WAY?
MOM?
PUT DOWN THAT WEAPON AND--
NO!
I'VE GOT NO IDEA WHAT'S GOING HERE, BUT I DON'T LIKE IT!
GOLEM, **GET CLOSE!**
WE'RE *OUT OF* HERE!
NO! STOP THEM!
DAMN IT!
BLINK
FRZZZAAT

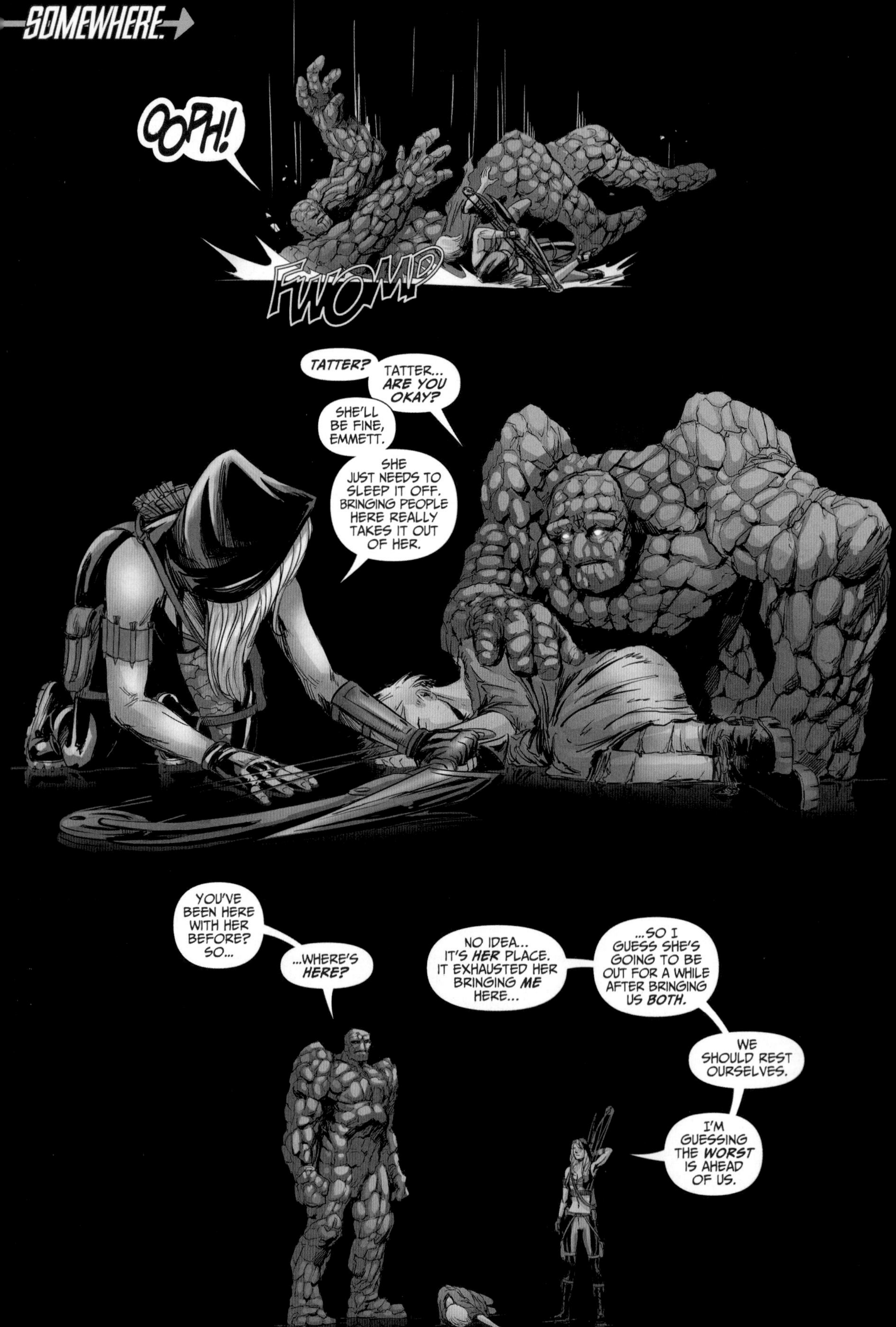
SOMEWHERE.
OOPH!
FWOMP
TATTER?
TATTER... ARE YOU OKAY?
SHE'LL BE FINE, EMMETT.
SHE JUST NEEDS TO SLEEP IT OFF. BRINGING PEOPLE HERE REALLY TAKES IT OUT OF HER.
YOU'VE BEEN HERE WITH HER BEFORE? SO...
...WHERE'S HERE?
NO IDEA... IT'S HER PLACE. IT EXHAUSTED HER BRINGING ME HERE...
...SO I GUESS SHE'S GOING TO BE OUT FOR A WHILE AFTER BRINGING US BOTH.
WE SHOULD REST OURSELVES.
I'M GUESSING THE WORST IS AHEAD OF US.

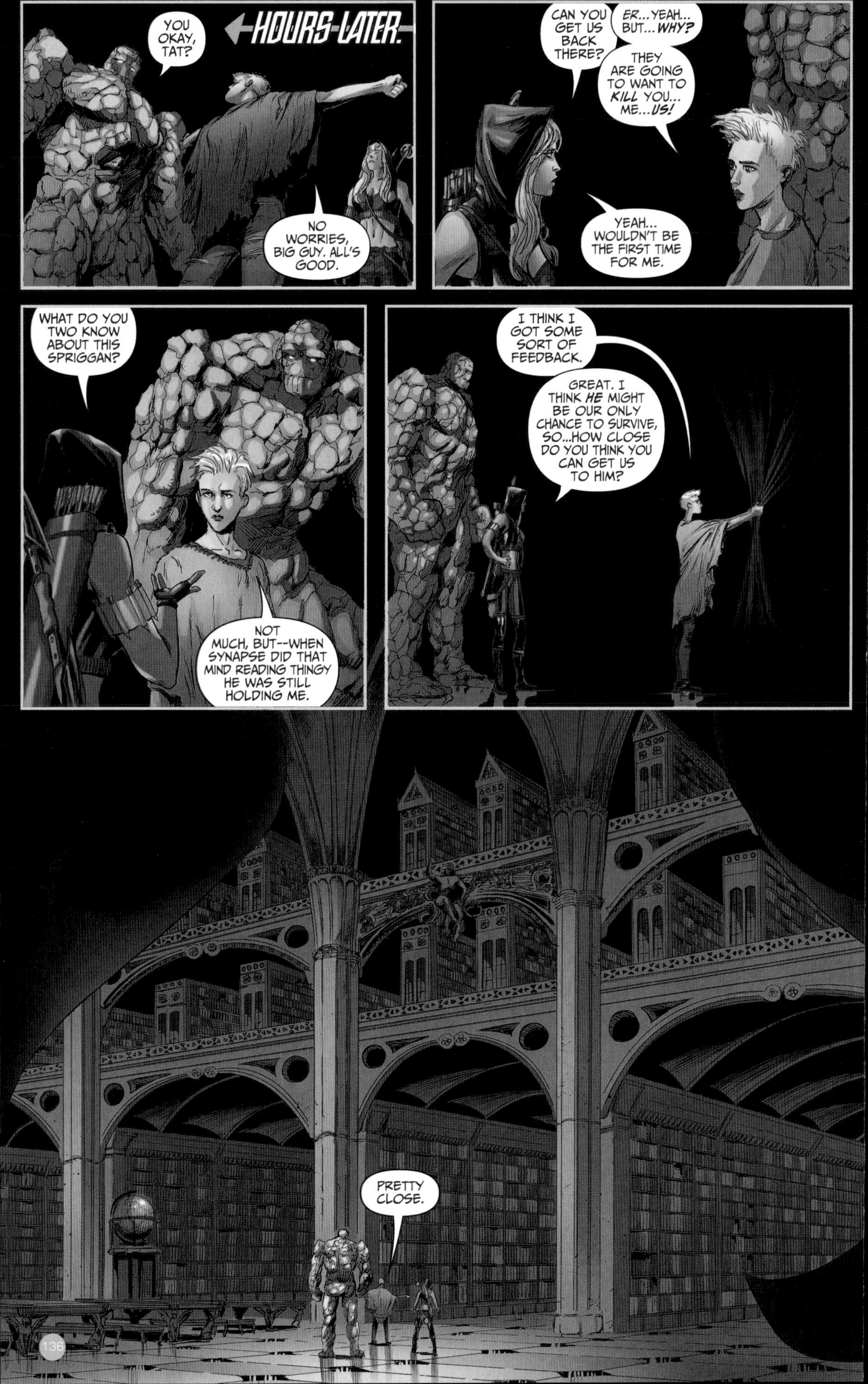
HOURS LATER.
YOU OKAY, TAT?
NO WORRIES, BIG GUY. ALL'S GOOD.
CAN YOU GET US BACK THERE?
ER...YEAH... BUT...WHY?
THEY ARE GOING TO WANT TO KILL YOU... ME...US!
YEAH... WOULDN'T BE THE FIRST TIME FOR ME.
WHAT DO YOU TWO KNOW ABOUT THIS SPRIGGAN?
NOT MUCH, BUT--WHEN SYNAPSE DID THAT MIND READING THINGY HE WAS STILL HOLDING ME.
I THINK I GOT SOME SORT OF FEEDBACK.
GREAT. I THINK HE MIGHT BE OUR ONLY CHANCE TO SURVIVE, SO...HOW CLOSE DO YOU THINK YOU CAN GET US TO HIM?
PRETTY CLOSE.

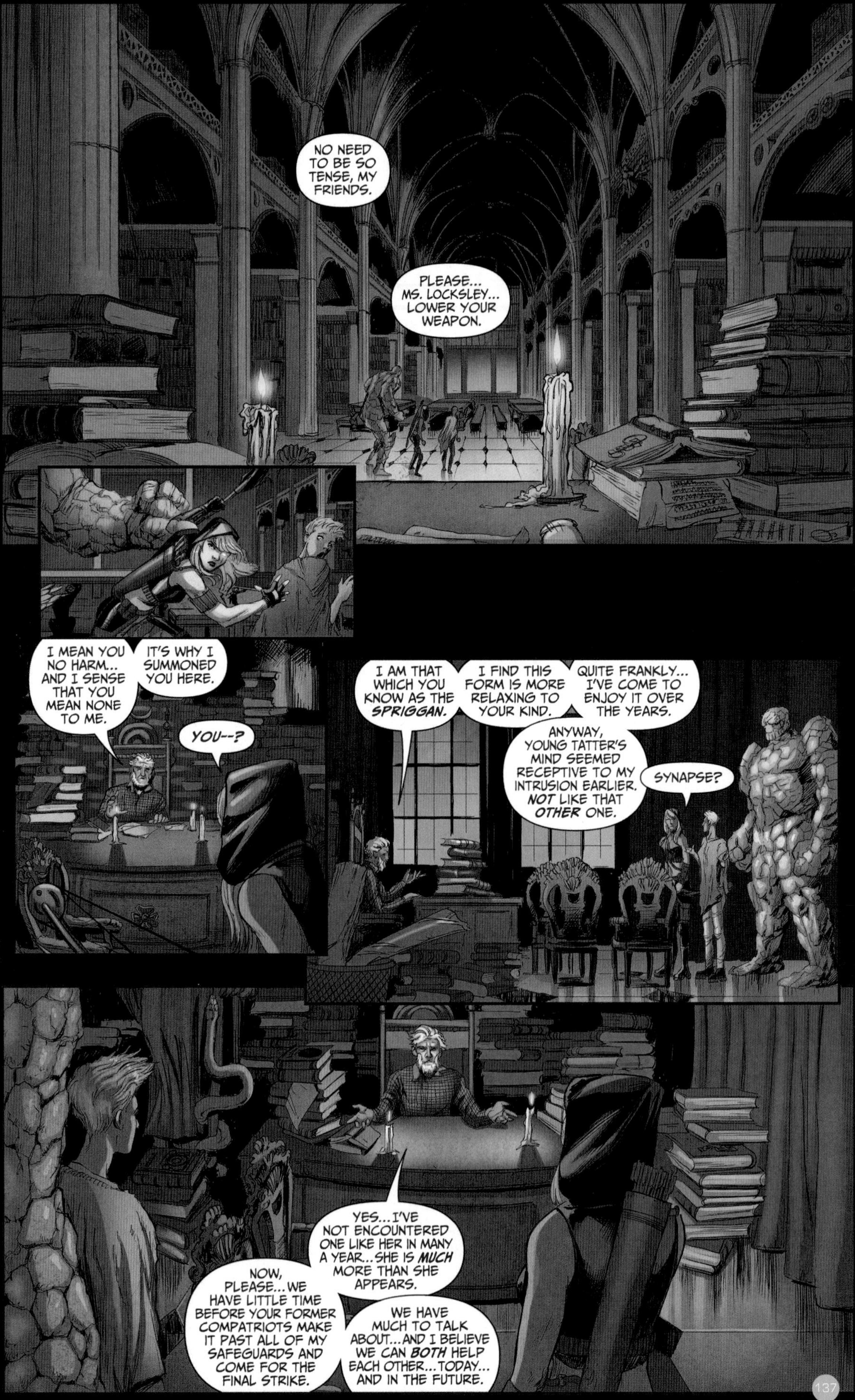
NO NEED TO BE SO TENSE, MY FRIENDS.
PLEASE... MS. LOCKSLEY... LOWER YOUR WEAPON.
I MEAN YOU NO HARM... AND I SENSE THAT YOU MEAN NONE TO ME.
IT'S WHY I SUMMONED YOU HERE.
YOU--?
I AM THAT WHICH YOU KNOW AS THE ***SPRIGGAN.***
I FIND THIS FORM IS MORE RELAXING TO YOUR KIND.
QUITE FRANKLY... I'VE COME TO ENJOY IT OVER THE YEARS.
ANYWAY, YOUNG TATTER'S MIND SEEMED RECEPTIVE TO MY INTRUSION EARLIER. ***NOT*** LIKE THAT ***OTHER*** ONE.
SYNAPSE?
YES... I'VE NOT ENCOUNTERED ONE LIKE HER IN MANY A YEAR... SHE IS ***MUCH*** MORE THAN SHE APPEARS.
NOW, PLEASE... WE HAVE LITTLE TIME BEFORE YOUR FORMER COMPATRIOTS MAKE IT PAST ALL OF MY SAFEGUARDS AND COME FOR THE FINAL STRIKE.
WE HAVE MUCH TO TALK ABOUT... AND I BELIEVE WE CAN ***BOTH*** HELP EACH OTHER... TODAY... AND IN THE FUTURE.

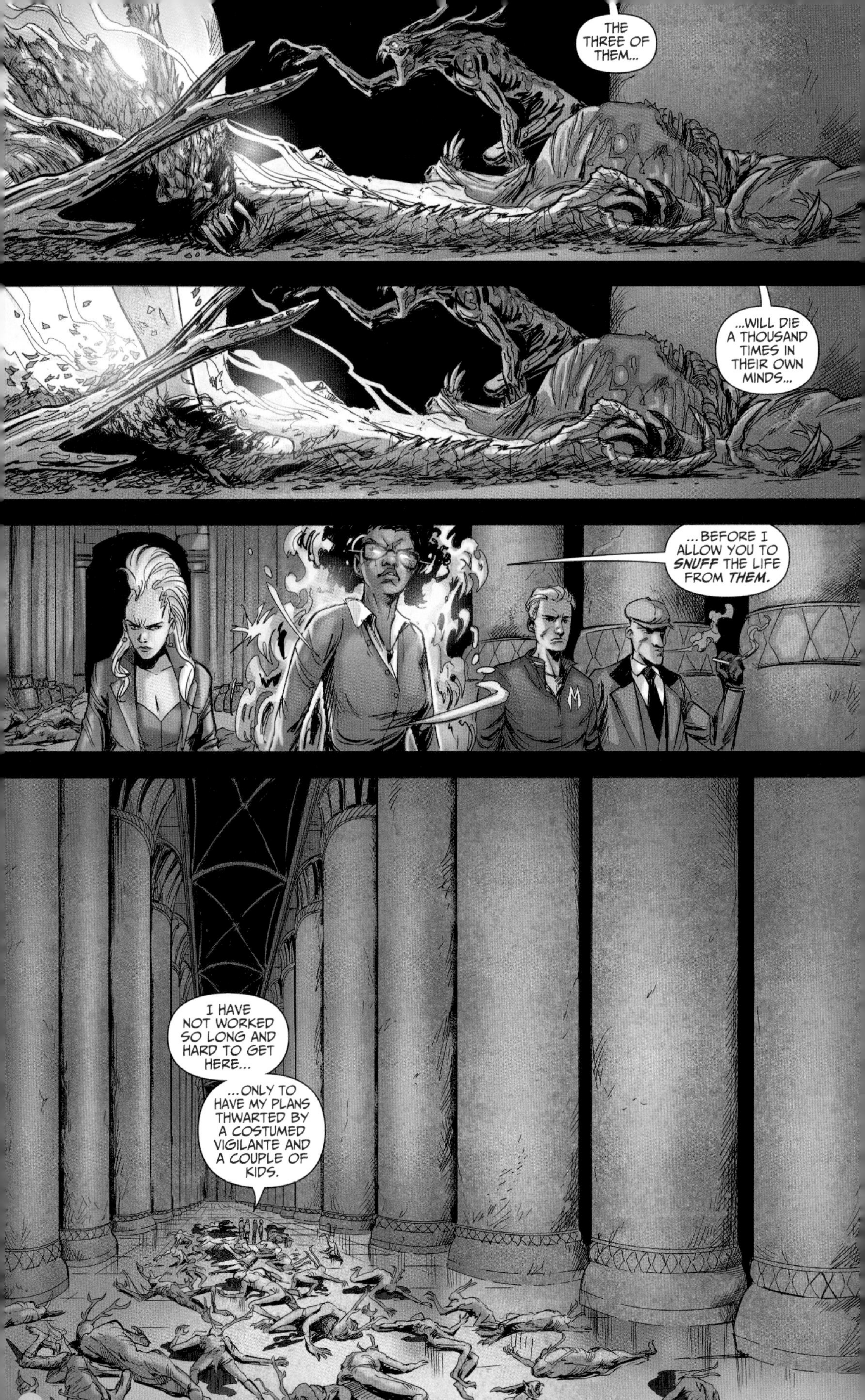
THE THREE OF THEM...
...WILL DIE A THOUSAND TIMES IN THEIR OWN MINDS...
...BEFORE I ALLOW YOU TO ***SNUFF*** THE LIFE FROM ***THEM.***
I HAVE NOT WORKED SO LONG AND HARD TO GET HERE...
...ONLY TO HAVE MY PLANS THWARTED BY A COSTUMED VIGILANTE AND A COUPLE OF KIDS.

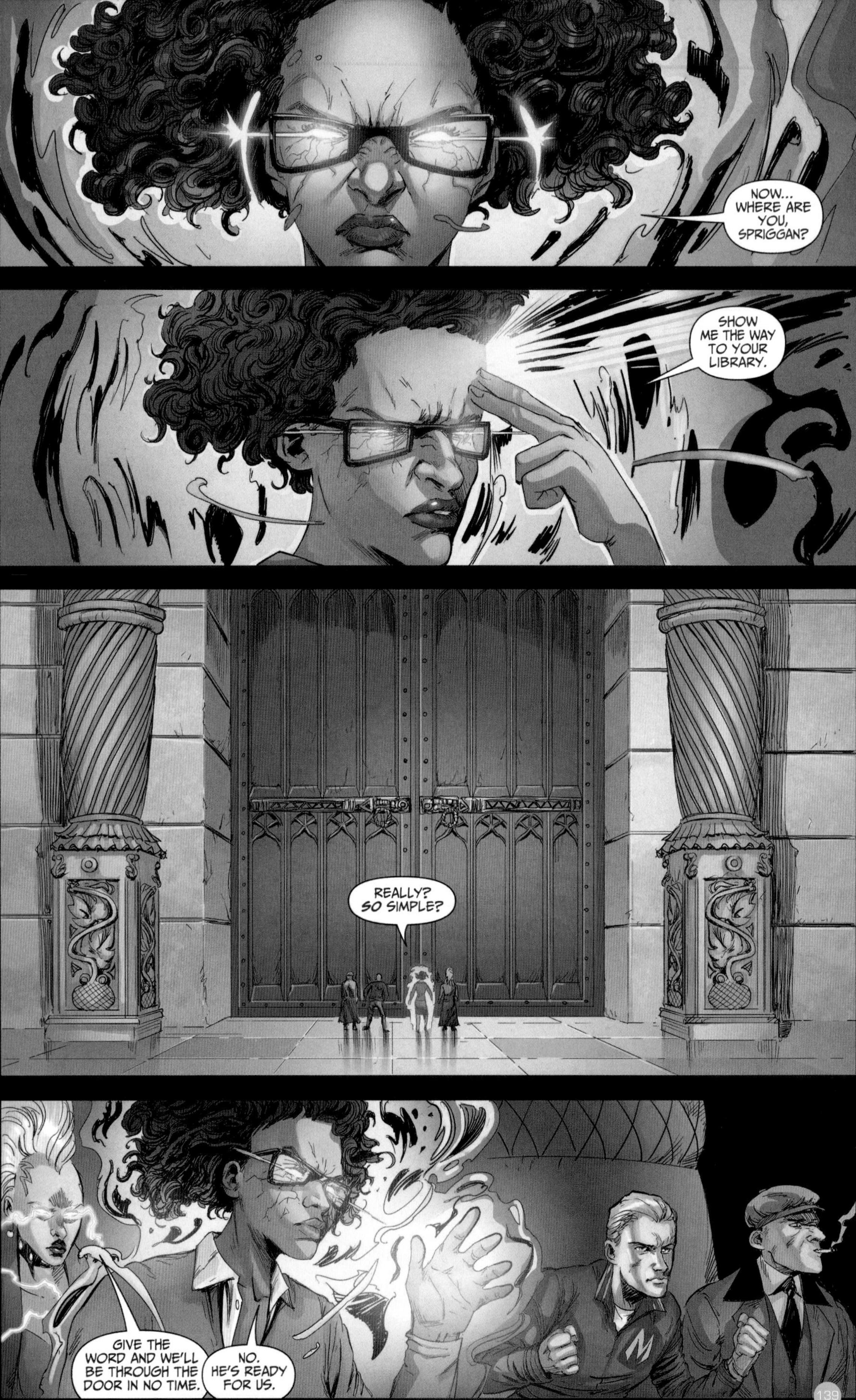
NOW... WHERE ARE YOU, SPRIGGAN?
SHOW ME THE WAY TO YOUR LIBRARY.
REALLY? SO SIMPLE?
GIVE THE WORD AND WE'LL BE THROUGH THE DOOR IN NO TIME.
NO. HE'S READY FOR US.

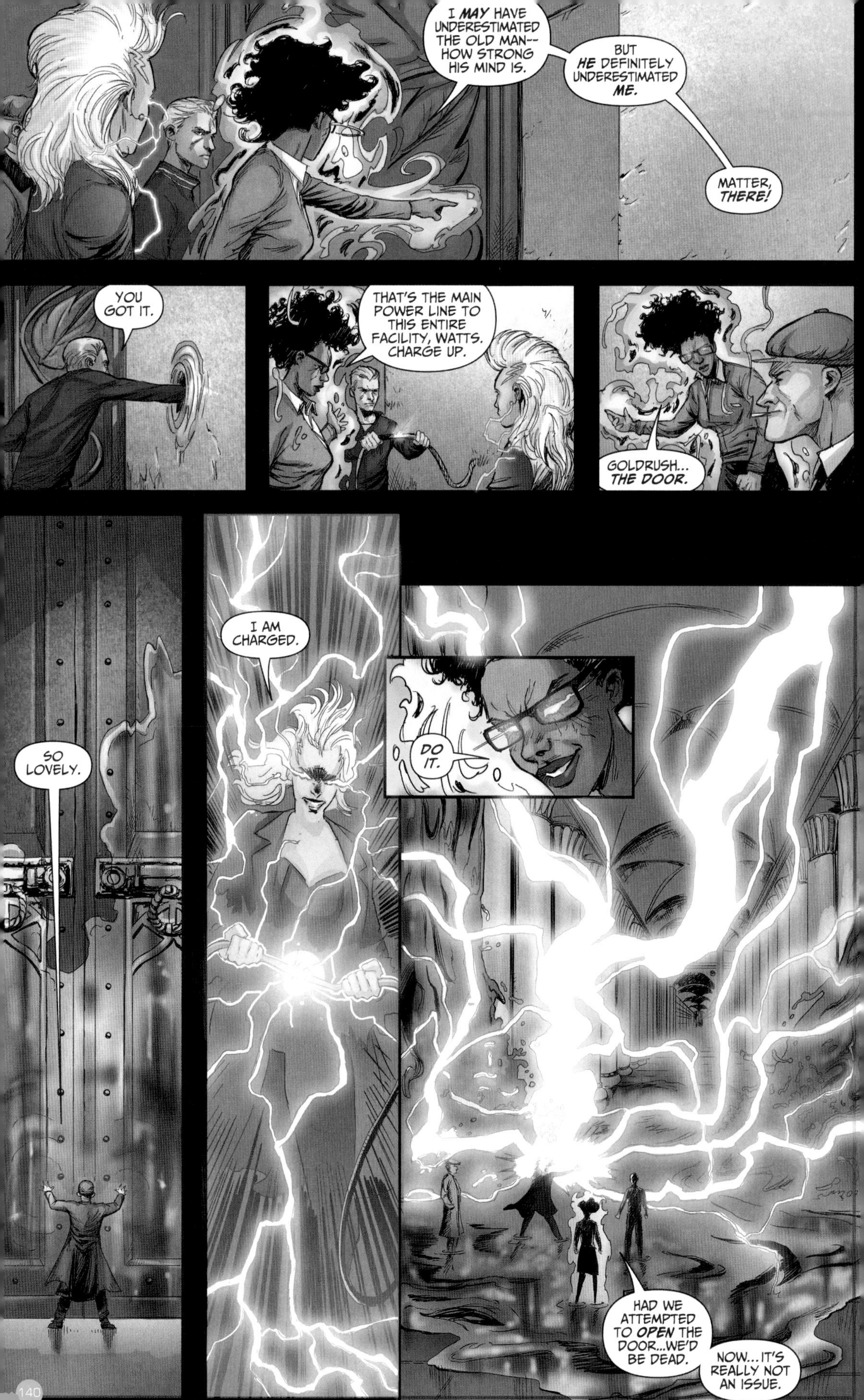
I *MAY* HAVE UNDERESTIMATED THE OLD MAN-- HOW STRONG HIS MIND IS.
BUT *HE* DEFINITELY UNDERESTIMATED *ME.*
MATTER, *THERE!*
YOU GOT IT.
THAT'S THE MAIN POWER LINE TO THIS ENTIRE FACILITY, WATTS. CHARGE UP.
GOLDRUSH... *THE DOOR.*
SO LOVELY.
I AM CHARGED.
DO IT.
HAD WE ATTEMPTED TO *OPEN* THE DOOR...WE'D BE DEAD.
NOW... IT'S REALLY NOT AN ISSUE.

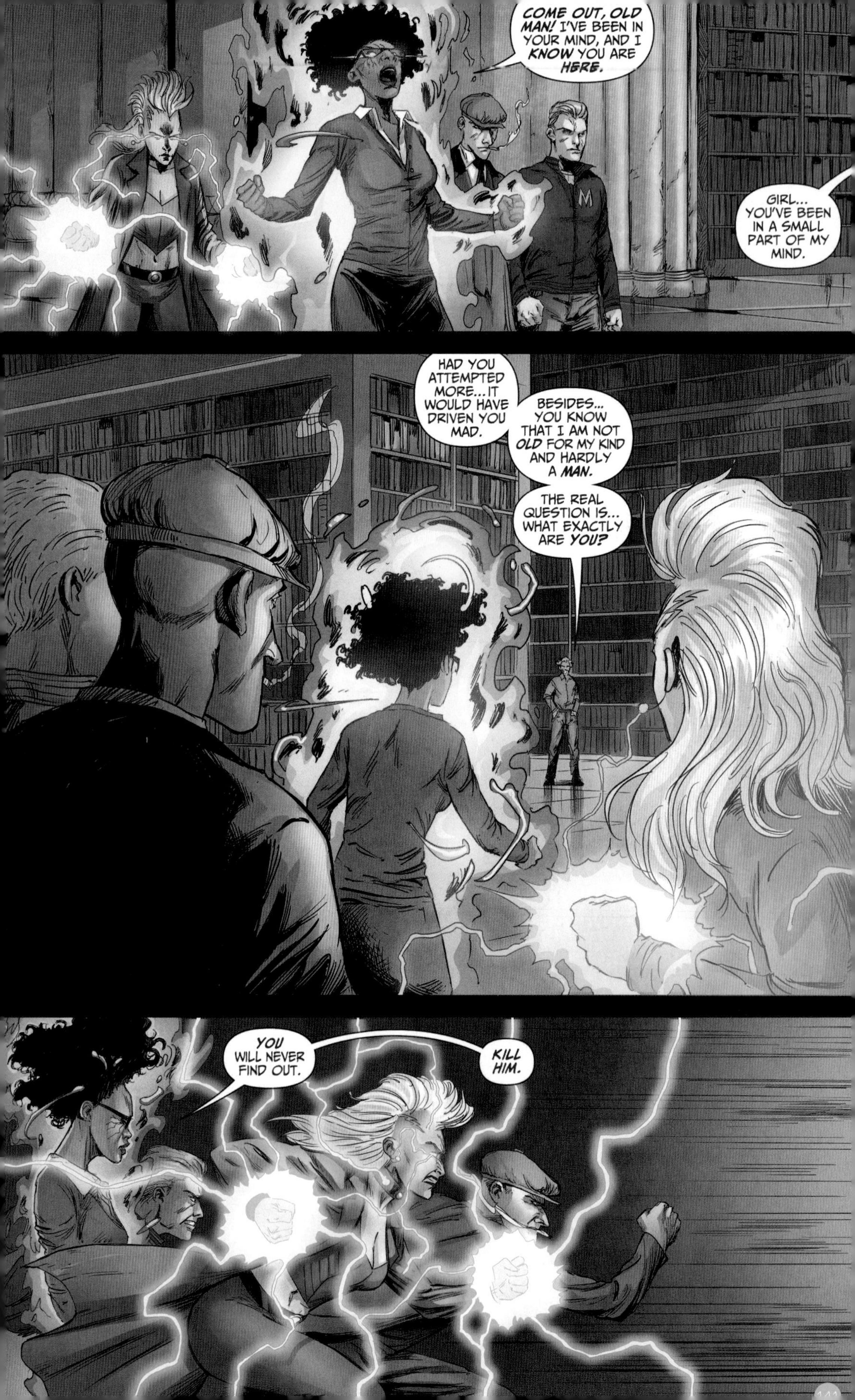
COME OUT, OLD MAN! I'VE BEEN IN YOUR MIND, AND I KNOW YOU ARE HERE.
GIRL... YOU'VE BEEN IN A SMALL PART OF MY MIND.
HAD YOU ATTEMPTED MORE... IT WOULD HAVE DRIVEN YOU MAD.
BESIDES... YOU KNOW THAT I AM NOT OLD FOR MY KIND AND HARDLY A MAN.
THE REAL QUESTION IS... WHAT EXACTLY ARE YOU?
YOU WILL NEVER FIND OUT.
KILL HIM.

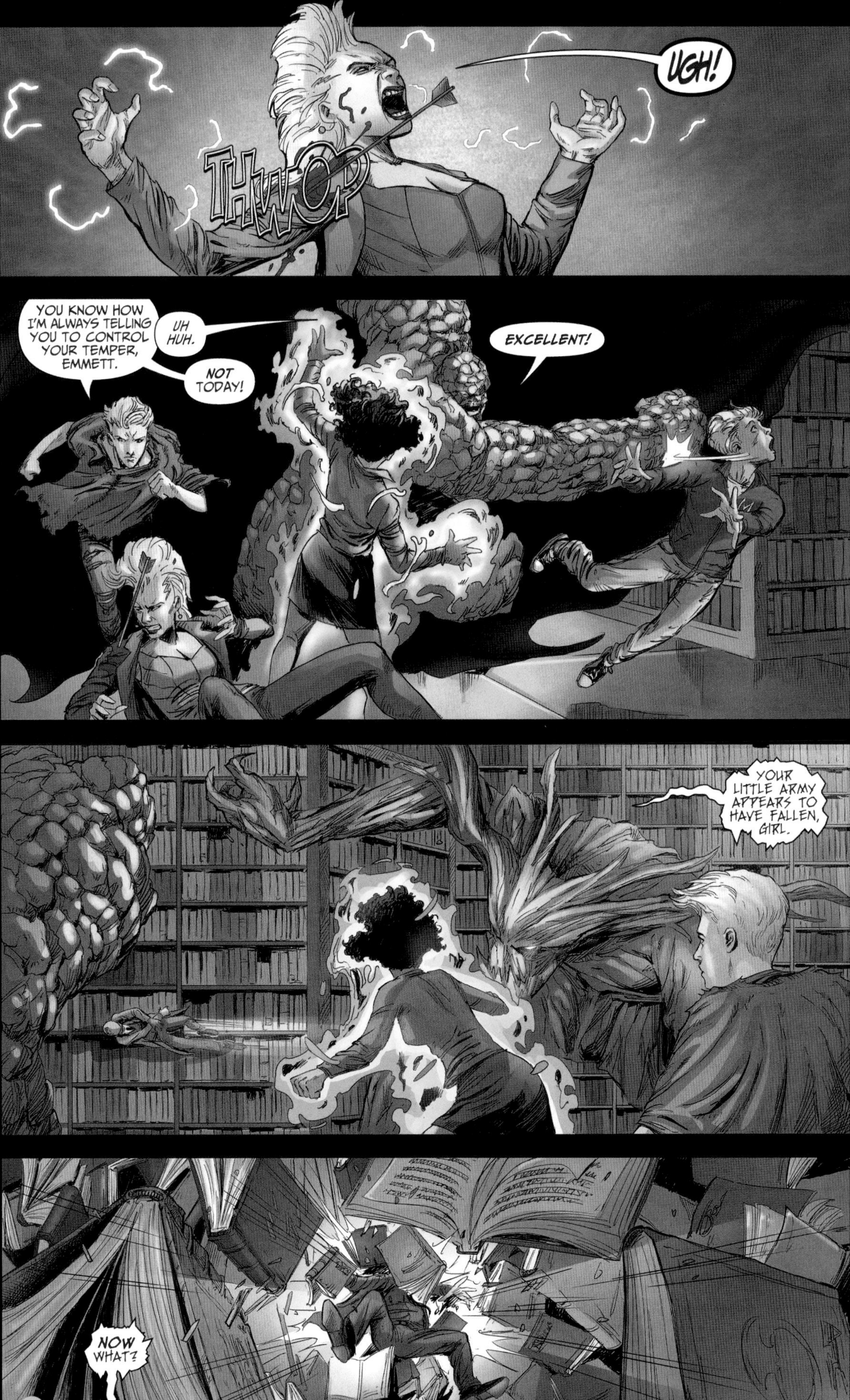
UGH!
THWOCP
YOU KNOW HOW I'M ALWAYS TELLING YOU TO CONTROL YOUR TEMPER, EMMETT.
UH HUH.
NOT TODAY!
EXCELLENT!
YOUR LITTLE ARMY APPEARS TO HAVE FALLEN, GIRL.
NOW WHAT?

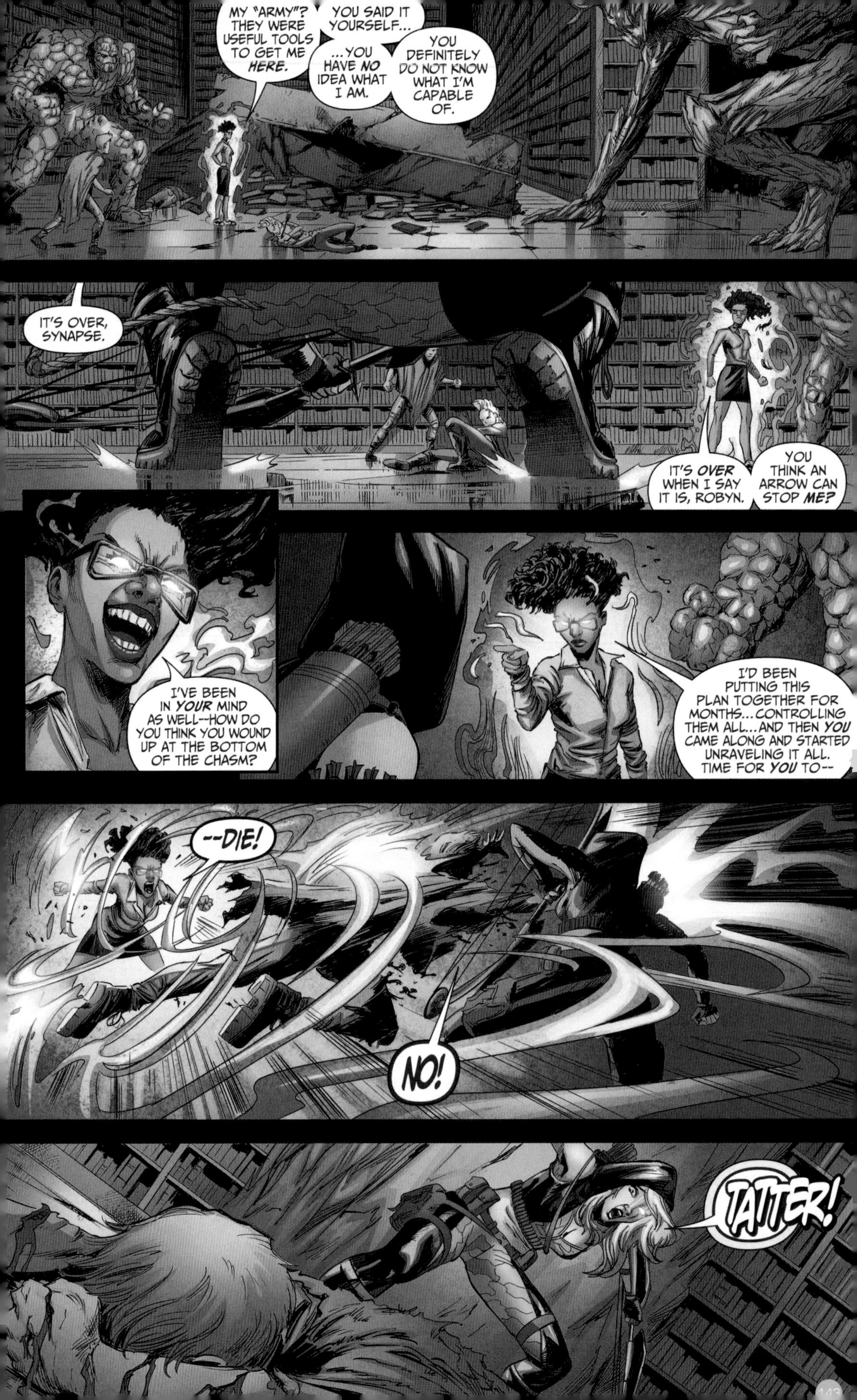
MY "ARMY"? THEY WERE USEFUL TOOLS TO GET ME **HERE.**
YOU SAID IT YOURSELF...
...YOU HAVE **NO** IDEA WHAT I AM.
YOU DEFINITELY DO NOT KNOW WHAT I'M CAPABLE OF.
IT'S OVER, SYNAPSE.
IT'S **OVER** WHEN I SAY IT IS, ROBYN.
YOU THINK AN ARROW CAN STOP **ME?**
I'VE BEEN IN **YOUR** MIND AS WELL--HOW DO YOU THINK YOU WOUND UP AT THE BOTTOM OF THE CHASM?
I'D BEEN PUTTING THIS PLAN TOGETHER FOR MONTHS...CONTROLLING THEM ALL...AND THEN **YOU** CAME ALONG AND STARTED UNRAVELING IT ALL. TIME FOR **YOU** TO--
--DIE!
NO!
TATTER!

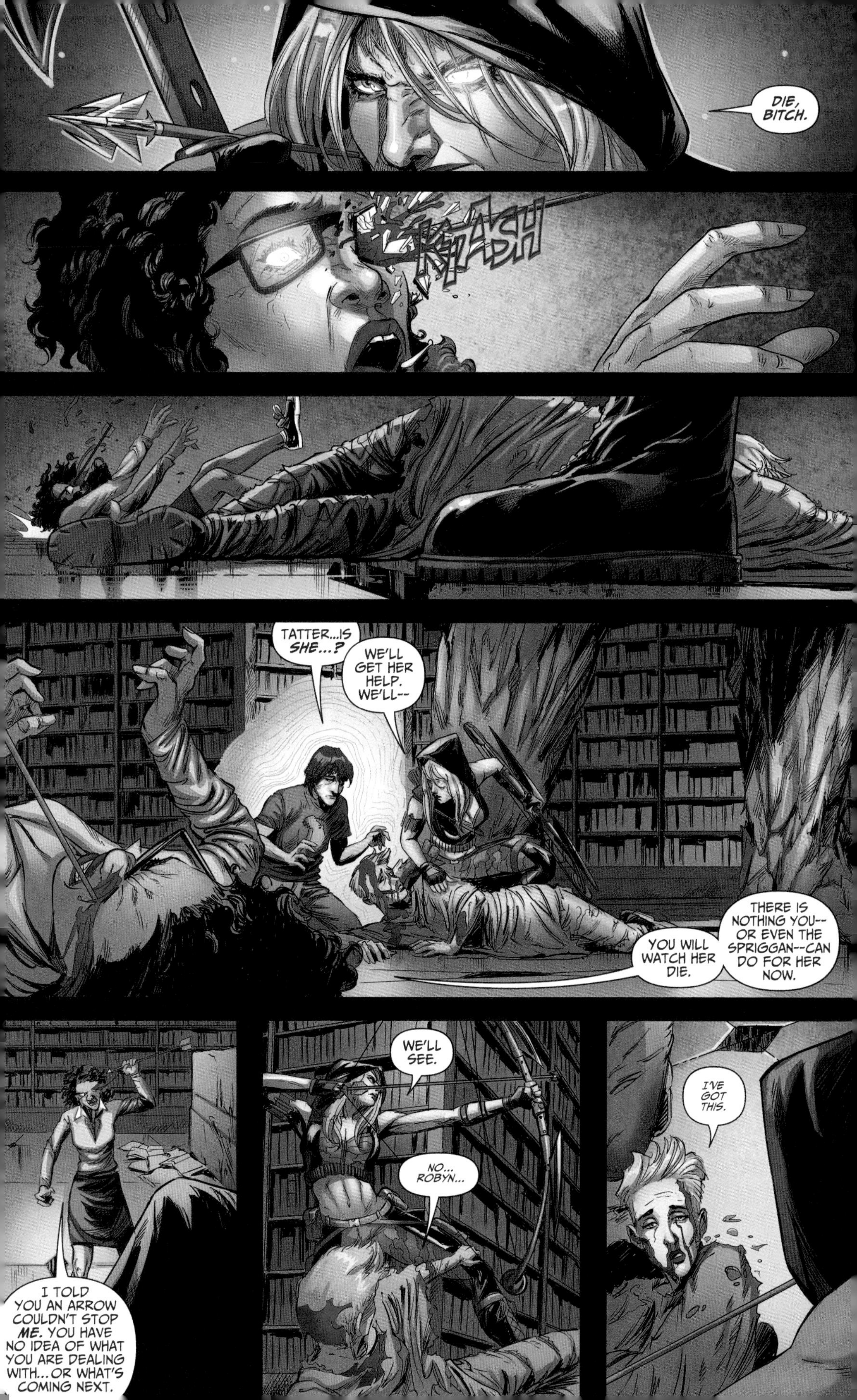
DIE, BITCH.
KRASH
TATTER...IS SHE...?
WE'LL GET HER HELP. WE'LL--
YOU WILL WATCH HER DIE.
THERE IS NOTHING YOU--OR EVEN THE SPRIGGAN--CAN DO FOR HER NOW.
I TOLD YOU AN ARROW COULDN'T STOP ME. YOU HAVE NO IDEA OF WHAT YOU ARE DEALING WITH...OR WHAT'S COMING NEXT.
WE'LL SEE.
NO... ROBYN...
I'VE GOT THIS.

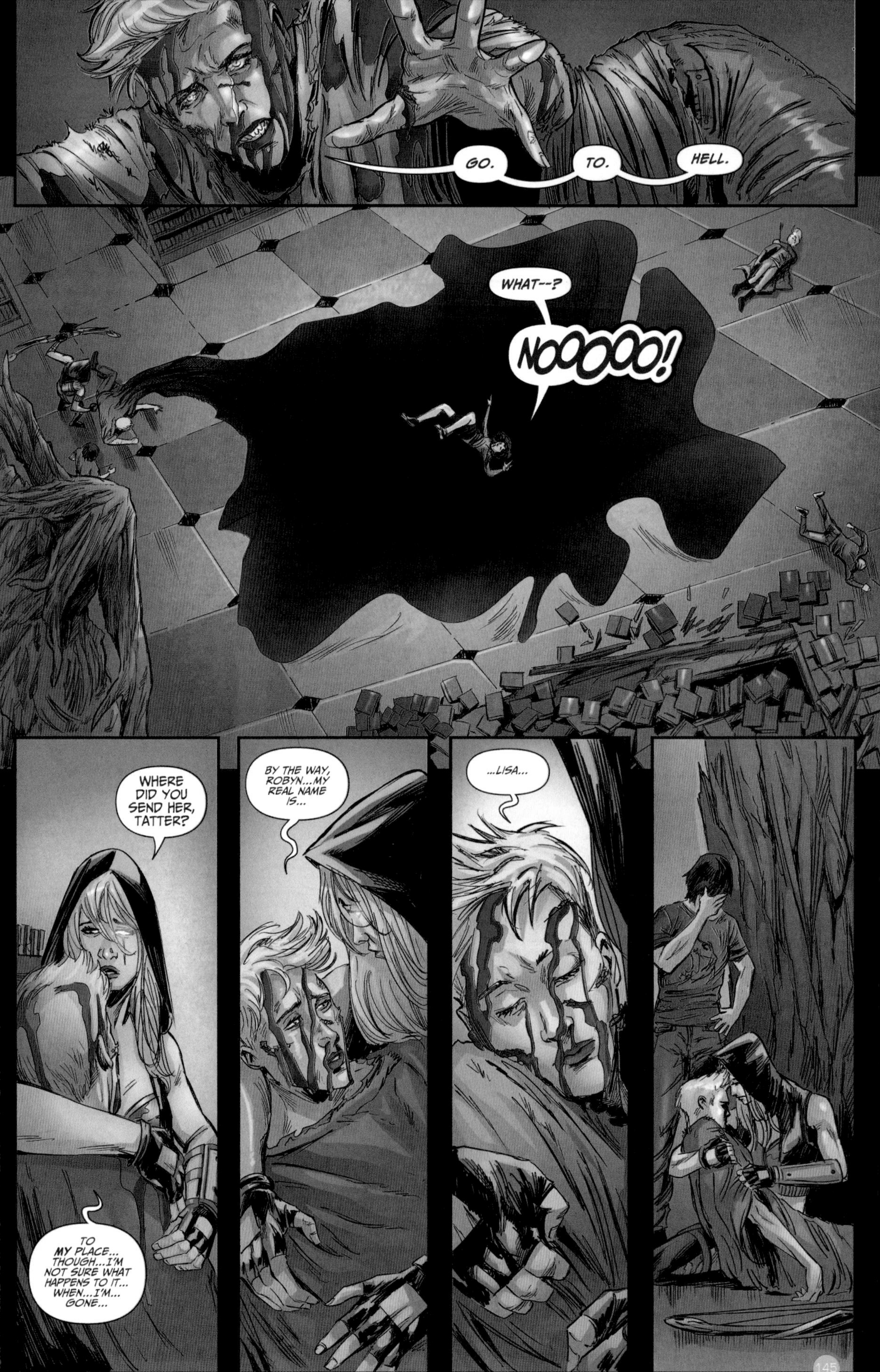
GO.
TO.
HELL.
WHAT--?
NOOOOO!
WHERE DID YOU SEND HER, TATTER?
TO MY PLACE... THOUGH...I'M NOT SURE WHAT HAPPENS TO IT... WHEN...I'M... GONE...
BY THE WAY, ROBYN...MY REAL NAME IS...
...LISA...

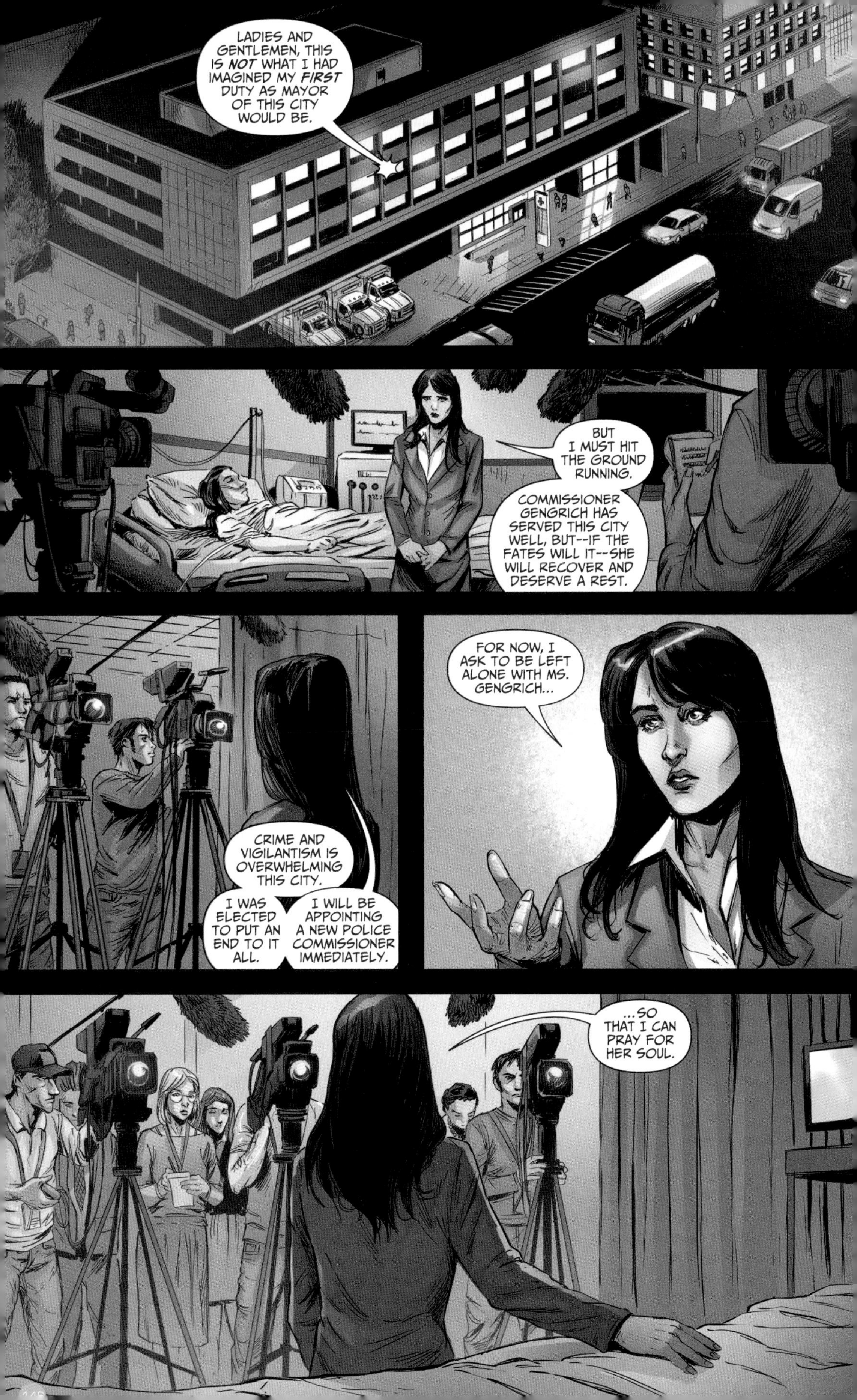
LADIES AND GENTLEMEN, THIS IS *NOT* WHAT I HAD IMAGINED MY *FIRST* DUTY AS MAYOR OF THIS CITY WOULD BE.
BUT I MUST HIT THE GROUND RUNNING.
COMMISSIONER GENGRICH HAS SERVED THIS CITY WELL, BUT--IF THE FATES WILL IT--SHE WILL RECOVER AND DESERVE A REST.
CRIME AND VIGILANTISM IS OVERWHELMING THIS CITY.
I WAS ELECTED TO PUT AN END TO IT ALL.
I WILL BE APPOINTING A NEW POLICE COMMISSIONER IMMEDIATELY.
FOR NOW, I ASK TO BE LEFT ALONE WITH MS. GENGRICH...
...SO THAT I CAN PRAY FOR HER SOUL.

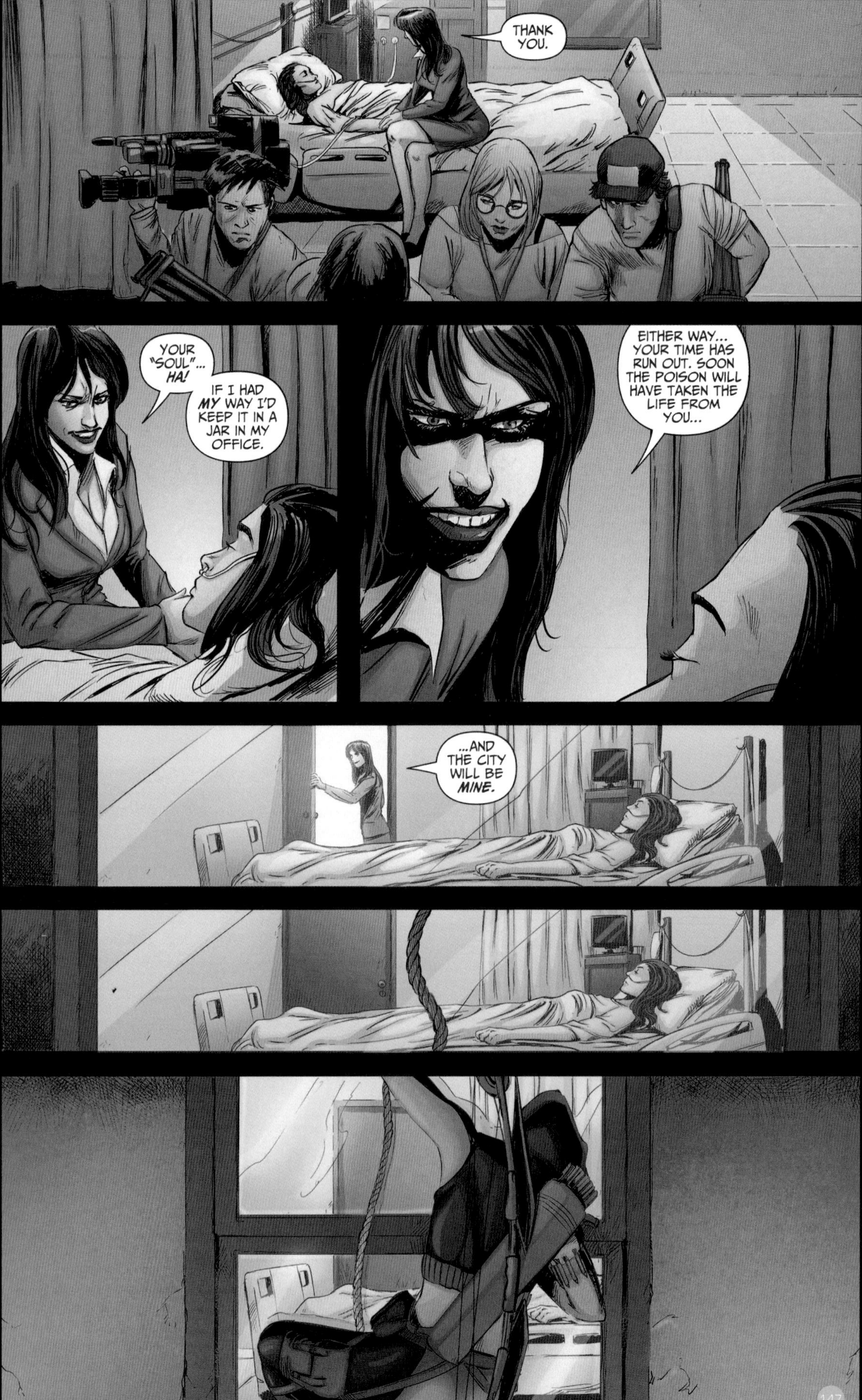
THANK YOU.
YOUR "SOUL"... HA!
IF I HAD MY WAY I'D KEEP IT IN A JAR IN MY OFFICE.
EITHER WAY... YOUR TIME HAS RUN OUT. SOON THE POISON WILL HAVE TAKEN THE LIFE FROM YOU...
...AND THE CITY WILL BE MINE.

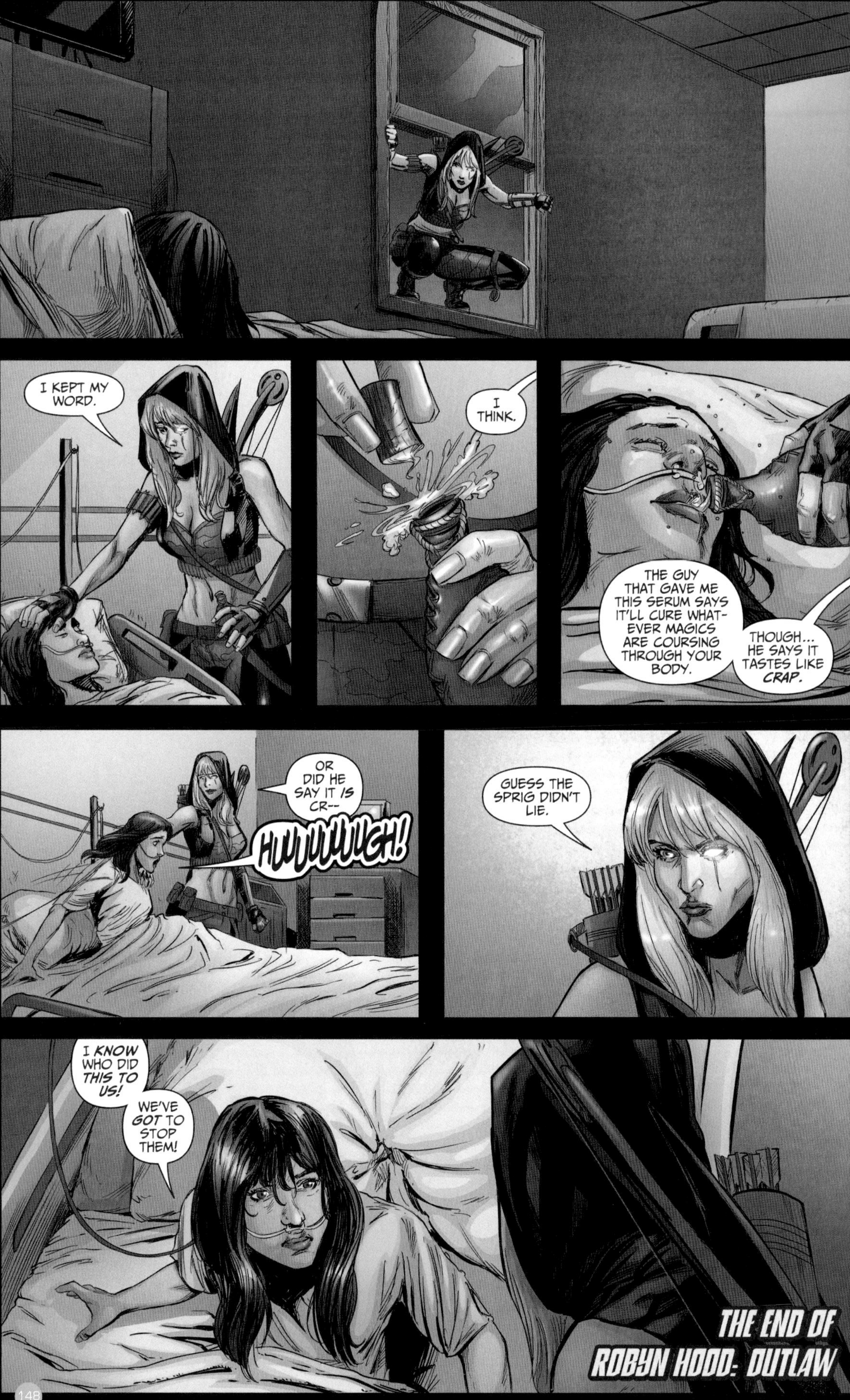

I KEPT MY WORD.
I THINK.
THE GUY THAT GAVE ME THIS SERUM SAYS IT'LL CURE WHAT-EVER MAGICS ARE COURSING THROUGH YOUR BODY.
THOUGH... HE SAYS IT TASTES LIKE *CRAP.*
OR DID HE SAY IT *IS* CR--
HUUUUUUUGH!
GUESS THE SPRIG DIDN'T LIE.
I *KNOW* WHO DID *THIS* TO *US!*
WE'VE *GOT* TO STOP THEM!
THE END OF
ROBYN HOOD: OUTLAW

ROBYN HOOD
OUTLAW

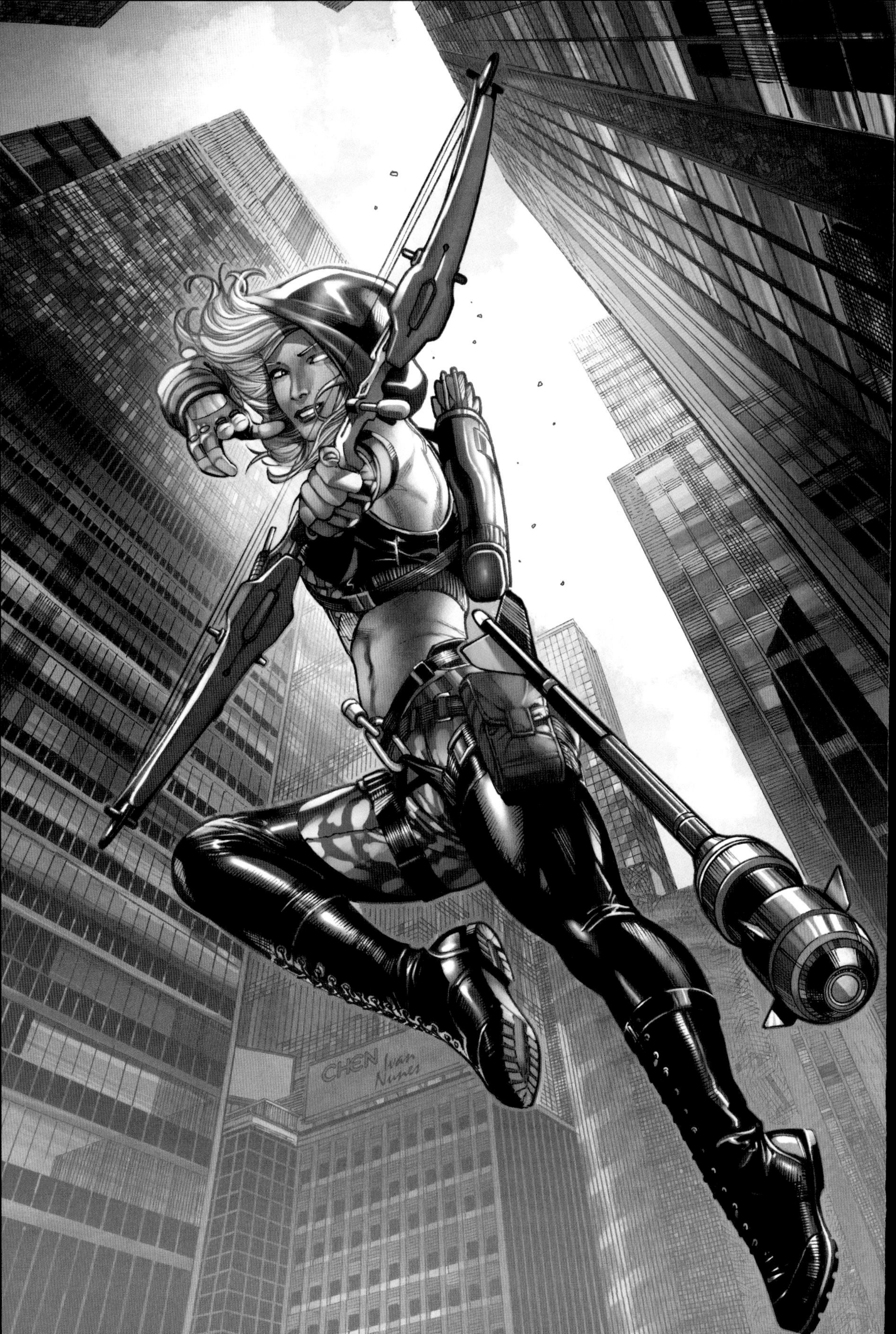
CHEN
Ivan
Nunes

ROBYN HOOD: OUTLAW 1 • COVER A
Artwork by Sean Chen • Colors by Ivan Nunes

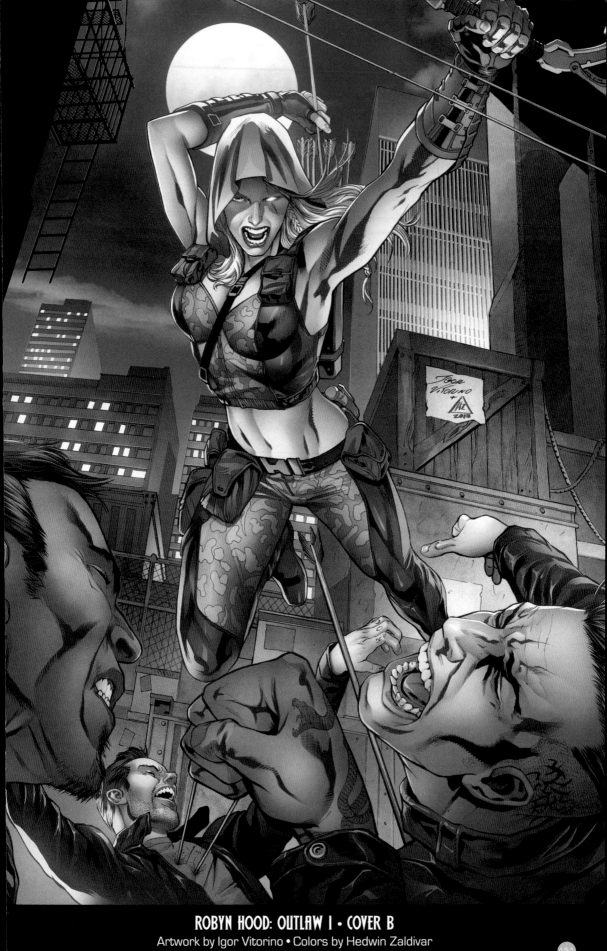

ROBYN HOOD: OUTLAW 1 • COVER B
Artwork by Igor Vitorino • Colors by Hedwin Zaldivar

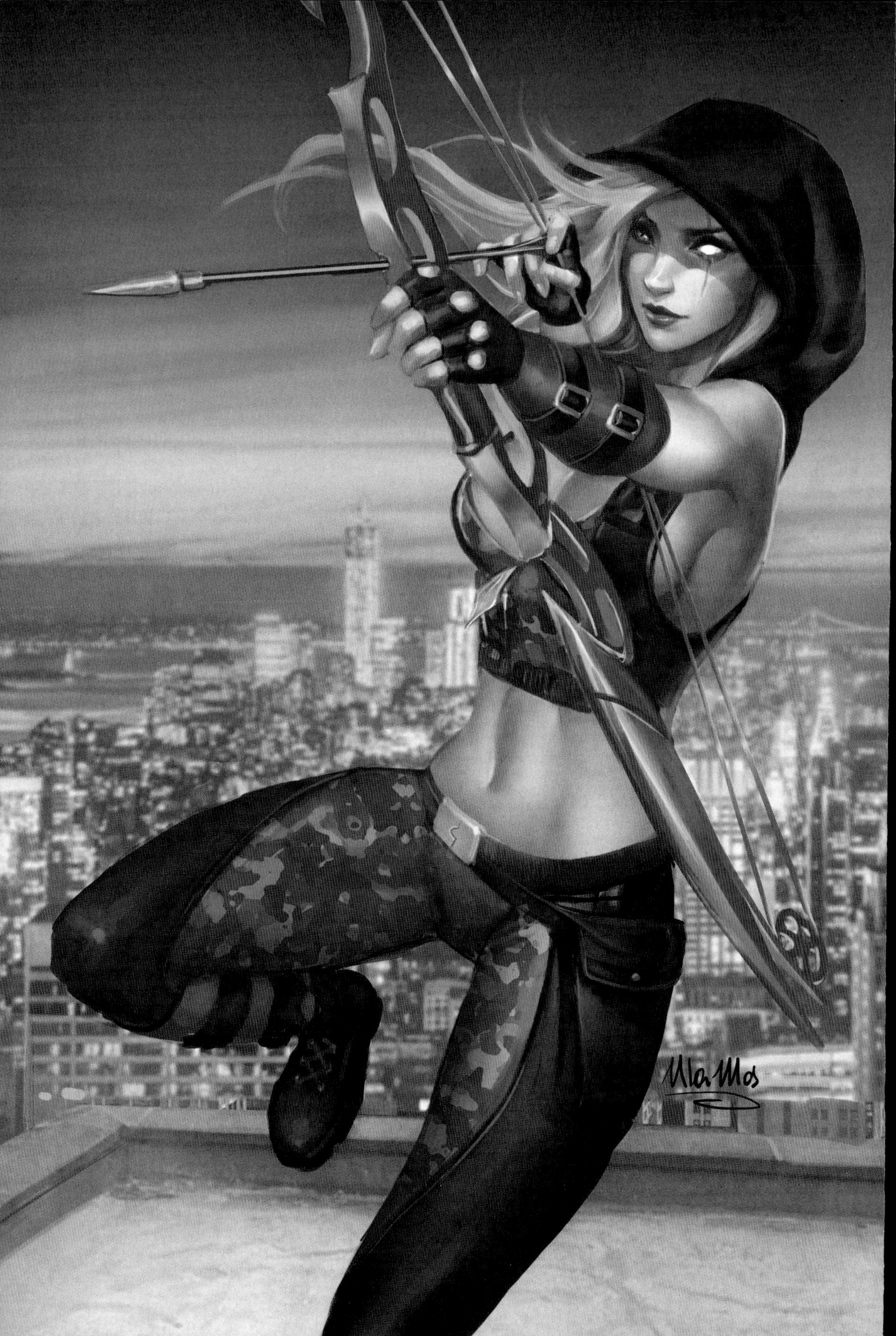

ROBYN HOOD: OUTLAW 1 • COVER C

Artwork by Ula Mos

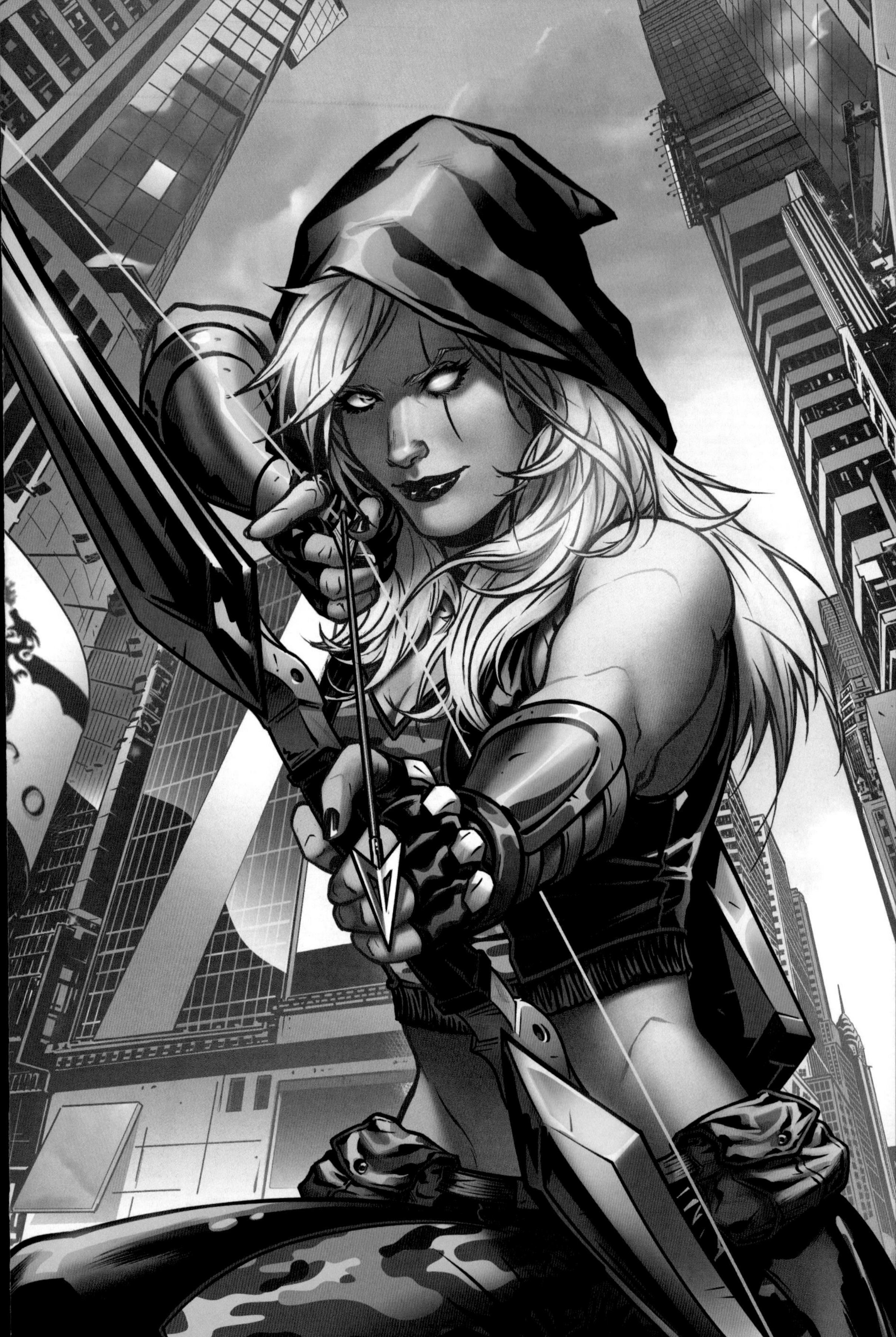

ROBYN HOOD: OUTLAW 1 • COVER D

Artwork by Riveiro • Colors by Ceci de la Cruz

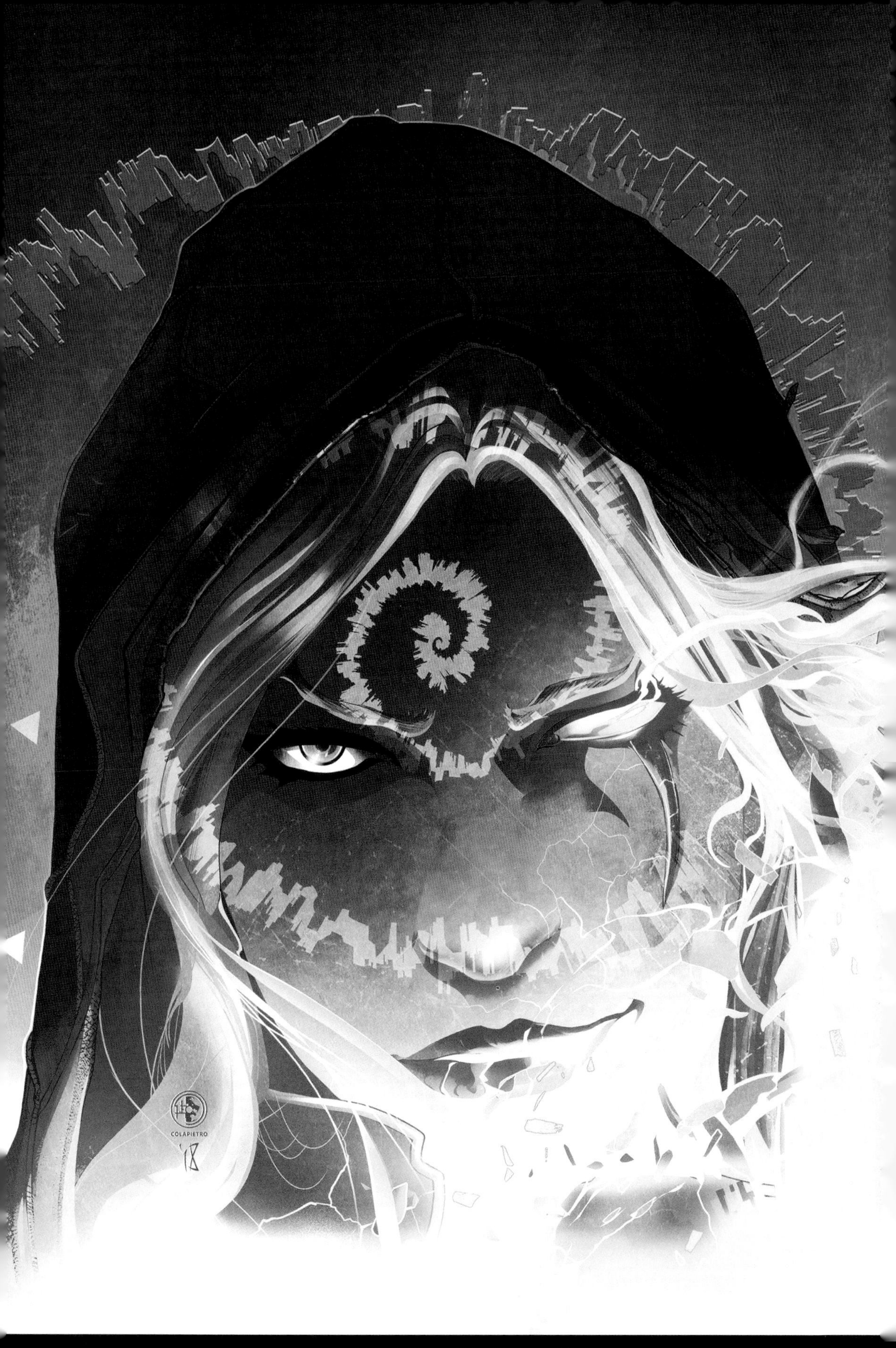
COLAPIETRO

ROBYN HOOD: OUTLAW 1 • COVER E

Artwork by Leonardo Colapietro

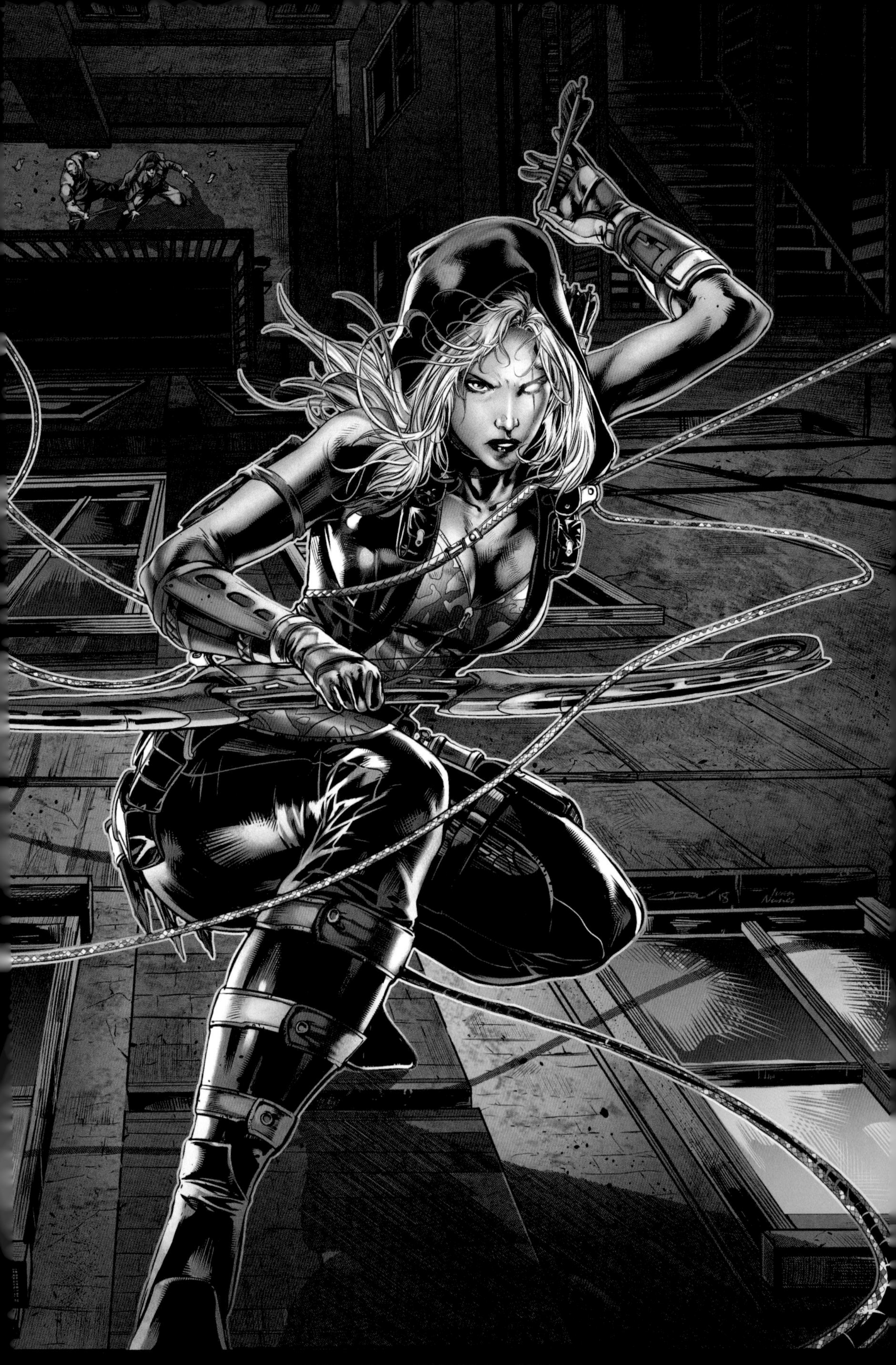

ROBYN HOOD: OUTLAW 2 • COVER A
Artwork by Caanan White • Colors by Ivan Nunes

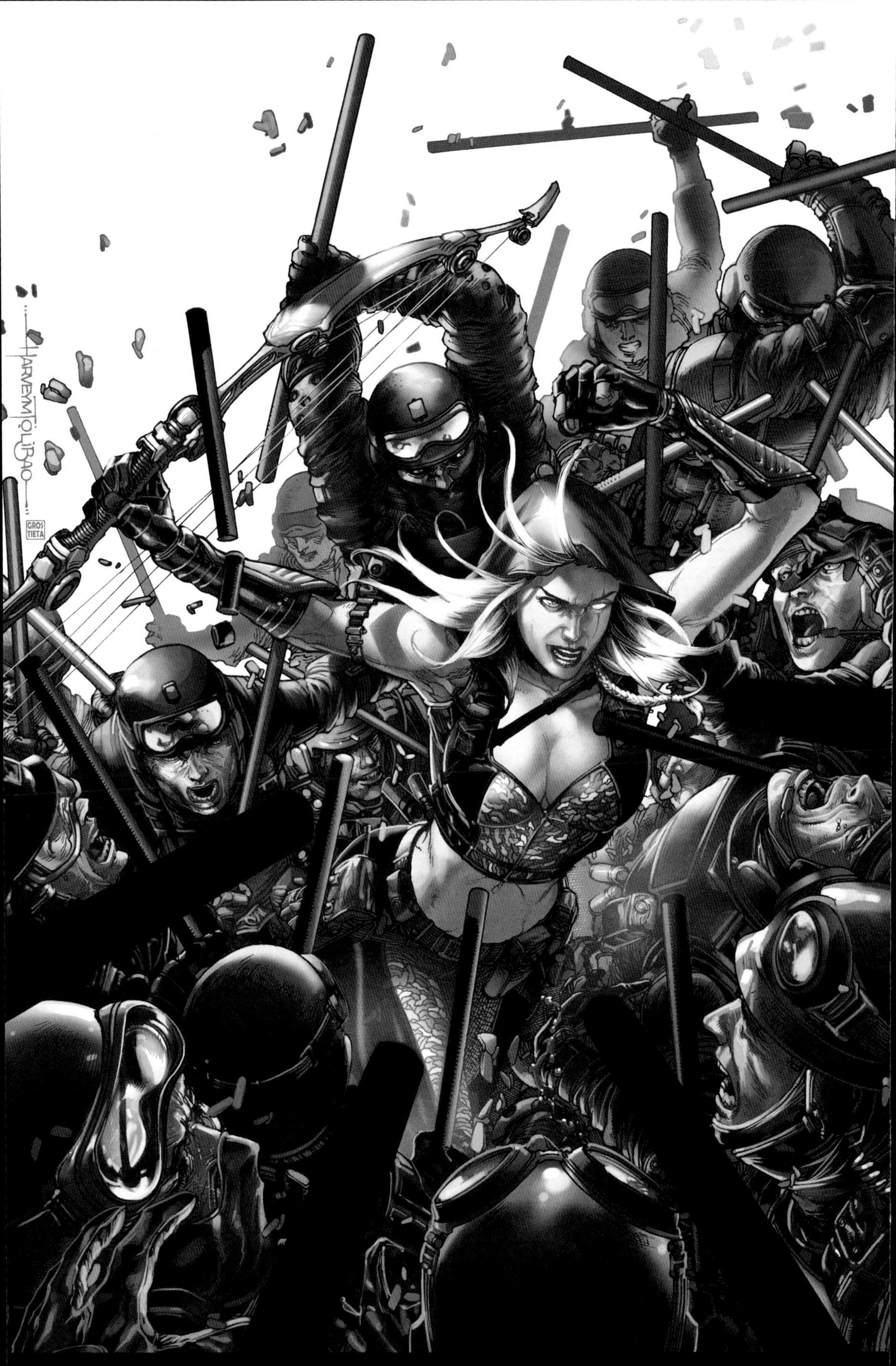

ROBYN HOOD: OUTLAW 2 • COVER B

Artwork by Harvey Tolibao • Colors by Grostieta

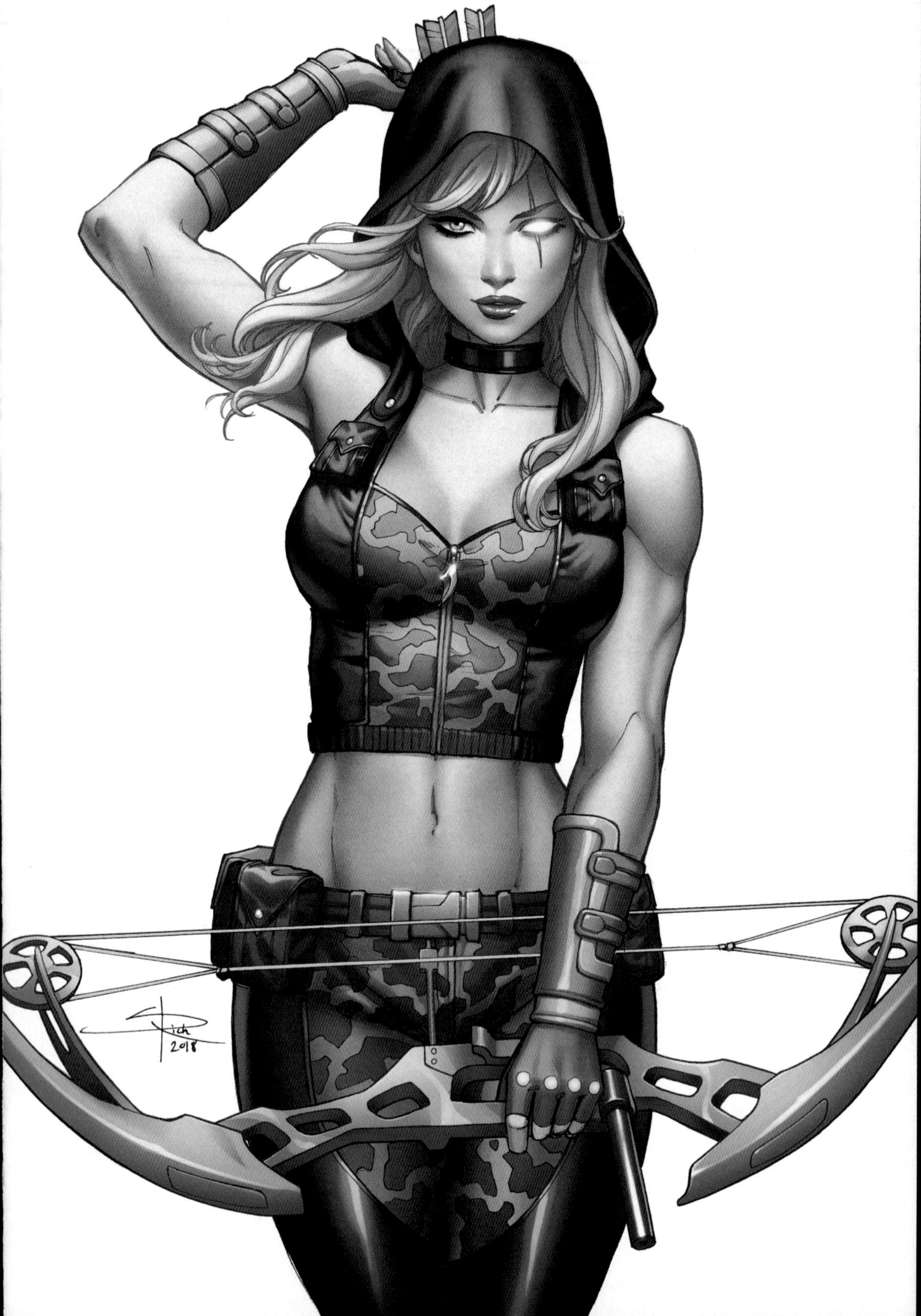
Rich
2018

ROBYN HOOD: OUTLAW 2 • COVER C

Artwork by Sabine Rich

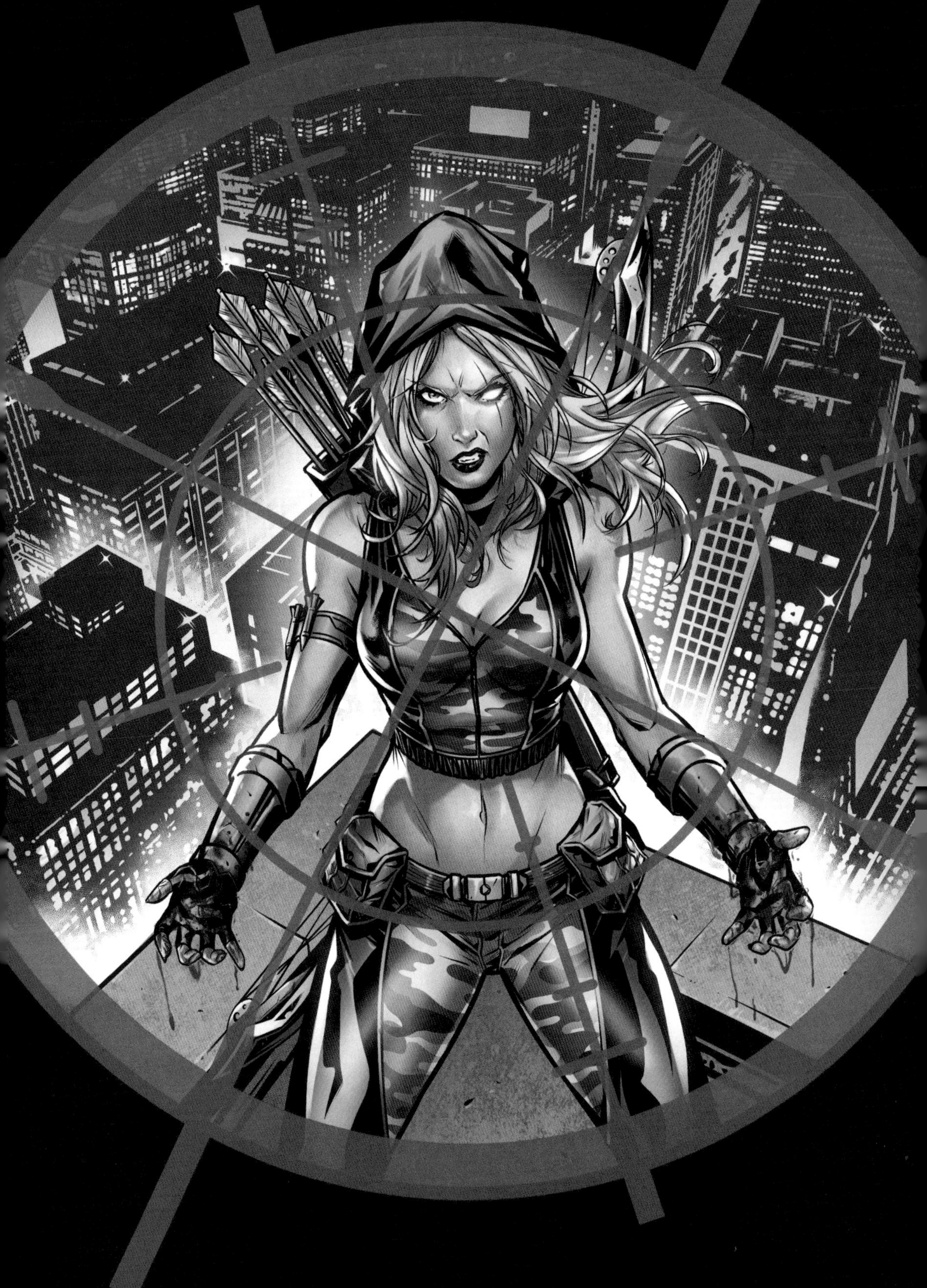

ROBYN HOOD: OUTLAW 2 • COVER D

Artwork by Riveiro • Colors by Mohan Sivakami

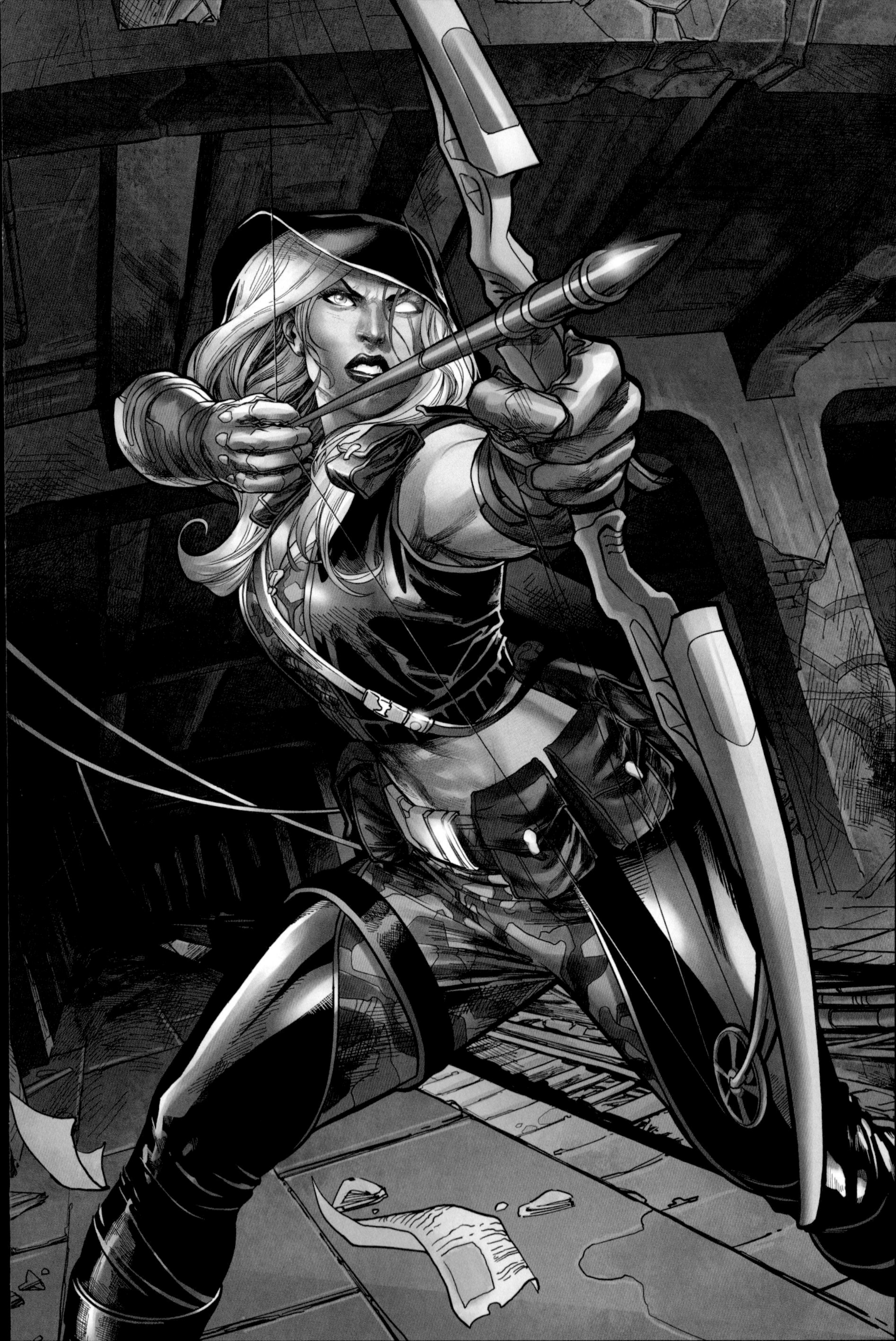

ROBYN HOOD: OUTLAW 3 • COVER A

Artwork by Martin Coccolo • Colors by Mohan Sivakami

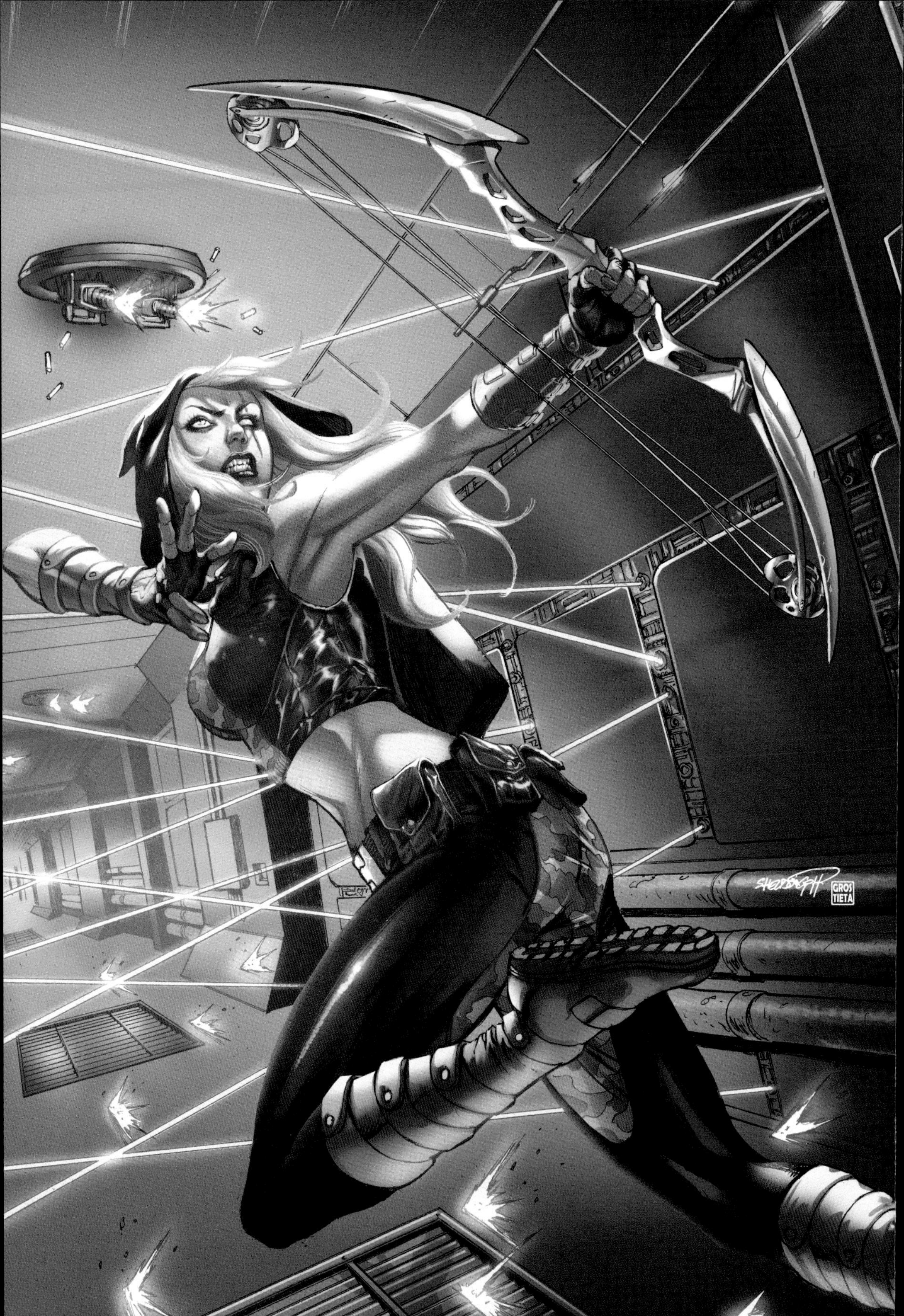
GROS
TIETA

ROBYN HOOD: OUTLAW 3 • COVER B

Artwork by Sheldon Goh • Colors by Grostieta

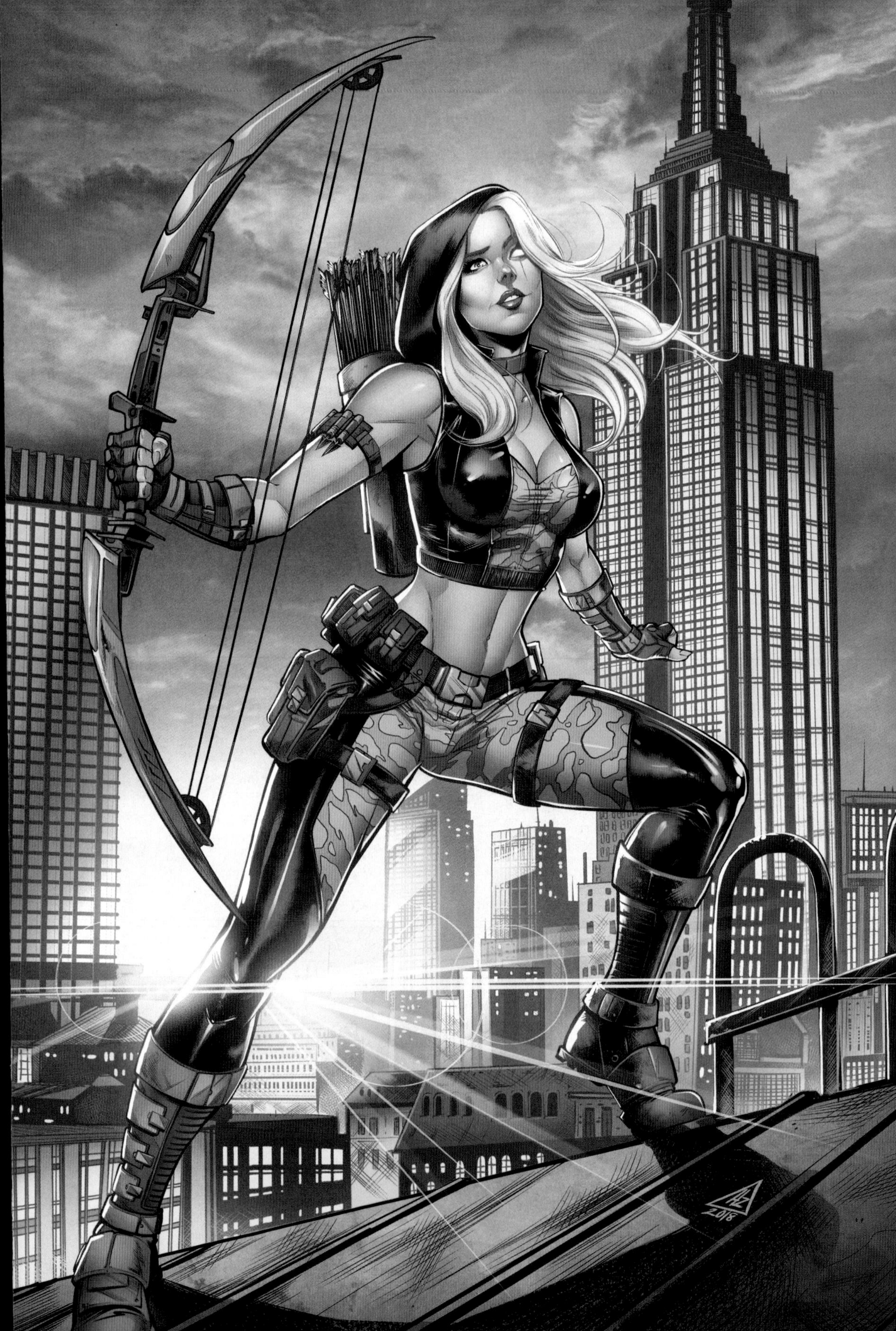

ROBYN HOOD: OUTLAW 3 • COVER C
Artwork by Hedwin Zaldivar

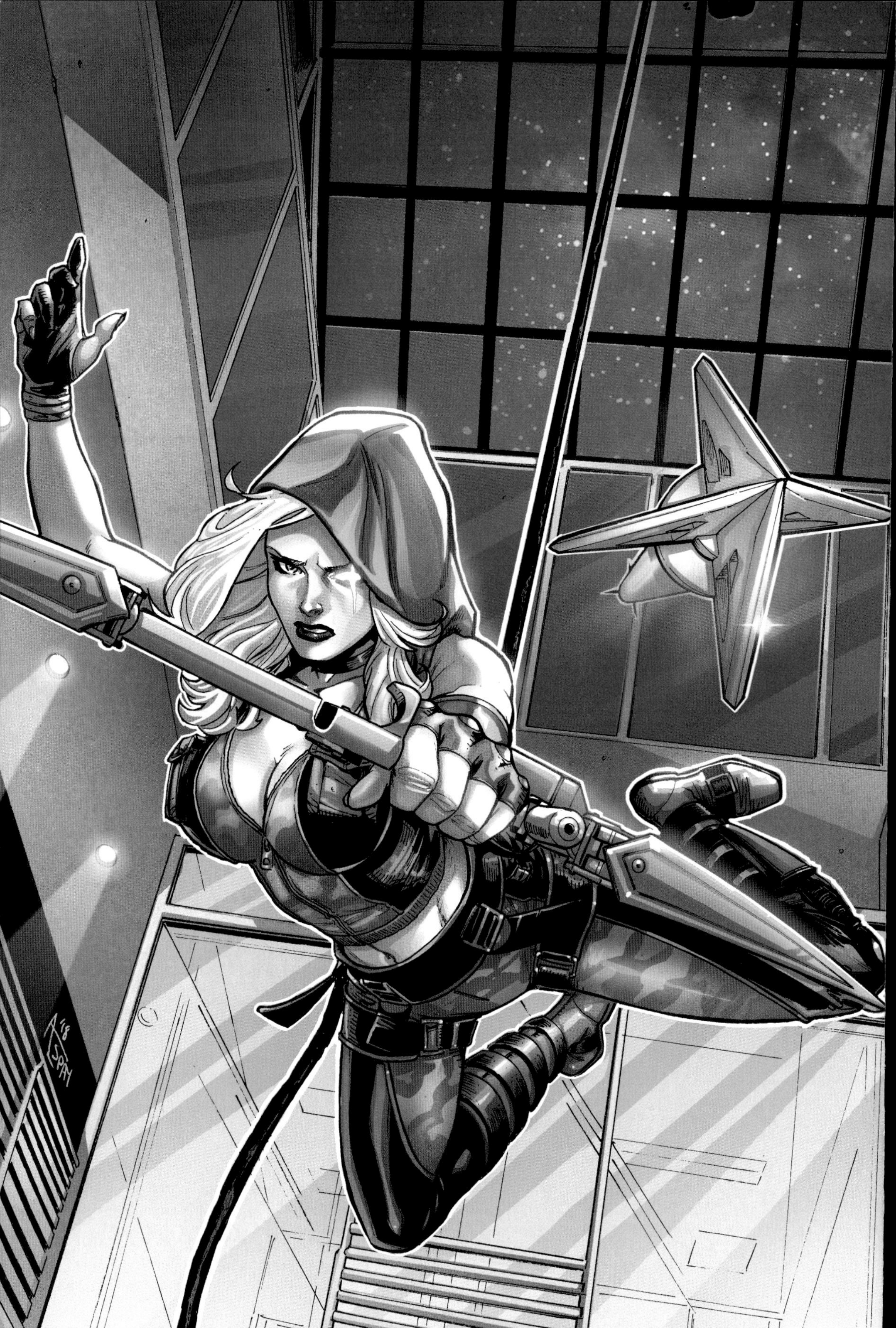

ROBYN HOOD: OUTLAW 3 • COVER D

Artwork by Anthony Spay • Colors by Juan Manuel Rodriguez

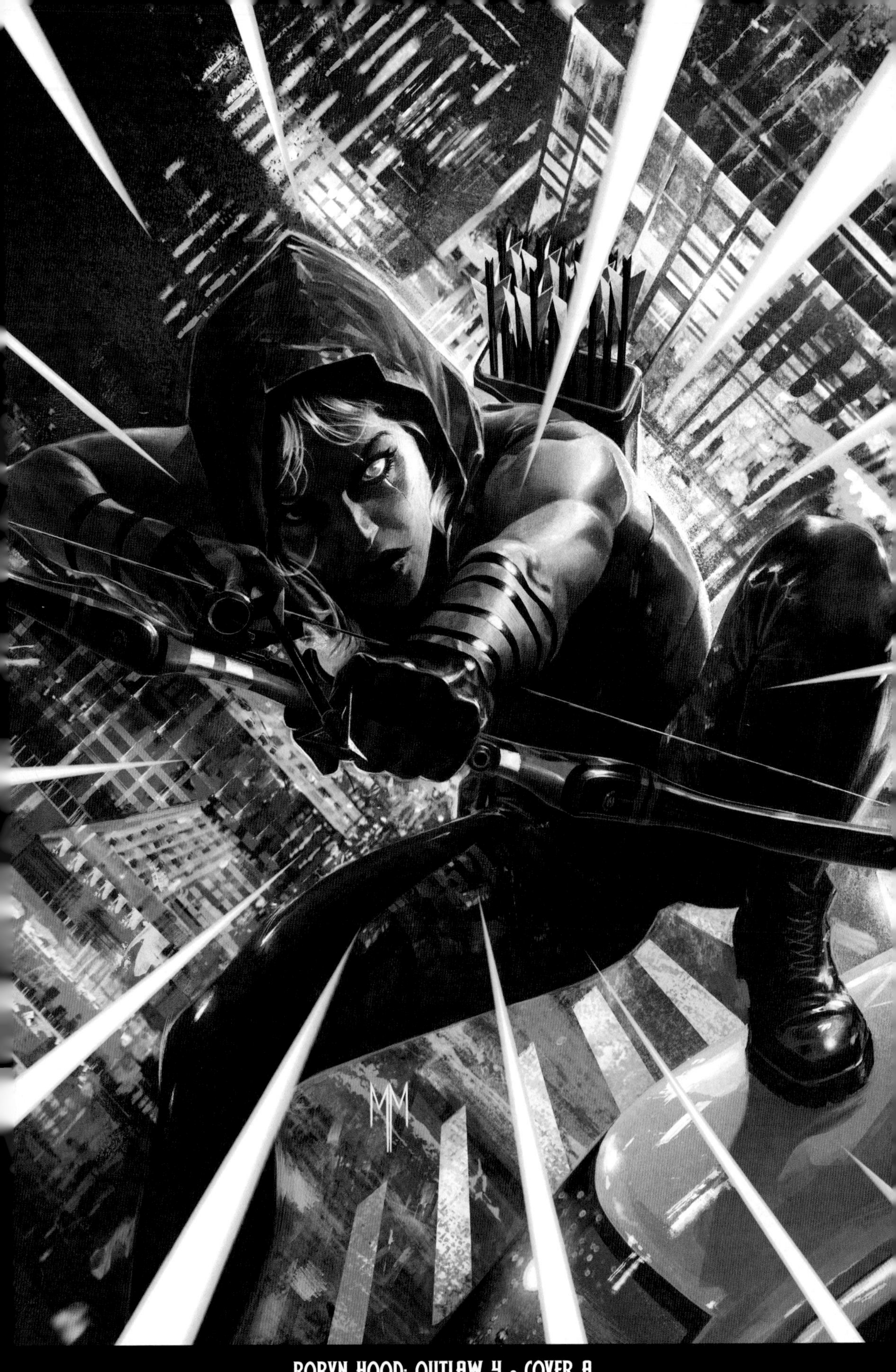
MM

ROBYN HOOD: OUTLAW 4 • COVER A
Artwork by Marco Mastrazzo

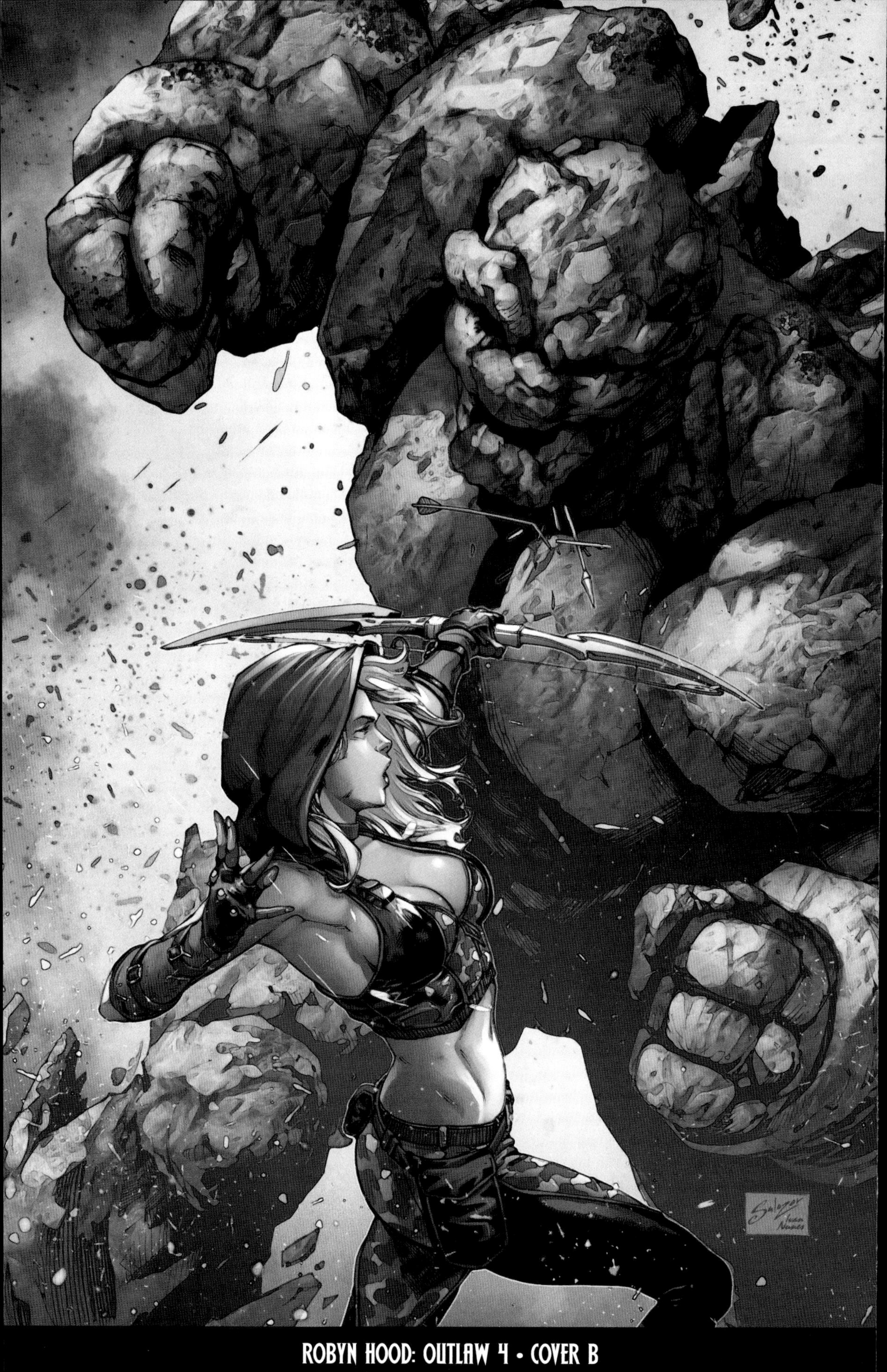

ROBYN HOOD: OUTLAW 4 • COVER B

Artwork by Edgar Salazar • Colors by Ivan Nunes

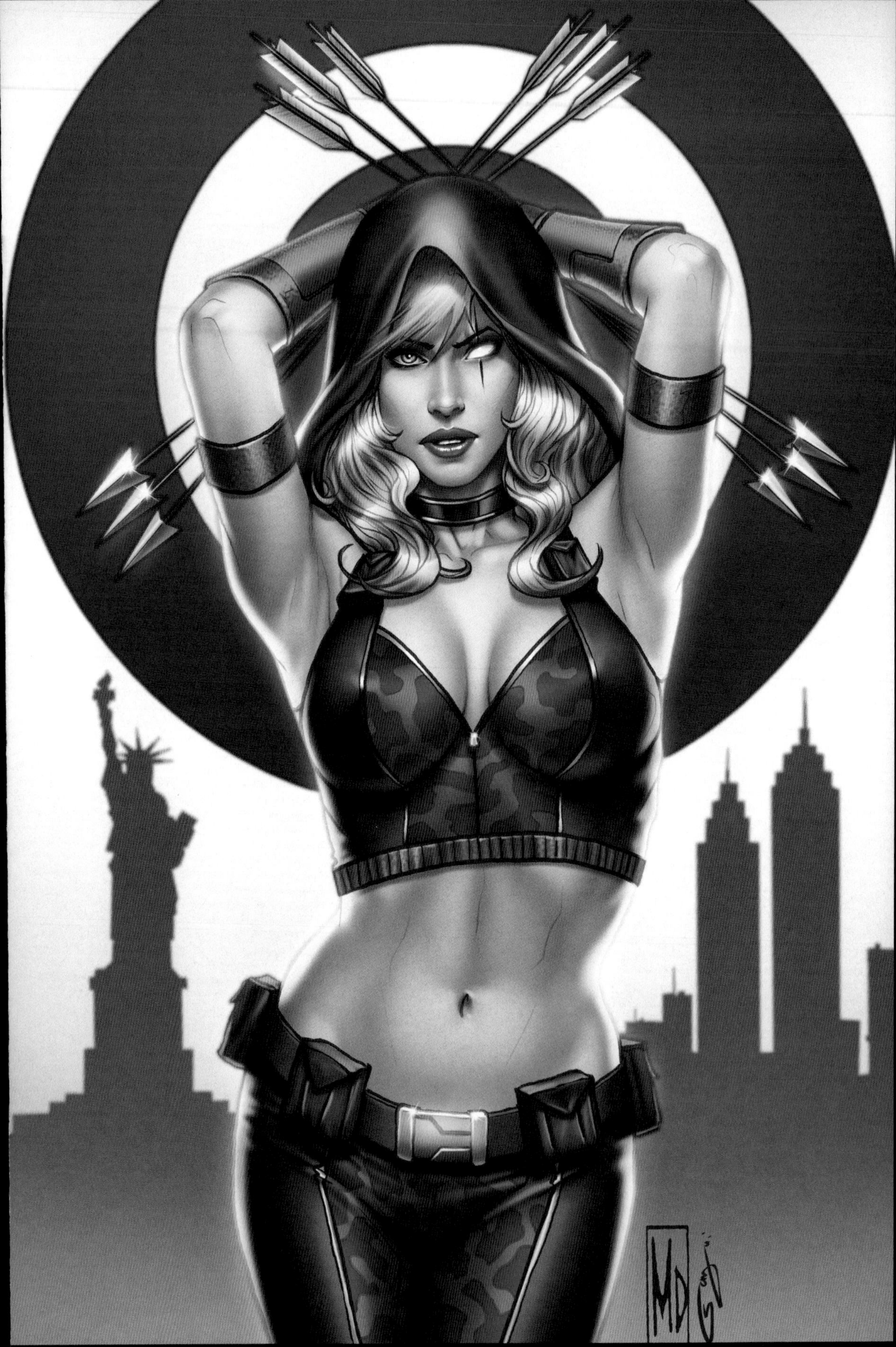

ROBYN HOOD: OUTLAW 4 • COVER C
Artwork by Michael DiPascale • Colors by Sanju Nivangune

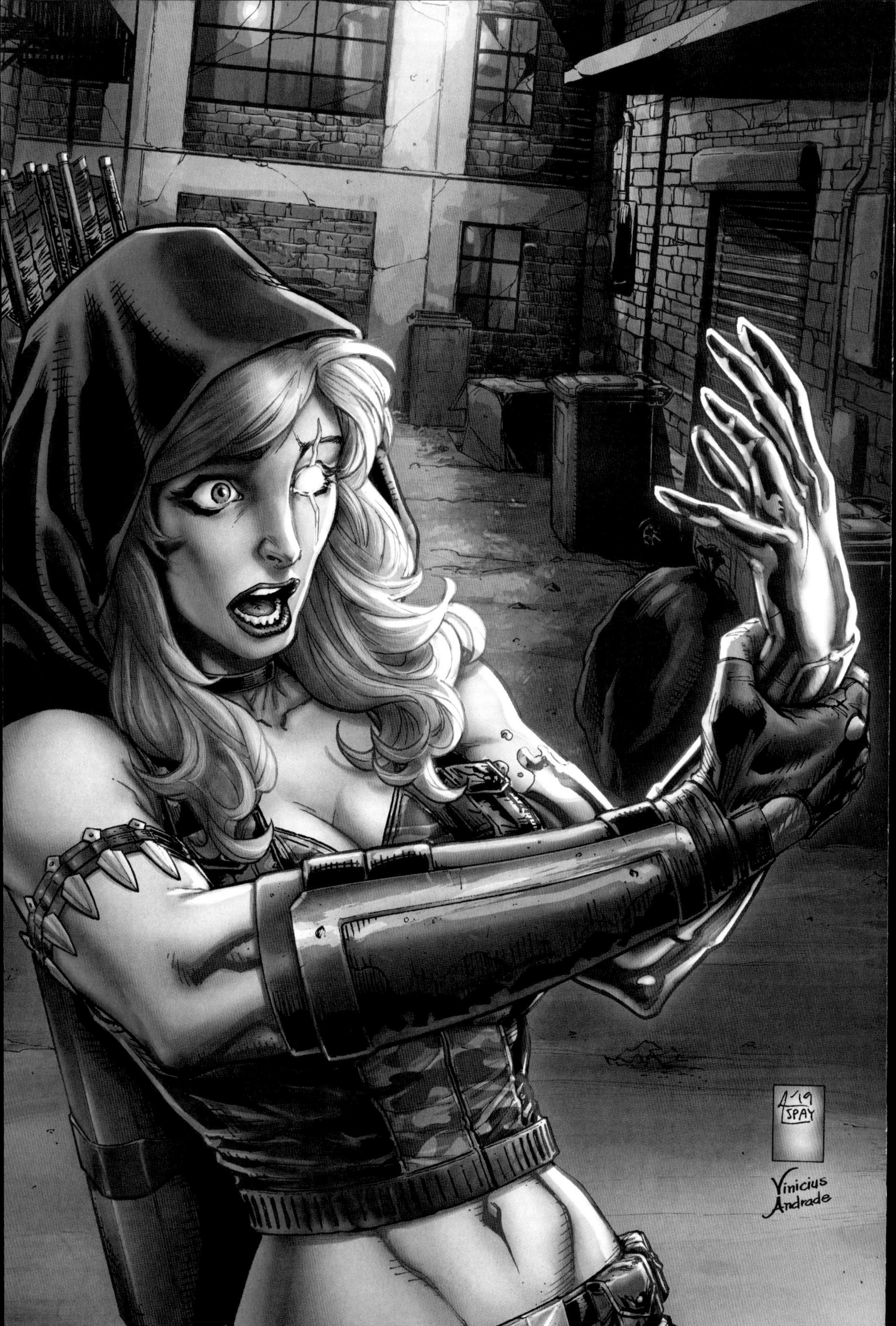
A '19
SPAY
Vinicius
Andrade

ROBYN HOOD: OUTLAW 4 • COVER D

Artwork by Anthony Spay • Colors by Vinicius Andrade

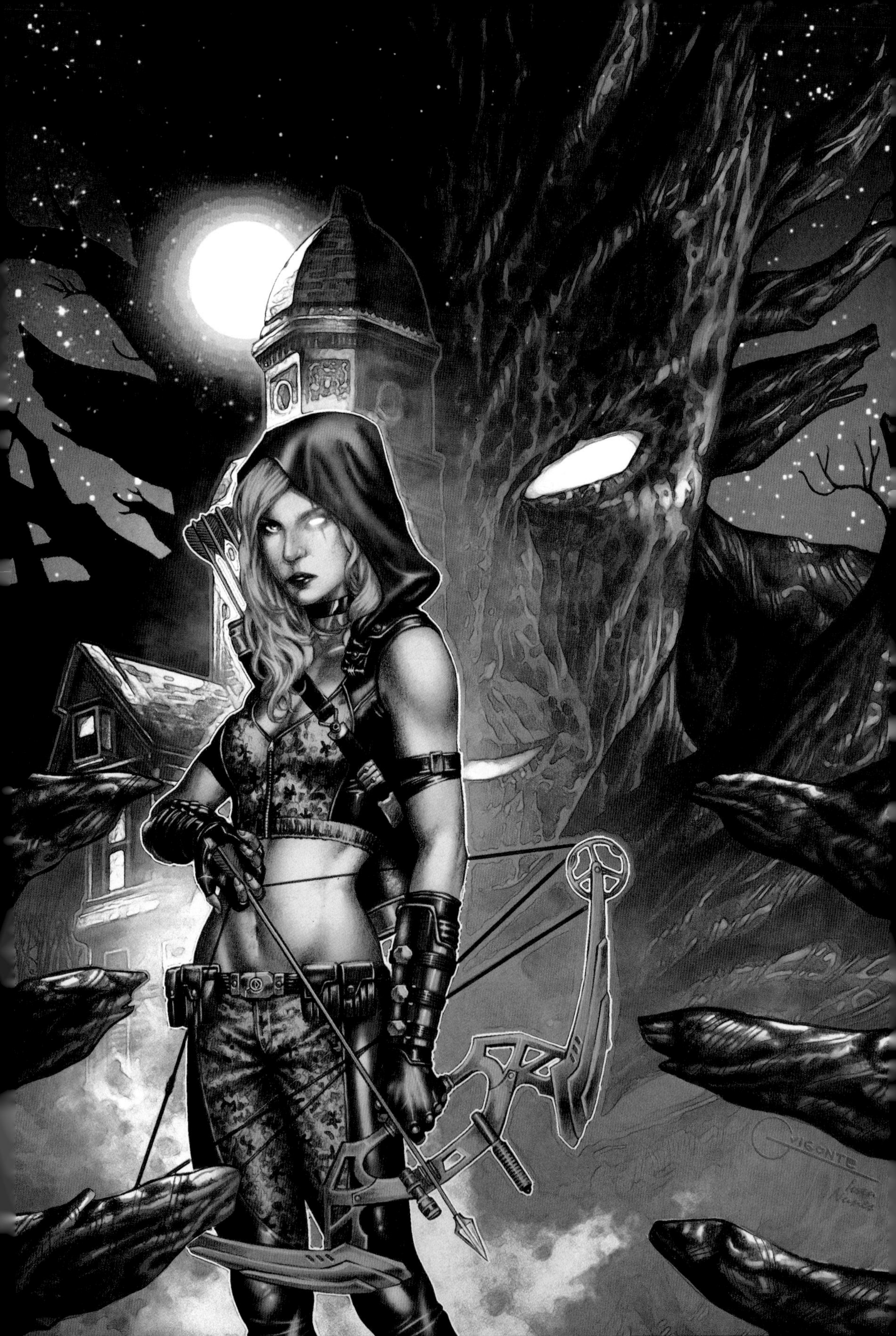

ROBYN HOOD: OUTLAW 5 • COVER A

Artwork by Geebo Vigonte • Colors by Ivan Nunes

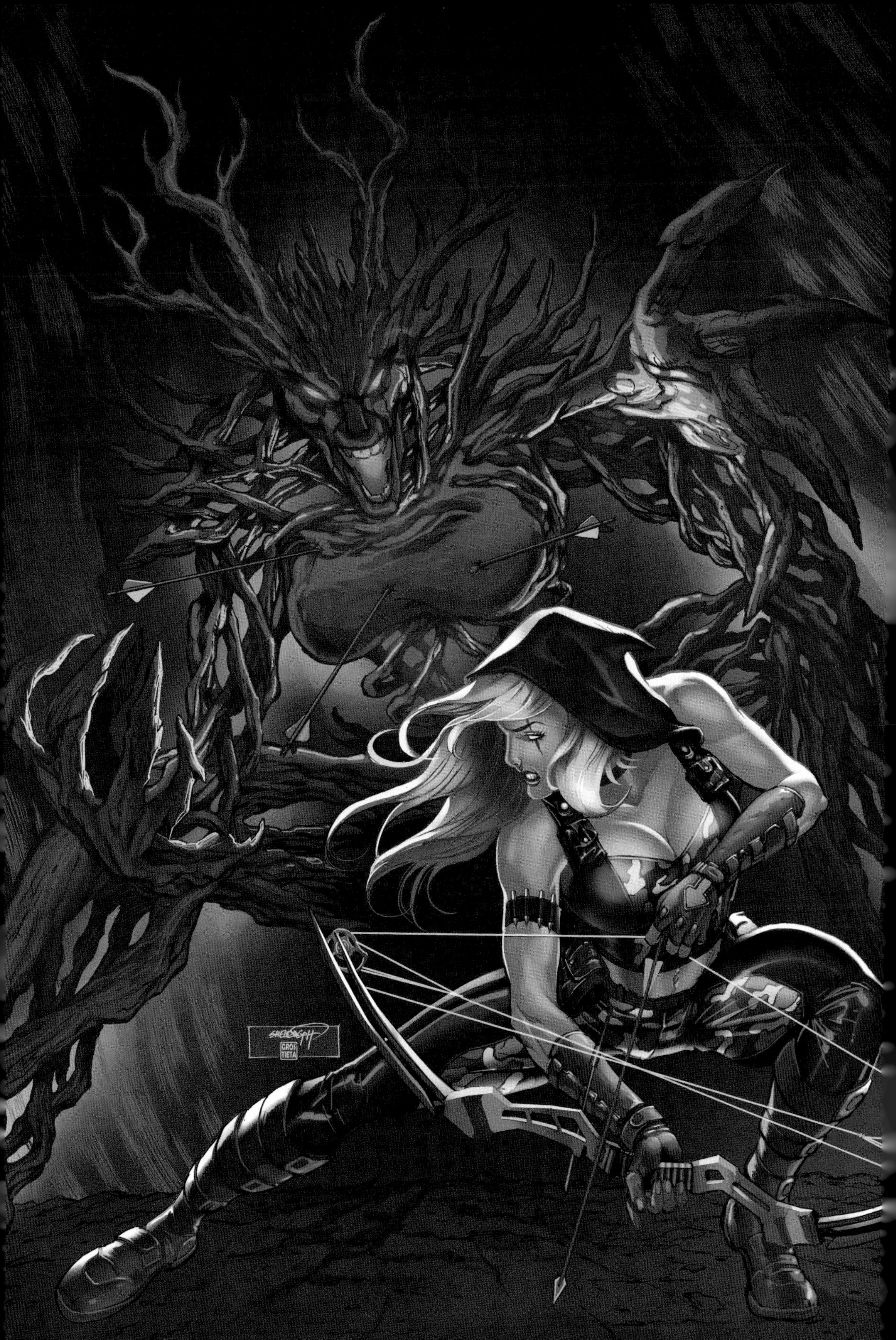

ROBYN HOOD: OUTLAW 5 • COVER B

Artwork by Sheldon Goh • Colors by Grostieta

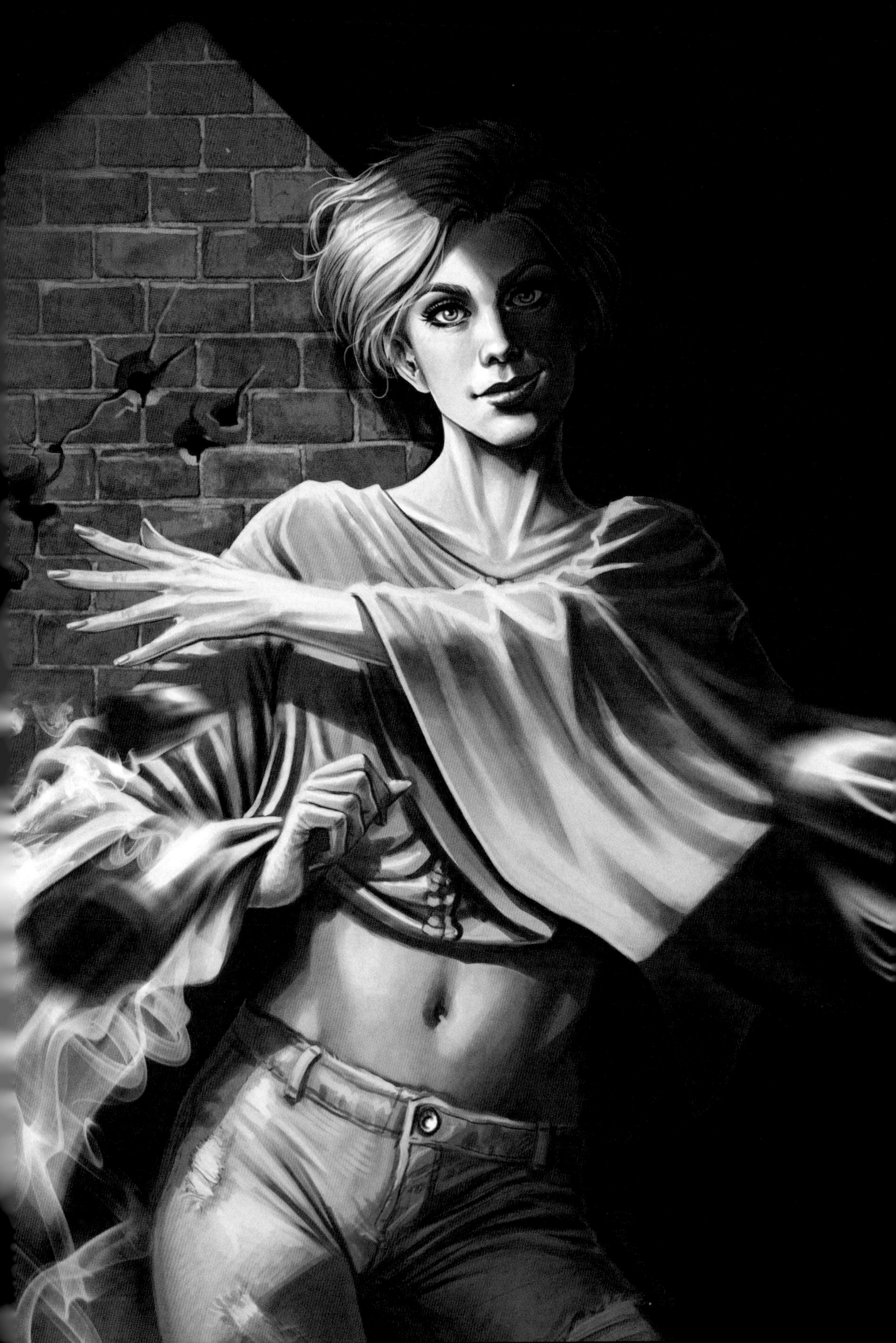

ROBYN HOOD: OUTLAW 5 • COVER C
Artwork by Claudia Iancello

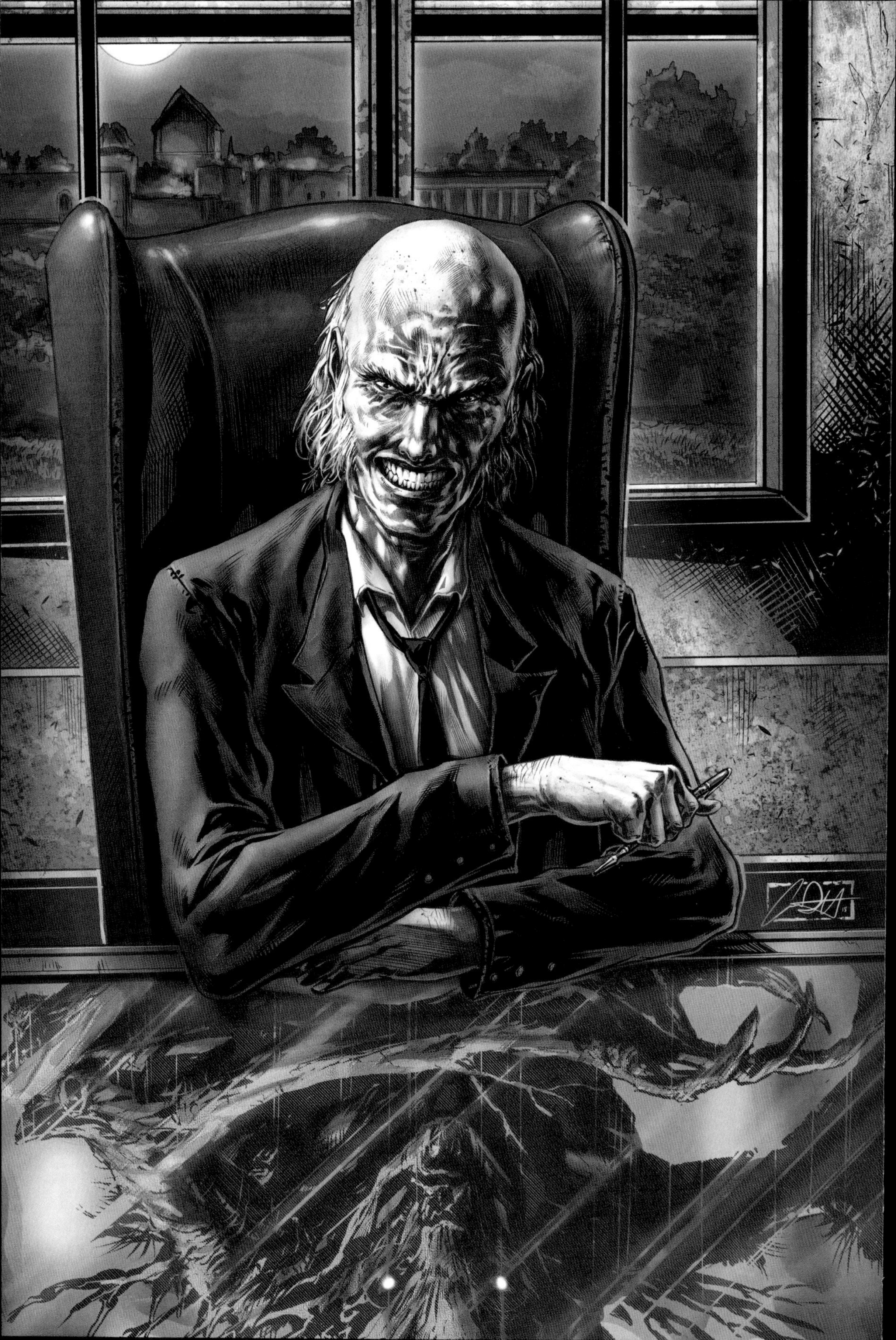

ROBYN HOOD: OUTLAW 5 • COVER D

Artwork by Caanan White • Colors by Vinicius Andrade

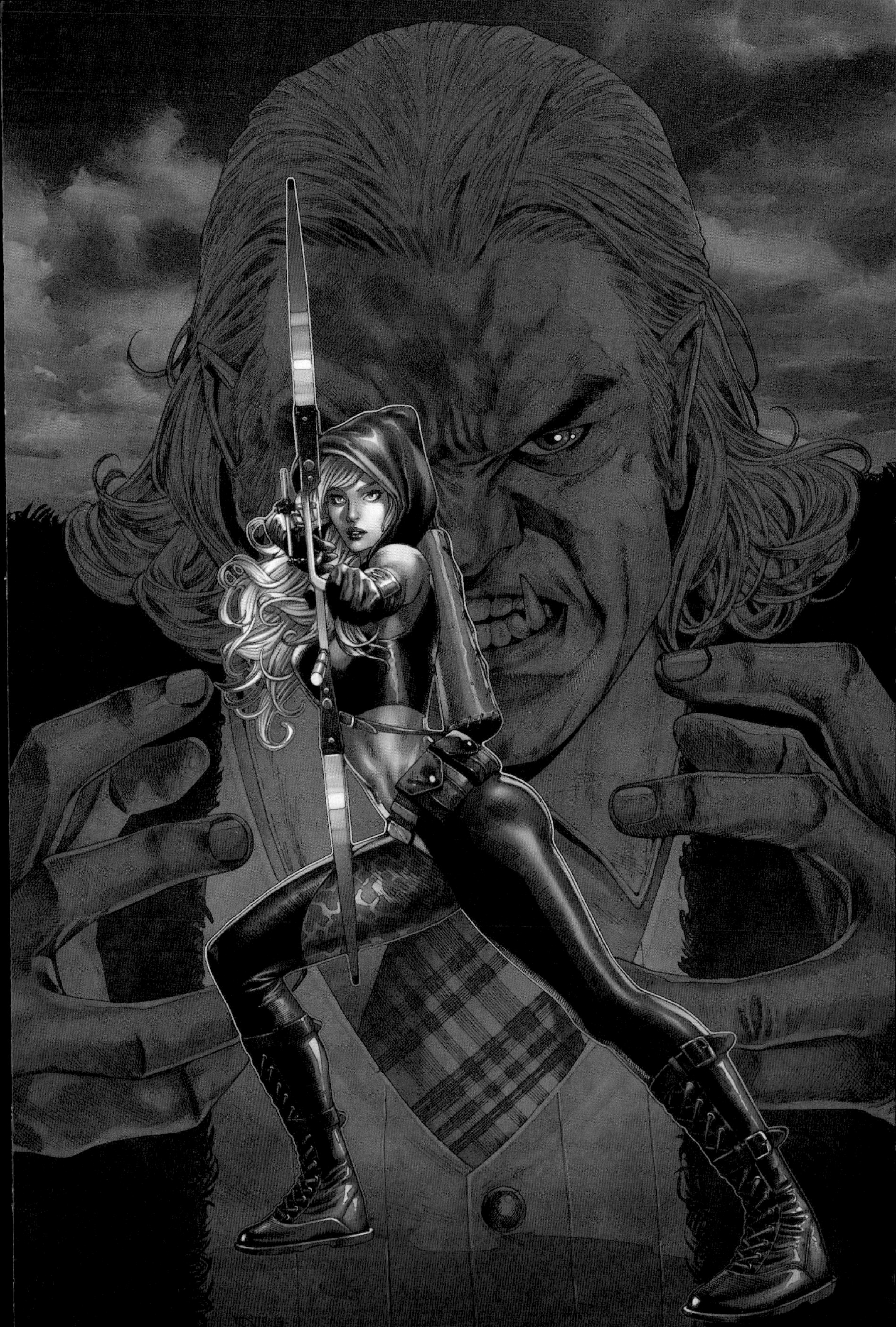

ROBYN HOOD: OUTLAW 6 • COVER A

Artwork by Michael Sta. Maria • Colors by Ivan Nunes

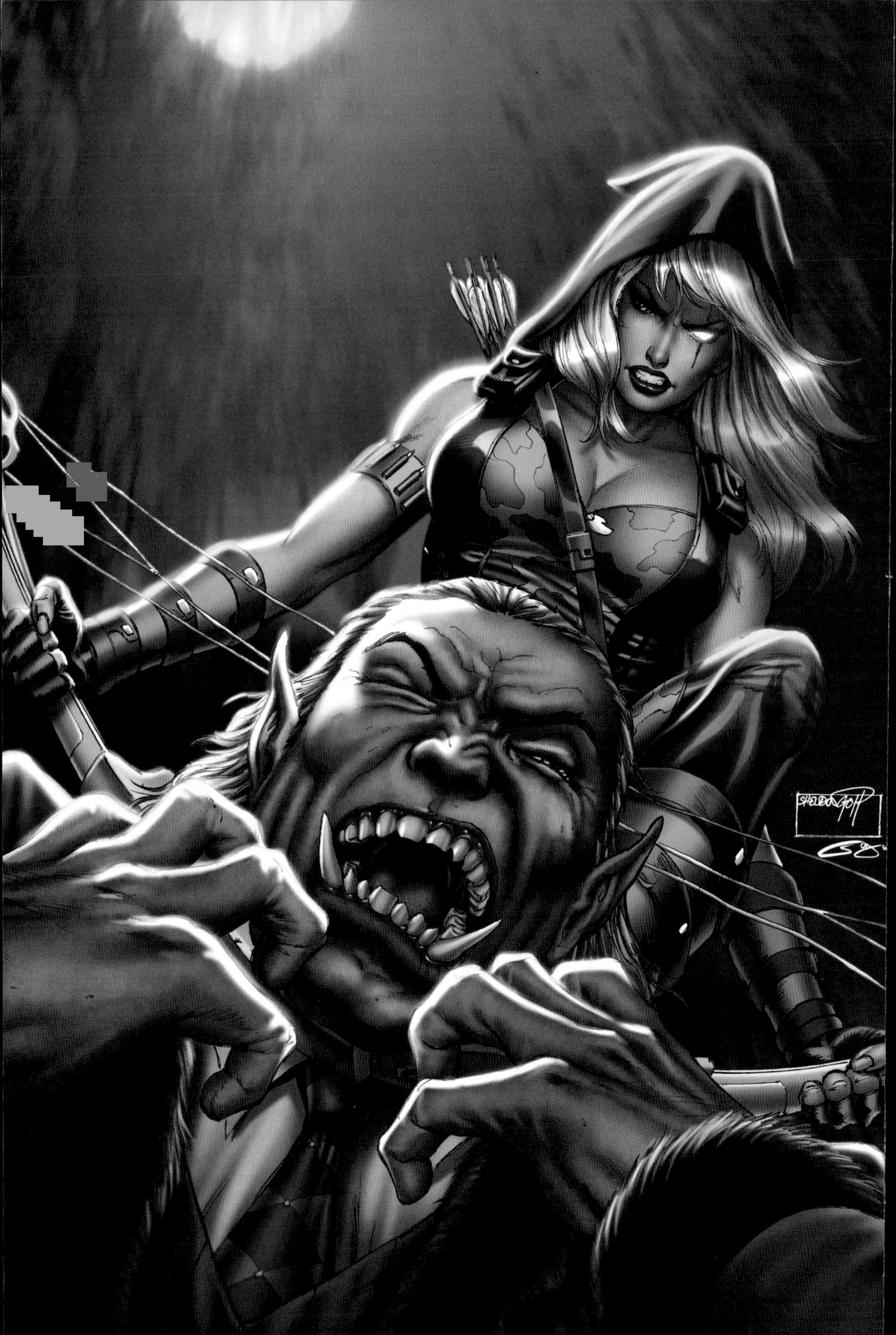

ROBYN HOOD: OUTLAW 6 • COVER B

Artwork by Sheldon Goh • Colors by Sanju Nivangune

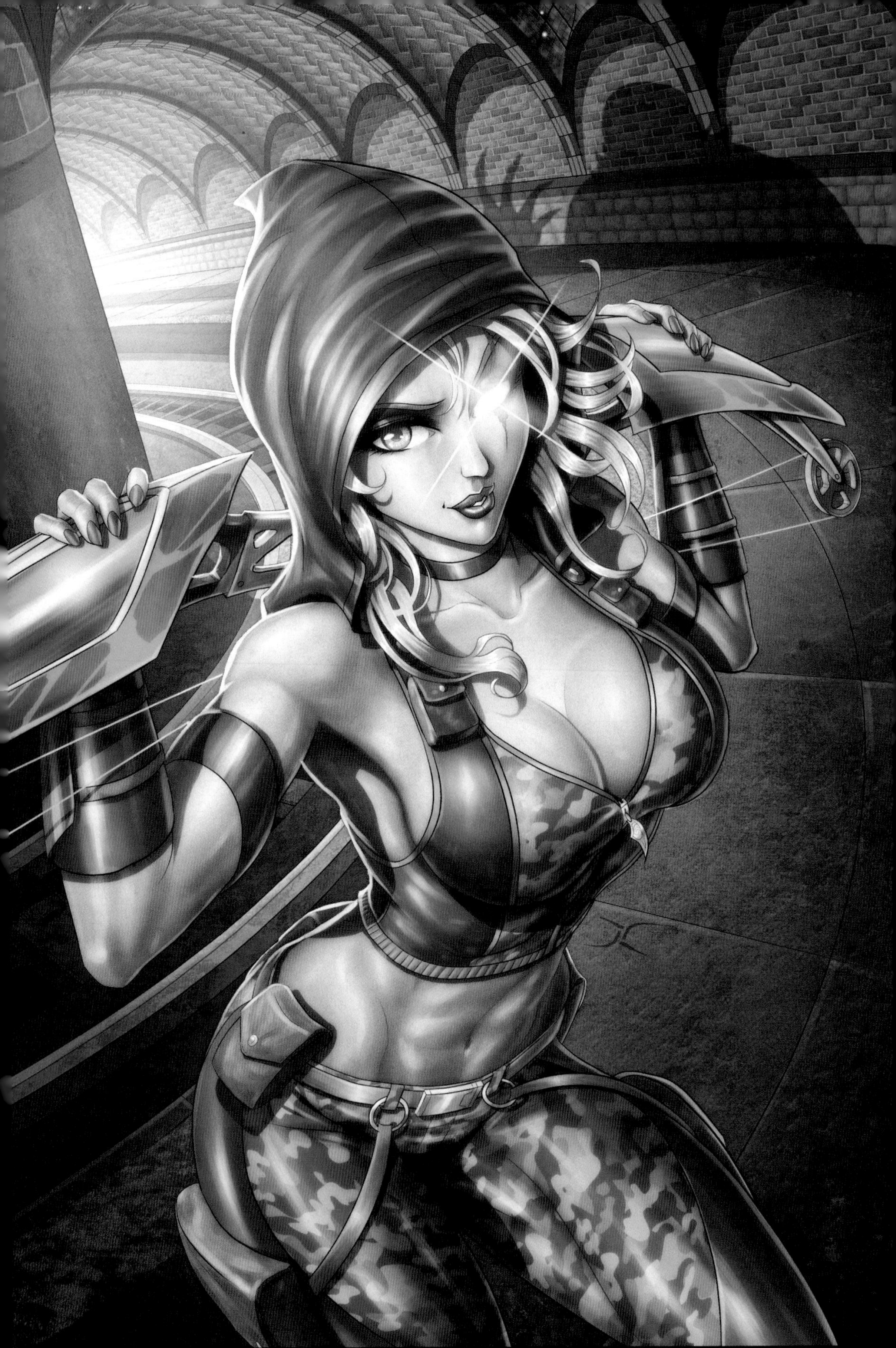

ROBYN HOOD: OUTLAW 6 • COVER C

Artwork by Jason Cardy

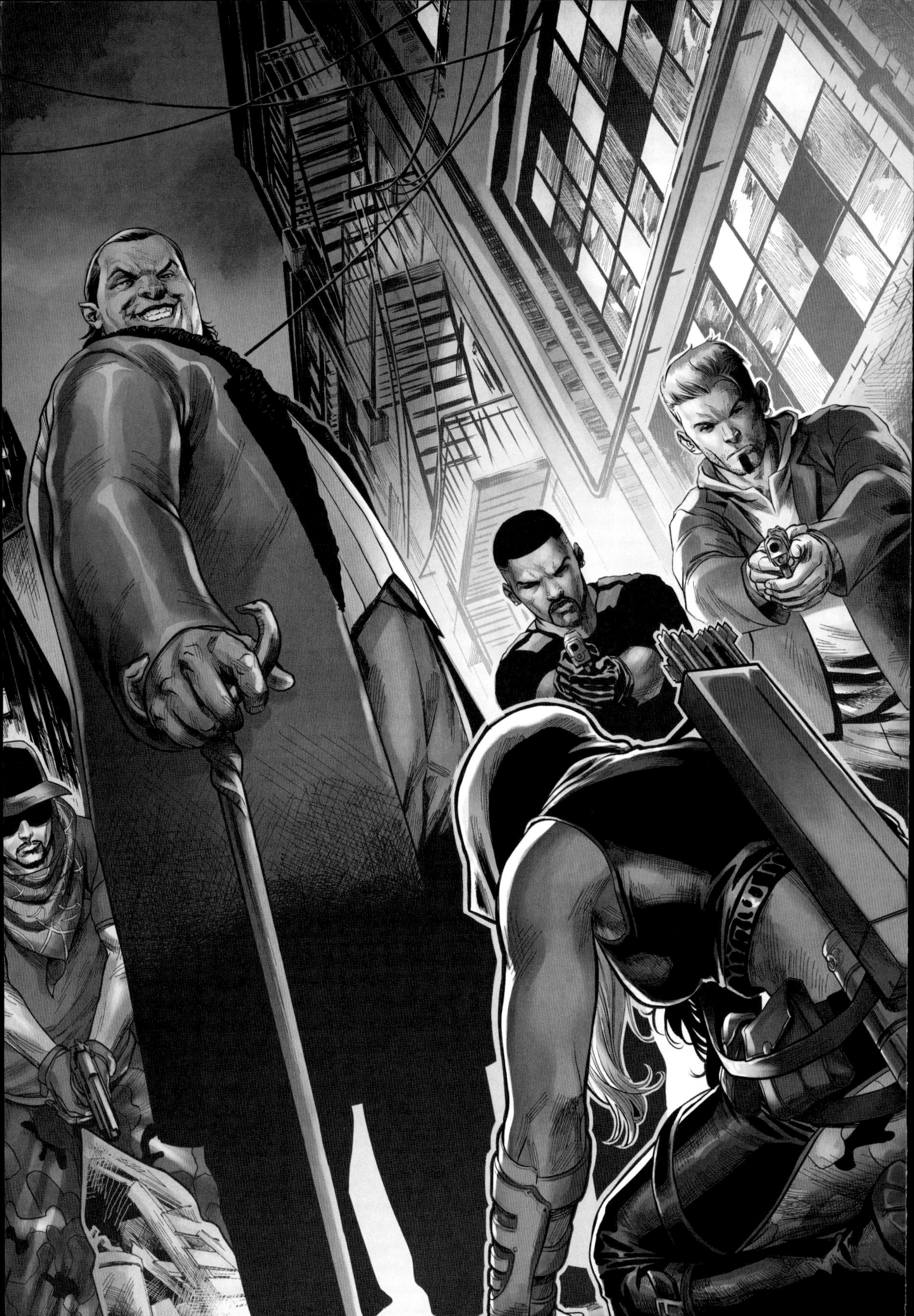

ROBYN HOOD: OUTLAW 6 • COVER D

Artwork by Martin Coccolo • Colors by Mohan Sivakami

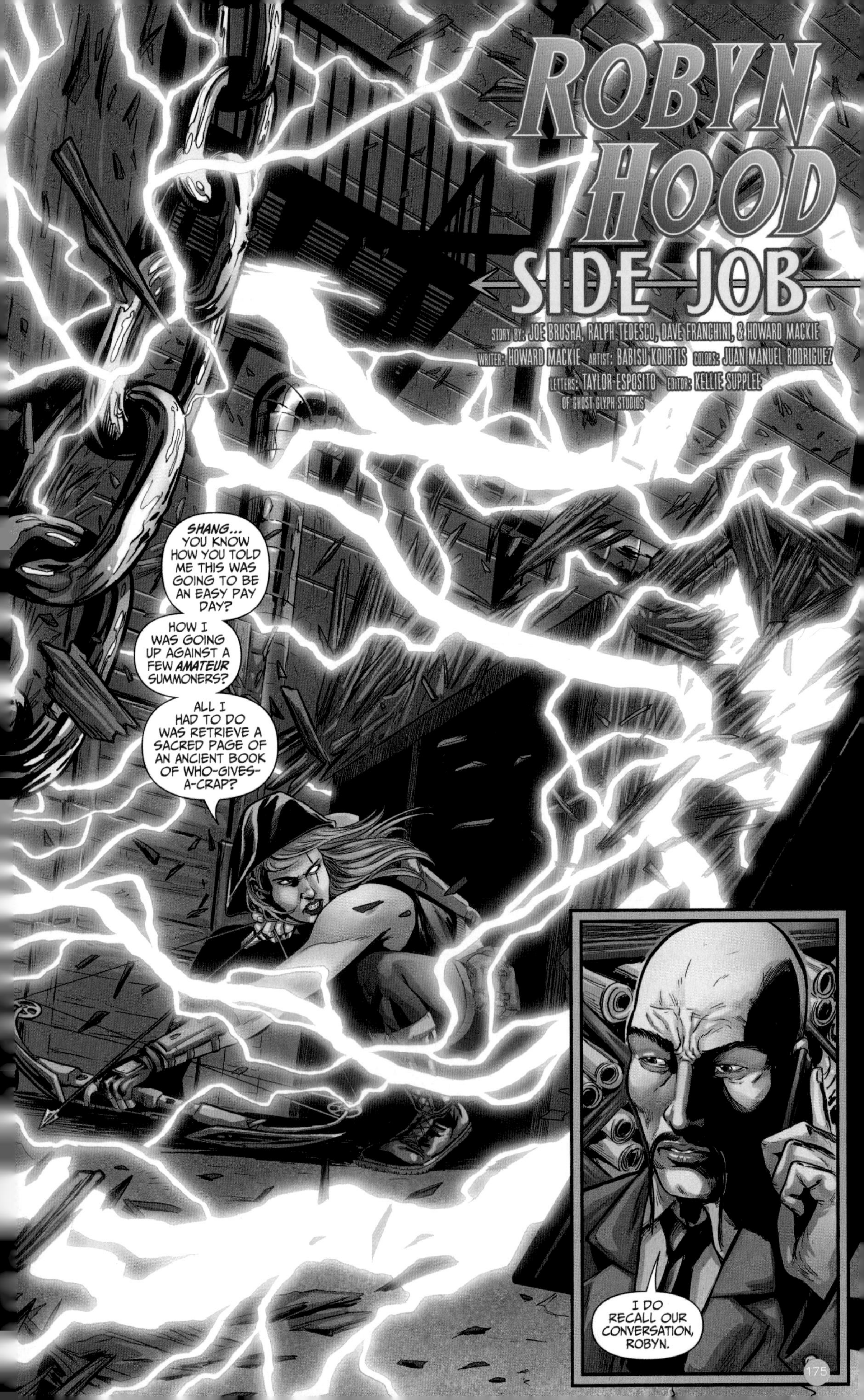
ROBYN HOOD
SIDE JOB
STORY BY: JOE BRUSHA, RALPH TEDESCO, DAVE FRANCHINI, & HOWARD MACKIE
WRITER: HOWARD MACKIE ARTIST: BABISU KOURTIS COLORS: JUAN MANUEL RODRIGUEZ
LETTERS: TAYLOR ESPOSITO EDITOR: KELLIE SUPPLEE
OF GHOST GLYPH STUDIOS
SHANG... YOU KNOW HOW YOU TOLD ME THIS WAS GOING TO BE AN EASY PAY DAY?
HOW I WAS GOING UP AGAINST A FEW *AMATEUR* SUMMONERS?
ALL I HAD TO DO WAS RETRIEVE A SACRED PAGE OF AN ANCIENT BOOK OF WHO-GIVES-A-CRAP?
I DO RECALL OUR CONVERSATION, ROBYN.

AMATEURS?

AMATEUR *SUMMONERS.* THEY'RE ACTUALLY PRETTY POWERFUL MYSTICS. WHY ELSE WOULD I NEED *YOU?* IF *ANYONE* COULD HAVE RETRIEVED THE PAGE--

OH, ROBYN...DID I MENTION THAT IT IS IMPERATIVE THAT NO BLOOD BE SPILLED ANYWHERE NEAR THE SCROLL.

IT WILL ONLY MAKE THE CREATURE THEY ARE TRYING TO SUMMON MORE POWERFUL.

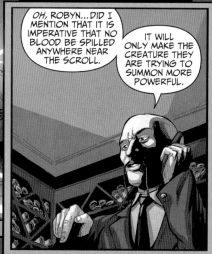

YOU DID *NOT* MENTION THAT EITHER, SHANG.

OOPS.

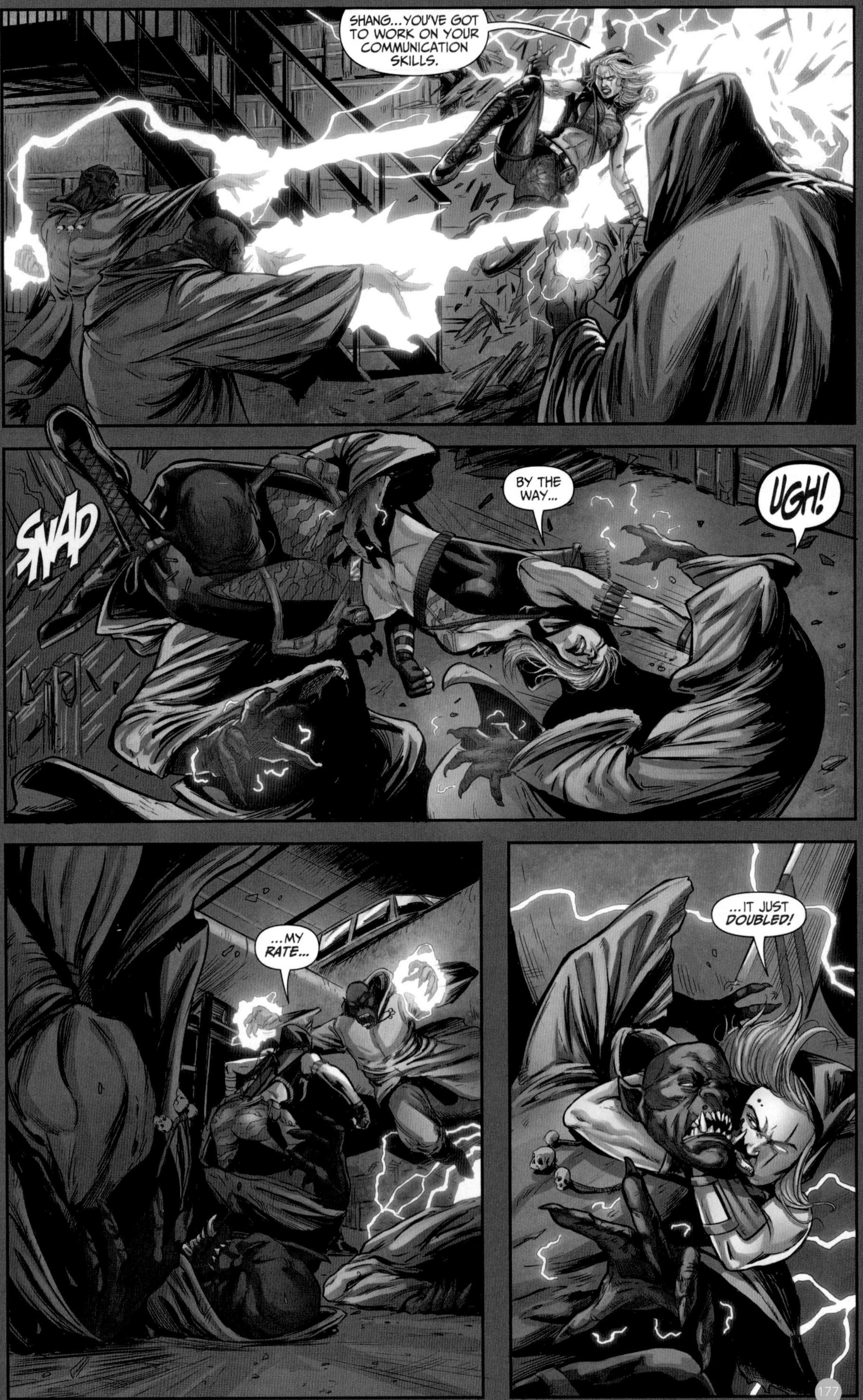
SHANG...YOU'VE GOT TO WORK ON YOUR COMMUNICATION SKILLS.
SNAP
BY THE WAY...
UGH!
...MY RATE...
...IT JUST DOUBLED!

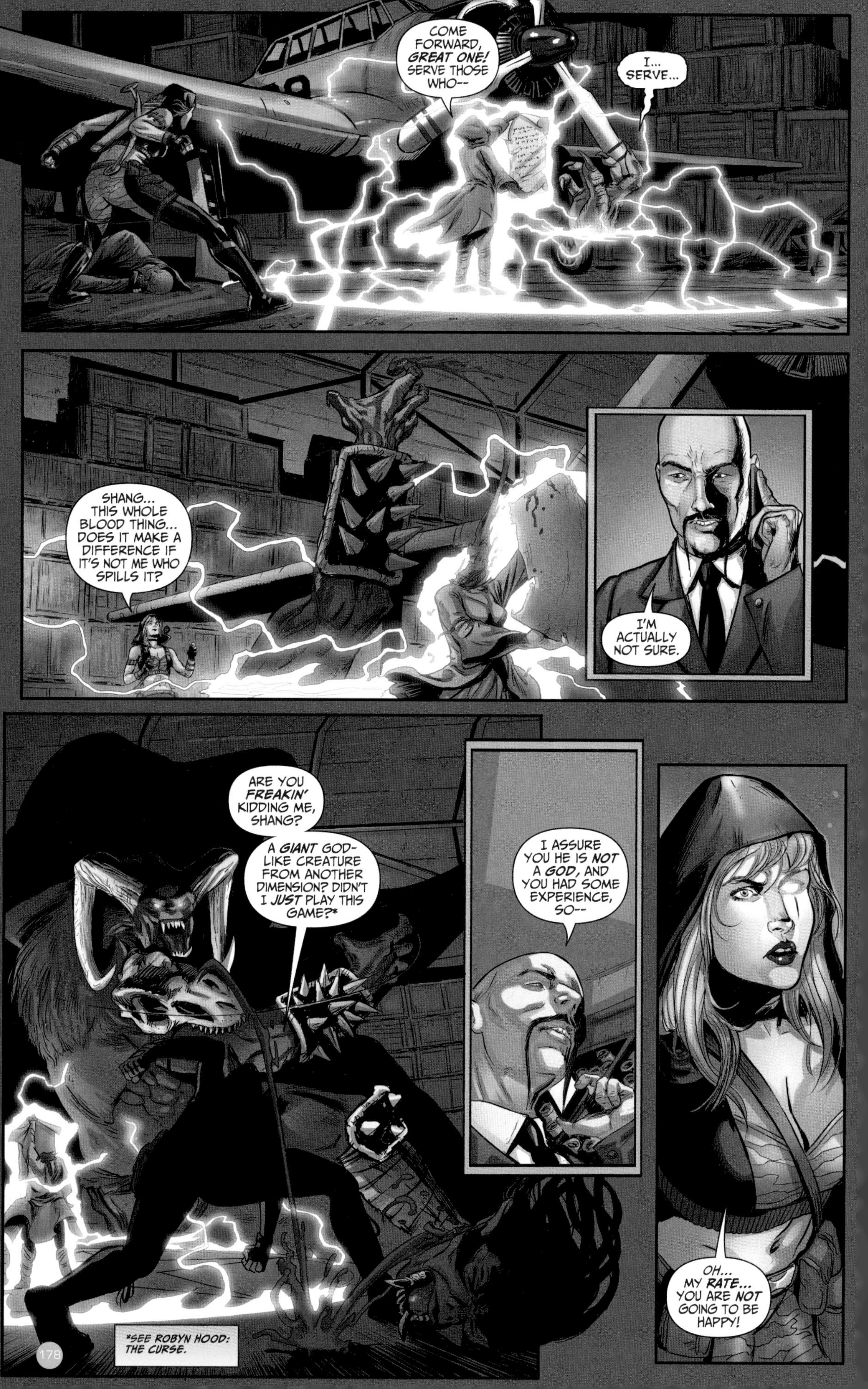
COME FORWARD, GREAT ONE! SERVE THOSE WHO--
I... SERVE...
SHANG... THIS WHOLE BLOOD THING... DOES IT MAKE A DIFFERENCE IF IT'S NOT ME WHO SPILLS IT?
I'M ACTUALLY NOT SURE.
ARE YOU FREAKIN' KIDDING ME, SHANG?
A GIANT GOD-LIKE CREATURE FROM ANOTHER DIMENSION? DIDN'T I JUST PLAY THIS GAME?*
*SEE ROBYN HOOD: THE CURSE.
I ASSURE YOU HE IS NOT A GOD, AND YOU HAD SOME EXPERIENCE, SO--
OH... MY RATE... YOU ARE NOT GOING TO BE HAPPY!

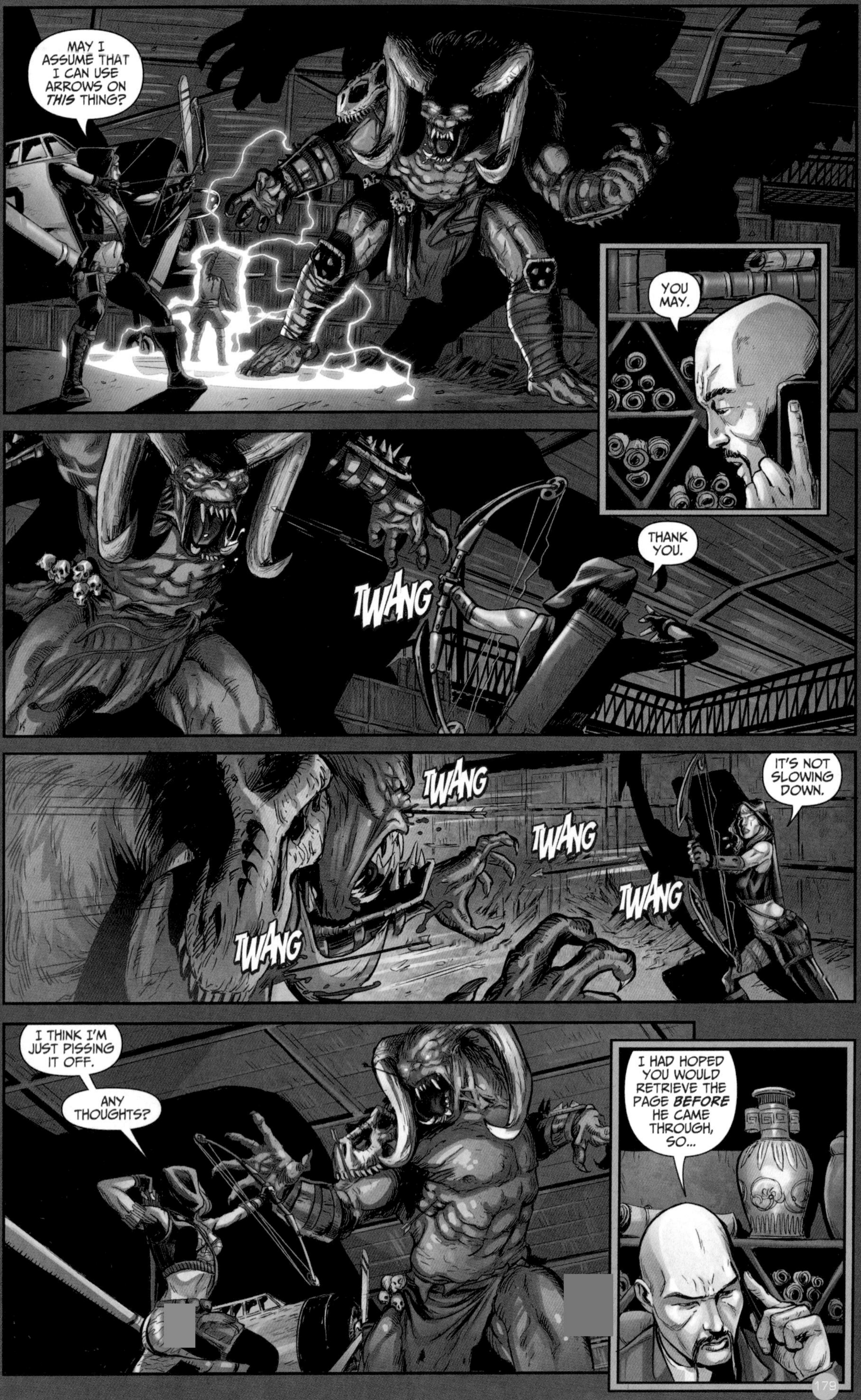
MAY I ASSUME THAT I CAN USE ARROWS ON *THIS* THING?
YOU MAY.
TWANG
THANK YOU.
TWANG
TWANG
TWANG
TWANG
IT'S NOT SLOWING DOWN.
I THINK I'M JUST PISSING IT OFF.
ANY THOUGHTS?
I HAD HOPED YOU WOULD RETRIEVE THE PAGE *BEFORE* HE CAME THROUGH, SO...

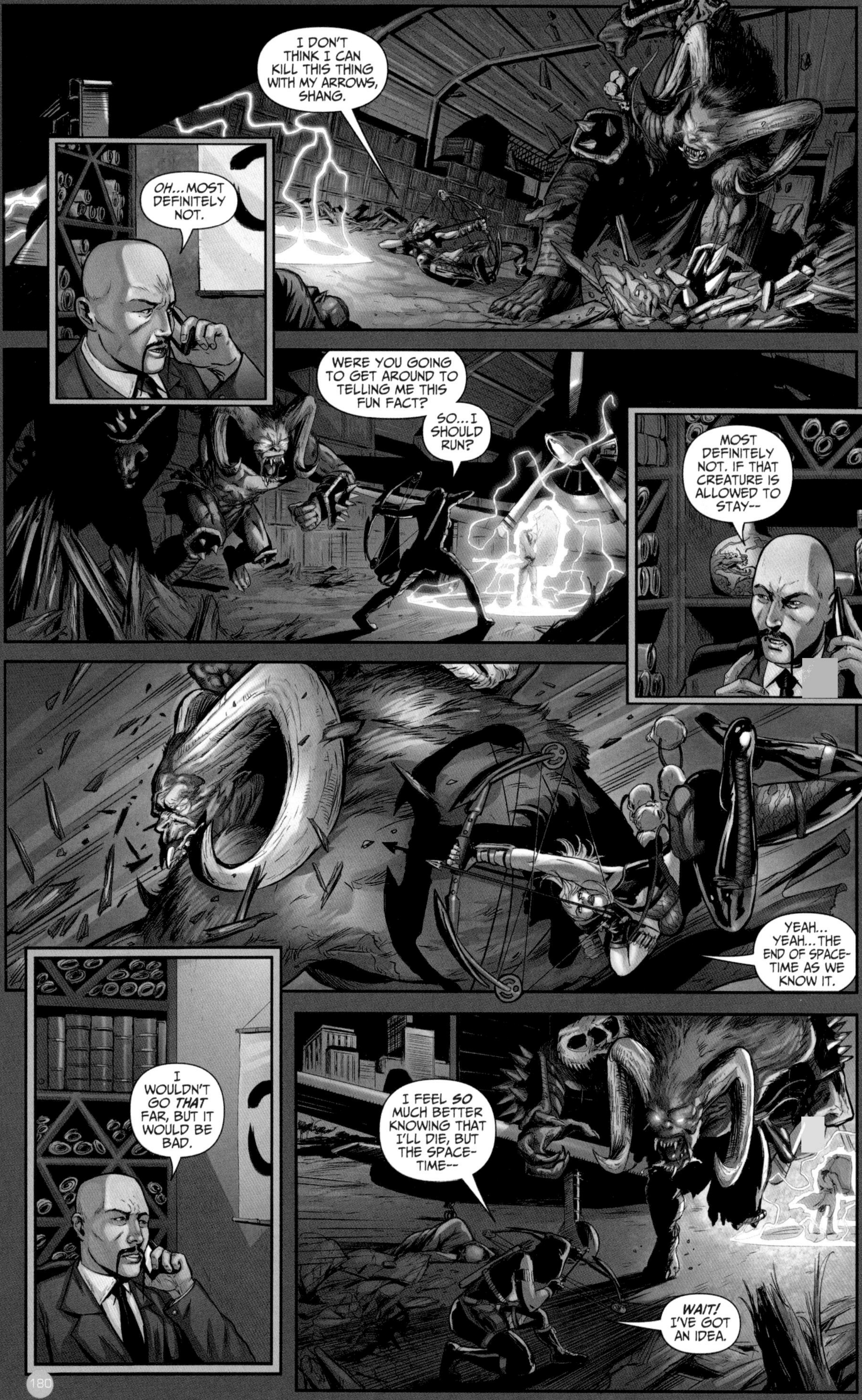
I DON'T THINK I CAN KILL THIS THING WITH MY ARROWS, SHANG.
OH... MOST DEFINITELY NOT.
WERE YOU GOING TO GET AROUND TO TELLING ME THIS FUN FACT?
SO...I SHOULD RUN?
MOST DEFINITELY NOT. IF THAT CREATURE IS ALLOWED TO STAY--
YEAH... YEAH... THE END OF SPACE-TIME AS WE KNOW IT.
I WOULDN'T GO ***THAT*** FAR, BUT IT WOULD BE BAD.
I FEEL ***SO*** MUCH BETTER KNOWING THAT I'LL DIE, BUT THE SPACE-TIME--
WAIT! I'VE GOT AN IDEA.

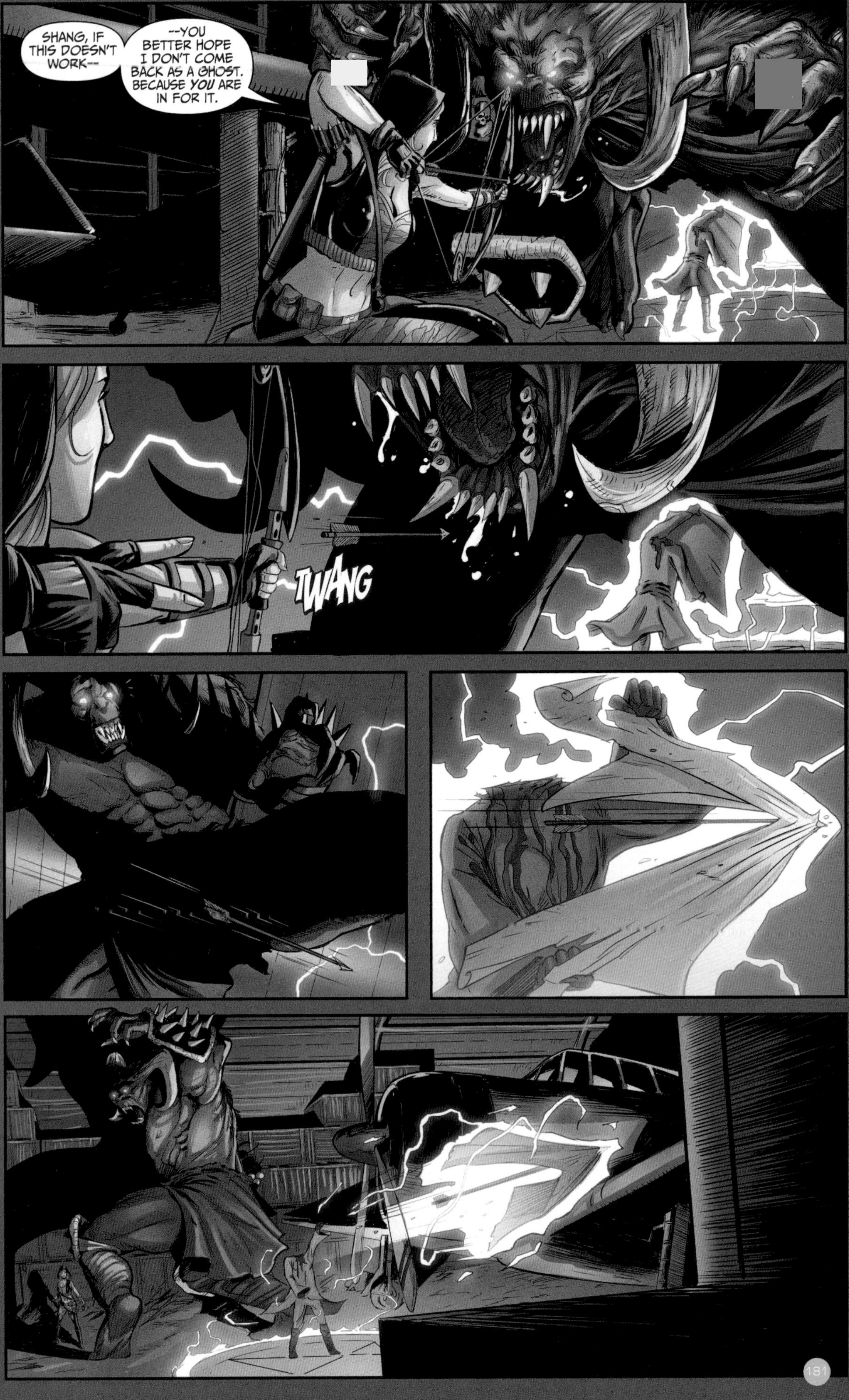
SHANG, IF THIS DOESN'T WORK--
--YOU BETTER HOPE I DON'T COME BACK AS A GHOST. BECAUSE *YOU* ARE IN FOR IT.
TWANG

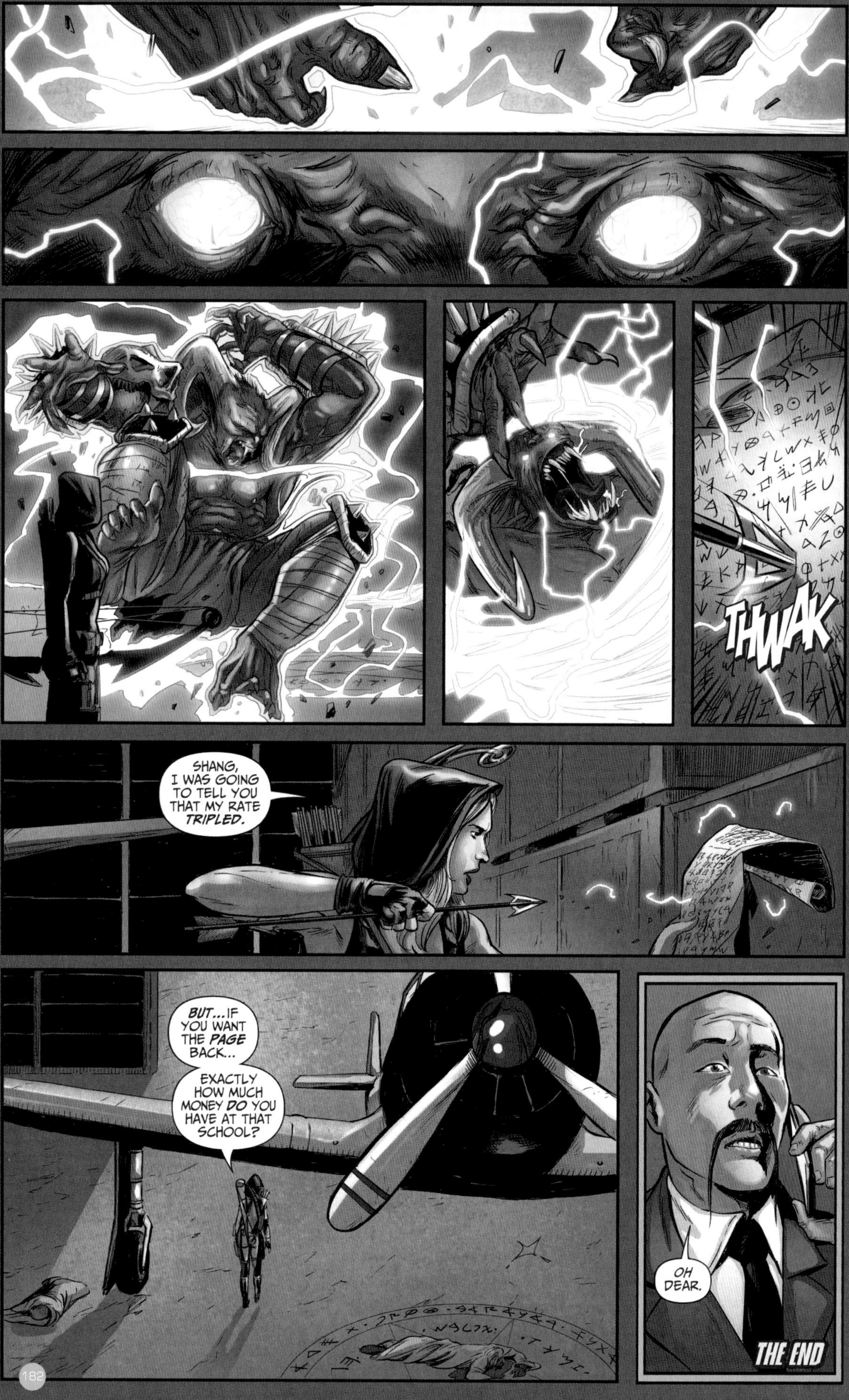
THWAK
SHANG, I WAS GOING TO TELL YOU THAT MY RATE *TRIPLED.*
BUT... IF YOU WANT THE *PAGE* BACK...
EXACTLY HOW MUCH MONEY *DO* YOU HAVE AT THAT SCHOOL?
OH DEAR.
THE END

ROBYN HOOD TRILOGY (2012)
Pat Shand (W) Larry Watts (A) Slamet Mujiono (C)
Inside the realm of Myst, a tyrant rules the city of Bree with an iron fist, leaving its citizens living in terror. But all hope is not lost as an orphaned teen from our world discovers her true destiny and becomes the legend she was meant to be.

ORIGIN ISBN: 978-1937068790
WANTED ISBN: 978-1939683045
LEGEND ISBN: 978-1939683885

> "The most bad ass archer in comics..."
> —**Word of the Nerd**

ROBYN HOOD: RIOT GIRLS SERIES (2014)
Pat Shand (W) Roberta Ingranata (A) Slamet Mujiono (C)
From drug lords, to corrupt politicians, to the things that go bump in the night, no evils that plague the streets of New York City will be safe as Robyn Locksley sets up shop as a private investigator. Joined by her best friend Marian Quin, a powerful witch from Myst, it's a whole new world for Robyn.

RIOT GIRLS ISBN: 978-1939683991
MONSTERS IN THE DARK ISBN: 978-1942275077
ATTITUDE ADJUSTMENT ISBN: 978-1942275152
UPRISING ISBN: 978-1942275312

ROBYN HOOD: I LOVE NY (2016)
Lou Iovino (W) Sergio Ariño (A) Grostieta (C)
This is the story of what comes next. It's the story of Robyn on her own for the first time, making her way toward an uncertain future. But most importantly, it's the story of a growing love affair between this unlikely outlaw hero and the greatest city on Earth, New York City—and how it saves them both.

ISBN: 978-1942275565

> "*Robyn Hood: I Love NY* is a marvelous new beginning."
> —**Fandom Post**

ROBYN HOOD: THE HUNT (2017)
LaToya Morgan (W) Daniel Mainé (A) Leonardo Paciarotti (C)
Robyn Locksley has finally taken down the monsters and villains that have plagued New York for far too long. Now, with the streets safe again, Robyn unfortunately isn't going to get to enjoy them. After being transported to an otherworldly, high tech, maximum security prison, she must fight for her life from some of the very creatures she has placed there.

ISBN: 978-1942275749

ROBYN HOOD: THE CURSE (2018)
Chuck Dixon (W) Julius Abrera (A) Robby Bevard (C)
After a daring and dangerous escape from a sadistic supermax prison, Robyn is finally back home where she belongs. But as she re-acclimates to her "normal" life in New York City, a new evil has been released and Marian Quin needs Robyn's help to send it back from where it came... But this battle is about to get more personal than either of these friends could have imagined, and nothing will ever be the same!

ISBN: 978-1942275817

GRAPHIC NOVELS

zenescope

ROBYN HOOD
HOOD
OUTLAW

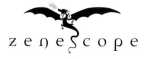

zenescope